THE
RORSCHACH SYSTEMS

JOHN E. EXNER, Jr., Ph.D.

DIRECTOR OF TRAINING IN CLINICAL PSYCHOLOGY,
LONG ISLAND UNIVERSITY, BROOKLYN, N. Y.;
FORMERLY DIRECTOR OF TRAINING IN CLINICAL PSYCHOLOGY,
BOWLING GREEN STATE UNIVERSITY, BOWLING GREEN, OHIO

GRUNE & STRATTON NEW YORK · LONDON

Library of Congress Catalog Card Number 68-31431

Printed in U. S. A.
(L-B)

To Doris

ACKNOWLEDGMENTS

In a book of this nature, extensive use of source materials must of course be made, frequently for the sake of accuracy in verbatum quotation form. Grateful acknowledgment is made to the following publishers and authors for such use. Precise identification of the various sources is made at appropriate points throughout the text by bibliographic reference.

American Journal of Orthopsychiatry: Beck, S.J., Introduction to the Rorschach Method © 1937

Child Development: Hertz, M., The Method of Administration of the Rorschach Ink Blot Test © 1936

Grune & Stratton: Beck, S.J., The Rorschach Experiment © 1960; Rorschach's Test I © 1944; Rorschach's Test II © 1945; Rorschach's Test III © 1952; Beck, S.J., and Molish, H.B., Rorschach's Test II © 1945; Schafer, R., Psychoanalytic Interpretation in Rorschach Testing © 1954

Harcourt, Brace & World: Klopfer, B., and Davidson, H., The Rorschach Technique © 1962

Journal of Consulting Psychology: Hertz, M., The Rorschach Method, Science or Mystery? © 1943

Journal Press: Hertz, M., Scoring the Rorschach Ink Blot Test © 1938

Macmillan: Piotrowski, Z., Perceptanalysis © 1957

Psychiatric Quarterly: Piotrowski, Z., Digital Computer Interpretations of Ink Blot Test Data © 1964

Rorschach Research Exchange, Vol. 1: Piotrowski, Z., On the Rorschach Method and its Application in Organic Disturbances of the Central Nervous System; The M, FM and m Responses as Indicators of Changes in Personality © 1936;

Vol. 2: Klopfer, B., The Present Status of the Theoretical Development of the Rorschach Method; The Technique of the Rorschach Performance; Loosli-Usteri, M., Letter to the Rorschach Research Exchange; Guirdham, A., Letter to the Rorschach Research Exchange; Beck, S., Some Present Rorschach Problems; Hertz, M., Comment © 1937;

Vol. 3: Hertz, M., On the Standardization of the Rorschach Method; Klopfer, B., Shall the Rorschach Method Be Standardized?; Frank, L., Comments on the Proposed Standardization of the Rorschach Method; Rapaport, D., Comments on Rorschach Standardization; Klopfer, B., The Theory and Technique of Rorschach Interpretation © 1939;

Vol. 4: Krugman, M., Out of the Inkwell © 1940;
Vol. 5: Hertz, M., Rorschach: 20 Years After © 1941;
Vol. 6: Piotrowski, Z., The Modifiability of Personality as Revealed by the Rorschach Method © 1942;
Vol. 9: Harriman, P.B., Book Review © 1945;
Vol. 10: Harriman, P.B., Book Review © 1946;
Vol. 29: Citation to Samuel Beck © 1965

State Hospitals Press: Piotrowski, Z., Rorschach Compendium © 1950

World Book Co.: Klopfer, B., and Kelley, D., The Rorschach Technique © 1942; Klopfer, B., Ainsworth, M.D., Klopfer, W.G., and Holt, R.R., Developments in the Rorschach Technique, Vol. 1: Technique and Theory © 1954

CONTENTS

FOREWORD   vii

1. INTRODUCTION   1
   THE BEGINNINGS   1
   THE RORSCHACH SYSTEMS   7

2. DIVERGENCE   15

3. DEVELOPMENT OF THE SYSTEMS   29

4. THE KLOPFER SYSTEM   52
   ADMINISTRATION   54
   SCORING   58
   INTERPRETATION   71
   QUANTITATIVE ANALYSIS   73
   SEQUENCE ANALYSIS   83
   CONTENT ANALYSIS   84
   SUMMARY   86

5. THE BECK SYSTEM   90
   ADMINISTRATION   92
   SCORING   94
   INTERPRETATION   97

6. THE PIOTROWSKI SYSTEM   121
   ADMINISTRATION   124
   SCORING   126
   DETERMINANTS   127
   INTERPRETATION   137
   COMPUTERIZATION   147

7. THE HERTZ SYSTEM   155
   ADMINISTRATION   158
   SCORING   160
   INTERPRETATION   168

8. THE RAPAPORT-SCHAFER SYSTEM   175
   ADMINISTRATION   178
   SCORING   181
   INTERPRETATION   188

9. THE SYSTEMS: PROCEDURES AND SCORINGS ... 201
   INSTRUCTIONS AND ADMINISTRATIVE PROCEDURES ... 201
   SCORING SYMBOLS AND CRITERIA ... 206
   LOCATION ... 206
   DETERMINANTS ... 210
   CONTENT ... 226

10. THE SYSTEMS: INTERPRETATION ... 228
    INTERPRETATION OF LOCATION COMPONENTS ... 232
    INTERPRETATION OF DETERMINANTS ... 234
    POPULAR AND ORIGINAL RESPONSES ... 242
    CONTENT SCORES ... 243
    VERBALIZATIONS ... 243

11. AN OVERVIEW ... 246
    ADMINISTRATIVE PROCEDURES ... 252
    METHOD OF SCORING ... 253
    INTERPRETATION ... 254
    TEACHING RORSCHACH ... 255
    SUMMARY ... 255

APPENDIX ... 257
   A KLOPFER INTERPRETATION ... 258
   A BECK INTERPRETATION ... 282
   A PIOTROWSKI INTERPRETATION ... 297
   A SCHAFER INTERPRETATION ... 315
   A HERTZ INTERPRETATION ... 321

AUTHOR INDEX ... 375

SUBJECT INDEX ... 377

FOREWORD

A number of studies have demonstrated that the Rorschach has been and continues to be one of the most commonly used instruments in psychodiagnostics. It is almost a half century since Rorschach's monograph was published on the technique. Since that time thousands of investigations have been published concerning its merits or lack thereof. It has been the subject of great criticism by many psychologists and colleagues from other professions. There are those who regard its worth with contempt and have advocated its complete abandonment. Many others defend the technique purporting it to be the most effective of the projective devices. While the controversy has raged, the test has not only survived but flourished even more intensely in the skilled hands of the practitioner so that today, Rorschach data is frequently given considerable weight in the final formulations concerning personality and behavior on which diagnoses are often based and recomendations postulated.

Unfortunately, the students of the Rorschach, both opponents and supporters, are often left with the notion that there is a single Rorschach orientation or system about which controversies are centered. That is only a partial truth. There are the ten Swiss inkblots. But there is not only one method of administration, or only one method of scoring, or only one method of interpretation. The fact is that there are several. In the United States there are at least five such orientations or systems and others can be found in Europe, Latin America, and Asia.

This work is devoted to the five American Rorschach systems. It has been precipitated by the many unanswerable questions asked by graduate students over several years in projective techniques courses but it was predisposed long before that by David Rapaport who, in 1955, encouraged a naive graduate student to "read all of the great people of the Rorschach." Among those he referred to Bruno Klopfer, Samuel Beck, Marguerite Hertz, Zygmunt Piotrowski, and Roy Schafer. Along with Rapaport, each has contributed much to the development of the Rorschach, both practically and theoretically. They are undoubtably among the giants of projective techniques. But they have not always agreed. Quite the contrary, they have frequently disagreed. Consequently, as each has committed a part of his professional life to the Rorschach, different approaches have evolved, approaches which have become relatively systematic and which are marked by the unique theoretical and/or methodological signatures of each. Each of the five systems, Beck, Klopfer, Hertz, Piotrowski, and Rapaport-Schafer, forms an overlay to the original work of Hermann Rorschach.

In the beginning it is doubtful that any one of these significant people really allied themselves closely with an approach designed to be different from the others. But each had a different training, and each had a different perception of the Rorschach as it might be applied by practical clinical psychology. The Rorschach seemed to provide a basic avenue for personality study which quickly became fertile ground for investigation, particularly in light of the fact that Rorschach died quite prematurely. Some of these Systematizers have committed themselves to a broad theoretical system, leaving the bulk of the task of validation to others. Others have built from the data structure upward, having been more reluctant to offer theoretical postulates for which no data exists.

The contemporary status of the technique is such that a student is ordinarily trained to approach the Rorschach by one System, usually the one which meets the needs and/or biases of his instructor. The remaining four Systems are typically given little or no consideration and thus, the student may complete his training with a naive assumption that he has "learned Rorschach." Some find themselves bewildered later in attempting to understand the other Systems. Others perseverate the naive assumption that the differences among the Systems exist only in minor scoring idiosyncrasies and that—on the broader level—there truly is a single Rorschach orientation. It is the goal here to contrast these Systems historically, methodologically, and theoretically so as to vanquish some of this naivity. The complexities of this undertaking have been eased considerably by the generous cooperation and encouragement offered by Systematizers and other Rorschach authorities. They have willingly participated in many interviews so as to offer clarification to material, and have devoted much time to the reading of parts of the manuscript for accuracy. They have willingly shared many personal ideas and memories. These have been very privileged experiences. Thus, to Samuel Beck, Bruno Klopfer, Zygmunt Piotrowski, Marguerite Hertz and Roy Schafer goes a very deep seated feeling of gratitude. And to David Rapaport, even though he did not live to see this work begin, a special indebtedness for forcing me to "look again" at the Rorschach. There have been many other special people, too numerous to mention, who have aided in the undertaking by supplying data or carefully reviewing parts of the manuscript. In particular I would like to thank Karl Bash for the precious Sunday which he took to share much historical data about Rorschach with me, and Franziska Baumgarten-Trammer, who most graciously surmounted a painful language barrier to share the Lipmann Collection with my wife and myself at her home in Bern. Finally, no work can be completed without willing and understanding secretaries. Three such people, Mrs. Connie Wearsch, Mrs. Janet Rader, and Mrs. Elaine Bond, have struggled with the peculiar language of the Rorschach world in a most commendable manner.

J.E.E.

CHAPTER 1

INTRODUCTION

There is little question that the Rorschach has become an integral part of clinical psychology. To suggest that it has been an instrument of controversy is indeed an understatement. An often stormy history may be observed during its development. And yet, it has survived. Its survival, much like that of psychoanalytic theory, has made a significant impact, not only on the clinical specialist, but probably on most all of psychology.

THE BEGINNINGS

The history of Rorschach development is not easily traceable. We know generally when Rorschach began his work and can trace his progress through his own writings and through those of Emil Oberholzer, Walter Morgenthaler, and Georg Roemer. It is uncertain, however, where the original ideas for his experiment were gleaned or when his decision to undertake the experiment occurred. As Zubin, Eron, and Schumer (1965) have indicated, the concept that formless stimuli could be used to stimulate the imagination can be traced back to Leonardo Da Vinci and Botticelli in the 15th Century. It is also important to note that in Europe, during the latter half of the 19th Century and the early part of the 20th Century, there was much public interest in inkblots, not as a test, but more as a game. For example, Justinius Kerner's book (1857) is sometimes referred to by historians of the inkblot techniques. This book contained a reasonably large number of inkblot-like figures, each of which was accompanied by a poetic-like association written by Kerner. It was also very common for inkblots to be used in a popular parlor game called "blotto" where the challenge was to "associate" to a design which might well be created there on the spot or used from the many inkblots and similar designs appearing in the contemporary books and magazines.

More formally, there was, both in Europe and the United States, considerable experimentation attempted with inkblots as tests of imagination, personality, and intelligence. Krugman (1940) cites the evidence that as early as 1895 Binet and Henri suggested that inkblots could be used for studying various personality traits, especially visual imagination. Tulchin (1940) indicates that Dearborn, then at Harvard University, published an article in 1897 discussing the potentials of employing inkblot techniques in experimental psychology. As Tulchin tells us, in 1898 Dearborn published the results of applying an inkblot technique to a group of 16 subjects, wherein he used twelve sets of inkblots, each having ten blots similar in nature. Tulchin also cites the pre-Rorschach work of Sharp, Kirkpatrick, Whipple, Pyle, Bartlette, and Parsons, all of whom published material between 1900 and 1917 concerning inkblot methodology in the United States and England.

Both Krugman and Tulchin indicate that much of the work done in the United States with inkblots was stimulated by Whipple who described his test as one of "active imagination" in which he used a series of twenty inkblots called "Test 45." His technique and data were described in a *Manual of Mental and Physical Tests* published in 1910.

In addition to the European layman's interest and the American and English studies, there were other experiments taking place in Europe. For example, Baumgarten-Traumer (1942) notes that in 1910 there appeared in Moscow an *Atlas for Experimental Research on Personality*. It was published by Theodore Rybakow, a Russian psychologist, who at that time was a tutor at the University of Moscow. In the *Atlas*, which like Whipple's *Manual* contained a large number of different types of tests, there was one test comprised of eight inkblots. The blots are all asymmetrical and reproduced in flat black, having no shading variations. Rybakow indicated that he used the test for the purpose of experimentation concerning the thought process as well as the depth of imagination. Since Rorschach worked in a private sanitorium in Moscow in 1913, and had himself experimented with inkblots some two years earlier, it is highly probable that he familiarized himself with Rybakow's work. Even if he did not do so in Moscow, his widow (1944) indicates that he was familiar with the work of Lipmann and Lipmann's collection of inkblots which included the Rybakow figures.

RORSCHACH

The real beginnings of the technique, as it is today, of course are directly traceable to the work of Hermann Rorschach who, in 1911 as a 27-year-old psychiatrist, began to experiment with inkblots. As has been suggested, he was much more than superficially aware of the previous experimental work done with inkblots. Olga Rorschach (1944) indicates that her husband's decision to work with inkblots was at least partially stimulated by the observations of a former classmate Konrad Gehring who, during the period of Rorschach's decisions, was teaching school in the intermediate level. Gehring had discovered that, while using inkblots which he ordinarily displayed on very large sheets of paper at the front of the classroom, certain children gave very similar responses to a variety of blots, even though the figures were quite different in their form and/or color. Roemer (1958, 1967) reports that, in the beginning, Rorschach had no intention of constructing a psychodiagnostic test series. According to Roemer, Rorschach's first purpose was to investigate reflex hallucinations and it was not until much later, around 1917, that he began to assemble material in a systematic manner for diagnostic purposes. Roemer also indicates that Rorschach discovered the diagnostic possibilities of the ink-blot technique somewhat accidentally while working at the hospital at Hersau, in Switzerland.*

Rorschach's interest in inkblots may have also been enhanced by his association with Hens. In 1917 Hens published a report concerning the use of inkblots with children, normal adults, and mentally ill subjects, based on research which was conducted at Bleuler's Clinic. Rorschach criticized Hens' work because of the limited analysis of his results and because of the classification of all of the responses of his subjects against the frame-work of vocational, social, and personal interests, and current events. It could be that the failures of Hens' approach, as perceived by Rorschach, stimulated Rorschach to deal more directly with the perceptual aspects of the blots rather than with their content.

The ultimate development of the techniques which Rorschach settled upon apparently was stimulated by a variety of sources. Inkblots were a "fad" of the times. Inkblots were being used in contemporary experimentation and Rorschach was encouraged by friends and colleagues. Possibly most important is the fact that Rorschach had a very inquiring mind which was dissatisfied with contemporary techniques of personality investigations. Roemer (1967) tells us that Rorschach never used more than 40 inkblots and that the final series was limited to ten because the publisher was unwilling to invest more money in the reproduction of additional plates. Whatever the cause of his initial interest, or the selection of his material, Rorschach clearly accomplished a major work in a relatively short period of time. His tragic and untimely death on April 2, 1922, after only a few days' illness, due to appendicitis complicated by peritonitis, created a void in inkblot research which could never be completely filled.

Very possibly, had it not been for the enthusiasm and dedication of Emil Oberholzer, Walter Morgenthaler, and Georg Roemer, Rorschach's work might well have gone unnoticed or at least unpopularized after his

---

* After working in Moscow in 1913, Rorschach received an appointment to the staff of the psychiatric clinic at the asylum at Bern-Waldau, and subsequently to the hospital at Hersau.

death. They continued to teach the techniques and encourage its use and investigation. Morgenthaler had previously been directly responsible for the publication of Rorschach's monograph, *Psychodiagnostik,* in 1921. As Bash (1965) points out, Morgenthaler had worked with Rorschach at the University Psychiatric Clinic at Waldau in Bern from 1914 to 1915. Bash indicates that during that year which was well before *Psychodiagnostik* was conceived, Rorschach was eagerly gathering material concerning the psychopathological features of certain sects of the Canton of Bern and their founders. Morgenthaler also shared a common interest with Rorschach in collecting artistic productions of psychotic patients.

According to Bash:

"Morgenthaler, as the editor of a series of 'Studies in Applied Psychology' for the newly founded, venturesome and soon afterward defunct Swiss publishing house of Bircher, recognized early the unique merit of Rorschach's discovery and pushed it through its publication against a certain reluctance of the publisher himself, a reluctance that is understandable to a degree when it is realized that Rorschach at first did not submit a complete manuscript, sketched the *Psychodiagnostik* only after its acceptance in what Morgenthaler himself called 'an incredibly short time, but in an unfinished state, then became impatient when the printing proceeded more slowly than he had expected, as if inwardly forewarned of his death a year later.' "

In addition to Morgenthaler's efforts, Oberholzer took it unto himself to publish posthumously an important paper of Rorschach's describing the inkblot technique and elaborating upon its potentials regarding personality diagnosis (1923). Certainly Oberholzer served as a significant stimulant to Samuel Beck, who refers to his "very instructive hours" with Oberholzer concerning the critical use of the Rorschach (1937). Later, Oberholzer was to provide similar encouragement to Zygmunt Piotrowski.

Rorschach did not postulate a specific theoretical position with regard to his inkblot technique and/or personality evaluation in general. His observations concerning the responses to the blots by both patients and non-patients led him to a variety of conclusions concerning the specific perceptual determinants of responses, i.e., color, movement and in particular, form; but he did not formulate a global theory concerning his test. His introduction to *Psychodiagnostik* points to the simplicity and intent of his experiment.

"The following pages describe the technique of and the result thus far achieved in a psychological experiment which, despite its simplicity, has proved to be of value in research and in general testing. At the outset it must be pointed out that all of the results are predominantly empirical. The questions which gave rise to the original experiments of this sort (1911) were of a different type from those which slowly developed as the work progressed. The conclusions drawn, therefore, are to be regarded more as observations than as theoretical deductions. The theoretical foundation for the experiment is, for the most part, still incomplete. . . .it must also be noted that there has been constant checking of the observations on normal subjects against observations of patients, and vice versa." (p. 13)

There did exist a fundamental assumption on Rorschach's part that the way in which the blot stimuli are interpreted somehow represents certain moods or styles of behavior. In this respect, it might be suggested that Rorschach inferred a typological approach which has inherent in it a fragmentary theoretical basis. It does seem certain that, at least in the beginning, Rorschach did not concern himself with the "projective" features of the responses. In *Psychodiagnostik* he refers to the work of Hens as being concerned with the problem of the content of percepts exclusively and not carrying interpretations beyond consideration of imagination, . . . "his conclusions (Hens), therefore, concern the content rather than the pattern of perceptive process which has been my principal concern" (p. 102). Actually, Rorscach offered a very conservative estimate concerning the use of the technique for diagnosis or personality evaluation.

"The inadequacy of the test in estimating the quantitative importance of findings can be so great that it cannot be said whether a symptom is manifest or latent. It is impossible to determine from the records of the test, in some cases, whether a schizophrenic reaction is manifest, latent, or dormant for the time being. . . .the content of the interpretations offers little indication as to the content of the psyche until it is considered in relation to the psychogram—granting that the results of this test for the discovery of patterns of thinking can be called psychograms." (p. 121)

Zubin, Eron and Schumer have raised a question concerning Rorschach's ultimate intentions for the technique. They suggest that Rorschach might well be appalled were he to perceive how the technique is utilized in contemporary psychodiagnosis. The implication here is that Rorschach would not have wanted the technique committed to projective theory nor psychoanalytic interpretation, especially of the content. Such a conclusion is very questionable. It is true that Rorschach questioned the value of the technique as directly applicable to psychoanalytic theory, especially the concept of the unconscious.

"The test cannot be considered as a means of delving into the unconscious. At best, it is far inferior to the other more profound psychological methods such as dream interpretation and association experiments. This is not difficult to understand. The test does not induce a free flow from the subconscious but requires adaptation to external stimuli, participation of the fonction du réel." (p. 123)

Rorschach suggested that if material were to be yielded from the unconscious or subconscious it would be manifest in the content, but cautioned that this would occur mainly as a function of neurotic inhibition or in some types of schizophrenic reactions. There is no doubt that he wanted the test fully investigated under well controlled experimental conditions but there is also no doubt of his familiarity, intrigue, and even commitment with psychoanalytic theory. He was a member of the Swiss Psychoanalytic Association, was well versed in Freudian theory, and had a very close association with Eugen Bleuler. Furthermore, this was an era in Europe when Freudian theory was having more than a casual impact. Rorschach was also very familiar with the work of Carl Jung, so much that he took great pains to point out carefully his use of the words introversion and extroversion was dissimilar to the definitions offered by Jung. He also cited a possible relationship between the *Erlebnistypus* (experience type) and the phenomenon of regression as described by Freud and suggested that the technnque could be useful in studying differences "after analysis."

If it is necessary to raise a question concerning Rorschach's probable reaction to the "projective hypothesis" as was delineated by Frank (1939) nearly twenty years later, it seems highly plausible to propose that he would have accepted the hypothesis as highly relevant and encouraged its investigation. Some support for this notion is found in Roemer (1967) who asserts that Rorschach endorsed the use of content analysis in 1921, ". . . a decision diametrically opposed to the opinion which he had expressed in his book, *Psychodiagnostik.*" Roemer also quotes from a letter, written in 1921, in which Rorschach states that the technique is based on the integration of the "analytical and professional" schools of psychological thought and that the combination of the two provide "a diagnosis so accurate that it strikes one with amazement."

That Rorschach failed to develop a broad theory pertaining to the test should not be surprising. In view of what is now known of him, it seems valid to speculate that had he lived to study the instrument over a longer period of time, a generalized theory would have evolved. Probably such a theory would have been based on the variety of hypotheses which he did formulate concerning the meaningfulness of the different types of precepts and more particularly with regard to the varieties of scoring categories and ratios. Conversely, it might have developed that, rather than construct a theory specific to the test, he might have woven the existing hypotheses into an existing theory of personality or behavior, most likely that of Freudian psychoanalysis.

It has been mentioned that Emil Oberholzer was among the senior advocates of the Rorschach. After Rorschach's death, Oberholzer became one of the main avenues through which Rorschach's ideas and work were made widely available. Oberholzer had a very strong psychoanalytic orientation. He trained David M. Levy in the use of technique, and Levy, in turn, was the first to bring the Rorschach to America. Beck, Klopfer, Piotrowski, and Hertz all attribute great significance to Levy's enthusiasm for the Rorschach. He organized the first Rorschach seminar in the United States, in Chicago, in 1925. A year later he offered the first publication concerning the Rorschach to appear in an American journal. It was a translation of a previously published work. Not long thereafter, it was his direct influence on Samuel Beck that provoked Beck's first steps into the world of the inkblot.

THE RORSCHACH SYSTEMS

In that the principal author of the Rorschach technique died prematurely, it seemed only natural that a variety of new investigators soon would come on the scene and, in turn, attempt to extend his basic work. Surely, this has been the case and has led to he development of a variety of Rorschach Systems. The word Systems is used here as contrasted with theories, in that each System represents an approach to the Rorschach. Each System has its own underpinnings in some other general or specific theoretical approach. Today, in America, there are five such Systems, none of which is completely different from the others nor from Rorschach's original conceptions.

The differences that exist in the present day Rorschach Systems seem to have been precipitated by two factors. First, none of the authors of the five Systems, Beck, Klopfer, Hertz, Piotrowski, Rapaport or Schafer, had any direct experience with Hermann Rorschach. In fact, only one of these Systematizers, Beck, studied under any person closely associated with Rorschach. For Beck, that person was Oberholzer, but his study with Oberholzer came only after completing his doctorate and having obtained Rorschach experience. This was eleven years after Rorschach's death. Beck completed his Ph.D. in 1932, having done the first doctoral dissertation on the Rorschach in America. Klopfer completed his Ph.D. in 1922, the year of Rorschach's death, but did not have any direct contact with the Rorschach *per se* until 1933. Piotrowski completed his Ph.D. in 1927 but was not formally trained in Rorschach until 1934, in Klopfer's first seminar. Marguerite Hertz also completed her Ph.D. in 1932 having developed an interest in Rorschach during her graduate work which became deep and prolonged. David Rapaport completed his doctoral work in 1938, and his protege, Roy Schafer, in 1950.

But chronology cannot be considered as the prime reason for differences in Rorschach orientations. The second, and much more fundamental cause appears to have been the general training and background in psychology to which each of the Systematizers was exposed. If a hypothetical continuum were drawn, placing the tenets of behaviorism on the far right and those of the more subjective phenomenology on the far left, the basic premises of each of the five Systems can be evaluated along such a line. The Beck System would fall near the extreme right while the Klopfer and Rapaport-Schafer Systems would fall near the extreme left. The Piotrowski System would be right of center, but not so much so as Beck. The Hertz System would be somewhat left of center but not so far as either the Klopfer or Rapaport-Schafer Systems. This should not be interpreted to mean that the Systems are completely different from each other for that is not the case. Although there are major differences, there are also major agreements. For example, all of the Systematizers endorse some form of psychoanalytic theory and all have accepted many of Rorschach's original interpretive hypotheses. Consequently, the continuum can only be used to denote the broader theoretical and operational base on which the Systems have developed.

Klopfer received his Ph.D. at the University of Munich in 1922. His dissertation was a comparative study on inhibition which offered a comprehensive review of work from Müller to Lewin and included the work of Freud, Adler, and Jung. His training was influenced by the "contemporary" German psychology as well as the growing psychoanalytic movement. He was strongly affected by both Eric Becker, who was Külpe's successor, and Morris Geiger whose orientation was strongly phenomenological. After taking his degree, Klopfer accepted a position at the Berlin Information Center for Child Guidance. It was during this time that he became aware of Rorschach's work but had no direct contact with the technique. In 1927, with the intention of becoming an analyst, he began personal analysis with Werner Heilbrun and accordingly became well indoctrinated in the Freudian movement. He was also encouraged to give careful reading of Jungian theory. In 1933, under the pressure of change in Germany fomented by Adolph Hitler, he went to Zurich where he gained personal experience with Jung. Subsequently, he became associated with the Zurich Psychotechnic Institute and began studying Rorschach under Alice Garbaski, who was an assistant to the Director of the Institute.

Klopfer's commitment to psychology and to the Rorschach has been from a phenomenological and Jungian psychoanalytic orientation. This follows mainly in the traditions of Descarte, Berkeley, Brentano, Stumpf, and Husserl. In general, this continental psychology is more prone toward the qualitative and subjective than the rigorous positivistic positions often assumed in American psychology. It has been only natural for Klopfer to approach the Rorschach in a manner which gives greater emphasis to subjectivity. This is not to infer that the Klopfer System is void in a normative base, for that is not true, and yet, the Klopfer approach to the Rorschach does encourage greater subjectivity than probably exists in any of the other Systems, except possibly that of Rapaport-Schafer.

The Beck System approaches the Rorschach much more conservatively than does the Klopfer System. Beck is clearly a behaviorist. He was born in Rumania but grew up in the United States, his parents having immigrated in 1903. He entered Harvard in 1912 to study the classics but withdrew in 1915 to accept a position as a newspaper reporter in Cleveland. He returned to Harvard in 1925 and took his A.B. in 1926. He then went to Columbia where he completed the doctorate in 1932 under the direction of Robert Woodworth and with the guidance of David Levy. Beck worked very closely with Levy, having been somewhat accidentally encouraged by Levy to do his dissertation on the Rorschach. This incident occurred one day when Beck's wife was late for an appointment with her husband, in turn providing time for a discussion on Rorschach with Levy. In 1927, Beck received a pre-doctoral fellowship in psychology at the Institute of Guidance where he worked with Levy. The Institute was under the direction of Lawson Lowery, who created an excellent atmosphere for teaching for psychiatrists, social workers, and psychologists. The Psychology Department at Columbia, chaired by Woodworth, was steeped in the traditional American behaviorism dedicated to scientific objectivity.

Shortly after his graduation, Beck accepted an appointment as a senior resident under F. L. Wells at the Boston Psychopathic Hospital and, shortly thereafter, an appointment to the Harvard Medical School. In 1933, he received a Rockefeller Foundation Fellowship which permitted him to go to Zurich to study directly with Oberholzer. Accordingly, the nucleus of Beck's approach to the Rorschach has been formulated during his years in the behavioristic environment of Columbia, his training under Levy, and his experience with the psychoanalytically oriented Oberholzer. It is also his association with Oberholzer that has probably made Beck most cautious about deviating from Rorschach's original concepts and procedures.

The Piotrowski System began through association with the Klopfer orientation, but, as it was developed, it has grown to a position more closely aligned with the Beckian behavioristic point of view. Piotrowski received his Ph.D. in 1927 from the University of Poznan, Poland. He did pre-doctoral studies at the Sorbonne in Paris and came to the United States for post-doctoral work in clinical psychology. In 1931, he accepted an appointment for one year as an instructor in the College of Physicians and

Surgeons at Columbia University. As an undergraduate, Piotrowski had specialized in mathematics but also maintained a very strong interest in the arts. As a graduate student, he trained in experimental psychology with major emphasis on perception and quantitative techniques, but also received, like Klopfer, a liberal exposure to the European traditions of phenomenological psychology. After completing his formal academic work he became quite interested in psychoanalytic theory and ultimately adopted a Freudian position toward the study of personality.

Although Piotrowski had been a subject for the Rorschach, as a curious graduate student, he had no formal training in Rorschach prior to his arrival in the United States. In fact, it was only due to the encouragement of Gladys Tallman, in 1934, that he decided to attend Klopfer's first Rorschach seminar to obtain first-hand information about the technique. Piotrowski had intended to remain in the United States for only one or two years; however, he was strongly encouraged by Elaine Kinder to accept a position at the Psychiatric Institute for further study. Later he moved to a position at the Columbia University Clinic in the College of Physicians and Surgeons. Strongly committed to the notions of mathematics and symbolic logic, Piotrowski perceived the Rorschach as an avenue to the study of personality in which deductive logic could be utilized fruitfully. His association with Klopfer as a "student" lasted for, at most, two years, wherein their basic differences in background and approach created schisms which neither could reconcile. As his System developed, Piotrowski became mainly concerned with the Rorschach as an instrument to be used in the study of psychopathology and the overall evaluation of personality and psychosocial interactions.

Hertz took her doctorate in 1932 from Western Reserve University. Her introduction to the Rorschach was almost as accidental as that of Beck. While working at the Brush Foundation,* Hertz found herself quite unimpressed with contemporary personality tests. The psychological unit at the Brush Foundation had previously experimented with the construction of their own tests, such as TAT-like pictures, hieroglyphics, etc. During a visit to New York, Hertz met David Levy and, as he had done with Beck almost four years earlier, suggested the Rorschach as being potentially useful for the study of children. Subsequently, during a social visit Beck showed her the Rorschach cards for the first time. The Psychology Department chairman at Western Reserve expressed considerable skepticism concerning the worth of the Rorschach but approved her study of it as a dissertation topic mostly to disprove its usefulness. While Hertz's initial Rorschach

---

* The Brush Foundation was an organization devoted to the total child, having special units for medical, dental, educational, and psychological care.

investigation, which involved the testing of 50 children did not disprove the usefulness of the technique, it did present her with the obvious problem of lack of normative data, leading in turn to many of her early post-doctoral investigations.

The early approach which Hertz took toward Rorschach study was consistent with her training, that being heavily oriented toward psychometrics. The consequent increase in her commitment to the Rorschach and the broadening of her associations with others likewise committed gradually caused her to take a more "clinical" approach, thereby temperizing her engrossment with psychometrics. The Hertz System began with a position very similar to that expressed by Beck but has gradually changed during its development to an approach more closely aligned with Klopfer. Nonetheless, Hertz has continued to disagree with Klopfer on many points. While endorsing the psychoanalytic approach, Hertz has seemed least strongly committed to psychoanalytic theory than any of the Systematizers.

David Rapaport and Roy Schafer first purported a formal approach to the Rorschach in 1946 in *Diagnostic Psychological Testing*. Rapaport had been researching with the Rorschach as early as the late 1930's and had published a paper on the principles underlying projective techniques in 1942. The Rorschach was carefully evaluated in that paper. He had received his Ph.D. in 1938, from the Royal Hungarian Petrus at Pazmany. Rapaport had studied under Paul Von Schiller and thus, had a very strong psychoanalytic orientation. He came to the United States shortly after taking his degree and accepted his first position at the Mt. Siani Hospital in New York City. After a year in New York, Rapaport assumed a position at the Oswatomi State Hospital in Kansas, which began for him a close tie with the Menninger Foundation, and subsequently, led to his appointment there. In 1948 he took a position at the Austen-Riggs Center where he remained until his premature death in 1960, at the age of 49.

Roy Schafer may well be Rapaport's most well known disciple. Schafer began his association with Rapaport shortly after receiving his Bachelor's degree from the City College of New York in 1943. He worked several years with Rapaport, first at the Menninger Foundation where he served as an intern, and later at the Austen-Riggs Foundation. Schafer graduated from Clark University in 1950, and is by far the youngest of the Systematizers, having been born in the year of Rorschach's death. Schafer published three important books after *Diagnostic Psychological Testing*. These are *The Clinical Application of Psychological Tests,* in 1948; *Psychoanalytic Interpretation in Rorschach Testing,* in 1954, a classic work giving emphasis to content analysis; and *Projective Testing and Psychoanalysis,* in 1967.

The Rapaport-Schafer System is probably least similar to any of the other Systems, using different procedures, different scorings, and giving major emphasis to the analysis of verbalizations. It also stresses the relationship between the examiner and the subject more than do any of the other Systems. It is the most clearly based on psychoanalytic theory giving a major role to the concepts of prototypes and the defense system.

It is arduous to predict the extent to which any of these Systems might have developed had Rorschach lived longer or had Oberholzer, Morgenthaler, or Roemer assumed a more active leadership in Rorschach research. It could be conjectured that the technique might have been modified significantly in light of Rorschach's desires for objectivity or possibly even abandoned because of its complexity. Conversely, it could be argued that the approach to interpretation might have become more firmly marked by an emphasis on content analysis, as has been suggested by Roemer, or inscribed by a greater emphasis on psychoanalytic theory, as later has been introduced by all of the Systematizers. But these things did not occur and consequently, the five American Systems of the Rorschach have developed. The obvious lack of agreement in approach and in theory, among Rorschach authorities, has given much cause for concern over a long period of time. Hertz, who has frequently acted as a Rorschach historian and evaluator, has pointed to the lack of agreement on many issues numerous times in the literature. The problem was also quite apparent to others during the 1930's. For example, in 1937, Marguerite Loosli-Usteri, a well-known Swiss psychologist, commented in an issue of the *Rorschach Research Exchange*:

"May I, however, first of all make a humble suggestion? Would it not be easier for all of us if we applied a uniform Rorschach terminology? We find already some difficulty in understanding each other, but what will it be in a few years' time? I am afraid, but if every investigator is using his own terminology, we shall soon have a babylonian (*sic*) confusion of languages which will make every understanding most difficult. Don't you think that a unified terminology, based on Latin, would be palatable to all Rorschach investigators all over the world?" (p. 73)

Obviously, her appeal for a common Latin terminology was not accepted by her colleagues, and even though she referred to language rather than theoretical and operational approach, her point was well taken and her prediction of a Babylonian confusion, at least partially, realized.

The differences which have evolved in theoretical and operational orientations have produced a broad variety of approaches to the Rorschach which encompass administration, scoring, interpretation, and research. These differences have often appeared based on legitimate intellectual considerations, but at other times the differences seem more based on affect than intellect. The differentiation in System development may have stimulated progress which otherwise might not have occurred. Obviously, healthy intellectual differences concerning most any matter can lead to deeper consideration. Conversely, when differences are too great to be reconciled, or when they persist over a lengthy period of time, they may serve to arrest the growth of an idea or operation. During a 40-year period of growth in the United States, the Rorschach has come to be one of the most commonly used psychodiagnostic techniques but it is also one of the most widely criticized tests of all times. There is still no clearly agreed upon theory of the test, no clearly agreed upon method of administration, no clearly agreed upon method of scoring, and approaches to interpretation continue to be heterogeneous. This may be the crux of the Rorschach problem, if indeed, there is a problem.

In the chapters that follow, the historical origins of the Rorschach divergence, the growth of the respective Systems, and an inter-System comparison will be considered with the goal of providing some clarification to these issues.

REFERENCES

Bash, K. W. In memoriam—Dr. Walter Morgenthaler. *J. Proj. Tech.*, 1965, 29, 267-270.

Baumgarten-Traumer, Franziska Zur Geschichte des Rorschachtests. *Schweiz. Arch. Neur Psychiat.*, 1942, 50, 1-13.

Beck, S. J. Introduction to the Rorschach Method. *Amer. Orthopsychiat. Assoc., Monog.*, 1, 1937.

Frank, L. K. Projective methods for the study of personality. *J. Psychol.*, 1939, 8, 389-413.

Hens, Szynon Phantasieprufung mit formlosen Klecksen be, Schulkindern, normalen Erwachseuen Und Genteskranken. (Dissert. Zurich, 1917.)

Kerner, J. Klexographien. Part VI in Pissen, R. (ed.). *Kerners werke.* Berlin: Boag and Co., 1857.

Krugman, M. Out of the inkwell *Ror. Res. Exch.*, 1940, 4, 91-101.

Loosli-Usterli, Marguerite. Letter to the Rorschach Research Exchange. *Ror. Res. Exch.*, 1937, 2, 73-74.

Rapaport, D., Gill, M., and Schafer, R. *Diagnostic Psychological Testing*, Vol. I and II. Chicago: Yearbook Publishers, 1946.

Roemer, G. Pour la Verite de Rorschach. *J. Med. Lyon*, 1958, 5, 521.

Roemer, G. The Rorschach and Roemer Symbol Test Series. *J. Nerv. Ment. Dis.*, 1967, 144, 185-197.

Rorschach, H. *Psychodiagnostics.* Bern: Bircher, 1921, (Transl. Hans Huber Verlag, 1942).

Rorschach, H. and Oberholzer, E. The application of the interpretation of form to psychoanalysis. *J. Nerv. Ment. Dis.*, 1924, 60, 225-248.

Rorschach, Olga. Uber des Leben und des Wesenart von Hermann Rorschach. *Schweiz. Arch. Neurol. Psychiat.*, 1944, 53, 1-11.

Schafer, R. *The Clinical Application of Psychological Tests.* New York: International Univ. Press, 1948.

Schafer, R. *Psychoanalytic Interpretation in Rorschach Testing.* New York: Grune and Stratton, 1954.

Schafer, R. *Projective Testing and Psychoanalysis*: Selected Papers. New York: International Univ. Press, 1967.

Tulchin, S. H. The pre-Rorschach use of inkblot tests. *Ror. Res. Exch.*, 1940, 4, 1-7.

Whipple, G. M. *Manual of Mental and Physical Tests.* (2 vols.) Baltimore: Warwich and York, 1914-1915.

Zubin, J., Eron, L., and Schumer, Florence. *An Experimental Approach to Projective Techniques.* New York: Wiley and Sons, 1965.

CHAPTER 2

DIVERGENCE

In the preceding chapter, it has been postulated that two elements, one chronological and the second based on theoretical differences, were essentially responsible for the divergence of Rorschach orientations into five similar but distinctly separate Systems. There is no single incident or time which can be designated as the point of divergence; however, there is a period that encompasses the years 1934-1940 during which time the seeds of divergence were sown. It was during this period that a number of Rorschach investigators sought to have their notions on administration, scoring, and interpretation known to colleagues. Differences of opinion were voiced and documented, schisms occurred, and some pleas for a common ground, such as that of Loosli-Usteri's, were formulated unsuccessfully.

Historically, the Beck System, or its key orientation, was the first to be documented. Its formulation was manifest in the compilation of some 14 articles beginning with the first American research report on the Rorschach, in 1930, and culminating in 1937 with the publishing of Beck's first book, *Introduction to the Rorschach Method*. This book was the first monograph of the American Orthopsychiatric Association and became known as "Beck's Manual." In it Beck defined his work as ". . . an effort to compile such a normative, objectively stable standard of procedure. . . ." He emphasized the necessity for normative data suggesting that those offered in the manual ". . . can in the present state of affairs, be only provisional and tentative in the extreme."

Well before the publication of Beck's "Manual" he had raised the flag of behaviorism on behalf of the Rorschach. His first salvo was fired in 1935 in an article appearing in the *American Journal of Orthopsychiatry*. In that article he summarized his reaction to Rorschach practice in Zurich, and stressed that a breadth and diversity of experience is essential to success in diagnosis. He expressed a feeling of distress that the Zurich procedures were marked too largely by the approach of the artist rather than the scientist and that an inconsistency of scoring was quite common. He appealed for research to be undertaken to find constant, experimentally tested, criteria for scoring of locations, standardizing the responses representing good and poor form, establishing frequency tables for color responses, and determining experimentally whether the tables or the subject's report is the more dependable criteria for color responses, experimentally

15

identifying the movement response, and possibly most important, determining how the various Rorschach responses point to the psychological processes. He also encouraged continued work with clinical groups, suggesting that the comparative values of the same trait in different types of personalities must be considered, and called for work to evolve concerning the significance of the content of responses. In the following year he published an article in *Character and Personality* (1936) entitled "Autism in Rorschach Scoring; a Feeling Comment." In this article he strongly criticized Bleuler and Bleuler for their suggestion that the Rorschach examiner should "feel himself into" every response made by the subject. By taking issue with the Bleuler position, Beck once again pointed to the need for fixed standards rather than greater subjectivity in scoring, emphasizing that it is the personality of the client and not that of the examiner that should ultimately be reflected in both the scoring and interpretation.

Klopfer's initial writings evolved from his direction of Rorschach training seminars in New York City while a Research Associate in Anthropology at Columbia University. These seminars, which first were formed somewhat loosely, gradually evolved into the development of the *Rorschach Research Exchange* and later the *Rorschach Institute*. Most of the beginning membership of the *Exchange* were from the Psychology Department of the Neurological Institute. In the first issue, which appeared shortly before the publication of Beck's Manual, Klopfer offered a refined scoring system for Rorschach (Klopfer, B. and Sender, S., 1936) based in part on his prior experience with the technique and in part on the seminar discussions which had occurred in New York City during the two preceding years. This scoring system was well organized but did not have the research base as did the data comprising Beck's *Introduction to the Rorschach Method*. It called for a greater diversification in the scoring, well beyond that which either Rorschach or Beck had gone.

In a later issue of the first volume of the *Rorschach Research Exchange*, Klopfer presented a paper, "The Present Status of the Theoretical Development of the Rorschach Method" (1937), in which he gave considerable space to reviewing the Beck Manual. The review was somewhat critical of Beck's failure to include the cut-off Whole response, to differentiate scoring movement, the limited scoring categories of Shading, and the general approach used by Beck in evaluating Form responses. The article naturally provoked reply from Beck which was published in the second volume of the *Rorschach Research Exchange* entitled "Some Rorschach Problems" (1937). Beck's reply, as might be expected, was equally critical; a criticism which might be pointed to as the first documentation of a real schism between the orientations. The breadth of the disagreements appears to have made the possibility of reconciliation at best quite difficult. Following Beck's paper, there appeared in the next issue of *Rorschach Research Exchange* a series of comments on the paper, which probably served to widen the schism.

Beck had made it very clear in his earlier writings that he was strongly committed to the Rorschach-Oberholzer tradition, wherein the approach to understanding personality combines both the nomothetic and idiographic methodologies. In all of his early publications, beginning in 1930, Beck took a strong position favoring standardization of procedures for administration and scoring. He consistently denounced subjectivity in scoring. Conversely, Klopfer expressed much more willingness for the individual examiner to use his own Rorschach experience as a guideline (Klopfer, 1937). This was one of the more essential points of disagreement between Beck and Klopfer. It focused on the appropriate procedure for scoring Form responses as plus or minus and, as facilitated by other differences, may have been one of the distinct factors causing a basic and unreconcilable divergence between the two. Some quotations from Beck's article, "Some Rorschach Problems" (1937), offer clarification concerning this issue.

"Doctor Bruno Klopfer's most recent discussion of Rorschach problems naturally provokes some comment. . . .the judgment of whether a response is to be scored plus or minus must be clinically validated. It cannot be the opinion of just one examiner however experienced with the Rorschach test he may be; or even of some group of examiners. . . . Once the response has been finally judged plus or minus, it must always be scored plus or minus. . . .the requirement here, in a word, is that of constant norms. . . .it would seem that Klopfer uses material that is extraneous to that properly belonging to F plus determination. . . .an individual may elaborate and integrate to his heart's content, but if he does not arrive at a FORM within the range of those found 'plus' he has not produced a clear or sharp perception."

In the same article, Beck delivered criticism towards Binder's scoring of Shading (1933), which had been supported earlier by Klopfer, and offered considerable disagreement with the methods suggested by Klopfer and Piotrowski (1937) for the scoring of movement responses. "Here (the M responses) the writer must seriously question the direction which Klopfer and his group are heading." Beck could not accept the postulate that Movement responses not involving humans or human capabilities should be scored as a special type of movement. Over some thirty years Beck has not changed in his opinion. Thus, while it might have been a disagreement over subjectivity in scoring Form responses that initiated the schism, the overall issue of Movement responses and scoring for Shading responses clearly substained and widened the schism. Quoting once again from the Beck article, "If this interpretation of M is based on Piotrowski's or

Klopfer's experience one is naturally interested in the evidence. It does not seem consistent with Rorschach's, Oberholzer's, Levy's or their close followers' understanding of the value of M."

Summarizing the 1937 article, Beck clearly specified the behavioristic orientation which his System was to follow, carefully spelling out that a certain subjectivity in Rorschach testing is acceptable but only as modified by serious strivings toward objectification.

"The Rorschach test, as a subjectively used instrument in the hands of individuals having experience with many clinical groups and themselves having good clinical insight, can be accurately used for an understanding of the whole personality. . . .this does not free any of us from the need, even obligation of making it less and less subjective and more and more objective; of looking for all methods in experimental psychology calculated to make it objective. . . .the objectification of the method cannot, it is admitted completely substitute for that insight that comes with much experience. . . .the best Rorschach experimenter—let us make a concession here, even to the term 'artist' and say that—the great Rorschach artist will be he who constantly tempers his accumulated subjective and intuitive knowledge with the restraints and correctives imposed by objectively recorded and rubricked experience."

The Beck article not only precipitated a reply from Klopfer but also a number of articles and letters of comment from many other Rorschach investigators including Hans Binder, Marguerite Hertz, Zygmunt Piotrowski, Gotthard C. Booth and Ernst Schachtel. In fact, the next several issues of the *Rorschach Research Exchange* were dotted with discussion papers about Beck's article, most of them critical, some even openly hostile. Possibly the strongest rejection is exemplified in a quotation in a letter from Arthur Guirdham, a physician in Bath, England (1937).

"I think that this search for objective validation goes too far. In our present state of knowledge, I think the Rorschach test is best used as an aid to typological investigation as a method of obtaining incidental data for analysis in individual cases. . . .most of the Rorschach norms have proved a useful working basis in orthopsychiatry, without attaining to the deadly accuracy of psychometry. (I sometimes think the word deadly here should be interpreted literally.) My argument that to be satisfied with the crude usefulness—and they are not by any means crude always—of the Rorschach norms in general may seem to be heresy. One uses a patellar hammer in medicine. A patellar hammer does not give one any indication of the extent of the length of extension under its stimulus; one doesn't measure mathematically the muscular tension present. But would one argue against its use in the practice of medicine from this point of view?"

Also offering negative criticism, but in a more compromising fashion, was Marguerite Hertz (1937).

"Inasmuch as Beck has pleaded persistently for objectivity in scoring and for scientific determinations, it is disappointing that he did not give the necessary information in respect to his procedure or to the sample of the population on which he based his results. . . .it appears to the writer that omission of experimental data is extremely serious especially in reference to an instrument which is still in its early state of development. . . .if norms are to be generalized for all subjects, examiners have the right to know something of the 'representativeness' and the 'appropriateness' of the subjects on which they have been determined. Klopfer is certainly justified, therefore in requesting the frequency figures on which the tables are based."

But Beck was not the only one which Hertz was willing to criticize in this article.

"Of course, Beck's desire to have adequate evidence before accepting Klopfer's conclusions in respect to these factors is commendable. These categories must be experimentally determined and validated as Beck says but there is no reason why Beck is willing to include FY and Y in his experiments and not categories suggested by other investigators especially when many of them have been partially validated. . . . In treating the M factor, Beck views with trepidation Klopfer's distinction of various kinds of M responses. The writer has on many occasions felt that Klopfer's group was refining the scoring to the extent of becoming involved in a maze of symbols. There are many of Klopfer's suggestions that she has not adopted, preferring to run down where possible existing categories and to validate them."

Possibly one of the most crucial statements in the entire Hertz article is her summary which seems to predict that she can never completely align herself with Klopfer after earlier in the article criticizing Beck too severely to suspect the possibility of future association.

"There is need to feel that subjecting the test to experimentation of this kind reduces its value as an artistic instrument. The interpretation of the psychogram will always demand intuition and skill on the part of the examiner. When Vernon suggests, however, that 'the application of the test from a clinical viewpoint is scientifically justifiable,' he may mean therapeutically justifiable, but not 'scientifically.' Only as a reliable and valid technique can the Rorschach method be a scientific clinical instrument."

Hertz had been writing about the Rorschach for nearly three years at this time. Her first article had appeared in 1934, followed by the publication of *Norms for Adolescents* in 1935, and a suggestion for a standard procedure for Rorschach administration in 1936. This latter article also reviewed the various techniques of Rorschach administration, deploring the lack of uniformity and calling for standardized procedures. Unfortunately, like the pleas of others for uniformity, this suggestion went unheeded. But it was not so much the failure to muster support for her suggestions that caused Hertz to continue developing a System of her own as much as it was her own basic Rorschach philosophy which was somewhat more liberal than the behavioristic approach suggested by Beck, yet more conservative than then phenomenological approach offered by Klopfer.

Similarly, when Beck took issue with Piotrowski's conception of movement, which had been regarded by others as a significant contribution to the Rorschach procedure, another seemingly unreconcilable divergence occurred. For Piotrowski, Beck was "unbending." The disagreement between Beck and Piotrowski on M was immediate and severe and has continued. To this day, their interpretations of the significance of Movement are far apart. At the same time, however, Piotrowski could not reconcile his psychopathological approach to the Rorschach, based on deductive logic, with the phenomonological approach of Klopfer. Hence, he began to draw into his own System shortly thereafter. Klopfer had previously struggled against Piotrowski's notions on Shading and Piotrowski also felt that Klopfer did not fully accept his ideas concerning Movement, that instead, Klopfer had presented Piotrowski's ideas in somewhat of a distorted form. While Piotrowski was impressed by Rorschach and *Psychodiagnostik*, he was nonetheless striving toward improvement of the technique rather than maintaining a static approach. He firmly endorsed Rorschach's notions of the importance of the Form association and in this respect agreed largely with Beck. When Oberholzer arrived in the United States, Piotrowski formed a relationship with him but did not maintain this relationship over an extended period of time for he felt that Oberholzer would not concede to changing any of Rorschach's basic ideas.

One of the most striking influences on Piotrowski's professional development in the United States was Kurt Goldstein. Goldstein had come to the United States as a refugee in 1938 and was working at Mt. Sinai Hospital. Piotrowski met him by attending an informal all-day seminar at Mt. Sinai each week and was immediately intrigued by Goldstein's logic and approach to problems of personality. It was through Goldstein's encouragement that Piotrowski utilized the Rorschach at Mt. Sinai and eventually evolved his Rorschach signs for organic invlovement. It seems well to ask why Piotrowski, having tentatively disassociated himself from Klopfer and being in disagreement with Beck did not lean toward the Hertz orientation. The answer is quite simple. In Piotrowski's thinking, Hertz was excessively concerned with standardization and minor details. While Piotrowski eventually accepted the importance of such concerns, at that time he perceived them as being less important than the more major problem of understanding the theory of the Rorschach and applying the technique in a manner compatible with a theory of personality.

In retrospect, it seems quite probable that none of the "Systematizers," including Klopfer, disagreed greatly with the summary statement in Beck's article. For example, the Rorschach problem for Klopfer was by no means one of objectivity versus subjectivity. And yet having a phenomenological rather than behavioristic orientation, Klopfer was much more willing to accept flexibility in scoring and interpretation which would facilitate an understanding of the unique characteristics of the individual. He consistently encouraged the collection of large samples from which to verify or reject qualitatively established Rorschach factors. Klopfer's point about Form responses, with which Beck so strenuously disagreed, was that *only* the most frequently given Form responses could be evaluated as plus or minus on a quantitative basis. He indicated that less frequently given, but more "keenly" perceived Form responses may still occur and they are quantitatively different from the common Form responses. He suggested three scorings for Form: F plus for high quality responses, F for the commonly perceived responses, and F minus for the response that did not fit the Form in the blot (1937). Klopfer was also very concerned with the Beck method of scoring Shading responses, feeling that the Beck method, or more appropriately the Rorschach technique, was too restricted. Klopfer conceived of the Shading response involving vista as being different from the flat-gray type of Shading responses. In 1937, he described four types of Shading responses and suggested scoring and interpretations for each. At that time, Beck was using only the symbols FY or Y for the scoring of all Shading responses. It is interesting to note that later Beck did modify his System to include appropriate symbols for vista and for texture as had previously been suggested by Klopfer although the symbols Beck adopted were different from that in the Klopfer System.

Beck reports, in a private interview (1966), of his feeling of disappointment at the apparent unwillingness of other Rorschachers to follow his suggestions concerning Rorschach problems and necessary research. The magnitude of this disappointment may be manifest by the fact that he did not accept membership in the Rorshach Institute (which became the Society for Projective Techniques) until 1950, and published nothing else in the *Rorschach Research Exchange,* (which became the *Journal of Projective Techniques*) until 1951.

Beck's failure to publish in the *Rorschach Research Exchange* did not diminish the intensity of the struggle which had evolved. In part, the controversy concerning objectification or standardization of the Rorschach probably continued because of Beck's early insistence on its necessity, but more likely it became magnified simply because the Rorschach represented a type of instrument foreign to the American traditions of psychometry. Especially Klopfer and his group used a basic phenomenological orientation in which there was no tendency to "kneel before the alter of standardization." To some American psychologists, it no doubt appeared that the Rorschach was spreading like a contagious disease which had certain charismatic qualities drawing people even closer to its use. Many disowned themselves completely from any interest in it. But others, even conservatives, beacme caught up in its potentials and it was this group, partially leader-less but certainly represented by both Beck and Hertz, that forced Klopfer and his followers to maintain a constantly defensive position toward their demands.

Whereas Beck withdrew from public battle preferring to publish his own research rather than commentaries on needs and problems, Klopfer was more willing to challenge his critics using his phenomenological base. In 1939, in his article "Shall the Rorschach Method be Standardized?," his position was made crystal clear.

"Orthodox 'experimentalists' demand that the Rorschach method be free of all 'subjective' elements. To reduce that point of view ad absurdum, we could say that they want to establish standardized tables where the scoring and interpretive value of every single Rorschach response could be looked up. They want to reduce the scoring and interpretation to a seemingly fool-proof mechanical, and therefore, 'objective' procedure. Even these extremists would concede that this procedure would be like an attempt to study the functioning of the human body by first cutting it up into pieces in order to find out afterwards how many pieces may have func-tioned together. . . .on the other extreme, where there are some Rorschachists who consider the procedure of scoring and interpretation a 'sacred art,' which should not be profaned by any attempt to rationalize it. At least, they are very hesitant to change anything in the procedure as it was left where Rorschach had to leave it at his untimely death 16 years ago. . . . In the first place, the term 'standardization' seems to be misleading, because it frequently implies a notion rigid schematization. Schematization would be incompatible with the Rorschach method, since it induces the examiner to pay less attention to all the individual nuances and facets of any given record. On the other hand, if the rational development of the method induces the examiner to observe what a Rorschach method offers more intimately and accurately than he could by relying merely on his personal skill and accumen, then 'such a rationalization' would have to be considered a decided advantage. To avoid misunderstanding it seems, therefore preferable to speak of 'refinement' or 'rationali-zation' rather than 'standardization.' "

In this article, Klopfer conceded a need for some quantification but only to the extent that quantification could assist in the comprehensive under-standing of the person, as a person, rather than a member of a group. He discounted the potential usefulness of the collection of hundreds or even thousands of records simply for the sake of setting up "imposing tables" without first having some clear idea about the meaning or significance of such categorization. He followed Rorschach's lead in supporting the notion of "blind diagnosis" as an appropriate research method through which clinical validation of the technique could be achieved.

Both Lawrence Frank and Marguerite Hertz wrote comments on the

Klopfer paper. Additionally the Rorschach Forum at the 16th annual meeting of the American Orthopsychiatric Association in February 1939, in New York City, concerned itself with the problem which Klopfer had posed. Frank found himself disposed to agree to a large extent with Klopfer (1939). He cited some of the limitations of traditional standardization procedures:

"While standardized tests are generally considered to be measures of individual differences, it would be more appropriate to say that they are ratings of the degree of likeness to cultural norms exhibited by individuals who are expected, as members of this society, to conform to those group patterns. In other words, the standardized test does not tell us very much about the individual, *as an individual,* but rather how nearly he approximates to a normal performance of culturally prescribed tasks for which a more or less arbitrary, but internally consistent, scheme of quantitative ratings is utilized. . . .this use of social norms of culturally patterned conduct by an individual tells us little or nothing about this 'private world' of his personality, how the individual feels about himself, his life, and social participation. We cannot therefore rely on his use of social norms of overt speech and conduct or upon conventional traits and motives if we are interested in the unique, idiosyncratic, *individual* personality and how he idiomatically 'structuralizes his life space,' as Kurt Lewin has expressed it. . . .the Rorschach method offers a procedure through which the individual is induced to reveal his 'private world' by telling what he 'sees' in the several cards upon which he may project his meanings, significances, and feelings, just because they are not socially standardized objects or situations to which he must give culturally prescribed responses. The Rorschach method is essentially a procedure for revealing the personality of the individual, as an individual, as contrasted with rating or assessing him in terms of his likeness or conformity to social norms of action and speech."

Hertz, in her paper (1939), persisted in her position favoring standardization yet not to an extreme:

". . .there is an ever-increasing group of Rorschach workers who object to exclusive reliance on the clinical approach because they fear the limitations and inconsistencies of subjective judgments. They see clinicians applying varying criteria to scoring and giving interpretations based on inconclusive evidence. They therefore demand some measure of objectivity in standardization in the procedure, and study those phases of the method which are amenable to such standardization and engage in painstaking statistical analysis where it is applicable. [She cites Beck, Vernon and herself as being among this group.] . . .too many Rorschach workers give the wrong impression as to the ease with which the test may be administered. . . .one has only to try to train Rorschach workers to realize the value of objective standards. If one relies exclusively on experience and personal judgment, one will find that few people will become proficient in the method. . . .one must conclude from the above discussion that the Rorschach method has been and should be further subjected to standardization. Klopfer, however, prefers to use the term 'refinement' or 'rationalization.' The writer prefers the term 'standardization' because it suggests not 'rigid schematization' as Klopfer fears, but scientific reliability and verification."

The papers and comments presented at the Rorschach Forum of the American Orthopsychiatric Association meeting in 1939 seemed, in the main, to support the Klopfer position. Formal contributions were made by Lois Murphy, Morris Krugman, David Rapaport, Douglas Kelley, Ludwig Hirning, Gotthard Booth, and Zygmunt Piotrowski (Miale, 1939).

At the Forum, Rapaport, having already been trained in Rorschach in Europe, injected some of the fundamental reasoning which would be a base for his System. Krugman agreed almost completely with Klopfer. He redefined standardization as having a special significance for Rorschach as not applicable to other psychometric instruments. Kelley pointed out the futility of attempting to standardize the Rorschach method in any manner similar to that of other psychometric tests. His notions were generally supported by Booth and Piotrowski, although Piotrowski did call for certain aspects of standardization, particularly the careful validation of some principles already having been formulated. Hirning made a direct case for overall standardization but tempered this considerably by suggesting that he spoke more of scoring symbols than interpretation.

Rapaport asked two basic questions, one concerning a definition of the standardization tasks and the second bearing upon the extent to which the Rorschach procedure is objectifiable. He commented on the three basic tasks known and recognized by most Rorschach workers concerning the question of good and poor Form responses, resolving of Location problems with details, and the question of popular Form. His ideas of objectification seem less clear. He discussed the problem of the relationship of the determinants to each other, rather than their statistical frequency, and made a suggestion that the longitudinal method would be applicable especially with regard to the antecedents of a response, indicating that instinct psychology, Gestalt psychology, genetic psychology, psychoanalysis and other new psychiatric findings could all furnish a basis for explaining and objectifying the Rorschach method. It seems, in retrospect, that the word objectification was being used quite differently by Rapaport than it was being purported by others, an element which may have contributed to the fact that his Rorschach System never really approximated any of the other Systems from its onset. Rapaport was less concerned with the Rorschach as a test than as an instrument to study the psychological process.

"Up to now clinical control, repetition of the Rorschach experiment, statistical standardization, were used as verification of the method. But the objectification of the procedure can be developed in an entirely different way as well. In my first point I referred to general psychological investigations on space rhythm and form genesis. Both of these problems can be investigated, for instance, under the aspect of the term 'pregnance' of Gestalt psychology. With the exception of the earliest attempts of Rorschach, Frankhauser, Furrer, etc., no efforts have been made to show the general psychological procedures underlying the Rorschach replies. We have to investigate these procedures and show how a reply is born and *why* it has the significance which it has according to the experience of all Rorschach workers." (1939)

After Volume 4 of the *Rorschach Research Exchange*, 1940, no additional clarification of disagreements is noted. In Hertz's presidential address, read at the Second Annual Meeting of the Rorschach Institute in April 1941, in New York City, entitled "Rorschach; Twenty Years After," she neatly covered the variety of work that had been done in the areas of standardization, administration, scoring, interpretation, the research in reliability and validity and offered an overall evaluation concerning the future needs for the Rorschach. One of the most distinct areas, which was not mentioned in the address, was the lack of common agreement between the various Systematizers.

At this point in time, probably only three Systems really existed, those of Beck, Klopfer and Hertz. Beck offered an approach that was quite different from that of Klopfer. Hertz had published several articles offering norms for different types of responses on different age groups and had, through a number of papers, made it rather obvious that while she agreed on some of Klopfer's scoring categories, she would not agree on his shading symbols nor some of his interpretations. Less than a year after her presidential address to the Rorschach Institute, Klopfer's first book, *The Rorschach Technique* (Klopfer, B., and Kelley, D., 1942) was published which compiled into one volume his overall System of scoring and interpretation of the Rorschach. Piotrowski was to continue his work independently of the other three for a number of years, finally crystalizing his ideas into his book, *Perceptanalysis*, which was published in 1957. It was evident, however, much before 1957 that Piotrowski's ideas were quite different from those of Beck particularly in the area of movement and the overall scoring dimentions and somewhat different from Klopfer in the scoring of shading and some general interpretative hypotheses. If his ideas were ever congruent wth those of Hertz, this congruency is difficult to distinguish. It should be noted, however, that Piotrowski remained "relatively" loyal to the Klopfer scoring orientation for some time. For example, in his comments on the 1937 Beck article, he clearly assumed the position congruent with that of Klopfer (1937). As the years passed, however, his research became more and more divergent from the interests and orientation of Klopfer and in many ways has almost progressed through a 180° shift. During the 1934-40 period, he was much oriented toward the implementation of his "deductive logic" with the phenomenological approach. As he grew more distant from Klopfer and became more intrigued by the microscopic quality of the

Rorschach as a visual stimulus, his own System gradually evolved. Piotrowski, in a personal interview, indicated that he was particularly impressed by
Homer and the conceptions in Homer about visual stimuli.* These concepts of visual stimuli formed a base for Piotrowski's System of Perceptanalysis, wherein he theorizes that the image is localized on an inkblot and
thus interpretable as a manifestation of the individual. In part, his notions
concerning the visual image being localized on an inkblot, evolved from his
relationship with Goldstein and his work with organics, and, in part, from
his involvement with the method of blind analysis which he utilized as a
teaching technique, and "to free myself from the anxieties of blundering
error" (1967). Piotrowski, like Beck, has methodically defended the point
that analyses done using a "non-blind" method always are prone to contamination by other data. Therefore, if an error does evolve, the responsibility of the Rorschacher is greater. His movement toward the use of the
computer as a blind analysis mechanism, into which Rorschach data could
be fed, was stimulated in part by frustration in which he seeks a technique
such as the machine and its undisputable characteristics, which can speak
for the Rorschach as an acceptable method for the evaluation of personality structure (1967). Hertz was also "in the think" of the divergence
situation. As early as 1938, the nucleus of her approach to Rorschach was
congruent with that of Klopfer with the exception of her emphasis on
normative data and her description of standardization requirements. While
working persistently on the development of normative data, she maintained reasonably close contact with both Klopfer and Beck. She was
neither convinced then or even now (1967) that the differences among
the Systematizers are very great. For a lengthy period of time after
completing her dissertation, Hertz had been involved in a Brush Foundation project collecting data on a variety of groups, including not only
instances of psychopathology but also heavily emphasizing children's
records (normal children), adolescent records, superior records, delinquent
records, racial differences, etc. This massive amount of data (nearly 3,000
protocols were involved) led to the writing of a manuscript concerning
Rorschach. Somewhat disasterously, as the Brush Foundation discontinued
operation and its records stored, these materials including the manuscript
were inadvertently destroyed.† Nevertheless, Hertz continued a steady

---

*Homer emphasized visual sensation and visual imagination in much of his work.
Like many Greeks of that period he offered descriptions of physical attributes,
stance, and movements to convey feelings and social behavior.

† Hertz indicates in personal correspondence that the manuscript was nearly completed. "I have not been able to duplicate such data. I am still unwilling to write a
book without relating what I say to my own research."

stream of Rorschach publications and in many respects seemed like a "conscience" for the Klopfer group, never actually joining the group but critical in a friendly manner. She identified less with Beck although frequently defending or concurring with Beck's ideas to the rest of the Rorschach world.

Rapaport was least directly involved in the era of divergence of any of the Systematizers. His early research on the Rorschach dealt with the fundamental principles underlying projective techniques in general, and the orientation that a variety of tests were required to obtain a thorough personality appraisal for any given subject. Rapaport was less committed to the Rorschach, as a test, during his professional life than any of the other Systematizers. He perceved the Rorschach to be simply another instrument which could be a focal point in a test battery through which accurate psychodiagnostic work could be accomplished. It must be quickly added, however, that Rapaport perceived the Rorschach as the most efficient single diagnostic tool possessed by clinical psychology and described it as an easily learned technique, the proficiency of which hinged on the examiner's clinical-psychological knowledge. He suggested that Rorschach was made more cumbersome by the extensions and refinements which in turn made it somewhat prohibitive for routine clinical use. He cautioned, as early as 1945, that extensions and elaborations on the Rorschach when not "excellently documented as valid and indispensable" be avoided, and encouraged that the diagnostic significance of the verbalization of the responses should be studied much further (1945).

It was along these latter lines of study that Schafer continued his Rorschach orientation. Rapaport, who was a professional godfather to Schafer, was strongly psychoanalytically oriented and devoted the major part of his professional life to the development and understanding of ego psychology. Schafer, in turn, pursued the basic ideas of his mentor in his own work with the Rorschach, concentrating largely on content analysis and psychoanalytic interpretation of responses. Schafer has also relegated a significant portion of his writing on the Rorschach to the relationship between the examiner and the subject, an area which had long been neglected by the other Systematizers. Thus, the evolution of the Rapaport-Schafer System was based on the principle that the Rorschach provided a type of "standardized interview" wherein the interpretive value is derived from the response rather than from the stimulus. Therefore, factors such as normative standards and refined scoring systems become less important.

And so, it was the destiny of the Rorschach in the United States to be developed by champions whose disagreements were deep seated and frequently intense. The chronology by which each System has developed varies markedly. In the next chapter, a study of that chronology will be offered so as to provide some additional clarification to the divergence phenomenon and its consequences.

REFERENCES

Beck, S. J. Problems of further research in the Rorschach test. *Amer. J. Orthopsychiat.*, 1935, 5, 100-115.

Beck, S. J. Autism in Rorschach scoring: A feeling comment. *Char. and Pers.*, 1936, 5, 83-85.

Beck, S. J. *Introduction to the Rorschach Method.* Amer. Orthopsychiat. Assoc., Monog. 1, 1937.

Beck, S. J. Some recent Rorschach problems. *Ror. Res. Exch.*, 1937, 2, 15-22.

Binder, H. Die Helldunkeldeutungen in psychodiagnostischen experiment von Rorschach. *Schweiz. Arch. Neurol. Psychiat.*, 133, 30, 1-67 and 233-268.

Frank, L. Comments on the proposed standardization of the Rorschach method. *Ror. Res. Exch.*, 1939, 3, 101-105.

Guirdham, A. Letter to the Rorschach Research Exchange. *Ror. Res. Exch.*, 1937, 2, 72-73.

Hertz, Marguerite. The reliability of the Rorschach inkblot test. *J. Appl. Psychol.*, 1934, 18, 461-477.

Hertz, Marguerite. Rorschach norms for an adolescent age group. *Child Develpm.*, 1935, 6, 67-76.

Hertz, Marguerite. The method of administration of the Rorschach inkblot test. *Child Develpm.*, 1936, 7, 237-254.

Hertz, Marguerite. Discussion on "Some recent Rorschach problems," *Ror. Res. Exch.*, 1937, 2, 53-65.

Hertz, Marguerite. On the standardization of the Rorschach method. *Ror. Res. Exch.*, 1939, 3, 120-133.

Hertz, Marguerite. Personal Communication, March, 1967.

Klopfer, B. and Sender, Sadie. A system of refined scoring symbols. *Ror. Res. Exch.*, 1936, 1, 19-22.

Klopfer, B. The present status of the theoretical development of the Rorschach method. *Ror. Res. Exch.*, 1937, 1, 142-147.

Klopfer, B. The shading response. *Ror. Res. Exch.*, 1937, 2, 76-78.

Klopfer, B. Shall the Rorschach be standardized. *Ror. Res. Exch.*, 1939, 3, 45-54.

Klopfer, B. and Kelley, D. *The Rorschach Technique.* Yonkers-on-Hudson, N.Y.: World Book, 1942.

Miale, Florence. The Rorschach Forum at the Sixteenth Annual Meeting of the American Orthopsychiatric Association, February 23, 1939, in New York City. *Ror. Res. Exch.*, 1939, 3, 106-119.

Piotrowski, Z. The M, FM, and m responses as indicators of change in personality. *Ror. Res. Exch.*, 1937, 1, 148-156.

Piotrowski, Z. Discussion on "Some recent Rorschach problems." *Ror. Res. Exch.*, 1937, 2, 68-69.

Piotrowski, Z. *Perceptanalysis.* New York: Macmillan, 1957.

Piotrowski, Z. Personal Communication, February, 1967.

Rapaport, D. and Schafer, R. The Rorschach Test: A clinical evaluation. *Bull. Menninger Clin.*, 1945, 9, 73-77.

CHAPTER 3

DEVELOPMENT OF THE SYSTEMS

As the seeds of divergence blossomed into seemingly irreconcilable schisms, the total Rorschach situation in the United States was definitely underpinned by quandry. Retrospectively, Beck's 1937 *Introduction to the Rorschach Method* was "too little and too late." For Beck, it was a first approach which would be the beginnings of a system. As F. L. Wells pointed out in his preface to the Beck book,

"It is Dr. Beck's purpose to offer a manual of practice upon which the clinical user and/or investigator can build his own experience as best suited to his purposes. In conformity with this the presentation has been kept at a concrete level, following so far as possible the case method."

In the book, Beck presented 59 cases representing ten basic groups,* plus a section on the basic fundamentals of scoring and administration which were clearly at an elementary level when contrasted with the later development of the Beck System.

Klopfer had already published his basic system for scoring with Sender in the first volume (1936) of the *Rorschach Research Exchange* which was different than that suggested by Beck. His review of Beck's book in the July, 1937 issue of the *Rorschach Research Exchange* (which he pointed to specifically as not being a review but rather as exemplifying the theoretical problems of the Rorschach) clearly implied his unwillingness to accept the Beck approach and his conviction that the *Exchange* should be the avenue through which any and all Rorschach problems should be resolved,

"The scoring and interpretation problems discussed here are only a selection on the basis of urgency. There are many other important problems which could be taken up, such as the problem of color shock, the significance of anatomical responses, the significance of the choice of a high number of inside details, the problem of original and popular answers, the significance of white space answers. Beyond that, there are the numerous problems connected with the administration of the test: . . .The Exchange will start, in its second volume, to devote its space systematically to a series of articles and discussions dealing with these theoretical problems, to present elaborate sample case studies as demonstration and training material, and to help in organizing coordinated efforts in problems where only the compilation of the

---

* These ten groups included healthy adults of superior intelligence, feeble minded, depressed states, hypomanic conditions, schizophrenics, neurotics, conduct disorders in adults, problem children, inadequate test records, and mental hygiene cases.

experience of a number of experts can assure the necessary material for statistical decisions. The readiness of some of the leading experts, such as Dr. Oberholzer of Zurich, and Dr. Beck of Chicago, to add their contributions to those made in the first volume, and the growing number of Rorschach investigators in all institutions, listed as our members, promises that the Exchange will be well able to serve its purpose."

Klopfer's hopes and intentions for the *Exchange* to be the main avenue for resolution of the Rorschach problems did not become reality. As previously mentioned in Chapter Two, Beck published nothing in the *Exchange* until 1951 other than his 1937 "reply article" which symbolically picked up the gauntlet of challenge that Klopfer had thrown down. Oberholzer never published in the *Exchange*. Both Hertz and Piotrowski continued to publish in the *Exchange* but in limited fashion. For example, Hertz and Piotrowski published more than 30 articles each on the Rorschach between 1936 and 1947 yet less than one-third of these appeared in the *Exchange*. It would appear that while Klopfer had reached out for a role of Rorschach leadership in America for himself and the *Rorschach Research Exchange,* his reach had been too forceful, or rigid, or both, thereby causing some of the significant Rorschach experts of the time to withdraw from him either partially or completely. But a leader he did remain. And of a strong group. Even though the group was not as all encompassing as he had hoped, the Klopfer group" as it was frequently referred to, did proceed forward to the ultimate development of the Klopfer System.

In the first issue of the 1937 *Exchange, Klopfer* added to his system of scoring with an article concerning basic administration, "The technique of the Rorschach performance," and in the 1939 volume published a forty-two page paper entitled "Theory and technique of Rorschach interpretation," in collaboration with Buchard, Kelley and Miale. It was subdivided into four chapters and touched on all of the fundamental interpretation problems which had been encountered to that time. A fourth article which is historically important to the development of the Klopfer System appeared in the 1940 volume of the *Exchange.* This article, "The technique of Rorschach scoring and tabulation," was written in collaboration with Davidson, Holzman, Kelley, Margulies, Miale, and Wolfson. The article offered a series of frequency tallies concerning Location scoring in the Rorschach and offered a base for Kloper's eventual discrimination of Location areas in the blots. The greater section of the article was headed "Chapter I, Scoring Categories for the Location of the Response" and was presented as the first of several such articles and requested that readers send to the *Exchange* their own frequency data for eventual inclusion. Subsequent articles did not appear however. Instead a book evolved.

Klopfer's first book, *The Rorschach Technique,* was published in collaboration with Douglas Kelley in 1942. The book, subtitled "A Manual for a Projective Method of Personality Diagnosis," is described by Klopfer in the forward as having "grew out of seven years of learning by teaching. My efforts to make the Rorschach more comprehensible and thus more teachable were supported by almost everyone of the more than 800 colleagues and students who participated in my seminars and classes."

But it was more than just a book on the Rorschach that Klopfer had published. It was clear, undisputed time advantage on the other Systematizers. Klopfer had already enjoyed this advantage to a large extent through the *Rorschach Research Exchange* in which his fundamental concepts about the Rorschach had been consistently disseminated and could be taught outside of New York rather easily using that material. The other active Systematizers, Beck and Hertz, had scattered their ideas in a variety of publications. Thus, for the first few teaching years of the Rorschach, if the prospective student were to be interested in the Beck System, he would go to Chicago or undertake the laborious task of accumulating Beck's ideas from his "Manual" plus articles from many other sources. The same was true for the Hertz System. Either study in Cleveland or accumulate material from a variety of sources. With Klopfer it was quite different. The prospective Rorschacher could study with Klopfer in New York or subscribe to the *Exchange* and partake in the majority of material to be published concerning the Rorschach. Another factor also gave Klopfer a significant time margin on his competition. He was unexcelled as an organizer. The loyality of those around him not only made it possible for the *Exchange* to become a success but also led to the formation of the *Rorschach Institute* in 1939, as an incorporated body dedicated to the study and teaching of the technique.

The *Rorschach Institute* set forth the first documented qualifications for the Rorschacher. Membership was available to psychiatrists, psychologists, sociologists, social workers "and other professional persons whose work and interests lie in the study and treatment of personality and its disorders, whose activities promise an enhancement of the scientific objectives of the Institute, and whose qualifications meet those set by the Institute." (Kelley, 1939) Qualifications included a minimum of three years graduate education; training in Rorschach by a "recognized instructor"; presentation of 25 Rorschach cases; and demonstration to an examining board competency in administration, scoring and interpretation of the Rorschach. Provisions were made for regional divisions and several evolved quite early. The *Rorschach Research Exchange* was, of course, the voice of the *Institute* and Klopfer its editor. As Krugman, the Institute's first president, cited in his presidential address in June 1940, 58 of the 93 Rorschach articles published in the United States between 1936 and 1940 appeared in the *Exchange*. Sixty-six charter fellows and members of the *Rorschach Institute* were listed in 1940 (Kelley, 1940). Beck's name was conspicuously absent.

In the Spring of 1940, Kelley (1940, p. 84) published a survey in the *Exchange* concerning the training facilities for the Rorschach in the United States. He noted that only two universities offered formal courses in the Rorschach method but that non-university seminars teaching the Rorschach method were being held throughout the United States. It is interesting to note that most of these were being given by charter members of the Rorschach Institute. Thus, the Klopfer System was being widely disseminated. Additionally, by this time, Klopfer had six Ph.D. candidates working at Columbia and one at NYU, all of whom were doing their dissertations on the Rorschach. He had conducted workshops and seminars during the previous year in Cleveland, San Francisco, Berkeley, Los Angeles, Pittsburgh, Denver, and Philadelphia, in addition to the regular workshop which he had established in Crafts, New York. By 1942 membership in the Institute had swelled in excess of 100 and regional divisions were listed in New York City, Connecticut, Massachusetts, Pennsylvania, Ohio, Kansas, the Southeast, Wisconsin, Texas, and on the West Coast. Overseas divisions were being formed in Canada, Australia, England, and South America.

When Klopfer's book appeared in 1942, the time and organizational advantage which he maintained over the other Systematizers was magnified several fold. For the first time since the publication of *Psychodiagnostik,* the person interested in Rorschach could purchase a manuscript complete in its description of the technique, including the methods of administration, scoring, *and interpretation*. Whether or not the Klopfer System was the best or most logical approach to the Rorschach, whether the Klopfer System truly represented Rorschach, it was clearly the system being used most widely. Even the war aided significantly in the dissemination of the Klopfer System. In 1941, some three weeks after the bombing of Pearl Harbor, the Executive Committee of the *Rorschach Institute* organized a Rorschach volunteer unit with Klopfer as its chairman. The idea underlying the unit was "such an organization would offer opportunities for a systematic cooperation between the fellows and members of the *Rorschach Institute,* who are now serving in the Armed Forces and those who want to do their part while they continue with their routine work. We hope to gain the cooperation of the various military authorities and as far as necessary the support of interested foundations" (1942, p. 39). The unit remained quite active throughout the war and did to a large extent fulfill the purpose for which it was established. Thus, Klopfer's organizational talents again paid off.

Klopfer's awareness of the importance of the *Rorschach Institute* and the *Rorschach Research Exchange,* in the development of his System, is noted in the introductory remarks in his book.

"After 1936 the method spread so rapidly, supported by the strong general interest in the study of personality, that in 1939 Rorschach workers in this country and abroad formed a professional organization, the Rorschach Institute, mainly as a clearing house for research and as a training center in order to help satisfy the growing demand for skilled Rorschach workers in medical, psychological, and educational institutions. Today, the skepticism which was quite prevalent as recently as five years ago, has been replaced in many instances by an interested and even enthusiastic acceptance of the Rorschach method."

While Klopfer was the catalyst for the foundation of the *Rorschach Research Exchange* and the *Rorschach Institute,* it should not be inferred that he in any way exerted absolute control over them. To be sure, people who were friendly toward Klopfer and/or oriented toward his System frequently published in the *Exchange* and sought membership in the Institute. However, a forum for disagreement with Klopfer was also provided. For example, the first president of the Rorschach Institute, Morris Krugman, in a strikingly well done review of Rorschach history entitled "Out of the Inkwell," summarized his presidential address by clearly siding with Beck's orientation:

"I should like to join Beck in his appeal for extensive and intensive training and experience in the various branches of psychology for all Rorschach workers. It is trite to say that the Rorschach is not a simple psychological test in which one can be specifically trained, regardless of background and experience, to obtain a composite score that has any meaning psychologically. I can claim only slightly more than half of Beck's 13 years of experience with the method, but I am convinced that his implication that a Rorschach diagnosis is only as good as the one who makes it, is true. I feel certain that the members and fellows of the Rorschach Institute agree on this. I believe that one of the major results of the organization of this institute will be the influence its members will exert to prevent the Rorschach from being misused by incompetents or charlatans. To this end, the Institute should exert every effort to avoid the misleading of innocents by permitting them to enter courses in the Rorschach method before they are prepared to benefit from them. Too many courses are now open to any who can afford the fee, without regard to their qualifications. I have heard some say that this is not a serious matter, and takes care of itself, since the method is so complex that the ill-prepared cannot use it properly. This is just the point—that they cannot use it properly, but they can misuse it, they can make unwarranted diagnoses, and they can mislead people and do damage. I feel certain that the Rorschach Institute will be very influential in keeping the Rorschach on the high professional level it deserves." (1940)

The second president of the Rorschach Institute was Marguerite Hertz. Her presidential address in 1941 entitled "Rorschach: Twenty Years After" also posed some disagreements with Klopfer. For example, wherein Klopfer had suggested that the word standardization was not applicable to the Rorschach, Hertz in her paper maintained:

"Hence, at the risk of heresy, I propose this evening to devote myself to the thought that standardization is no longer debatable, that the extent that it is either possible or desirable, standardization is the outstanding feature of the 20 years since Rorschach. I propose to content myself with a brief survey of our progress toward standardization and toward the establishment of reliability and validity."

But then in tempering the strength of her remark she stated:

"But, again risking heresy, I emphasize, I do not mean standardization in either the sense of rigidity or inflexibility. I use the term because our emphasis has been upon the development of our method as an art at the expense of those considerations which in the last analysis, would place the Rorschach method within the bounds of reliability and practicability. If, in this brief survey, I emphasize certain studies and overlook others, it is only because preference has been given to systematic treatments and to studies with research orientation."

In effect, Hertz was continuing her disagreement with Klopfer's notion of standardization of the technique. At the same time, she was cautiously, almost tenuously, voiding herself of a commitment toward the type of objectification which was common for the time. She spoke favorably of the use of blind analysis as a method for testing both reliability and validity. She also expressed the necessity for continuing the emphasis on the "unique idiomatic characteristics of the personality" without losing sight of generalizations or uniformities. In a sense, however, her disagreemnt with Klopfer was stronger than possibly even she realized. In one of her summary paragraphs she states:

"Our immediate obligation is to continue the process of standardization in form and character that will best serve our method. It is our function to organize coordinated research projects, to make a concerted drive on the same problems at the same time, to infuse with meaning the empirical facts which we have amassed, and thus to add scientific results to our store of knowledge." (1941)

While the words were probably acceptable to Klopfer, the intent behind the words was probably not. To him, phenomenology was in and by itself a science and problems of standardization, reliability, and validity fell more toward the Guirdham description of "deadly psychometry" for which Klopfer was totally unprepared. In fact, it is evident in tracing the development of the Klopfer System that the basic problems of standardization, reliability or validation never seem to slow down the progress of development nor create significant alterations in the System.

When the Klopfer and Kelley book was published in 1942, **Klopfer was** by no means adverse to mentioning standardization or statistical methodology. He confronted it directly and almost grandiosely. Having found himself consistently challenged by the criticisms and demands of other psychologists, he pointed out that the term objectivity, as applied by his contemporaries, was based on two technical prerequisites: first, that the results obtained by an objective procedure could be measured or counted; and secondly, that most experimenters with necessary skill and experience would arrive at the same or similar results. Applying this criteria of objectivity to the Rorschach, Klopfer in turn announced the Rorschach to be objective. He did temper his pronouncement by indicating that in terms of structural interpretation of scoring data there was an important difference between the Rorschach procedure and that of the more usual psychometric instruments. Whereas psychometric instruments achieved their results by adding their scores in a summative manner, this procedure was inappropriate to the Rorschach. He re-emphasized that Rorschachers adequate interpretations would be contingent not only on the use of quantitative results but interpretation of the overall record through the store of clinical knowledge available to the interpreter. He strongly maintained that it is a combination of the quantitative and qualitative data which permit the examiner or the interpreter to arrive by inference at a complete individual personality picture. Thus with a suaveness which might almost be considered admirable, even for a phenomenologist, Klopfer dealt with his most intense critics.

Klopfer also reaffirmed his notions that any attempt to standardize or routinize the preliminary or pretest phase of the Rorschach administration would be impossible. He cited the fact that the Rorschach deals with individuals and each must be treated uniquely, with the end goal of providing a relaxed atmosphere.

"In mechanical standardization as, for instance, the use of written instructions, is in reality a pseudo-standardization, since instead of controlling the experimental situations such a procedure actually has different and unmeasurable effects on different subjects. [He also cautioned against providing the subject with unnecessary sets in the instructions.] . . .It is very important that the instructions simply set the task and leave the choice of procedure entirely to the subject. Therefore a formulation such as 'look at each card as long as you like, only be sure to tell the examiner everything you see on the card as you look at it,' . . .seem to emphasize the quantity of interpretation, which involves a restriction of the conditions."

It would appear that this may be interpreted as a "backhanded slap" at the Beck procedure which is quoted almost verbatim there. Again he seems to take difference with both Beck and Hertz by his encouragement:

"Some Rorschach practitioners have over-emphasized the necessity for the accumulation of great numbers of records, as if the accumulation and summarization of these records would lend at least the appearance of objectivity to the method."

Of course at this time both Beck and Hertz were strongly encouraging this very procedure. Klopfer emphasized his disdain for this approach, much like he contended with the entire problem of standardization by saying, "It scarcely seems ncessary at this time to suggest the futility of such a procedure."

Klopfer tempered his position considerably on the matter of blind analysis. Previously, he had strongly supported the blind analysis technique; now he suggested that its greatest worth was in research methodology. He strongly cautioned that probably the more comprehensive and worthwhile Rorschach interpretations would be derived, where the Rorschach material was combined with material from all other sources, such as clinical observations, case histories, and psychometric results.

The basic symbols which Klopfer offered in 1937 were not altered markedly in his 1942 text. In fact, the 1942 scoring formula is essentially the same. The system of symbols is also essentially the same as used in the current Klopfer System with some minor modifications. Possibly the most significant change made in the Klopfer System after 1942 was the introduction of the Form Level Rating, which permitted Klopfer to discard the system of scoring good and poor Form responses plus or minus, a technique which he consistently disliked. The Form Level Rating, which was first published in 1944 as a preliminary proposal in the *Rorschach Research Exchange,* was later incorporated as a permanent part of the 1946 revision of the 1942 text. This same approach to Form persists in the contemporary Klopfer literature. It is also worth noting that in 1942 Klopfer spoke out directly against the use of multiple determinants as had been suggested by Beck, Piotrowski and Hertz.

"The questions may be raised why in such cases of ambiguity we must establish a rank order among determinants; why can't we have two main determinants—for instance, a movement and a color combination in the case of the above mentioned clowns? The answer is that rigid adherence to the principle of giving one and only one main score for each independent concept in each of the three scoring areas (location, determinant, content) seems to lead to a clearer focusing of the structural personality picture. As a by-product we gain an important arithmetical check on our computations, since the total number of main scores in the location, determinant, and content areas will be equal and can serve as a check on computational errors."

Possibly the major impact of the 1942 Klopfer book was the section on interpretation which comprised over 100 pages. It elaborated to a great extent on the 1939 article and supplemented this with exemplary chapters which dealt with organic pathology, dementia praecox, mental deficiency, convulsive states, psychoneurosis, depressive states, and miscellaneous clinical problems. Nowhere was such a comprehensive body of Rorschach information available to the reader in one package. Therefore, Klopfer's book in addition to yielding a time advantage, offered what could easily have evolved into "the" permanent Rorschach handbook in America. No doubt, it did manifest an enormous influence on many students of the Rorschach trained during the period from 1942 to 1945.

But the other systematizers and their followers were neither detracted nor subdued by Klopfer's time advantage or the dominance of a journal by one individual. In 1944 Beck published *Rorschach's Test: Vol. I: Basic Processes*. W. L. Valentine's foreward to Beck's 1944 book bespeaks Beck's role in the behaviorism versus phenomenology struggle.

"In the seven years since the publication of the *Manual* (referring to Beck's *Introduction to the Rorschach Method*), arguments about whether the Rorschach method was a scientific method or an art of practice, whether standardization should be imposed or whether it should not, whether the technique was communicable or whether it depended on a mysterious clinical insight, have given way to the general acceptance of Beck's viewpoint that the method is public, repeatable, and objective.

A third period of significance in Rorschach history will develop around the year 1944, corresponding with the appearance of this volume. The requirements of the pioneer era have been served; we now get down to the details of development."

The fact that Beck's importance to the Rorschach world had in no way been diminished by the Klopfer time advantage is manifest in Philip Harriman's review of Beck's new book which appeared in the first issue of the 1945 *Rorschach Research Exchange*.

"If one were to list the three Americans who have done the greatest work to establish its (The Rorschach) scientific respectability, by *consensus gentium* Beck, Hertz, and Klopfer would be the first choices. Consequently, Beck's new volume is certain to attract thoughtful attention from everyone who has a genuine interest in the Rorschach test. . . .It is probably that upon the day of its arrival in the mails all students of the Rorschach were tempted to be truant from work and to begin at once their perusal of the volume. It is also likely that hundreds of students have spent these long winter evenings in hours of collating the Beck volume and the Klopfer-Kelley textbook." (p. 41)

By this time Beck had published some 24 articles plus his 1937 manual. Even if one were to be "Klopfer-oriented" it would be impractical to think that the Beck writings could somehow be avoided. The basic text of the Harriman review was not especially complimentary to Beck and observed that Beck held himself aloof from some of the innovations of others.

"That the initial enthusiasm for Beck's new book wanes the more carefully one reads it is attributable to two factors: first, the book is so weighty that it demands sober reflection—it is decidedly not light and superficial; and secondly, grave omissions, as well as occasional lapses from sound judgment, mar the exposition. . . .A well known experimental psychologist—Dr. Willard Valentine—contributes a foreward in which he states (a) Beck's point of view is now generally accepted, and (b) the reader sits beside an expert and watches him score. Beck declares his purpose 'to demonstrate the processes used in evaluating Rorschach test responses.' If this statement were amended, the reviewer would agree that the purpose has been accomplished. This phrase, however, has been omitted: 'an expert who regards all dissenters as up-start innovators.' Beck's attitude towards 'the new idiom that has appeared in recent years' is somewhat reserved. . . ."

In the review, Harriman suggested that Beck had utilized very little of the Rorschach literature, remarking on Beck's unwillingness to score animal movement, criticizing the complexity of the Beck score for Organizational activity, disregarding the phenomenon of color naming, and offering a limited scheme for the scoring of shading responses. Although concluding that the work would provide an important contribution to the understanding of the Rorschach, Harriman's review left no question that he felt the Beck approach to be too narrow and, more importantly, disregarding of the work of others, especially Klopfer and Hertz. Any shortcomings that the 1944 Beck text may have had were far outweighted by its overall importance in the continued development of the Beck System. He had made an important step toward closing the time advantage which Klopfer maintained. But even more important is the consideration that he now had in publication an updated manual, of sorts, through which his System could be taught on a broader geographic basis. In the preface to the text, he reaffirmed his commitment to Rorschach, to Oberholzer, to behaviorism, and also clarified or re-emphasized his disagreement with the Klopfer System.

"The scoring demonstrated will be recognized as only slightly modified from that which I have previously published. It will show little influence deriving from the new idiom that has appeared in recent years, only in America, reporting studies in which the Rorschach inkblot figures were used. This is not to minimize the value of such investigations. Some will prove significant because of the areas they explore, such as important clinical and other personality groups. Especial interests attaches to the application of the test stimuli, or derived material, to avoid problems. One watches at present with close attention, even if with skepticism, the effort to use the test figures as a group technic. . . .But as one studies these wide departures from Rorschach's fundamentals in evaluating the individual responses and in interpretation, two questions arise: (1) Do the new symbols and categories achieve anything that is an advance on Rorschach test procedures? (2) Are the new doctrines validated, either by specific ad hoc investigations or by other, established principles of personality structure, whether derived clinically or in psychologic experiments?

Examination of the published evidence does not result in conviction. The authors of the innovations have not published proofs that demonstrate their method as more soundly established than that worked out in Psychodiagnostik. In the absence of such proofs in the newer literature, my sanctions continue to be the experience of Rorschach, Oberholzer, and Levy."

There would be no reconciliation for Beck. Nor would he modify significantly his own commitment to Rorschach's thinking. To be sure he had created a new symbol for dealing with dimensional effects created by the shading of the blots and he had undertaken greater elaboration of the quality of the Form of a response but these were in essence minor modifications in areas which Rorschach touched lightly upon in his original writings.

Somewhat quickly, Beck extended the teachability of his ideas and his System. In 1945, shortly after Harriman's review appeared, *Rorschach's Test: Volume II: A Variety of Personality Pictures,* was published. As Beck points out in his acknowledgements, "the present volume takes up the Rorschach test at the point where Volume I leaves off—at the stage of interpretation."

Volume II is, in essence, an elaborate updating of the 1937 manual. In fact, six of the 47 cases reported in Volume II were taken directly from the 1937 manual. The unwritten "motto" of the development of the Beck System had been "cautious conservatism." A reflection of this conservatism is manifest in Roy Grinker's foreward to Beck's Volume II.

"What has been accomplished up to the present has not been the result of wider use of the test by men qualified only by short courses of instruction, not of the long-anticipated accumulation of "normal standards,' and not of artificial mutilation of the method for the purpose of quickly obtaining 'good' or 'bad' responses. Progress has resulted only from the increased depth of vision and broadening perspective of a few investigators capable of such growth, who have the humility to study their material carefully and repetitively, to use every assistance from clinical psychiatry, psychoanalysis, and sociology, and to publish their results only after considerable and cautious reflection. These words have really described the author of this book, whose development I have watched as he has worked closely with the members of the Department of Neuropsychiatry of the Michael Reese Hospital. The reader of this volume will not be instructed as to the results of a 'test' for various clinical conditions, but he will have the opportunity to visualize through a master's eyes the dynamic forces operating in normal living beings of varying levels of accomplishment, and he will see clearly in the pathological material how these same dynamic forces are in disharmony."

Harriman also reviewed Volume II for the *Rorschach Research Exchange.* His review appeared in the first issue of the 1946 volume. Once again Harriman's review was not especially flattering although considerably less scathing then his review of Volume I. Harriman's basic objection to Volume II seemed to lie in the fact that Beck had not developed a tenable theory of personality. He also suggested, as a negative factor, that Beck had not included material indicating his own awareness of the extensive literature, particularly experimental findings concerning personality.

"The case materials are all here from which one of the most substantial contributions to the theory of personality might be written. Unfortunately, Beck has expounded his theory of personality in the beginning of his book. In none of his seven footnotes to this chapter does he reveal an acquaintance with the extensive literature, particularly the major experimental findings and the newer points of view expounded in books and journals, that have been published in recent years. His own theory seems, at least to this reviewer ,to be a hodge-podge of speculation and dogmatism. Does he lack the frame of reference for his appraisals of Rorschach records, or is he hesitant about expounding his views?

Harriman went on to praise some chapters and punish others. Although in no way speaking officially for the Rorschach Institute or the *Rorschach Research Exchange,* (in fact, in his introduction to his review of Beck's Volume I, Harriman carefully noted no formal association with any of the editors of the *Exchange*), his summary of the review to Volume II quite probably manifest the feelings of the Klopfer group toward the Beck System.

"After studying this volume carefully, one must agree that the Rorschach technique is largely an art, far less objective than the Terman-Merrill, even in the hands of a neophyte. To be sure, the experiments in 'blind diagnosis' have brought convincing proof of agreement among experts in the Rorschach test; but the interpretations of a beginner would inevitably be far removed from those of an experienced Rorschach worker. Beck has added little of value for the expert, and his procedures would be disasterous in the hands of one who would learn the method by self-study. The readable, fluent style in which he writes his interpretations is deceptively simple to the earnest but unqualified young student who would 'practice' the method. On the other hand, the patient student can learn a great deal by taking a set of cards and working out each of the scorings which Beck has given. Only after a full year spent in this laborious research can he hope to be ready to piece the records together. Then, he must gain a knowledge of 'reaction types' and 'clinical pictures' before starting on the more stimulating task of interpretation."

There would, of course, be those who would take serious issue with Harriman's criticisms of both Volumes I and II; for example, Piotrowski's review (1946) was considerably more on a positive side as was that of Rabin (1946), but, concerning the growth of the Beck System, that is unimportant. The importance of Volume II is that it completed the mold of the System. Whereas Beck had started in an almost disorderly fashion, by using a case method approach in 1937 that was lacking the systematization of a well-documented scoring scheme and was not accompanied by any lengthy interpretive material, Volumes I and II remedied that deficit. Now

Beck was not only able to take a firm stand on his System of scoring and his administrative approach but also could document, in an interactive fashion, his interpretive approach to the Rorschach. From this point, although additional changes would be made both in scoring and interpretation, the fundamental structure of the Beck System was available to the student in written form. The Klopfer time advantage had now, to a large extent, been neutralized although to be sure the Systems themselves were growing further and further apart. In 1949, when Beck revised Volume I, he finally added a texture symbol which made the scoring for his System complete.

Where during this period of development of the Klopfer and Beck Systems was Hertz? What was her relationship to Klopfer? And to Beck? And at what point might it be said that a Hertz System began its own evolution? The answers to all of these questions are not as well defined by historical material as is available in tracing the development of the Klopfer and Beck Systems. To be sure, Hertz was avidly interested in Rorschach. Her first publication on the Rorschach occurred in 1934 and concerned itself with the reliability of the technique using a sample of 100 high school students and applying a split-half method. In 1935, she published what was to become, for a short time, a classic series of norms for adolescent age groups and also provided a historical summary of the Rorschach. In that summary she covered the areas of administration, reliability, norms, and the current status of the test. She quite accurately pointed to the fact that in spite of increased interest and innumerable investigations, the procedure of giving the test still showed considerable variability and was indefinite. She also noted that the scoring of responses was still very poorly defined and highly subjective depending upon the experience and clinical intuition of the examiner. Hertz also indicated that only two studies had been published dealing with reliability, the results of which contradicted one another, and in the area of validity, found little or no evidence to support the use of the Rorschach, either with regard to intellectual or nonintellectual factors of personality. Her conclusions, though in retrospect not necessarily earthshaking, did nonetheless demonstrate to the Rorschach world that she was highly knowledgable about the technique. It was clear from her summary that the Rorschach had not gained the professional status, as defined by traditional psychometric standards, as had other psychological tests of the era. She summarized many of the obstacles to such status but held out considerable hope for the future of the Rorschach in light of Rorschach's own early work, subsequent "preliminary" investigations, contemporary criticism of other psychological tests, and possibly most of all, the fact that "various investigators who have applied the test practically claim that it works." She prophesied that although the Rorschach was still in its infancy, its future would be distinguished.

"The Rorschach test is still at the beginning of its history. Much remains to be done before it can be accepted in full. That it has a future, however, cannot be denied."

The Hertz prophesy was obviously an accurate one. The actual impact of her own work on the post-1935 development of the Rorschach is more difficult to gauge. Two factors, one of interest area, the other concerning the nature of applicability, manifested an important role in determining the Hertz impact on Rorschach development and particularly as her own System related to that of Beck and Klopfer. The interest area factor is quite simple. Much of her early work with the Rorschach was concentrated with children, adolescents, and normals, thus fell outside of the main stream of diagnostic and personality interest that was pervading the Rorschach world from the period of 1935 through 1945. Secondly, and probably much more important was the manner which Hertz chose to present her thoughts and findings concerning the Rorschach. After her original Rorschach manuscript was tragically and inadvertently destroyed, she never wrote a book, although the quantity of her writings which comprise some 50 articles on the Rorschach alone, not to mention other subjects, could have at any one of a variety of intervals been incorporated into a major work such as the 1942 Klopfer text or the 1944 Beck Volume. Unfortunately, however, Hertz chose not to do this, and instead relied on the massive number of publications in her name concerning the Rorschach technique, plus her own teaching methodology at Western Reserve University, to convey to the Rorschach world the aspects of what is now the Hertz System.

While vitally interested in the development of her own System, she played another role which was equally important to the Rorschach world. As mentioned earlier, that role might well be considered as one of a "conscience" for the other Systematizers. At times she took a strong stand in favor of Beck or against Beck. The same was true for Klopfer. Possibly one of her most interesting commentaries on Rorschach problems concerned the matter of standardization of the Rorschach method which appeared in the 1939 *Rorschach Research Exchange*. Here, in responding to Klopfer's suggestion for refinement rather than standardization, she methodically approached the data heretofore published, neatly combining statistical and objective examination of the technique as well as opinion. She defined the requirements for standardization as including a uniformity in procedures of administration, objectivity in scoring, the establishment of normative data for different age groups and for different personality and clinical types, and the formulation of a standard procedures of interpretation. Not only did she disagree with Klopfer's notion of "refinement" but also indirectly criticized his method for establishing scoring categories.

"Before attempting to verify the psychological significance of a category, one must first isolate it and then identify it. Then we engage in scientific research. But we have to start counting sometime and it seems that Rorschach workers delay in this latter enterprise. . . .For example, Klopfer has presented the hypothesis for M, FM and m. Theoretical and psychoanalytical explanations have been offered by Piotrowski. To the writer's knowledge no acceptable evidence has yet been presented to justify inclusion of this differentiation of the M in a final scoring system. Patterns such as these must be isolated and identified as they show up in personality or clinical types. Their reality, the principles and conditions of their occurrence, their systematic relations to other patterns should be scientifically studied without delay in order to establish them on a firm and reliable foundation."

She also expressed her own feeling about the place of the Rorschach in the overall scheme of test and measurements.

"If the psychological instruments of personality description could be viewed on a scale, at one extreme would appear tests standardized to a maximum degree, at the other, methods which are not amenable to any form of standardization. . . .The intermediate range on the scale would contain those instruments of personality description differing in degree of refinement, standardization and use of subjective judgments. These differences may be due to the fact that the method has not been sufficiently developed as yet. Or, the method may elicit material of such a nature that it defies measurement. However, the finer and more exact the instrument, the more it approaches the possibility of standardization. . . .The Rorschach method is intermediate on this scale. It is more on the qualitative side—an art, if you will—which requires a maximum amount of ingenuity, insight, and intuition in its application. At the same time, there are parts of it which may be reduced to quantitative measurement. This phase of its development has been delayed. However, the method should be viewed as an instrument which may apply quantitative method to qualitative-subject matter and which may yield results which will stand on the firm basis of objectivity without sacrificing those elements which defy measurement. . . .In a recent presidential address delivered before the American Psychological Association, Dashiell in discussing contemporary developments in psychology, stressed particularly the signs of reproachment between the experimental and clinical attitudes. He described the present tendency to study experimentally and clinically prsonality mechanisms, neurotic behavior, even psychoanalytic concepts, experimental psychologists, psychiatrists and psychoanalysts all cooperating in joint projects. It is the hope of the writer that there will be a similar interpenetration of these same attitudes in reference to the Rorschach method. Clinicians will place more emphasis on standardized procedure and will subject their clinical observations to scientific validation. Experimentalists will cease refinement and quantification absurdum and will emphasize more insight and intuition in the application of the method. Then, indeed, the Rorschach method will be unique in steering a safe course between the Scylla of quantitative fallacy and the Charybdis of qualitative subjectivity."

It was under the flag of this basic philosophy that the Hertz System did evolve, constantly oriented toward standardization and objectification where possible, yet rarely, if ever, losing sight of the necessity for subjective intuition to be offered into Rorschach interpretation. While this approach seems highly congruent with that of Beck and not extremely dissimilar with the early writings of Klopfer, there was nevertheless a distinct difference. Beck, as has been pointed out, was committed to Rorschach and to Oberholzer. He was cautious to change, preferring instead to concern himself with Rorschach's basic hypotheses. Thus, in an overview, he might be considered more conservative or cautious than Hertz in his readiness to depart from the basic postulates offered in *Psychodiagnostik*. Conversely, Klopfer was quite willing to add as many accoutrements to the fundamentals of Rorschach as seemed clinically or phenomenologically appropriate. In fact, Hertz criticized him in one of the above statements for neglecting the quantitative characteristics of the Rorschach. This failure on the part of Klopfer's group caused Hertz to avoid a more complete commitment to Klopfer and instead worked on the development of her own System.

The Hertz System developed slowly but definitely. In fact, if one were to review the major Rorschach influences in the United States in 1941, as did Krugman in his Presidential address to the Rorschach Institute, it is inconceivable that Hertz's ideas would be considered unimportant as contrasted with either those of Beck or Klopfer. But with the publication of the 1942 Klopfer-Kelley book and the advent of the Klopfer time advantage, the relative importance of the Hertz System quickly fell behind on the national scene. Where Beck made up this difference, Hertz did not. In all fairness to both Hertz and Klopfer, it should be quickly added that quite probably Hertz *was not* as much in disagreement with Klopfer as had been Beck and therefore there was no real need to attempt to compensate for the Klopfer "time advantage." The basic difference at that time between the Hertz and Klopfer Systems was in the use of scoring symbols, a phenomenon which Hertz did not perceive to be a major item. Also this was an era in which Hertz herself was "re-thinking" her approach to the Rorschach. During her first decade of Rorschach experience, Hertz had been strongly committed to a psychometric approach. Gradually, however, it would appear that her writings become more marked by subjectivity and more concerned with the qualitative aspects of the methodology as had been suggested for years by Klopfer. Also Hertz considered Klopfer to be the teacher par excellence and in this sense "the Rorschach leader." As the mid-1940's passed, her interests and research appears to turn from the areas of isolated scores or patterns consistent with the applied normative approach to broader interpretive patterns. In doing this, she shifted further away from the Beck System and allied herself much more closely with the Klopfer and peripherally with the Rapaport-Schafer type of Rorschach approach. She now became more concerned with the integration of Rorschach data with social history and less concerned with the utilization of "blind analysis" or the establishment of normative data in the "traditional" sense of psychometry.

The total evolution of the Hertz System has been somewhat sporadic and has shifted emphasis at least once, if not more so, over a 30-year period. It has never achieved the level of organization that is enjoyed by the Beck, Klopfer, or Piotrowski Systems and possibly not even as much organization as the Rapaport-Schafer System, mainly because of the lack of a single manual or text. Nevertheless, her writings have continued to be influential in the Rorschach world and she unquestionably must be considered as one of the major figures in the overall Rorschach development in the United States.

The Piotrowski System grew in a reasonably methodical manner. Whereas Piotrowski was initially introduced to the Rorschach by Klopfer, his tendencies away from Klopfer may be noted rather early. In part, the divergence from Klopfer was caused by differing interests in the utilization of the Rorschach. Klopfer emphasized teaching of the technique and its general implementation for personality evaluation and Piotrowski emphasized the psychodiagnostic aspects of the Rorschach specifically as related to psychopathology. Somewhat narrowly at first, Piotrowski concentrated his early research efforts on work with organics. Secondly, however, the theoretical differences between Klopfer and Piotrowski were quite sharp in some respects. As early as his 1937 paper concerning the M, FM, and m responses as indicators of changes in personality, there is indication that he and Klopfer would eventually disagree on FM and m. Of course, in that this conception of movement differed from that of Beck and was subsequently rejected by Beck, it was difficult to conceive that Piotrowski could ally himself strongly with the Beck System.

Piotrowski's original conception of FM and m were that:

"The FM, being less integrated with the total personality, represents tendencies which originated early in life but which have not fully matured. It may be considered, then, as a less developed form of the M. Consequently, the FM does not have the same stabilizing value for the relationship between the subject and his environment. It may be thought of as representing those parts of the personality which have not been fully utilized for the purpose of facilitating the subject's relationship with the environment. This would indicate that we do not develop adequately all our potential capacities. The m is an unfavorable sign. While the M and the FM point in varying degrees to reality, the m does not point anywhere, so to speak. The m represents tendencies which are not expressed outwardly and constructively. Since these tendencies are not tested in practical life by the individual, they lack adaptation to reality, and thus develop in a distorted fashion. The attitudes expressed through the m may be thought of as being incompatible with the predominant tendencies of the personality. Thus, the m is an attic, as it were, where those trends of the personality which would otherwise lead to inner conflicts are stored away." (1937)

Later (1947), Piotrowski modified his conception of FM to the extent of suggesting that FM was directly related to the unsophisticated energy level of the individual, that m revealed a subject's conception of a role of life which that individual feels very desirable but which he considers unattainable because of external difficulties or personal incapacity. This was contrasted with Klopfer's interpretation of m which was interpreted as the subject experiencing promptings from within as hostile or uncontrollable, working on him rather than as sources of energy at his disposal (1942).

While such disagreement of a theoretical nature was in and by itself insufficient to create a schism between Klopfer and Piotrowski, it did form the cornerstone of their divergence. Later a new issue widened the schism. It was that of the scoring and interpretation of shading. In 1942 Piotrowski compared his own System of scoring with that of Rorschach, Binder, Beck, and Klopfer. He found the Klopfer-Binder approach to shading too complex and lacking a valid base for interpretation. By 1942, Piotrowski had made it very clear that he could not accept the Klopfer approach to the Rorschach on several basic issues and therefore a separate System, different from Klopfer and Beck and certainly from that of Hertz, would evolve. Adding to his differences with the other Systematizers, Piotrowski found himself quickly engrossed in the theoretical aspects of the test as a method based on perception. In fact, he suggested (1947) that Rorschach might well have named the technique "Perceptanalysis" rather than "Psychodiagnostik." For Piotrowski then, the true interpretation of the subject is yielded by an understanding of the subject's visual percept and his interpretation as verbally reported about that percept. To this extent Piotrowski becomes much more concerned with the stimulus characteristics of the blot in his System than do any of the other Systematizers.* Consequently, Piotrowski assumed a sign approach to the Rorschach wherein the combination of verbally reported visual images create a descriptive pattern of the individual. To this end, Piotrowski would be considered an operationalist, describing behavior in a Beckian fashion but keeping the description rela-

---

* Beck being concerned with the degree to which the subjects' responses are similar to others, Klopfer being concerned with the nature of the association, and Rapaport-Schafer being concerned with the technique as is utilized as a structured interview.

tively free of any given personality theory. Correspondingly, Klopfer approaches the interpretation of the response pattern from a psychoanalytic theory, as does Rapaport-Schafer and also, though to a lesser extent, does Beck.

The Piotrowski System has taken longer to develop in its comprehensive form than any of the others. His book *Perceptanalysis* was not published until 1957, partly because he devoted a great deal of time prior to 1957 to research in diagnosis of psychopathology, but also in part because the basic theoretical scheme of the Rorschach did not evolve itself in his thinking until that time. Before 1957, the Piotrowski System clearly existed but in a less formally articulated manner, being scattered throughout journals and monographs in a manner very much like that of the Hertz System.

For David Rapaport, the systematization of the Rorschach came more quickly and more simply than probably for any of the other Systematizers. His notions concerning Rorschach were well established prior to his entry into the United States and his commitment to psychoanalytic theory was long and firm. For him, Rorschach was one of many techniques available for personality evaluation. He considered it a basic association technique, more complex in its structure and in the material which it provoked, but in the overall sense forming the basis for a structured interview. Rorschach then was one of many potentially useful instruments through which the projections of the subject could be viewed. Rapaport referred to this orientation in his comments on standardization problems in 1939. In 1942 in his article "Principles Underlying Projective Techniques," he set forth the principle under which his System evolved, "projective procedures imply a general projective hypothesis: behavior manifestations of the human being, from the least to the most significant ones, are revealing of his personality— that is, the individual principle of which he is the carrier." In reviewing the concept of the projective hypothesis and projective procedures, Rapaport expressed the belief that all tests could be arranged on a hierarchy, the criteria for which would be the extent to which a given technique would provoke projection by the subject. He maintained that the tests, such as the Rorschach, the Szondi, and the Thematic Apperception test, would clearly stand at the top of such a hierarchy because they satisfied the requirements in the criteria to the greatest extent.

By 1944, only five years after his entry into the United States, and only six years after the completion of his Ph.D., Rapaport and his collaborators had completed the first volume of Diagnostic Psychological Testing as a result of a farreaching project to study the usefulness of the test battery in psychodiagnosis. In that project seven tests were investigated concerning their clinical usefulness. Among these instruments was the Rorschach. In

1945, in a brief publication with Roy Schafer, Rapaport devoted himself exclusively to the Rorschach and its clinical efficiency as contrasted with other instruments in the test battery. They described the Rorschach as the most efficient single diagnostic tool, being easily learned, but one the proficiency of which hinges, to a large extent, on the examiner's clinical-psychological and psychiatric knowledge. Also in that article, Rapaport and Schafer suggested that extensions or refinements of the technique tended to make it cumbersome, time-consuming and more prohibitive for clinical use. Thus, they discouraged such extensions unless they could be demonstrated to be indispensable to the technique. In this respect, Rapaport was disagreeing with all of the other Systematizers, probably less so with Beck than any of the others, in terms of their general approach to the Rorschach, but even with Beck to the extent that Beck was not utilizing the technique as a "structured interview."

In 1946, with the publication of Volume II of *Diagnostic Psychological Testing,* Rapaport was somewhat critical of those who attempted to differentiate the usefulness of the Rorschach as something other than a unique type of social history.

"The concept of projective testing has been overused, and yet limited to a relatively small set of procedures in the minds of those working in this field. It is sometimes forgotten that the central and time-honored procedure of personality study—namely, case history—is a 'projective procedure' too. The tendency is to forget that the term 'projection' in connection with projective tests' is not identical with the psychoanalytic concept of projection as a defense mechanism central to the nosological picture of paranoid disorders, nor even with the popularized and emasculated version of that concept denoting any attribution of one's own intents, thoughts, and feelings to another person. . . .The projective hyypothesis can therefore be applied into any segment of human behavior; and in Volume I we have shown that it can be applied profitably to the diagnostic analysis of intelligence test results. Therefore, the projective hypothesis, far from differentiating projective from non-projective procedures, shows rather that any procedure investigating human behavior can be looked upon from this point of view. . . .Therefore, when a procedure is so designed as to enable the subject to demonstrate his psychological structure unstilted by conventional modes, it is projective."

In Volume II of *Diagnostic Psychological Testing,* Rapaport also established himself as clearly disagreeing with the procedures of the other Systematizers by suggesting that the several requirements for validation and clinical standardization had not been met regardless of a vast amount of research that had already been published by that time on the Rorschach.

He described four steps prerequisite to clinical standardization and validation: (1) study of all major types of psychopathological groups, (2) a unitary nosology by which all groups are well defined, (3) the use of a well-defined, thoroughly studied control group of "normals," (4) administration and scoring by a single set of criteria and practices.

"One must not be surprised, then, that isolated attempts at mechanical-statistical standardization have not taken all these complexities into consideration; nor that the attempt to standardize signs of maladjustment in the Rorschach test in the Armed Forces was not successful, and that the test was abandoned as useless for military selection purposes; nor that a critical reaction against the tests persists with a consequent undue defensiveness among its promulgators, and that in general a somewhat unhealthy atmosphere has begun to surround the Rorschach test in which its diagnostic limitations have been sufficiently emphasized, looked for, caught, or kept in the foreground of investigation."

It would seem that for Rapaport and Schafer, the general approach to Rorschach had been erroneous, the expectencies too high, the demands too great; all leading to an engendering of skepticism toward the overall usefulness of the instrument.

After the publication of Volume II of *Psychological Diagnostic Testing*, Rapaport elaborated very little on the Rorschach approach, instead becoming more involved with general developments in ego psychology. Schafer did not elaborate to a great extent on the Rapaport model as much as he did to clarify it. First, in 1948 he published the *Clinical Application of Psychological Tests* which may be considered as a sequel to the two volumes of the *Diagnostic Psychological Testing*. In this text, Schafer presented a collection of individual case records demonstrating how the data which comprised the final diagnosis are elicited from both the separate and overall test findings. Later, in 1954, Schafer published *Psychoanalytic Interpretation in Rorschach Testing*. As he noted in the preface:

"This book is written for those who have completed at least their basic clinical training in administering, scoring, and interpreting Rorschach test results; preferably the reader should also have clinical testing experience beyond the doctoral level. The traditional, more or less established significances of scores and score configurations will not be reviewed here. Rorschach, Beck, Klopfer, Piotrowski, Schachtel and Rapaport have all presented major expositions of Rorschach technique. While their many differences in individual points of administration, scoring and interpretation cannot be overlooked, each presents a broad, helpful introduction to the test. All of these discussions, Rapaport's—and my clinically focused summary of it—provide the best introduction to what follows here. Unless the reader is intimately familiar with at least one of the major expositions listed above, he is certainly to be confused by the present works variations on basic Rorschach themes."

Schafer also assumed familiarity on the part of his reader with psychoanalytic theory.

And so, over a period of slightly more than twenty years (1936-1957) five American Rorschach Systems developed. Three Systems, those of Beck,

Klopfer, and Hertz, had crystalized by 1945, the Piotrowski and Rapaport-Schafer Systems being formulated shortly thereafter. None has remained static since its inception. Quite the contrary, all have been marked by significant additions and modifications continuing into the current decade. The Piotrowski System is probably the least static of any with the current attempts to computerize the technique. The Rapaport-Schafer System has experienced the least modification but this is, at least in part, because neither Rapaport nor Schafer had intended a formally structured System of the Rorschach. Both were more interested in the broad techniques of psychodiagnostics and the application of psychoanalytic theory to these techniques of which the Rorschach merely represents one of many useful tests.

Before attempting to compare the Systems for similarities and differences, it seems important to study each with regard to its respective development so as to gain some appreciation for the events and decision which led to the contemporary status of the System. The next several chapters are oriented toward that goal. Subsequently, the Systems will be compared, but with some limitations which will become obvious as each System is studied in depth.

REFERENCES

Announcements of the Rorschach Institute. *Ror. Res. Exch.*, 1942, 6, 39-41.

Beck, S. J. Introduction to the Rorschach Method. *Amer. Orthopsychiat. Assoc.*, Monog. 1, 1937.

Beck, S. J. Some recent Rorschach problems. *Ror. Res. Exch.*, 1937, 2, 15-22.

Beck, S. J. *Rorschach's Test: Vol. I: Basic Processes.* New York: Grune and Stratton, 1944.

Beck, S. J. *Rorschach's Test: Vol. II: A Variety of Personality Pictures.* New York: Grune and Stratton, 1945.

Harriman, P. Beck, Samuel J. Rorschach's Test: I: Basic processes. *Ror. Res. Exch.*, 1945, 9, 41-45.

Harriman, P. Beck, Samuel J. Rorschach's Test: II: A Variety of personality pictures. *Ror. Res. Exch.*, 1946, 10, 37-39.

Hertz, Marguerite. The reliability of the Rorschach ink-blot test. *J. Appl. Psychol.*, 1934, 18, 461-477.

Hertz, Marguerite. Rorschach norms for an adolescent age group. *Child Developm.*, 1935, 6, 69-76.

Hertz, Marguerite. The Rorschach ink-blot test: historical summary. *Psychol. Bull.*, 1935, 32, 33-66.

Hertz, Marguerite. On the standardization of the Rorschach method. *Ror. Res. Exch.*, 1939, 3, 120-133.

Hertz, Marguerite. Rorschach: Twenty years after. *Ror. Res. Exch.*, 1941, 5, 90-129.

Kelley, D. By-laws of the Rorschach Institute. *Ror. Res. Exch.*, 1939, 3, 92-100.

Kelley, D. Survey of the training facilities for the Rorschach method in the U.S.A. *Ror. Res. Exch.*, 1940, 4, 84-87.

Kelley, D. Announcement of the training committee. *Ror. Res. Exch.*, 1940, 4, 88-89.

Klopfer, B. and Sender, Sadie. A system of refined scoring symbols. *Ror. Res. Exch.*, 1936, 1, 19-22.

Klopfer, B. The present status of the theoretical development of the Rorschach method. *Ror. Res. Exch.*, 1937, 1, 142-147.

Klopfer, B. The technique of the Rorschach performance. *Ror. Res. Exch.*, 1937, 2, 1-14.

Klopfer, B., Buchard, E., Kelley, D. and Miale, Florence. Theory and technique of Rorschach interpretation. *Ror. Res. Exch.*, 1939, 3, 152-192.

Klopfer, B., Davidson, Helen, Kelley, D. and Miale, Florence. The technique of Rorschach scoring and tabulation. *Ror. Res. Exch.*, 1940, 4, 75-83.

Klopfer, B. and Kelley, D. *The Rorschach Technique*. Yonkers-on-Hudson, N. Y.: World Book, 1942.

Krugman, M. Out of the inkwell. *Ror. Res. Exch.*, 1940, 4, 91-101.

Piotrowski, Z. The M, FM, and m responses as indicators of changes in personality. *Ror. Res. Exch.*, 1937, 1, 148-156.

Piotrowski, Z. Rorschach's Test: I: basic processes. II. A variety of personality pictures by Samuel J. Beck. *J. Consul. Psychol.*, 1946, 10, 375-376.

Piotrowski, Z. A Rorschach compendium. *Psychiat. Quart.*, 1947, 21, 79-101.

Piotrowski, Z. *Perceptanalysis*. New York: Macmillan, 1957.

Rabin, A. Rorschach's Test: II: A variety of personality pictures by S. J. Beck. *J. Abnor. and Soc. Psychol.*, 1946, 41, 233-236.

Rapaport, D. Comments on Rorschach standardization. *Ror. Res. Exch.*, 1939, 3, 107-110.

Rapaport, D. Principles underlying projective techniques. *Charact. and Personal.*, 1942, 10, 213-219.

Rapaport, D. *Manual of diagnostic psychological testing. I: Diagnostic testing of intelligence and concept formation.* Chicago: Josiah Macy Found., 1944.

Rapaport, D. and Schafer, R. The Rorschach test: a clinical evaluation. *Bull. Menning. Clinc.*, 1945, 9, 73-77.

Rapaport, D., Gill, M. and Schafer, R. *Diagnostic Psychological Testing*. Vol. II. Chicago: Yearboko publish., 1946.

Schafer, R. *The clinical application of psychological tests.* New York: Internat. Univ. Press, 1948.

Schafer, R. *Psychoanalytic interpretation in Rorschach testing.* New York: Grune and Stratton, 1954.

Schafer, R. *Projective testing and psychoanalysis*: Selected Papers. New York: International Universities Press, 1967.

CHAPTER 4

THE KLOPFER SYSTEM

The development of a Klopfer System of the Rorschach was almost inevitable from the time of his introduction to the technique in 1933 in Switzerland. As a scholar, teacher, and dedicated psychologist, he quickly became highly enthusiastic about the potentials of the Rorschach. In the many interviews conducted in regard to this text, both those who agree and those who disagree with his approach, described his enthusiasm for the Rorschach as overwhelming and almost charismatic. What did Klopfer bring to the Rorschach? Certainly no strong commitment to projective methodology. Definitely no strong commitment to Freudian psychoanalysis. Not even the eagerness of conquering the unknown psychology. Instead, he brought himself and his dedication to teaching. It was this dedication which predisposed his eventual Rorschach role. The aura of his excitement carried the thrust of Rorschach innovation into the United States in a manner much different than that which had been conveyed by either David Levy or Samuel Beck. Klopfer fully believed in the Rorschach. And his belief combined with his teaching and organizational talents, led him to be a leader in the field.

In 1966, the Society for Projective Techniques conferred upon him "The Great Man Award." The citation of the Society is brief and to a large extent underplays the importance of this individual in the development of Rorschach in the United States.

"For his unique contributions to the field of projective techniques, the society honors its founder. Bruno Klopfer: teacher par excellence, scholar, innovator, founder of this journal and of this society whose birth, development, and maturity made possible. It seems quite impossible to contemplate the impact of projective techniques on American psychology, apart from our founder's contributions. For these contributions to our society, to the field of projective techniques, especially to our knowledge of the Rorschach, and to clinical psychology generally, we are grateful to Bruno Klopfer."

One must also recall that Klopfer manifest his regard for the Rorschach in an atmosphere which at best might be described as cautious regarding new innovations. American psychology looked askance on phenomenology in those years and had established itself as closely allied with the demanding notions of "pure science." Behavorism was the byword. And anyone willing to depart from behaviorism or unwilling to accept its basic tenets would be regarded with somewhat of a jaundice eye.

52

But the American atmosphere was by no means completely hostile. It must be remembered that David Levy had already established a good relationship for the Rorschach in the United States and that Robert Woodworth had endorsed Beck's doctoral research on the technique. Following the completion of his dissertation, Beck's work at the Harvard University Medical School had also generated additional interest and respect for the inkblot method. Also, the approach with which Levy and Beck utilized the technique in those years was not inconsistent with the notions Rorschach conveyed in his original experiment and thus not alien to the fundamentals of behaviorism.

A liability for Klopfer in the development of his Rorschach System was the fact that frequently, he was too willing to place his faith in a phenomenological or intuitive concept concerning the Rorschach. As a consequence, his eagerness to develop the Rorschach often was perceived by those around him, for example Beck, as a too rapid or liberal departure from Rorschach's original ideas with little justification. To some extent, such a notion is probably accurate, but at the same time, it should be noted that Klopfer perceived his role not as one of perpetuating Rorschach's ideas as much as enhancing the Rorschach as a test.

His organization of the *Rorschach Research Exchange* exemplifies his perceptiveness as a teacher. Without the *Exchange* playing a major role in the formulative years of Rorschach in the United States, it is quite likely that Rorschach literature would have been scattered through many journals too numerous for a single student to attend to. The most unfortunate feature of Klopfer's organizational activity was that he could not bring himself to reconcile his ideas with those of Samuel Beck. Had this occurred, the whole history of American Rorschach might well have been changed and this text quite unnecessary. Several writers, including Beck, Hertz, Piotrowski, and Rapaport, at times, suggested that the "Klopfer group" was developing its modifications of the Rorschach too rapidly without adequate justification. That criticism was probably very valid and it appears that even Klopfer became aware of its validity eventually, but possibly too late, for reconciliation to occur. The organization of the Klopfer System, which might be said to have begun with the 1936 publication of scoring symbols, was as much as 90 per cent complete with the publication of the 1942 Klopfer and Kelley text. Thus, in a period of some eight years, a system materialized and received extensive elaboration.

It seems most appropriate to study the development of the Klopfer System, or for that fact, of any system in terms of three basic components: administration, scoring, and interpretation. As has been noted, the fundamentals of the Klopfer System evolved between 1936 and 1942. It is easiest to deal with the first two categories, those of administration and scoring in light of their evolution during these years, than is the third, that of interpretation which has continued to change in some respects to the present day.

ADMINISTRATION

Rorschach, in the monograph *Psychodiagnostik,* suggested as a basic administrative procedure the following:

"The subject is given one plate after the other and asked, what might this be? He holds the plate in his hand and may turn it about as much as he likes. The subject is free to hold the plate near his eyes or far away as he choses; however, it should not be viewed from a distance. The length of the extended arm is the maximum permissible distance. Care must be taken that the subject does not catch a glimpse of the plate from a distance since this would alter the conditions of the experiment. . . .An attempt is made to get at least one answer to every plate, though suggestion in any form is, of course, avoided. The answers are taken down as long as they are produced by the subject. It has proved unwise to set a fixed time for exposure of the card. Coercion should be avoided as much as possible. Occasionally it becomes necessary to show a suspicious subject how the figures are prepared, ad oculos. In general, however, rejection of the test is relatively rare, even among suspicious and inhibited patients."

It is also worth noting that in Rorschach's original monograph, he indicated that most all subjects regard the inkblots as a test of their imagination. He felt that it makes little difference whether the examiner encourages the subject to give free reign to his imagination or not. This hypothesis of Rorschach's will prove interesting when the Beck and Klopfer Systems of administration are compared.

In the *Psychodiagnostik,* Rorschach did not outline, in his procedure for administration, the necessity for a formal Inquiry. He did, however, suggest that it is at least sometimes necessary and, in fact, seemed to imply that a thorough Inquiry could evolve:

"Sometimes it is difficult to determine whether an answer is of F or M. Intelligent subjects can generally say with reasonable certainty whether or not kinaesthetic factors have contributed to the response; one should wait until after the completion of the test before asking the question, however; otherwise attention is drawn to kinaesthetic factors too strongly. Occasionally unintelligent subjects and patients will give clues on careful questioning. In other cases, comparison of the interpretation under question with answers clearly F or M will make differentiation possible."

It is also implied in *Psychodiagnostik,* that Rorschach utilized some question procedure to determine the location of the response, as the protocols included in the text typically give the location used by the subject, and the relation of color to the response.

In the September, 1937 issue of the *Rorschach Research Exchange* ("The Technique of Rorschach Performance") Klopfer elaborated on his administrative procedure. He reviewed the suggested procedures of Rorschach, Schneider, and Beck and concluded that the basic Rorschach instructions should be followed.

"The subject is given one plate after another and is asked, 'What might this be?' This formulation, 'What might this be?' is the only standardized verbal instruction given by Rorschach himself. It seems worthwhile to keep exactly this formulation, which conforms best to the basic conditions of the method; to set a task and leave the procedure entirely to the subject. . . .In dealing with intelligent subjects, I usually emphasize that there are no further regulations in fulfilling the task, and that this lack of regulation is essential for the test. In the same way, questions by the subject, such as, 'Shall I say the first thing that comes to my mind?' or 'Shall I say what it reminds me of, or what it looks like?' have to be answered persistently, 'That is all up to you.' "

Klopfer also expressed his belief that it was permissible for the subject to sit beside the examiner, although agreeing with Rorschach's original suggestion that it is preferable that the examiner sit somewhere in back of the subject and is not to disturb him. In all other respects Klopfer, in essence, agreed with the basic Rorschach procedure for the "Free Association" portion of the test. He elaborated considerably on the problem of Inquiry.

"A satisfactory inquiry is impossible without a thorough acquaintance with the scoring system and its interpretive value, since the first function of the inquiry is to make the scoring and the interpretation of the spontaneous reactions possible. The second function of the inquiry is to give the subject a chance to supplement and complete spontaneously the responses given in the performance proper. This function is of particular importance where subjects of a high intellectual level are hampered by embarrassment or negative attitudes in expressing their faculties adequately during the first encounter with the cards. The third function of the inquiry is to enable the examiner to test the limits of the subject's capacities by tapping faculties which have not been used in spontaneous reactions. The fulfillment of this latter function will as a rule constitute a separate phase, after the inquiry has completed its first two tasks. These two tasks are usually intermingled."

To the extent that Klopfer defined the first purpose of the Inquiry, to make adequate scoring possible, he does not appear to have deviated from Rorschach and certainly not from Beck, at least in intent. However, with the inclusion of two other functions for the Inquiry, obtaining supplementary information and testing limits, Klopfer departed sharply from both the Rorschach and Beck methodologies. In fact, the emphasis on the first function given by Klopfer appears to exceed the method, although not the intent, of either Rorschach or Beck. Klopfer described the basics of the Inquiry procedure which he recommended to include much more direct questioning than would be permissible for either Rorschach or Beck. For instance, suggesting that the examiner begin the Inquiry directing his questions to the location of the response on the card, Klopfer cautions:

"The general location is not sufficient for accurate scoring of the responses. We must also be informed about the elaboration and inner organization of each response. . . .We may get spontaneously a pointing out of the head, the body, and the wings as an answer to our question, 'Describe the bat to me.' If not, we may proceed to ask for the head, the body, and the wings. . . .Even so, we are not yet satisfied. The subject has pointed out a great or small number of details, explaining and elaborating the figures seen in the response. But there are a number of important elements in almost everyone of the ten cards, the reaction to which is very interesting. Thus, for instance, a 'bat' is very frequently seen in the whole of Card I. We may have received some information about the body and the wings, the claw-like extensions at the upper center, and some embarrassed remarks about the invisible head. Now we are interested in what the subject has to say about the four white spots, about the ragged lower edge, about the peculiar lower center protrusion, and the tiny spots around the main blot. Correspondingly, subjects giving the 'clown' response to Card II, usually skip in their explanation the lower center red spot, or in seeing two figures in action on Card III, will not mention the three red spots there. Most subjects in most of their responses will commit such minor omissions, and it has proven very useful to pin them down on just these points. . . .Such inquisitive questions may frequently stimulate additional responses which either add something to a response given before, or use the omitted parts for independent responses. We have to ask whether or not the subject saw these things in the performance proper, and, if he did, why he didn't mention them in his spontaneous explanation. Thus we receive information about the different types of mental behavior under pressure for explanation, but we do not count such responses as spontaneous additions."

Whereas Klopfer seemed to be much more involved in location scoring than either Rorschach or Beck, he was in fact somewhat more conservative about determinant scoring than either Rorschach or Beck.

"As to the inquiry in regard to 'What qualities in the selected figures are utilized in determining the response?', we can only give some general technical hints, because the specific directions for this part of the inquiry are fully dependent on the scoring and interpretive values. . . .The main difficulty is the avoiding of leading questions. . . .Let us take, for example, an inquiry about the 'butterfly' response to Card II lower center red, or Card III center red. Should the formulation mentioned by Beck, 'What about that reminds you of a butterfly?' elicit only answers like, 'The shape of the wings,' 'The feelers,' etc., we may continue, 'Is it only the form that reminds you of a butterfly?' (I prefer this negative formulation to the more positive one mentioned by Rorschach and Beck, 'Suppose this were all grey, or black, but the same shape it is now, would you think it is a butterfly?'). . . .For very stubborn color-evaders we not infrequently give responses like, 'What other than the form should it be?'. . . .I find it advisable in such cases not to press the inquiry further at this point, but rather to wait until the color is spontaneously mentioned in a response in the inquiry about Cards VIII, IX, and X. Then we can go back to the 'butterfly' response saying, 'Here you used form and color—how about that in the butterflies?'."

While Klopfer suggested conservatism with regard to color, be became much more liberal with regard to the texture element.

"Occasionally we find such responses determined exclusively by the form. A good trick for getting spontaneous information here after the more general questions have failed, is to ask, 'Do you see this rug or skin, right-side-up or up-side-down?' If the texture has been used, the subject will invariably mention the hairiness or skin texture quite indignantly."

Klopfer was also willing to go one step further, than either Rorschach or Beck, by encouraging at the beginning of his inquiry additional responses: "We will now go over your responses, but if something else comes to your mind that you should like to add, or if you would like to change some of your responses, don't hesitate. . . ." He suggested the use of testing the limits so as to provoke additional responses to determinants not used in the performance proper. His basic contention here was that, in some instances, determinants may have been neglected and an approach to testing the limits would be in order, to determine whether there is an unwillingness on the part of the subject to articulate these determinants or whether there is simply an inability to use them.

In the 1942 Klopfer text, the fundamentals for instructions and administration were not changed significantly. He stressed the general preparation of the subject as being probably more important than for many other types of psychological tests and also reaffirmed the basic notions on seating arrangements that he had in the 1937 article. While also reaffirming the three main aspects of the Inquiry, he elaborated in greater detail on the importance of testing the limits, separating this from the Inquiry proper, and modifying it by indicating that it would not necessarily be required for all subjects.

"The accumulated experience of the last few years has given more and more emphasis to this phase of the administration of the Rorschach method. Naturally the importance of this phase is in inverse proportion to the richness of the other two phases, the performance proper and the inquiry. The more results these phases yield, the less important testing the limits becomes. . . .As a rule, testing the limits will be particularly necessary where the performance proper and the inquiry produce few and meager responses."

The extensiveness of location inquiry and the basic cautiousness for determinant inquiry were not essentially changed in the 1942 volume. In the 1954 Klopfer text, no consideration to the seating arrangements was given, however, it should not be assumed that this was suddenly considered unimportant. Quite the contrary as in the 1962 Klopfer and Davidson Rorschach Manual, the notion that the examiner, as well as the subject, should be able to see the cards during the administration of the test, was reaffirmed. Also, in the 1954 volume, there was considerably less material on inquiring for location. Whereas in 1937 and again in 1942, Klopfer had felt the necessity for an elaborate location inquiry, both the '54 and '62 volumes define location inquiry as simply determining the basic area used by the subject, as contrasted with the detailed Inquiry concerning portions of the area used which had been previously suggested. It should be noted that the modification of location Inquiry probably evolved with the inception of the location sheet wherein the blot could be shown in miniature to the subject. The Rorschach Record Blank, which was devised for the 1942 book, included a location sheet, thus making the overall task of inquiring for location much easier.

In 1942 Klopfer and Kelley noted:

"Very often the subjects themselves offer the necessary cues in some later responses. For instance, let us assume that no clear information has been elicited as to the use of color or action elements in some responses. In one of the other cards the subject mentions spontaneously something about color or action. This gives the examiner the opportunity to say, 'In this case you said the color made you think of. . . ; how was it here?' "

This type of questioning which was encouraged in the 1937 procedures as a basic part of the Inquiry was now dealt with under the heading of "analogy questions." The inference was made that analogy questions should be used "late" in the inquiry after the less directive methods failed. To offer clarification, the 1954 volume, and subsequently in the 1962 manual, the analogy procedure was considered as a separate methodology from the Inquiry which would follow the Inquiry.

"The analogy period is optional, used only where the inquiry has not fully clarified the scoring problems. It consists of asking the subjects whether a determinant admittedly employed in connection with one response is applicable to others." (1954)

SCORING

The transition of the Klopfer System of scoring for Location is shown in Table 1. It will be noted, from examination of Table 1, that by 1936 with the publication of the Klopfer-Sender article on scoring that he had already added to the basics of scoring Location as described by Rorschach. Rorschach had used six Location symbols. In the 1936 scoring, Klopfer and Sender agreed in essence with Rorschach's concept of W but modified or supplemented all of the other Location scorings. The Rorschach scoring of DW was not included. The Rorschach scoring of S was included but modified to pertain only to First Grade Normal Details and a new symbol, s, used when white space involved other than First Grade Normal Details. The symbol Dd was not used as such nor was the Do. In scoring detail responses, the Klopfer group preferred to use D only when First Grade Nor-

TABLE 1

A Comparison of the Evolution of the Klopfer Method of Scoring Location from 1936 to 1962 with that Originally Suggested by Rorschach

Symbol	Rorschach	Klopfer & Sender—1936	Klopfer & Kelley—1942	Klopfer & Others—1954	Klopfer & Davidson—1962
W	(G) plate interpreted as whole	Same	Same	Same	Same
W	Not used	Not used	Intended use of whole blot but part or parts omitted or cut-off	Where S uses at least two-thirds of the blot but makes a point of omitting or disregarding certain portions which do not fit the concept	When S designates at least two-thirds of the blot with the intention of using as much of the blot as possible
DW	Plate interpreted as a whole secondarily, the answer based primarily on a detail	Not included	A detail interpreted and its meaning assigned to the whole blot without justification	Same, always involves a minus form level	Same
S	White intermediate figures (space detail)	Same (Must involve first grade normal details)	Any use of white space	Same	Same
s	Not used	White space involving other than first grade normal details	Not used	Not used	Not used
D	A normal detail of the plate	First grade detail	Large usual detail	Same	Same
d	Not used	Second grade detail	Small usual detail	Same	Same
Dd	An unusual or small detail	Not used	Not used	Not used	Not used
dd	Not used	Third grade detail	A tiny detail	Same	Same
de	Not used	An edge detail	An edge detail	Same	Same
di	Not used	An inside detail	An inside detail	Same	Same
dr	Not used	A rare detail	A rare detail	Same	Same
Do	A detail is interpreted in place of a whole	Not used	Not used	Not used	Not used

mal details were used.* Klopfer and Sender preferred to use the symbol d for Second Grade Details.† The 1936 Sender and Klopfer article described First Grade Normal Details from the ten test plates formulated in collaboration with Dr. Maria Rickers, who at that time was working at Worcester State Hospital in Massachusetts.

Klopfer and Sender used the symbol dd to describe Third Grade Details. In their earlier article concerning the detail answers, this scoring was also subdivided into four sub-categories. The first was for tiny details "with about the same insular or penninsular pattern as the 'd' jutting out from the edge of some larger part or isolated small dots, as at the bottom of Card I, but so tiny that the normal person usually overlooks them. The appropriate symbol according to the degree of smallness would be 'dd' or 'ddd.' " The second of these categories pertained to inside details described as "parts taken from within a blot on the basis of differences in shading without using the outer edge," and were suggested to be scored 'di.' The third subdivision concerned edging details, where interpretations were based only on the contour and a suggestion that these be scored 'De' or 'de' depending on whether the edging occurred in a First or Second Grade Detail. Finally, it was suggested that rare details could occur not covered by other scorings and should be scored either Dr or dr.

Although the 1936 Klopfer and Sender article did not include the symbol for a cutoff-Whole, it is certain that Klopfer scored cutoff-Wholes during this period, as one of his comments on Beck's 1937 manual, in his 1937 paper, specifically refers to that problem.

"The problem of the cutoff-Whole (W̶) (responses which omit deliberately or neglect unwittingly some part of it which does not fit in with the given interpretation), has not been dealt with in publication thus far. Dr. Beck discards even Rorschach's own approach to this problem, (his proposal to call the two figures in

---

* First Grade Normal Details were defined in an earlier article, (Sender and Klopfer, 1936) as "the obvious 'normal' details. . . .These parts, therefore, have the general properties of relatively independent 'sub-wholes' in the sense of that term used by the Gestalt psychology. They are: (a) insular or almost insular in their positions, for example, the black and red spots in Cards II and III and the various colored parts in VIII, IX, and X; (b) if not completely separated by white space or color they are the large parts of the black spots with an almost independent contour surrounded by white space or by parts of different shading as the middle and side parts in Card I."

† Second Grade Details were described as ". . .The Second Grade Details are found in a penninsular-like position. They are not as large, or as definite or as indispensable with regard to the whole blot as the D's but they are nevertheless obvious and easily recognizable parts; (a) jutting out from the edges of the larger blots; (b) obtainable through the breaking up of a D into its natural divisions; (c) smaller parts outstanding because of their particular color or shading."

Card III a Whole in spite of the omission of the red spots). Furthermore the scoring of main responses and their elaborations is not settled."

By 1942, with the publication of the Kelley-Klopfer text, Klopfer scoring for Location was complete. The concept of DW was included and modified only slightly in 1954 by suggesting that it always involves a minus Form Level. The notion of the cutoff W had been fully elaborated although continuing to be refined in the 1954 and 1962 texts of Klopfer and his colleagues. The use of s as had been suggested in 1936 was discarded and the concepts of First, Second, and Third Grade Details had been converted into the concepts of large usual, small usual, and unusual details respectively.

The procedure for scoring determinants was also reasonably well crystalized in the Klopfer System by 1942. Subsequent to 1942, minor modifications occurred, although no major changes evolved with the exception of the Form Level Rating which was first proposed by Klopfer in 1944 and was formally included in the second printing of the Klopfer and Kelley text in 1946. Table 2 shows the evolution of the Klopfer System of scoring for determinants as contrasted with those originally suggested by Rorschach.

The problem of scoring Form had been one of the basic disagreements between Klopfer and Beck. Rorschach had suggested in *Psychodiagnostik*:

"Most interpretations are determined by the form of the blots. This is the case generally as well as in each individual test. The evaluation of these form responses thus becomes a significant problem; in order to avoid subjective evaluation statistical methods were used. Form answers given by a large number of normal subjects (100) were used as the norm and basis. From this a definite range of normal form visualization could be defined, and a large number of frequently recurring answers were collected. These were called 'good forms' (F+). In this process, many forms which would not, on subjective estimation, have been called good, were so designated. Those answers which are better than these, are called F+ also, those which are less clear are F-. Even though the normal range is statistically fixed, judgment of what is better or worse than the good normal response remains a matter for subjective evaluation to a certain extent. However, this evaluation can be made with relative certainty."

Klopfer considered Rorschach's method as only preliminary leaving the final determination to the examiner. In that Beck had attempted to follow the Rorschach method of statistical determination of good and poor form specifically, Klopfer raised this issue in his 1937 commentary on the Beck manual.

"The third serious problem in this area involves the differentiation of F+ and F-. Publication of the frequency figures on which Dr. Beck's lists are based would be of great help in recognizing the line between a quantitative and a qualitative determination of F+ and F-. Dr. Beck has recognized that F responses given to rare details cannot be determined quantitatively as F+ or F-. In passing, we may

TABLE 2

A Comparison of the Evolution of the Klopfer Method of Scoring of Determinants from 1936 to 1962 with that Originally Suggested by Rorschach

Symbol	Rorschach	Klopfer & Sender—1936	Klopfer & Kelley—1942	Klopfer & Others—1954	Klopfer & Davidson—1962
F	Form Answers. (Scoring of + or − based on frequently recurring answers, allowing for subjective evaluation where statistical data insufficient)	Discussion of F not included. In 1936 Klopfer used scoring of + and − based on subjective evaluation. In 1937 Klopfer offered "rules" by which F+ might be scored and used scoring of F and F− in protocols	Form answers (F+ to be used where Form accuracy is better than commonly given Form answers. F to be used for commonly given Form answers and F− to be used for answers where Form accuracy is less than that used in commonly given responses.) In 1944, with Davidson suggested Form Level Rating where all responses would be rated from +5.0 to −2.0 depending on accuracy, organization, and specification	Form answers (Only symbols F and F− used in conjunction with the Form Level Rating)	Same as 1954
M	Movement answers involving kinaesthetic influences (restricted to humans or human behaviors)	Same as Rorschach	Same as Rorschach	Same as Rorschach	Same as Rorschach

		Animal Movement		
FM	Symbol not used. (In Rorschach's 1923 paper reference is given to Form tending toward Movement which could involve either human or animal figures)	Form tending toward movement. Designates action of animals	Same as 1942	Same as 1942
→M	Not used	A tendency toward M where the kinesthetic projection is hesitant or vague	A tendency toward M where it is elicited only under fairly direct questioning, where live posture is attributed to a human but then qualified, where elicitation is reluctant or vague, or where doubtful human action is portrayed in animals	Same as 1954
→FM	Not used	A tendency toward FM	A tendency toward FM where animal movement acknowledged with reluctance, doubt or only after considerable inquiry	Same as 1954
m	Not used	Minor movements i.e. expressive qualities in Hd and Ad (pointing finger), and passive happenings (explosions, collisions). May be combined with F dependent on degree of Form involvement	Minor movements involving expressive descriptions (masks), natural forces (flames, smoke), abstract forces (phallic force), or ambiguous dynamic terms (hanging) may be combined with F dependent on degree of form involvement	Inanimate movement. Essentially the same as 1942

TABLE 2 (*Continued*)

A Comparison of the Evolution of the Klopfer Method of Scoring of Determinants from 1936 to 1962 with that Originally Suggested by Rorschach

Symbol	Rorschach	Klopfer & Sender—1936	Klopfer & Kelley—1942	Klopfer & Others—1954	Klopfer & Davidson—1962
C	Color answer, interpretation, based on the Color of the blot alone	Same as Rorschach	Pure Color response almost mechanically associated with a concept and no attempt to associate this concept with other interpretations	Pure Color response which is totally undifferentiated without any organizational relationship to any other percept and is repetitive	Same as 1954
Cn	Not used. (In Rorschach's record #17 he used the symbol CC to denote Color naming and counted it as a C response)	Not included, however, reference was made to necessity for distinction between C responses and Color denominations which were scored Cn by Piotrowski, 1936	Color naming	Same as 1942	Same as 1942
Cdes	Not used	Not used	Color description referring to the variety of colors or degree of brightness or differences in surface appearance of the different colors. Usually not meant as responses	Color description which must be intended as a response and must not be used as an elaboration of another type of Color response	Same as 1954
Csym	Not used	Not used	Color symbolism as a response giving an abstract association to Color	Same as 1942	Same as 1942

CF	Color-Form answer determined primarily by the Color, secondarily by the Form	Same as Rorschach	Essentially same as Rorschach except some responses which might be scored a C by Rorschach are scored CF here due to requirements for scoring C. Symbol C/F included where use of Color is arbitrary	Same as 1942 with inclusion of symbols C→F where Color is forced plus use of CF sym.	Same as 1942
FC	Form-Color answer, interpretation based primarily on Form, Color secondary	Same as Rorschach with notation that where Color is artificially connected with Form the symbol F/C should be used	Same as 1936 with addition of symbol F↔C where use of Color is forced	Same as 1942 with inclusion of symbol FCsym where Color is used symbolically where form is definite	Same as 1954
(C)	Chiaroscuro responses	Not used	Not used	Not used	Not used
K	Not used	Chiaroscuro responses wherein a tendency exists to dissolve ink blots because of Shading (clouds, smoke, perspective, light shadows). May be combined with F depending on degree of Form involvement	Shading as depth impression or diffusion with FK used for vista, linear perspective, reflections, and landscapes or maps and K or KF used for diffusion and darkness responses	Same as 1942	Same as 1942

TABLE 2 (*Continued*)

A Comparison of the Evolution of the Klopfer Method of Scoring of Determinants from 1936 to 1962 with that Originally Suggested by Rorschach

Symbol	Rorschach	Klopfer & Sender—1936	Klopfer & Kelley—1942	Klopfer & Others—1954	Klopfer & Davidson—1962
c	Not used	Texture; may be combined with F depending on the degree of Form involvement	Texture where Shading is used as a surface impression (texture) or as a transparency. May be combined with F depending on the degree of Form involvement	Where the surface or texture effect is possessing textural or reflective qualities with F being combined depending on the degree of Form involvement and pure c being scored only when S completely disregards the F element and uses the shading mechanically	Same as 1954
k	Not used	Not used	Toned-down Shading effects where S reacts strongly to Shading but is unable to form a definite picture i.e. landscapes (topographical maps) and x-rays. Combined with F depending on the degree of Form involvement	Responses in which a three-dimensional expanse is projected on a two-dimensional plane (topographical maps and x-rays), Combined with F depending on the degree of Form involvement.	Same as 1954
C'	Not used	Not used	Use of achromatic Color. May be combined with F depending on the degree of Form involvement	Same as 1942	Same as 1942

state that they are keener more frequently than the popular form answers, and only rarely poorer or directly violating the given forms. These F responses to rare details are, however, only an extreme case showing most clearly the limitations of a clearly quantitative determination of F+ and F-. Rorschach obviously restricted quantitative determination of F+ to F responses with highest frequencies, taking this type of F answer not as an optimum, but as a minimum requirement for the borderline between good and poor forms. Thus, in regard to all F responses with a medium or small frequency, we have to determine whether they are somewhat keener or somewhat poorer than the most frequent F answers. The elaboration of qualitative determinants for keen and poor forms should therefore be delayed no longer. As a preliminary suggestion I might mention the following distinctions. Increase of keenness in form perception can be based on: (1) choice of form interpretation of a W or D fitting altogether more closely than the usual answers. . . (2) elaboration and integration of more details than the usual within a popular interpretation. . . (3) the selection of unusual details or unusual combinations of details because of specific form patterns thus gained. . . .Negative qualities in form interpretation are: (1) The confabulatory approach. The scoring of a DW with F+ in Dr. Beck's experiment 8, response 2, seems to be excluded by definition. . . .(2) Form interpretation based on blind guessing, vaguely in the direction of the given form. In these cases the subject is unable to explain in the inquiry the reason for his interpretation, or to give any explanatory details. . . .Should such a form answer be at least somewhat in the neighborhood of one of the usual form interpretations, it may be scored F±. . . .(3) The contaminatory approach, a typically schizophrenic type of response. . . .(4) Complete perseveration. . . .(5) Position responses. . . ."

While Klopfer does show scoring of F+ as well as F− in an article on chronic arthritis with Gotthard Booth in 1936, the remainder of the protocols included by Klopfer, in various publications subsequent to that time, do not show extensive use of the + symbol. In his 1937 article, Klopfer suggested that the symbol F+ might be used only for scoring the most superior form answers, with a scoring of F used for normally acceptable responses where popularly used forms were used and F− in the tradition of Rorschach. In 1942, in elaborating on the scoring of form responses Klopfer indicated:

"The problem of form accuracy and scoring have been central issues in the Rorschach literature almost from the very beginning. Rorschach made some very valuable suggestions as to determination and interpretation of form accuracy, which unfortunately were so vaguely expressed that they led to rather fundamental misunderstandings. As a clinician, Rorschach was particularly interested in the pathological significance of intellectual disorders and deteriorations as expressed in inaccuracies found in the subject's concept formations. He was less interested in exact distinctions between inaccurate and non-commital form responses, or between fairly accurate form responses and concepts of a superior form keenness. These differences could not be discovered and described in detail before a systematic inquiry provided the necessary evidence."

Klopfer conceded that the standards used by different examiners to judge the accuracy of Form show considerable variation. He maintained that it was because of this variation that Rorschach recommended the use of the degree of accuracy in the responses of a sizable majority of many subjects as a comparative base. Klopfer asserted that Rorschach did not suggest a correlation between frequency and accuracy, that instead, Rorschach meant for the frequency of 'popular' form interpretation to be a 'yardstick' of comparison. Klopfer postulated that the most accurate Form responses are given less frequently than the more mediocre, but 'popular' Form answer. Using this as his basis for argument, Klopfer then proceeded to elaborate on his 1937 suggestions, wherein the use of the symbol F+ would be used only for the most accurate Form answer which would be characterized by above average accuracy, good organization, and would be atypical with regard to commonness in a normal population. The symbol F then would be used for all other Form responses not meeting this criteria but not being marked by a discrepancy between conventional concepts or the actual Form of the blot. He defined F− responses as those marked by these latter characteristics or any which were completely arbitrary, mechanical, perseverative, confabulatory, or based simply on position.

The Klopfer technique of scoring movement has undergone a gradual transition from 1936 to 1954. Klopfer's original scoring for human Movement (M) has been reasonably consistent with that first suggested by Rorschach, who indicated that the M scoring should be restricted to humans or human behaviors and involve Movement answers which demonstrate kinesthetic influences. The 1962 Klopfer requirement for scoring Movement still sets forth the same prerequisite. It would not be interpreted, however, that Klopfer has been content to score Movement responses only as defined by Rorschach, for this has not been the case. It will be noted in Table 2 that, in 1936, Klopfer had already added the symbols FM and m, the latter being combined with F in a manner dependent upon the definiteness or vagueness of form.

The symbol FM was used by Klopfer in 1936 to denote instances where Form tended toward Movement and also provided for scoring when the action was specified for animals. Klopfer's justification ftr the use of the symbol FM was based on Rorschach's 1923 article in which he referred to special scoring consideration for responses primarily of Form but tending toward Movement or primarily of Form and tending toward Color. Since some of the examples included animals involved in Movement, it was natural for Klopfer to include the designation of animal Movement under the FM symbol. By 1942, Klopfer and his group had decided that the symbol FM should be used exclusively for animal Movement and have continued this type of scoring to the present.

The symbol m was suggested by Piotrowski in a 1936 seminar and adopted by the Klopfer group. Piotrowski elaborated on the significance of this in 1937. In essence, a similar rationale was used by Klopfer and Piotrowski in adopting m as was there for the adoption of FM. Rorschach in the 1923 article had referred to "m's" which were Movements occurring in tiny or unusual detail areas. He interpreted these as minor in terms of importance as contrasted with regular Movement responses. Thus, in 1936, m was designated as minor Movement, referring to expressive qualities in human and animal details and for passive happenings. By 1942, the definition of m had been modified slightly so as to be applicable to any expressive description such as masks, natural forces such as flames or smoke, abstract forces such as the sex drive, or ambiguous or dynamic terms. The symbol was renamed "inanimate movement" in the 1954 Klopfer publication with the description remaining the same as for 1942. By 1942, Klopfer had elaborated on the responses characterized by a tendency toward a determinant to the extent that he began using an arrow to indicate this factor. Thus a tendency could exist toward Movement ($\rightarrow$M), toward animal Movement ($\rightarrow$FM), toward Color ($\rightarrow$FC, $\rightarrow$CF), or toward any of the various Shading components. Once again, his rationale was that such scoring would be consistent with Rorschach's original notions, wherein a clear determinant does not exist but is vaguely inferred by the subject and should not be neglected.

Klopfer's 1936 scoring for Color was essentially the same as that given by Rorschach. However, as early as 1936, Piotrowski began scoring Color naming with the symbol Cn which was later adopted in the Klopfer System. Klopfer also elaborated on Rorschach's symbol FC, noting that wherever Color is artificially connected with Form, the symbol F/C would be appropriate. By 1942, the scheme for scoring Color had been expanded not only to include the symbol for Color naming but also appropriate symbols for Color description (Cdes) and Color symbolism (Csym). He also expanded on the artificial use of Color, calling it "arbitrary use of color" and expanded the scoring of F/C to include the possibility for C/F. In studying that phenomenon, he also encountered the situation where Color is forcibly used by the subject and created the symbol F$\leftrightarrow$C. Also by 1942, Klopfer had seriously departed from Rorschach's original interpretation of the pure C response. Whereas he agreed with Rorschach in 1936, by this time he began defining the pure Color response as one which is almost mechanically associated with the concept and where there is no attempt to associate the percept with other interpretations given to the blot. This same criteria was set forth in the 1954 scoring with some slight elaboration. In all other respects, the 1942 scoring for Color and its variations has continued to remain essentially the same through the 1962 Klopfer and Davidson edition.

A transition similar to that which occurred for Color scoring also occurred in the scoring of chiaroscuro responses. While Rorschach did not score chiaroscuro or Shading responses in the original *Psychodiagnostik,* he did offer some elaboration on such responses in the 1923 article. Here he included the scoring of (C) whenever Shading was involved in a response. This concept was elaborated on considerably by Binder in 1932. Klopfer, however, preferred not to use the Rorschach (C) because of the similarity to the Color symbol and instead, selected the symbol K representing the sounding of the word chiaroscuro. In 1936, he defined the K response as one wherein a tendency exists to dissolve the inkblot because of the Shading, suggesting that the symbol could be used with the symbol F depending upon the degree of Form involvement. In 1942, the definition of the symbol K was modified to include only those responses where Shading was used for diffusion and/or darkness responses. In these instances, the symbols K or KF would be used. However, where Shading was used to formulate a depth impression, reflection, or linear perspective, the symbol FK would be used. This definition has continued in the Klopfer System to the present.

In 1936, Klopfer introduced the symbol c to denote texture responses. No such determinant had been recognized by Rorschach. As with Color responses, Klopfer denoted that the symbol F might be combined with the c depending upon the degree of Form involvement. By 1954, Klopfer had made the criteria for scoring pure c essentially the same as that for scoring pure C—that is, where the subject completely disregards the Form element and used the Shading mechanically or perseveratively.

Whereas Klopfer used only two symbols for scoring of Shading responses in 1936, he included four in 1942, K, c, k, and C'. k responses were described as toned-down Shading effects where the subject reacts strongly to the Shading but is unable to form a definite picture. This was later defined in 1954 as responses in which a three-dimensional expanse is projected on a two-dimensional plane and restricted primarily to topographical maps and x-rays. The symbol C' was actually introduced by Klopfer and Davidson as a part of the 1937 Record Blank to be used for scoring achromatic Color. The 1942 text offered elaboration and clarification of this phenomenon. No change in the definition of C' has occurred since 1942.

Although Klopfer has proliferated in detail concerning the scoring for Location and Determinants of a response, this has not been the case for scoring Content. In 1936, he introduced the symbol Aobj to denote animal objects such as fur rugs, animal skulls, etc. Otherwise his scoring for Content has remained consistent to Rorschach's basic suggestions through 1962, although other Systematizers have elaborated considerably on symbols for content.

In the 1923 article, Rorschach referred to "vulgar" responses as those interpretations which occur once in every three records. Thus, he formulated the notion of the popular response. By 1942, Klopfer selected ten popular responses, admitting that they were substitutes for statistically verified "populars" because "a frequency tabulation of universal validity is not available, . . ." Since that time, there has been very little elaboration in the Klopfer System concerning the notion of popular responses and the same ten populars continue to be utilized through the 1962 Klopfer and Davidson edition.

INTERPRETATION

From the very beginning of Klopfer's writings concerning Rorschach interpretation, he stressed the fact that interpretation would be a complex process in which there would be no room for a rigid "sign approach." In his 1939 article, "Should the Rorschach be Standardized," he suggested that there should be in reality two levels of interpretation. The first of these would be based specifically on a "blind" approach to the raw data. Using this approach to interpretation, the interpreter is forced to structure his evidence for each conclusion which he would draw about the fundamental personality structure of his subject. In this manner, Klopfer believed that the interpreter could offer hypotheses concerning intellectual level, mode of dealing with problems or conflicts, maturity, general level of adjustment, balance between control and spontaneity, and other important characteristics of personality. He encouraged that, at a second level of interpretation, a fusion should occur between the hypotheses generated from the "blind analysis" of the raw data and "any other information about the subject." Klopfer maintained that, by following this procedure, the mass of information accumulated concerning the subject, both from the Rorschach protocol and the other sources, could be formed into a clearer picture "explaining many of the peculiar behavior patterns by linking them with the personality structure, and showing the impact of decisive experiences in the case history upon the personality development." Klopfer indicated that the Rorschach could be the revelation for the deeper conflicts or emotional strains existent within a personality yet not manifest overtly in behavior.

Not only did he discourage a rigid "sign approach" to the Rorschach interpretation, but also reacted favorably toward the analysis of the content of responses in terms of "symbolic significance." He pointed out that some persons using the Rorschach attempt to deal with the material as simply as free association or day-dream responses are interpreted analytically. While offering no strong objection to this, he cautioned that the true value of Rorschach data would evolve where the interpreter used both Rorschach and analytical interpretation of material. Although strongly committed to the Jungian Analytic Psychology, Klopfer was careful to avoid basing his technique of Rorschach interpretation solely or even largely on that approach. Instead, he preferred to limit his orientation to a few basic and well accepted assumptions.

"There is no need for us to get entangled in the warring camps fighting for their particular theories of personality structure. The general psychological assumptions we have to make are so few and simple that nobody will have any compunction about accepting them. First, we assume that actions and reactions of human beings are stimulated or promoted from without as well as from within. The stimulation from without has never been doubted. There probably has never been any psychologist either, who has not assumed promptings from within as a working part of actual life. There has only been doubt about the possibility of observing these promptings from within in an objective way." (1939, p. 161)

The fundamentals of the Klopfer approach to Rorschach interpretation were well defined in the 1939 article. While rejecting the rigid "sign approach," he by no means discarded the importance of signs. He advocated that adequate interpretation required consideration of three basic Rorschach characteristics. First would be the configuration principle which required, "we cannot draw any conclusions from any one factor unless we receive confirmation from several others." Klopfer maintained that the principle of configuration would guarantee the "intrinsic objectivity" of the Rorschach method, wherein a configuration of traits would be found in the raw material and ultimately through the skill of the interpreter, be molded into one definite personality picture.

The second fundamental step in interpretation was described as "proportional occurrence." For Klopfer, this meant comparing the traits of an individual as they are manifest in any Rorschach category on an interpersonal basis. That is, the extent to which those traits occur in other individuals. But this approach was not to be concerned only with interpersonal or normative comparisons but also on an intrapersonal basis.

"Proportional occurrence has a double aspect. We are always interested in the proportional occurrence of one Rorschach category as compared with others within the same record; this is the numerical expression of what we just called the configuration of traits. On the other hand, we are also interested in the proportional occurrence of one category in one record as compared with the proportional occurrence of the same category in other records, to discover the relative strength or weakness of any given personality trait. In order to construct our personality picture, we use the combination of both proportions; the inter-individual proportion (indicating, for instance, the keenness of the mind of the subject, the strength or weakness of his vitality or impulsiveness, the richness or poverty of his imagination), and the intra-individual proportion (indicating, for instance, whether the mind is keen enough to control a very rich imagination, the vitality is strong enough not to be subdued by a very keen mind, the desire for adaptation and the interstability are strong enough to control a strong impulsiveness)."

The third fundamental for interpretation was that of sequence analysis. By this Klopfer meant a response by a response analysis of the dynamics which lead from one response to the next within a single record. Klopfer suggested in the 1939 paper that sequence analysis would not only be concerned with what Rorschach had called succession, that is, the question of whether a subject tried to start with a W and proceeded to larger and then smaller details, but also may go beyond the formal scoring elements or manner of approach and include the potential symbolic meaningfulness of the response for the subject.

In the 1942 Klopfer and Kelley text, these essentials were reaffirmed and elaborated upon in somewhat more detail so that instead of having three basic principles they were subdivided into seven.

"(1) The quantitative results of the tabulation, representing the crude totals for the major scoring categories. (2) The configurational results of the tabulation, showing some important inter relationships, . . . (3) The distribution of the quantitative scoring results for all ten cards. . . (4) The sequence analysis of the scoring list, showing the succession of various location and determinant scores within each card. . . (5) The qualitative analysis of all individual responses as to organization, form accuracy, and integration of various determinants. . . (6) Analysis of the general symbolic characteristics of the content. . . (7) The use of conspicuous behavior exhibited during the Rorschach administration. . . ."

In the 1954 volume, these fundamentals have been neatly crystalized into three broad categories, one for quantitative analysis, one for sequence analysis, and one for content analysis. While the titles changed over the fifteen-year period, the basic requisites of interpretive procedure which they represented did not. Thus, during that fifteen-year period, elaboration rather than change occurred.

Quantitative Analysis

Some of the major interpretive hypotheses which Klopfer has suggested follow. Each section begins with the 1939 postulate (where one was offered) and is carried forth through the appropriate period of its elaboration.

Whole Responses. W must be interpreted in light of the quality as well as quantity. Klopfer disagreed with the Rorschach hypothesis that a relatively high number of W's represented an emphasis on the abstract forms of thinking and the higher forms of mental activity. Instead, he suggested that some W's of a "simple variety" would be vague or non-committal. These types of responses are not applicable to the standard Rorschach interpretation and instead indicate a mental inability to organize the whole card into its subdivisions. Therefore, a high number of such simple or popular W's may represent a pathological condition. He estimated that the normal proportion of W in a record should be approximately 20 per cent. In the 1942 text, these same hypotheses are incorporated and not elaborated upon. In fact, much of the wording is identical with that of the 1939 article. The 1954 text, however, did produce greater elaboration with specific hypotheses being offered where the percentage of W is either lower or higher than the expected 20 to 30 per cent range and also hypotheses are offered concerning the ratio between W's and M's, (that a natural proportion W to M would be 2 to 1 indicating an organizational interest with enough creative potential to maintain this interest).

Detail Responses. The detail response was interpreted as representing a "sense for a clear recognition of crude facts, rather than a drive for daring combinations, or a sense for the unusual aspects and nuances." Having differentiated D and d permitted the Klopfer group to elaborate further on the detail hypothesis. It was considered a normal emphasis if D would approximate between 45 per cent and 55 per cent of a record whereas d responses would compromise 10 per cent to 20 per cent of a protocol. It was assumed that a relationship existed between D and a "common sense" approach to life. The d was interpreted to imply a critical attitude which is considered healthy if maintained in adequate proportion to other location scores. An overemphasis on d might suggest hypercriticality or even obsessiveness. There is no essential alteration or elaboration on the interpretation for detail responses in the 1942 text. In 1954, it is suggested that an average amount of D could be interpreted as "a practical, everyday, commonsense application of intelligence, an interest in the presented, obvious facts, without much drive to seek relationships between these presented facts of experience. Conversely, where the proportion of D is lower than expected, the implication could be that the subject lacks recognition of everyday problems or facts or is unable to differentiate between the obvious facts presented by the world around him due to intellectual deficit or emotional disturbance. The d response is reaffirmed as criticalness and interpreted if overemphasized as "an insecurity against which the individual defends himself by clinging to limited areas of certainty for fear of losing his bearings," while an underemphasis is interpreted as "a low level of interest in the minutia of experience." These hypotheses are reaffirmed in the 1962 manual.

White Space Responses. Klopfer noted that the S factor had been one which received considerable attention in the literature. Most of this discussion centered around Rorschach's hypothesis that overemphasis on white space indicates some sort of oppositional tendency. Klopfer took issue with these interpretations suggesting that:

"They mistook these oppositional tendencies for behavior. They were always surprised when they did not find negativistic behavior in subjects producing a lot of S or vice versa. This mistake is based on a variety of psychological constellations, from unbearable extraneous pressure to the seemingly unreasonable negativism of a deeply insecure individual. Secondly, the oppositional tendency indicated in S is not necessarily directed against the environment."

Accordingly, Klopfer laid the groundwork for the idea that S could reveal simply individualistic tendencies. He did concede that the pure S response usually indicates a compulsive reaction or inhibiting ambivalence but only when overemphasis is the case. In the 1942 text it is stated, "preference for the use of white space left by the blots may indicate some oppositional tendencies," suggesting that Klopfer had modified his view on the significance of white space considerably. This was the only comment of substance concerning S in the 1942 text other than to describe the manner in which S might be scored. In the 1954 text an emphasis on S is interpreted to mean an oppositional tendency in the intellectual sphere the strength of the tendency being related to the daringness in use of white space, "S implies an intellectual kind of opposition, a putting of the self across, it is the competitive or self-assertive aspect of intellectuality."

Movement Responses. A large number of the Klopfer hypotheses concerning quantitative data have, in one way or another, involved M. The basic M hypothesis, as manifest in 1939, represented a slight deviation of Rorschach's initial notions. M for Klopfer could only be properly assessed in terms of number and quality which existed. The meaningfulness of M was made quite clear:

"The differentiation between higher and superior levels can be based on the strength or obviousness of the stimulus to see M in any card. Card III has, naturally, the first place here. Card II, Card VII, Card IX seem to vie for second place. Card I, Card IV rank next. . . .The greater the number of M responses, and the further they go beyond these most obvious M stimuli, and the richer the original variations from the usual responses to these obvious stimuli, the more the M's are indicative of a really brilliant mind. Beck's assumption that one to zero M represents a low; two to four a medium; and five and more a high level agrees with our experience if we take as a medium level what we usually call the higher average intelligence. . . .The quality of M is intellectually important in one point; in the question of whether the form elements of a blot or blot proportion used for M is well integrated into the M concept. Rich M responses, with elaborate form elements within them, indicate, naturally, the optimum of cooperation between rich imagination and keen thinking. Definitely inaccurate forms in M usually indicate some hypomanic state, where the imagination overwhelms rational thinking, or they indicate a psychotic lack of control over one's imagination."

Klopfer noted that M's are rarely found among children up to eight years of age and strongly maintained, as did Rorschach, that M's seem to be the basic indicator of the substance or richness of the inner life, manifesting creative capacities and the acceptance of one's own self and inner promptings. Concerning the problem of Movement expressed in animal action, however, Klopfer clearly disagreed with Rorschach in the 1939 article.

". . .Almost without exception, Rorschach experts follow Rorschach's lead in excluding animal action from the category M. However, there is the end of unanimity, as no agreement whatsoever exists about the question of what is to be done with the excluded animal action. Rorschach gave a hint as to how to use it in his posthumous paper. . . .This setting is a background for the selection of the symbol FM. . . .It seems now quite safe to assume that they (FM) represent the influence of the more instinctive layers within the personality. At least, that is the most simple explanation for the fact that children are quite free in seeing animals in action while they do not usually see humans in action in their responses to the cards. Naturally, it is also mentally easier to see animals in action, since animal shapes offer themselves more readily in all blots. . . .There is another more decisive and empirical confirmation of the role of FM. Invariably, while we have reason from other sources to assume that the subject was emotionally infantile, living in a level of instinctive prompting below his chronological and mental age, we find in the Rorschach records of such subjects a predominance of FM over M.

Klopfer was even more adamant in 1939 concerning the meaningfulness of the m response. He suggested that it represented mainly the effects of uncontrollable forces working upon the objects or figures.

". . .We may say that we find such m where the subject experiences his promptings from within, as hostile and uncontrollable forces working upon him, rather than as sources of energy at his disposal. A few such m, alongside with a far greater number of M and FM don't seem to be indicative of a real disturbance within the inner life of the subject. . . .If m reaches or outnumbers, either M or FM, then it seems to be a danger signal that these inner conflicts are too strong to guarantee a close cooperation between the inner and outer life. Whether these conflicts lead to actual disturbances in the subject's relationships with the environment depends upon the balance between the control and spontaneity. If the control is too rigid or ineffective, then these inner conflicts are likely to permeate the whole life situation of the subject."

Klopfer was careful to point out that the interpretation of either FM or m must be in light of the number and proportion of the total responses of M. M for Klopfer remained among the most important features of the entire psychograph. At the same time, Klopfer was unwilling to accept

Rorschach's basic formulation of the personality configuration which Rorschach himself had suggested. This was incorporated in the term *Erlebnistyp* (translated as experience type) which for Rorschach indicated a fundamental characteristic of the individual.

"The introversive and extratensive features of a subject comprise independent groups of psychisms, the relations of which determine the experience type of the individual. These features must have an entirely different mental basis from the conscious, disciplined thinking of the subject. . . .It indicates how the person experiences, but not how he lives, or toward what he is striving. An individual with very predominant introversive features may be decidedly extratensive in his behavior where the extratensive features are less in evidence in the test than the introversive. . . .These discrepancies between the experience type and actual living can only be explained by the fact that the 'active energy,' the effective energy at the moment, the will, the libido, or whatever else it may be named, is so oriented as to allow only a part of the faculties for experiencing to be in operation. . . .In the discussion above it has been shown that personality and talents, perceptive, and probably, imagery-type, and significant elements of affect and intelligence are all direct outgrowths of the experience type of an individual."

Rorschach believed that the Erlebnistyp is revealed in the Rorschach test by the ratio of human movement to Color responses (M: Sum C). Klopfer, in turn, believed that this ratio by itself would be insufficient for the derivation of such information, "These confusions have been enhanced by the fact that the indicators for Erlebnistyp as Rorschach left them, has proven to be much too crude, unless an interpreter is familiar enough with the Rorschach method to weigh and consider all the other inponderables not included in the rough quotation. . . ." While questioning the absoluteness of the M to Sum C ratio, Klopfer maintained that the accurateness or inaccurateness of this ratio could be "checked" through two other ratio formulations which he offered. The first of these concerns the ratio of non-human Movement tendencies (FM's plus m's) to the sum of the texture and achromatic Color responses (c's plus C' 's). The second of such checks is the proportion of responses to Cards VIII through X as compared with the number of responses in the total record (8—9—10 per cent). Thus for Klopfer, as contrasted to Beck, the Erlebnistyp is insufficient for the indication of basic personality configuration. In 1942, Klopfer elaborated on the importance of M as it might be manifest in the M tendency. In all other respects, the interpretation of M, FM, and m remained essentially the same. By 1954, the hypotheses concerning M had been more fully crystalized. M is interpreted in the following manner:

". . .Perhaps the most significant and yet, interpretively, the most elusive single determinant. . . .As a start in understanding the complex body of interpretive hypotheses that has been built up around the M response, it should be pointed out the M concept implies three main features: (1) A kinesthetic projection—an enlivening of the blot material by reading into it movement that is not there in fact. . . .(2) A human concept . . . , which implies an ability to see one's world as peopled and consequently to feel empathy with others; . . . (3) Perception at a highly differentiated and unusually well integrated level. . . .The M response touches upon all of the most important aspects of the well functioning personality, bridging the gap between inner resources of drive and fantasy and the outward orientation of reality testing and object relations."

The 1954 text indicates that at least three M's are necessary for interpretation; that the appearance of M's of good Form level is a contraindication of low intellectual level in that the extent to which M's appear manifest the individual's freedom to use his imaginal processes; that M's occurring in conjunction with a minus Form level rating can serve to distort reality to the extent that the ties with reality are seriously loosened. M is also perceived in the 1954 interpretation as a manifestation of inner stability, representing a system of values, and indicative of the degree of self acceptance or self concept of the individual. FM responses are interpreted as indicating an awareness of impulses, to immediate gratification, as contrasted with the more intellectually delayed goals manifest in the M response. FM is described as follows:

"These impulses stem from the most primitive or archaic layers of the personality, either having an instinctual basis or having been acquired very early in the life of the individual. . . .Sometimes they have a manifestly hostile and aggressive content; sometimes they are overtly helpless, succorant, and presumably indicate dependency needs. Content analysis of the record as a whole, not merely of the FM rsponses, is often of assistance in rounding out the picture; . . .The presence of FM in large numbers does not necessarily mean that the individual in fact indulges his impulses to immediate gratification, but rather that he feels such impulses whether or not he expresses them in action. A clue to the behavioral expression of these impulses may be found in the FC:CF balance."

The response m is interpreted in the 1954 text similarly to the 1939 and 1942 interpretations. It is suggested that while m involves a projection of movement into the blot material, it is marked by a feeling of inanimate or abstract force. The hypothesis offered is that m, in numbers over one or two in a record, reflects an awareness of forces outside control of the subject which threaten the overall stability or composition of the personality organization.

The Form Response. Klopfer had made much of his differences with Beck concerning the plus or minus Form quality. In his 1939 article on interpretation, he described the Form response as related to intellectual capacity. He cautioned that the evaluation of Form level must not only come in pure F responses but also those where F is combined with some other determinant. He perceived the F response as being related to constriction or lack thereof, and identified a F per cent which is different than "the traditional F+ per cent." "It is obvious that the traditional had nothing in common with our F per cent, since it refers to the proportion of accurately seen forms among all forms. It is less obvious that our F per cent is not applicable to the traditional system of scoring as Rorschach left it at his death." For the Klopfer group, any subject who gives more than 50 per cent F in a record demonstrates signs of rigidity. Accordingly, constriction, or lack thereof, could be defined in terms of this base figure. He noted that minus responses given to Form indicate damage to the effectiveness of overall control indicators. He reaffirmed his belief that only the most intelligent or most well organized and healthy individuals would give Form responses of excellent or original quality. Conversely, he suggested that where no high level Form quality existed, that some process of mental deterioration might exist. He was careful to point out, however, the relationship of Form to the utilization of Color. In this respect, he suggested that when Color existed without the element of Form being predominant, the individual would be more impulsive in his behaviors than the individual who displayed Form-dominated Color responses. In 1942, Klopfer referred to the number and quality of the Form responses as the interpretive "keystone" to an understanding of the relationship between the intellectual and emotional aspects of personality. He postulated that the "healthy balance" between these elements is probably lost when an overemphasis on Form occurs in a protocol. He also suggested that the evaluation of Form responses is the most important supplement to Location data concerning the mental approach of the subject toward life situations. In the 1954 text, the section on Form interpretation is reduced substantially as contrasted with his previous expositions on the subject and the interpretive significance of the Form response is modified somewhat. Here, Klopfer indicates that the F response represents an impoverished or somehow limited mode of perception wherein the individual restricts himself at the expense of his own emotional and/or affectual nuances which ordinarily occur in the form of Color and/or Shading responses. He hypothesizes that when F occurs in an appropriate relationship to Movement, Color and Shading, it manifests the individual's ability to divorce himself from affect and interact with the environment in an impersonal, "matter of fact" way. He suggests, however, that when the F response occurs in greater abundance, at the expense of Movement, Color and the Shading components, the degree of impoverishment is critical in that it produces some lack of awareness of inner impulses even though maintaining some emotional reactivity to the impact of the environmental influences.

Color Responses. Klopfer's 1939 interpretation of Color responses did not vary significantly from that offered by Rorschach. Klopfer accepted the general postulate that Color responses are indicative of the emotional ties of the individual with external reality, FC responses being interpreted as meaning the degree of emotional adjustment which the subject manifests to his external reality. In other words, the subject manifests a semblance of ego control over his emotion when dealing with the outside world. Klopfer and his group added to Rorschach's interpretation of the FC response by denoting two special categories, F/C and FC–. The F/C response was explained as being an adjustment "expressed in the form color combination . . . as less personal, less full-bodied than the genuine FC." The FC– response was interpreted as a more immature and probably less efficient emotional adjustment because of the limitations of the ego control.

In 1939, Klopfer suggested the CF combination is not more unusual than the FC combination. "In it the consideration of rational elements in our behavior is not thrown overboard altogether. However, the emotional stimulus has assumed a dominating role." This explanation offers the concept that the CF dominated subject is more impulsive than the average individual. Klopfer cautioned, however, that an evaluation of the CF responses would be required before deciding whether this impulsiveness would be destructive or detrimental to the personality, or constructive, as the individual was psychologically organized. It was pointed out that the CF type Color reaction should be regarded as "destructive" where the content of the response is loosely organized, as in the instance of blood responses, or the like, which might indicate confusion. The C/F response was conceived as indicating those instances of personality organization where "a feeble attempt to hide confusion intellectually" occurs. The notions of Color description, Color symbolism and Color naming were also dealt with in 1939. Color description responses were suggested to indicate instances where "subjects who are at odds with their strong inclination to react to emotional stimuli from without" . . . whereas color symbolism was represented as a manner of "dealing with the color stimulus which technically belongs to the pure color response . . . their psychological significance belonging to the CF combination." Color naming was interpreted as "seems to have a magic function. The emotional stimulus implied in the color represents a deadly enemy threatening to break into the carefully isolated inner world of the patient and engulfing him with the dangerous whirlpools of reality relations he cannot master." The crude pure C response was noted to be "very rare." This was explained as "the last remainders of a rational permeation have been extinguished in the emotional reactions represented. . . ." We may see that this interpretation is reasonably close to that given by Rorschach:

"C answers are seen, first, in the irritable and sensitive, and increase in number in manics where irritability and instability are features. . . .The primary C answers are representatives of impulsiveness. The more C's, the greater the tendency to impulsive actions. The C and CF answers express the more egocentric affective responsiveness, while the more adaptive affective rsponsiveness is expressed in the number of FC's. . . .A better way of saying this is that the FC answer is the expression of the desire to adapt, for the FC may be poorly visualized. . . .The logical conclusion to be drawn from this discussion is that the relationship of the three types of color answers in a given protocol is significant. FC (capability for formation of rapport), CF (affective lability), and C (compulsiveness) may be united in widely varying proportions."

Klopfer did not, in effect, change his interpretation of color answers in the 1942 text. Instead, these interpretations, as given in 1939, are reaffirmed. It is interesting, however, to note that his reaffirmation of the pure C response, when combined with its definition for scoring, served to magnify its significance regarding the existence of pathology. In this respect, he went well beyond that implied by Rorschach and delineated an almost new category wherein the subject would have to clearly "reveal that the last remainders of a rational permeation have been extinguished in the emotional reactions represented by such responses." In 1954, clarification of the interpretive hypothesis for color responses is offered. The FC response is described as indicating a ready control of affect without any loss of affective responsiveness. Such control is perceived as still providing ventilation of impulse, but in such a manner as is appropriate to the situation. Klopfer also speculates that such responses give indications of a social dependence as well as social awareness. Conversely, the CF type response is seen as manifesting some loss of intellectual control over affect. Klopfer cautions that the true nature of this loss of control can only be evaluated against the framework of the total protocol and in reference to the particular content of the response. The pure or Crude C response is specifically interpreted as meaning pathology. "a pathological lack of emotional control, emotionality of an explosive, hair trigger variety."

The 1954 text also offers elaboration on the interpretation of forced Color and arbitrary Color responses. The arbitrary Color answers indicate that responses to the emotional impact of the environment is superficial, generating behavior which does not represent the true feelings experienced. The forced Color responses represent an effort toward smooth affective control which is unnatural and lacks success because of tensions implicit in the social relationships of the individual. The 1954 interpretations of Color naming, Color symbolism, and Color description remain essentially unchanged from those offered in 1939.

Shading Responses. In 1939, the significance of the FK type response was described as a failure or inability to use the imagination freely. Such responses were conceived as representing a cautiousness and self concern relating to "inner promptings," which appear best described by the ideas of introspection. The Fc type response was also interpreted as a type of cautiousness but different than manifest in FK. Klopfer believed that the texture response gives indication of a careful, sometimes painful, preoccupation with the activity in the environment which results from a need to protect oneself from his own feelings of insecurity. Texture then, represents a striving for social tactfulness. This same interpretation was offered in the 1942 text but modified to some extent in the 1954 volume. In 1954, it was interpreted as meaning an acceptance of affective needs related to the desire for approval and belongingness, "refined beyond a craving for physical contact" and pre-requisite to the establishment of deep and meaningful object relations. Conversely, the cF and c type responses are postulated to represent this same need but at a much more primative level of functioning, i.e., cF indicating a need for closeness and fondling of an infantile sort, c indicating the undifferentiated need for affection, mostly of a "physical contact variety."

Thus, over a period of some 15 years, Klopfer changed his interpretation of the texture response from one indicating a relationship of tact or tactlessness in the environment, to one representing need for dependency and closeness.

Similarly, a modification of the interpretation of K responses occurred in the 1942 text. Therein, K or KF responses were interpreted as manifestations of insecurity and anxiety of the "free-floating type." Similarly, the FK response was regarded as representing introspectionism. However, the more diffuse use of shading as manifest in KF or a pure K response was suggested as the manifestation of anxiety or insecurity. In 1954, this interpretation is modified to, "K and KF indicate an anxiety of a diffuse and free-floating nature, reflecting a frustration of affectional satisfactions." The FK continues to be interpreted much like the 1939 version. "FK indicates an attempt by the person to handle his affectional anxiety by introspective efforts, by an attempt to objectify his problem by gaining perspective on it, by putting it at some distance from himself so he can view it more dispassionately."

The symbol k was not included in 1939. By 1954, the pure k response was hypothesized to mean "affectional anxiety behind a good front of outward control and is found with subjects who cover up their anxiety with an intellectual cloak. . . . Fk has also been found with extremely busy people of the executive type; the implication is that the compulsive work may constitute a defense to prevent an awareness of affectual anxieties from breaking through."

The C' was first interpreted in 1942. It was perceived much like the k response as relating to K, that is of toned down emotionality.

"Achromatic tendencies in general are indicative of depressive tendencies only if they outnumber bright color responses. . . .C' responses are found mainly in two situations. First they occur in records of subjects of the very rich and variegated reaction to all sorts of stimuli from without. This combination clearly represents an artistic impressionability. Second, when they represent a 'burnt child' reaction, the reaction of people who are basically responsive to emotional stimulation from outside but have experienced a series of traumatic experiences. Such subjects tend to withdraw from the 'hot' bright-colored area into the safer realm of the less affective grey, black, and white hues."

No essential change in this interpretation occurred in either the 1954 or 1962 texts.

Ratios. The 1939 article called attention to three basic ratios; the M to Sum C, one pertaining to the sum of nonhuman movement to texture and achromatic Color responses, and the 8-9-10 per cent. In 1942, the listing of ratios and percentages was increased considerably. In addition to the basic three, Klopfer suggested the utilization of a ratio of FK plus F plus Fc divided by R, the ratio of animal to total response, average reaction time for the colored versus non-colored cards, the W to M ratio, and the average time per response. In the 1954 volume each is elucidated in some detail and some additional ratios are suggested, such as the relationship between M and FM, M, FM plus m, FK plus c divided by F, and the ratio of FC to CF plus C responses. Each of these is given some interpretive hypothesis. Yet several, especially those developed in the 1954 text, are pointed to as more speculative than "firm" in terms of interpretive significance.

What seemed to occur between 1939 and 1954, in the Klopfer utilization of quantitative data, was that more details were being involved and tentatively interpreted. It is interesting to note that where the 1954 volume includes a reasonably large number of hypotheses for these ratios and percentages, the 1962 text is more conservative, offering, instead, the more traditional ratios and percentages found in the 1942 text, and suggesting interpretive hypotheses reasonably consistent with those found in 1942.

SEQUENCE ANALYSIS

In 1939, Klopfer was somewhat vague on what Sequence Analysis might involve. He discussed the manner of approach to the cards, suggesting a specific proportion of W to D, which should evolve in a normal record. He was concerned also with the number and quality of S responses as well as the number and quality of M responses. He pointed out that the quality of the M's would, in part, be differentiated by the obviousness, or lack thereof, with which Movement can be perceived on the various cards, suggesting that it occurs most easily to Cards II, III, VII, and IX, and least easily to Cards V, VI, and X. He indicated that the "brilliant mind" would produce M's beyond those most easily perceived and that the quality of the productions would be obviously rich.

Likewise, Klopfer was concerned with the Form Level. As previously noted, he considered the interpretation of the popular Form, higher quality Form, and original Form, versus the inferior or originally inferior Form responses. His basic interpretation of Sequence, however, was relegated to those considerations of succession as had been described by Rorschach. A rigid succession presupposes a higher intellectual capacity, wherein the individual does not make for a higher efficiency. Orderly succession manifests some variation of logical order, whereas a loose succession might be interpreted as, "to be found where mental capacity is not high enough to grasp the logical order fully, or where the mental control for maintaining such an order is weakened either through pathological conditions, or through emotional interferences." A confused succession was interpreted to be a clearly pathological sign. In 1942, the ideas about succession and sequence were essentially the same as those offered in 1939. Some elaboration was given to the importance of the W response and to the balance of form responses. Similarly re-emphasis was given to the movement response. However, added to this were indications concerning the balance of Color to Form, and Shading to Form.

By 1954, elaboration on a sequence component of interpretation became more succinct. Each card is listed together with the hypothesis concerning what it might facilitate in terms of responses. Determinants are considered individually in light of their proportional significance to the overall record and their individual meaningfulness as occurring within a card. Sections on reaction time and response time are also included. The section on color dynamics, while not unlike that of the 1942 text, is expanded considerably as is the section on shading dynamics. Also for the first time, a segment is included concerning the relationship between subject and examiner whereby some concessions are made as to the impact of the examiner on the subject's responses to the blots.

CONTENT ANALYSIS

A specific section dealing with Content Analysis was not included in 1939. In 1942, a brief section was included concerning the variation of content suggesting that subjects of a higher intellectual potentiality should not produce more than 50 per cent animal responses and that as a rule, animal, human, anatomy, geography, and a few plant and object contents would be typical in a great majority of records. It was hypothesized that a minimum of 25 per cent of responses outside of the four basic categories

(H, Hd, A, Ad) could be indicative of higher intelligence but that overall the breadth and depth of content analysis "must be carefully studied, for often a subject tries to impress the examiner by displaying his far-reaching education, and responses in these categories may be quite shallow and evasive." By 1954, the general principles for content analysis were more firmly specified. Klopfer emphasized that any clinical interpretation would necessitate the constant formulation of hypotheses, which require additional information before their ultimate acceptance or rejection. He suggested two methods which could be relevant to the final decision, one calling for a comparison with other test data such as sentence completion tests or with case history material, the second recommending comparison with results obtained concerning feelings, attitudes, and/or needs from material such as thematic content analysis tests.

Subsequent to this introductory material, specific hypotheses are offered concerning the content analysis, wherein human figures, animals, anatomical contents, sexual symbolism, evasive responses, or miscellaneous categories such as masks, emblems, clothing, and the like occurred. Additionally, a section was included pertaining to the content most frequently elicited by the cards. Thus, specific standards are established for content toward which the examiner should direct his attention. Where these standards are not met, the procedure of "Testing the Limits" is suggested. Where the content deviates from that hypothesized, it is suggested that the interpreter concern himself with the specific symbolic meaning to the subject.

"These conditions require that the individual constantly check himself by comparing the hypotheses formed on this basis with one another, with hypotheses derived from analysis of structure, and with hypotheses found on the basis of other tests and case history materials. The result will be a series of formulations which will permit a rather thorough assessment of the personality and will be of considerable aid in clinical diagnosis."

This approach is reaffirmed and to some extent clarified, in the 1962 text.

"The qualitative aspects of the responses have become an integral part of the interpretive process as a result of the work of Klopfer and Beck. The content of the responses—that is, what the subject sees in the blot material—is the most recent factor to attract the attention of the Rorschachers. . . .An analysis of the content of responses offers clues concerning the symbolic meaning of the subject's concept formations. The significance of the most frequently occurring content has been briefly discussed elsewhere in this volume, primarily from a quantitative standpoint. Some qualitative aspects will be considered in this section. In addition, a selection of some of the less frequently occurring content including interpretive meanings is listed. It may be well to reiterate that original concepts and repetitive concepts are particularly revealing. Also relevant is the question of the significance of the area selected in relation to the content. . . .It suffices to say that the problems involved in the interpretation of content are many and that the meanings attached to the several contents offered here must be used with caution. The hypotheses presented below are based on dynamic personality theory as well as clinical experiences. They are presented not as facts, but as working hypotheses, hunches, or guesses."

SUMMARY

The evolution of the Klopfer system was not simply the work of one man. Although Bruno Klopfer was the central figure in its development, the overwhelming number of his works were collaborative efforts. First with Sadie Sender, in 1936; then with Burchard, Kelley, and Miale in 1939, Kelley in 1942; Ainsworth, Walter Klopfer, and Holt in 1954; and Helen Davidson in 1962. In the intervening years many other co-authors, too numerous to mention, were involved. But the catalyst was Klopfer. Klopfer the organizer, Klopfer the teacher, Klopfer the phenomenologist; all facets of this man are manifest one way or another in the System.

It appears to have evolved methodically. Yet, possibly, at times, prematurely. It began with broad-based hypotheses and developed toward the more specific details. Klopfer and his group seemed unexpectedly willing to depart from some of the fundamentals which had been postulated by Rorschach. Changes in scoring occurred early (1936 through 1942). Changes in interpretation also seemed to occur early when contrasted with the limited amount of data available on which to base these changes. And yet, the methodology of the evolution cannot necessarily be criticized. As Klopfer and his group found themselves limited in scoring and/or interpretation, new things were added. New interpretive hypotheses were offered and "tested" clinically. If there is a basic criticism it must be directed toward the phenomenological approach which was consistent with changes in the techniques of administration, scoring, or interpretation which occurred without the rigid demands of experimentation or even the compilation of frequency data. Of course, experimentation was not the orientation of Klopfer. Nor was it his intention to restrict the development of the instrument and/or System by an adherence to traditional psychometric or experimental procedures.

It is interesting to note that while Klopfer disavowed himself from a "sign approach," he did give some emphasis to signs, at least as they might be used in an overall configurational analysis. Later, however, the total impact of phenomenology began to prevail more and more in the Klopfer writings. More hypotheses were offered with seemingly less data on which to base them. To be sure, they were offered with words of caution, but the fact that they were offered, nevertheless brought them into the System.

But let this not be interpreted negatively. The System, whether or not valid, has been rather thoroughly refined. And as the System matured, greater emphasis was given to the actual content of the responses, with no less emphasis on the psychogram. Over these years of transformation, Klopfer naturally disavowed some of his early thinking. For instance his interpretation of texture, animal and inanimate movement, white space, and color, have all been altered remarkably. He also disavowed the limited use of the Rorschach such as in blind analysis, which he had previously encouraged in his early writings. Klopfer's change in orientation towards the comprehensiveness of the Rorschach is possibly best portrayed by a quotation from the 1962 text.

"Some workers have stated that the Rorschach can, better than other devices, tap something called the total personality or the whole person. Anything so complex as personality, however, cannot be studied as a whole. It is rather foolhardy to think that any one instrument can catch the whole personality in one measure. Neither the Rorschach nor the psychoanalyst, neither the clinical psychologist nor the experimentalist, can get at the entire person directly. . . ."

Although that is a conservative statement, Klopfer lists a variety of personality characteristics such as feelings about the self, responsiveness to people, reaction to emotional stress, intellectual status and functioning, etc. which may be revealed in the Rorschach. He makes no claims for validity, carefully pointing out "the literature on validation highlights a few seemingly positive findings in a context of many apparently negative findings and contradictory results," but suggests the traditional validating procedures are not necessarily applicable to projective methods. While his words may seem conservative, the approach of the Klopfer System is quite liberal.

It is, of course, premature to attempt an evaluation of the impact of the Klopfer system on psychodiagnosis or clinical psychology. Its relevancy to other systems will be studied later. For the moment it seems best to suggest that, for better or worse, a monumental accomplishment did occur.

REFERENCES

Booth, G. C. and Klopfer, B. Personality studies in chronic arthritis. *Rorschach Res. Exch.*, 1936-1937, 1, 40-49.

Booth, G. C., Klopfer, B. and Stein-Lewinson, T. Material for a comparative case study of a chronic arthritis personality. *Rorschach Res. Exch.*, 1936-1937, 1, 49-55.

Davidson, H. H. and Klopfer, B. Rorschach statistics. Part I: Mentally retarded, normal, and superior adults. *Rorschach Res. Exch.*, 1937-1938, 2, 164-169.

Davidson, H. H. and Klopfer, B. Rorschach statistics, Part II: Normal children. *Rorschach Res. Exch.*, 1938, 3, 37-42.

Faterson, H. F. and Klopfer, B. A survey of psychologist's opinions concerning the Rorschach method. *Rorschach Res. Exch.*, 1945, 9, 23-29.

Goldfarb, W. and Klopfer, B. Rorschach characteristics of "institution children." *Rorschach Res. Exch.,* 1944, 8, 92-100.

Hackbusch, F. and Klopfer, B. The contribution of projective techniques to the understanding and treatment of children psychometrically diagnosed as feeble-minded; with sample case studies. *Amer. J. Ment. Def.,* 1946, 41, 15-34.

Kelley, D. M. and Klopfer, B. Application of the Rorschach method to research in schizophrenia. *Rorschach Res. Exch.,* 1939, 3, 55-66.

Klopfer, B. and Sender, S. A system of refined scoring symbols. *Rorschach Res. Exch.,* 1936-1937, 1, 19-22.

Klopfer, B. Discussion of M. R. Hertz's "The normal details in the Rorschach ink-blot test." *Rorschach Res. Exch.,* 1937, 1, 119-120.

Klopfer, B. The present status of the theoretical development of the Rorschach method. *Rorschach Res. Exch.,* 1936-1937, 1, 142-148.

Klopfer, B. The technique of the Rorschach performance. *Rorschach Res. Exch.,* 1937, 2, 1-14.

Klopfer, B. and Davidson, Helen. Record Blank for the Rorschach method of personality diagnosis. *Rorschach Res. Exch.,* 1937, 2, No. 1, Appendix.

Klopfer, B. Discussion on "Some recent Rorschach problems." *Rorschach Res. Exch.,* 1937, 2, 66-68.

Klopfer, B. The shading responses. *Rorschach Res. Exch.,* 1937-1938, 2, 76-79.

Klopfer, B. and Miale, F. R. An illustration of the technique of the Rorschach interpretation: the case of Anne T. *Rorschach Res. Exch.,* 1937-1938, 2, 126-153.

Klopfer, B. and Tallman, G. A further Rorschach study of Mr. A. *Rorschach Res. Exch.,* 1938, 3, 31-36.

Klopfer, B., Krugman, M., Kelley, D. M., Murphy, L. and Shakow, D. Shall the Rorschach method be standardized? *Amer. J. Orthopsychiat.,* 1939, 9, 514-529.

Klopfer, B. Should the Rorschach method be standardized? *Rorschach Res. Exch.,* 1939, 3, 45-54.

Klopfer, B. and Davidson, H. H. Record blank for the Rorschach method of personality diagnosis. New York: *Rorschach Inst.,* 1939.

Klopfer, B., Burchard, M. L., Kelley, D. M. and Miale, F. R. Theory and technique of Rorschach interpretation. *Rorschach Res. Exch.,* 1939, 3, 152-194.

Klopfer, B. Personality differences between boys and girls in early childhood. *Psychol. Bull.,* 1939, 36, 538.

Klopfer, B. Personality diagnosis in early childhood: The application of the Rorschach method at the pre-school level. *Psychol. Bull.,* 1939, 36, 662.

Klopfer, B. The interplay between intellectual and emotional factors in personality diagnosis. Proc. 6th Inst. except Child, *Child Res. Clin.,* 1939, 41-47.

Klopfer, B. Personality aspects revealed by the Rorschach method. *Rorschach Res. Exch.,* 1940, 4, 26-29.

Klopfer, B., Davidson, H., Holzman, E., Kelley, D. M., Margulies, H., Miale, F. R. and Wolfson, R. The technique of Rorschach scoring and tabulation. *Rorschach Res. Exch.,* 1940, 4, 75-83.

Klopfer, B. and Margulies, H. Rorschach reactions in early childhood. *Rorschach Res. Exch.,* 1941, 5, 1-23.

Klopfer, B. Pseudopsychotic reactions in Rorschach records of preschool children. *Psychol. Bull.,* 1941, 38, 597.

Klopfer, B. and Kelley, D. M. *The Rorschach Technique.* Yonkers-on-Hudson: World Book, 1942.

Klopfer, B. and Hirning, L. C. "Signs," "Syndromes," and individuality patterns in Rorschach reaction of schizophrenics. *Psychol. Bull.*, 1942, 39, 513.

Klopfer, B. Instruction in the Rorschach method. *J. Consult. Psychol.*, 1943, 7, 112-119.

Klopfer, B. and Davidson, H. H. Form level rating; a preliminary proposal for appraising mode and level of thinking as expressed in Rorschach records. *Rorschach Res. Exch.*, 1944, 8, 164-177.

Klopfer, B. Personality diagnosis in children. In Lewis, N.D.C. and Pacella, B. L. *Modern trends in child psychiatry.* New York: Internat. Univ. Press, Inc., 1945, Chapter 5.

Klopfer, B. Comments on "The Case of Gregor." *Amer. Psychologist,* 1950, 5, 462.

Klopfer, B., Ainsworth, M. D., Klopfer, W. G. and Holt, R. R. *Developments in the Rorschach Technique.* Vol. 1 Technique and theory. Yonkers-on-Hudson, N. Y.: World Book Co., 1954, x 726.

Klopfer, B., et al. *Developments in the Rorschach Technique*: Vol. II. Fields of application. Yonkers-on-Hudson, N. Y.: World Book Co., 1956, xx, 828.

Klopfer, B. Psychological variables in human cancer. *J. Proj. Tech.,* 1957, 21, 331-340.

Klopfer, B. and Boyer, L. B. Notes on the personality structure of a North American Indian shaman: Rorschach interpretation. *J. Proj. Tech.,* 1961, 25, 170-178.

Klopfer, B. and Davidson, H. *The Rorschach Technique.* New York: Harcourt, Brace & World, 1962.

Rorschach, H. *Psychodiagnostics.* Berne: Bircher, 1921. (Transl. Hans Huber Verlag, 1942.)

Rorschach, H. and Oberholzer, E. The application of the interpretation of form to psychoanalysis. *Neurol. U. Psychiat.,* 1923, 82, 240-274.

Selinsky, H., Klopfer, B. and Emery, M. Inferences drawn from Rorschach tests in convulsive states. *J. Nerv. Dis.,* 1936, 84, 322-323.

Sender, S. and Klopfer, B. Application of the Rorschach test to child behavior problems as facilitated by a refinement of the scoring method. *Rorschach Res. Exch.,* 1936-1937, 1, 5-17.

Sender, S., Klopfer, B. and Rickers, M. Description of the first grade normal details for the ten test plates. *Rorschach Res. Exch.,* 1, 1936, 16-17.

Troup, E. and Klopfer, B. Sample case studies. *Rorschach Res. Exch.,* 1936-1937, 1, 121-140.

Wood, A., Arluck, E. and Margulies, H. Report of a group discussion of the Rorschach method. *Rorschach Res. Exch.,* 1941, 5, 154-165.

CHAPTER 5

THE BECK SYSTEM

Samuel J. Beck's transition to psychology took longer than any of the other Systematizers. He had been a scholar of the classics as an undergraduate at Harvard and a newspaper reporter in Cleveland. The decision to study psychology in graduate school seemed natural to him, coinciding with his interests in people and their personalities. At first, his graduate studies at Columbia University were committed to "general psychology," with major emphasis on learning the skills of the experimentalist. As an adjunct, he became quite interested in children and gradually became more interested in the growing field of abnormal psychology. It was through his chance conversation with David Levy that he was drawn to the Rorschach. The Rorschach represented a challenge to Beck as a tool for exploring the unknowns of the individual. He conducted his dissertation on the Rorschach, the first to be done on the technique in America, under the direction of Robert Woodworth and the advice and encouragement of Levy. From 1928 to the present, Beck has worked tirelessly to develop the Rorschach as a scientific tool which would have meaningfulness for all of psychology. As both teacher and researcher his productivity can be perceived as commendable. It is of interest to note that by 1933, Beck had published eight articles on the Rorschach. Hertz had finished her dissertation on the technique the previous year and was researching with it at the Brush Foundation. Klopfer was receiving his training with the technique in Switzerland. Piotrowski had yet to become interested in the test, and Rapaport had not yet begun graduate training. Thus, Beck had some just cause, at least from a historical point of view, to feel some dismay when, some short time later, others began promulgating distinctly different Rorschach approaches. In any event, there is no question but that his early work with the Rorschach contributed significantly, not only to the development of his own System but to the encouragement of others to explore the potential utilization of the Rorschach as a instrument for the evlauation of personality.

In 1965 the Society for Projective Techniques (which had previously been the *Rorschach Institute* and the *Rorschach Research Exchange*) awarded their first citation for outstanding achievement in the field of projective techniques. This citation went to Samuel Beck.

"For his sustained pioneering and indefatigable research and teaching in the field of projective techniques. Throughout a long career, beginning with the first American Research report on the Rorschach, 35 years ago, he labored fruitfully and successfully in narrowing the gap between projective methods and the field of scientific psychology. Over many years he has contributed greatly, directly and indirectly, to the science and art of projective techniques and personality assessment, blending successfully the nomothetic and idiographic approaches. In addition, his continuous efforts at delving into the mysteries of personality structure and the processes of schizophrenia have been marked by scientific vigor and clinical insight, which have enriched the field of psychopathology."

It might be suggested that in awarding the first citation for achievement in projective techniques to Beck, the American Rorschach world, including the Klopfer group, was bowing in deference to the distinction of a pioneer.

The very beginning of Beck's work with Rorschach exemplified the training for systematic investigation that he had received at Columbia. His first article concerned the use of the Rorschach for personality diagnosis and was very cautious in its prediction. That article, published in 1930, explained the use of the Rorschach as a measure of intelligence and as a potential means of indicating emotional stability and/or instability. He presented four illustrations, using the case study method which was to typify a large number of his publications through the 1930's. Later, in 1930, he published data concerning the use of the Rorschach with feebleminded children. Once again, his cautiousness prevailed as he indicated, even though presenting data from 69 cases, that norms were wholly insufficient for the derivation of conclusions, but held out the promise that the technique could be used successfully as an index of intellect or for the probing of personality. An elaboration of that article appeared in 1932 in which he directly presented his data as a test of five Rorschach indices of intellectual functioning, W, F, M, A, and O. In 1931 he published two articles. The first of these offered evidence that the Rorschach could be used to diagnostic advantage with problem children. In the second, he presented typical responses obtained in the Rorschach from manic-depressive psychotics.

By 1933, Beck was prepared on the basis of his previous work, to offer material on "Rorschach theory," as related to the understanding of personality. In the first of three articles appearing that year, he attempted to demonstrate that the problem of balance in personality may be approached by means of the analysis of the quantitative measurement of four fundamental Rorschach processes. He speculated that personality evaluation could be ascertained in terms of the balance between the manifestations of form perception, organizational behavior, creativeness, and affect. He suggested that certain patterns were recognized as stable, whereas other patterns would be clearly indicative of psychopathology. In a second 1933 article, he elaborated on this same concept. It was his contention that the unitary personality (culturally and intrapsychically stable) evolves from the organization of the four basic psychological processes, form recognition, organizing energy, affective drive, and creative activity. In a third 1933 article Beck contended with the configurational tendencies in the Rorschach. He questioned whether the capacity to see the Rorschach blots as wholes is a more significant sign in the test, as Rorschach had suggested, or whether other methods of perceiving the blots may indicate a higher organizational capacity. It was on the basis of this work that the eventual scoring for organizational activity, the Z score, evolved.

Whereas Beck had published a number of articles prior to 1937, the first culmination of his work was experienced in *Introduction to the Rorschach Method*, which was the first monograph of the American Orthopsychiatric Association. *Beck's Manual*, as it came to be known, manifests the extent of his work with the Rorschach technique to that point. Rather laboriously, he offered the protocols of some 59 cases together with their interpretations for the reader. The last three chapters of the *Manual* (12, 13 and 14) are possibly of greatest interest here. In these three chapters Beck outlined the "experimental technique" in detail, giving his prerequisites for administration, scoring, and the fundamentals for interpretation. While many of these procedures and interpretive suggestions were by no means new, they were, nonetheless, crystallized for the first time into an integrated manual to which the student could turn.

The elementary level of this era of Rorschach development might be best exemplified by one of the beginning statements of Chapter 12 concerning the test material.

"Usually the test figures are now sold mounted on card-board facilitating their handling. Should it be necessary for an experimenter to mount them himself, he had best use a stiff card-board. Soft board will buckle and spoil the material for purposes of testing. The cards had also best be exactly the size of the paper on which the figures come, thus avoiding overlapping. Care should be taken that the paste leaves no small particles bulging, since it is not unknown for a schizophrenic patient to select these bulges to react to."

Such primitive conditions for experimentation are, of course, striking today. Yet it was in this world of the unknown that the early researchers were forced to work.

ADMINISTRATION

In the 1937 manual Beck sugested a standard procedure of instructions using written material which would be handed to the subject.

". . .The following standard instructions, typed on a white card, have proven satisfactory: You will be given a series of ten cards, one by one. The cards have on them designs, made up of ink-blots. Look at each card and tell the examiner what you see on each card, or anything that might be representative. Look at each card as long as you like, only be sure to tell the examiner everything that you see on the card as you look at it. When you have finished with the card, give it to the examiner as a sign that you are through with it. If these directions are not clear, ask any further questions that you wish. Are you ready?"

These same instructions have been in essence, perpetuated by Beck through the development of his System. Beginning with the first edition of *Rorschach's Test—Volume I* in 1944, the use of the written instructions was dropped although the verbalization of the material remained the same. It should be noted however, that Beck carefully elaborated on the instructional procedure in the 1944 volume to suggest that "paraphrasing of this language may be very liberal. . . .It must be emphasized that the essence of Rorschach Test Procedure is to leave S entirely free." Even with the 1961 fully revised third edition of this text, the instructional procedure has not been changed. In 1937, Beck affirmed his notion that the subject should be seated in front of the examiner with no distractions. This was traditional with Rorschach's suggestion.

The Free Association procedure recommended by Beck is similar to that described by Rorschach wherein the examiner should not interject any comment or response other than to reply to the examinee's questions in a nondirective or "nonleading" manner. In the 1937 Manual Beck indicated his endorsement of Rorschach's format for Inquiry as opposed to that suggested by Oberholzer.

"After O has given his final response to card X, and not until then, is it necessary to go over the record, response by response and ascertain (a) what portion of the figure has been reacted to; (b) what qualities of the selected figures were utilized by O in determining his response. . . .The writer deviates from Oberholzer but finds support in Rorschach who is very specific on this point in his practice. Oberholzer, and some American experimenters, inquire for each test figure before the next one is presented. They maintain that in waiting until the end of the experiment, O may forget the response source or its determinant. In the writer's experience there has been so very few instances of such forgetting that this factor seems negligible. The need to wait until the end of the free association period rests in the probability that questioning as to any response in the earlier portion of the test will influence O's reaction to portions following. What seems to me to be at stake is one of the most essential elements of the Rorschach method—mainly, complete freedom of O in his associations."

Beck has reaffirmed this methodology in all of his subsequent texts dealing with procedure. Beck also requires that every response be inquired. Rorschach had not emphasized this specifically. In fact, Rorschach had been somewhat vague on this point. F. L. Wells, with whom Beck worked at Boston Psychopathic Hospital, had suggested inquiring every response to avoid errors in examiner judgment. Wells also formulated the introductory statement to the Inquiry which Beck adopted for his System and included Rorschach's caution that questioning is kept non-directive, and non-leading. Beck has emphasized that the Inquiry may be almost as important as the Free Association, citing the fact that it is the Inquiry which leads to a specific identification of the Location of the response plus information clarifying the Determinants of the response.

Unlike Klopfer, Beck has not endorsed an Analogy Period or a Testing of the Limits procedure. He has, under very special circumstances, such as with feeble-minded subjects, indicated the permissibility of asking such questions as, "What else do you see?" and cited instances wherein encouragement is permissible. However, these require much more stringent conditions than those necessary for either the Analogy or Testing of the Limits procedures as described by Klopfer.

SCORING

The Beck scheme for scoring Rorschach responses has never deviated drastically from that originally suggested by Rorschach in *Psychodiagnostik*. Table 3 shows the evolution of the Beck method for scoring Location from 1937 to 1961 as contrasted with the original scoring for Location described by Rorschach. From an examination of Table 3, it will be noted that in only two instances did Beck modify Rorschach's suggestions for Location scoring. These are the S response which Rorschach used by itself for scoring Location and Beck described as only being used when combined with a W, D, or Dd, and the elimination of the use of Do for scoring location and instead including this in the scoring for content.* A third deviation not really inconsistent with Rorschach's thinking occurs in the criteria for the scoring of D or Dd. Rorschach had described the D response as a normal detail of the plate and the Dd as an unusual or small detail. Beck carried Rorschach's thinking further by actually utilizing frequency distributions to determine those areas of the blots to which responses would be most frequently given. In the 1937 text, he was able to outline areas, both large and small in size, which were frequently responded to and thus, included in his category of D. In doing this he made a slight alteration from Rorschach's original notion that Dd could be scored for small detail. As Beck's studies of frequency distributions of Location responses ensued, any area, whether large or small, which was responded to infrequently would then be scored Dd.

---

* Beck used the symbol Dr rather than Rorschach's Dd for the scoring of unusual details in the 1937 Manual but reverted to the symbol Dd in the 1944 text.

TABLE 3

A Comparison of the Evolution of the Beck Method of Scoring Location
from 1937 to 1961 with that Originally Suggested by Rorschach

Symbol	Rorschach	Beck—1937	Beck—1944	Beck—1949	Beck—1961
W	Plate interpreted as a whole	Same	Same	Same	Same
DW	Plate interpreted as a whole secondarily, the answer based primarily on a detail	Same	Same	Same	Same
S	White intermediate figures (space detail)	S used to denote white space detail and always combined with the symbol W, D or Dr	Used for white space detail but always combined with the symbols D or Dd (by this time Beck was convinced that S would be used with D in only three instances on Cards II, VII & IX. All other S responses were considered by Beck as Dds)	Same	Same
D	A normal detail of the plate	A frequently selected detail (as established by a frequency distribution)	Same	Same	Same
Dr	Not used	Reaction to a rarely selected detail	Not used	Not used	Not used
Dd	An unusual or small detail	Not used	Rare detail as defined by infrequent use	Same	Same
Do	A detail is interpreted in place of a whole	Not used (X was added to content of Hd or Ad to denote this process)	Same	Same	Same

The scoring of Determinants for responses has also remained relatively consistent with that described by Rorschach. Table 4 provides a comparison of the Beck System for scoring Determinants as it has evolved from 1937 to 1961 with those Determinant scorings used by Rorschach. In addition to the basic scoring for Determinants listed in Table 4, Beck also provided for other features of the response to be quantitatively evaluated. These include the Z score for organizational activity, and the scoring of blends. Rorschach had also considered the scoring of blend responses.

"Now and then interpretations are seen which appear to be conditioned both by kinesthesis and color, either with or without consideration of form. These occur quite rarely. It usually happens that most answers which appear to be in this group at first glance show, upon closer examination, that either M was primary and C secondary, or vice versa. . . .Those rare answers in which movement and color appear to influence the answers simultaneously may be called MC's."

In 1937 Beck provided for scoring of only three blend responses (M.CF, M.FC, and M.FY), suggesting that they usually occurred in "very superior or rich mentalities." By 1944 the importance of scoring blends was more notable, and differentiated the Beck System significantly from all other Systems. In 1944 Beck included a separate chapter on "Diverse Determinants" in which the problem of the blend response was given the majority of space. He noted that such responses presented the dilema of whether to score twice, thus loading the record with too many responses, or to score only once, (as was advocated by Klopfer), thereby omitting the other score and possibly losing the impact of its importance.

"Many responses occur in which M, C, Y, or any of their variations blend. . . .The most satisfactory solution has been to enter both, as a multiple determinant. . . .In commenting on the coincidence of M and C in the same responses, Rorschach states this circumstance to be rare. This is inconsistent with later experience."

Thus, Beck provided for the specialized scoring of any combination of determinants, even including those where two different types of shading would occur, as for example, Y.V, although noting that blends of shading responses are extremely rare.

From examination of Table 4 it is also interesting to note that Beck approached the problem of shading more conservatively than did Klopfer. For instance, in 1937 only two symbols, Y or FY, were used for shading. By 1944 Beck had become convinced of the necessity of a separate scoring for depth responses and therefore incorporated the symbols V, VF, and FV and redefined FY so as to exclude interpretations based on depth or distance. It was not, however, until 1949 that Beck incorporated a new symbol for scoring of the texture response, T, TF, or FT. The apparent slowness with which Beck did incorporate a texture symbol, as contrasted with Klopfer's suggestion of such a symbol as early as 1936, indicates the reluctance of Beck to make significant modifications in Rorschach's original System.

It is also important to mention that Beck has persistently maintained the requisite for scoring on an "all or none" basis. Whereas Klopfer and some of the other Systematizers have been prone to score "tendencies," Beck has preferred to maintain a neatness of scoring wherein either a determinant "occurs or does not occur." Even Rorschach's 1923 discrimination of tendencies toward movement or color have not been included by Beck. Instead, Beck has maintained what he considers to be the Oberholzer tradition, wherein the decision to score a determinant other than F in a questionable response will be made in light of the total record. Thus, if many M's occur in a record, a response which seems to be movement would be scored M. Conversely, if few or no M's occur in a record, such a debatable response would be scored F.

Whereas Beck has been conservative in limiting the number of symbols for scoring location and determinants, he has been one of the most liberal in increasing the formal symbols available for scoring Associational Content. Klopfer, by 1954, had developed some 25 such symbols ranging from the commonly used H for human to N for nature concepts with many man-made articles included in the general category Obj (Object). By 1949 Beck had increased his list of symbols for Associational Content to some 36 separate abbreviations also ranging from H, to more specific items such as Pr for Personal, Ru for Rural, Vo for Vocational, Hh for household, and the like.

It seems appropriate to question why some of the symbols selected by Beck are so different from those selected by Klopfer and/or some of the other Systematizers. According to an interview with Beck (1967) the symbol Y was selected primarily by chance, in that it was a letter not already used by Rorschach, and one which would not be easily confused with other symbols that were being used. V and T were both selected as the first letter of the characteristics to which they referred, Vista and Texture respectively.*

INTERPRETATION

Beck's approach to the interpretation of Rorschach data consistently has utilized the case study method. Until 1945 Beck offered no methodical elaboration on interpretation in a manner similar to Klopfer's 1939 article

---

* Klopfer has also reported in an interview ((1966)) that he selected his symbols K and k as they represented the sound of the beginning of the word chiaroscuro and that his decision to use c and C' were based on his notion at that time that they were based on the same psychological process as Color.

TABLE 4

A Comparison of the Evolution of the Beck Method of Scoring Determinants from 1937 to 1961 with that Originally Suggested by Rorschach

Symbol	Rorschach	Beck–1937	Beck–1944	Beck–1949	Beck–1961
F	The Rorschach Form answers (scoring of + or − based on frequency of recurring answers allowing for subjective evaluation where statistical data insufficient)	Same as for Rorschach (by this time Beck had developed a frequency distribution on which + and − scoring was based. In those instances where frequency data was inadequate. Beck suggested the scoring of F without the + or − sign)	Same (by this time the frequency tabulation on which the + and − signs were based had been expanded to a much larger sample)	Same	Same (by 1961 the N of the same was again enlarged)
M	Movement answers involving kinesthetic influences (restricted to humans or human behaviors)	The experience of felt Movement involving an action physically possible for a human. (In essence the same definition as that described by Rorschach	Same (the definition for M was elaborated on to the extent that animal and inanimate Movement were reaffirmed as not being M; and the notation that M does not require vigorous activity but could involve a pose or attitude such as sleeping)	Same	Same (considerably more elaboration on the definition but no change in requirement or intent)
C	Color answer, interpretation based on the Color of the blot alone	Same	Same	Same	Same
CC	Not actually described by Rorschach. Used in his record No. 17 to denote Color naming and counted as equivalent to a pure	Not included	Not included	Not included	Not included

CF	Color-Form answer determined primarily by the Color, secondarily by Form	Same	Same	Same	Same
FC	Form-Color answer, interpretation based primarily on Form, Color secondarily	Same (elaboration included concerning significance of the inquiry to determine FC from CF responses)	Same	Same	Same
(C)	Chiaroscuro Responses	Not used	Not used	Not used	Not used
Y		Responses containing grey only, without Form elements	Same but not including those light determined responses involving vista	Same but not involving those responses including vista or texture	Same
YF		Not used	Light determined responses where Shading is primary, Form is secondary	Same	Same
FY		Chiaroscuro, or vista responses determined by differential grey with Form always present and usually interpretations of depth or distance	Light determined response not involving vista wherein Form was primary, Shading secondary	Same	Same
V		Not used	Vista responses based solely on Shading and giving the impression of depth or distance with no Form involved	Same	Same
VF		Not used	Shading responses of depth or distance where Shading is primary, Form is secondary	Same	Same

TABLE 4 (*Continued*)

A Comparison of the Evolution of the Beck Method of Scoring Determinants
from 1937 to 1961 with that Originally Suggested by Rorschach

Symbol	Rorschach	Beck—1937	Beck—1944	Beck—1949	Beck—1961
FV	Not used	Not used	Same as 1937 definition for FY (Chiaroscuro or vista response determined by differential grey with Form always present and usually interpretations of depth of distance) By 1944 the FV requirement included an absolute necessity of depth or distance	Same	Same
T	Not used	Not used	Not used	Texture responses based on the Shading component where no Form is present	Same
TF	Not used	Not used	Not used	Texture responses based on Shading where Shading is primary, Form is secondary	Same
FT	Not used	Not used	Not used	Texture responses based on Shading where the Form is primary, Shading is secondary	Same

or the material in his 1942 text. Prior to the 1945 text all of Beck's interpretive conclusions were offered in separate publications. The introductory sections concerning the psychologic significance of Rorschach test factors in *Rorschach's Test: Volume II* (1945) and *Rorschach's Test: Volume III* (1952) do represent somewhat of a methodical approach to the problem of interpretation.

Whereas Beck had published eight articles by 1933, his first article dealing specifically with an interpretive approach occurred in 1937, "Psychological Processes in Rorschach Findings." Prior to this time, he had offered case studies of the Rorschach with the feeble-minded, problem children, manic depressives, and had discussed the phenomenon of "balance in personality" especially as applied to the healthy personality. It was the 1937 article which clearly offered interpretive suggestions which were differing from, or added to, those of Rorschach. In that article, Beck described "neutral" psychological processes, discussing them in terms of four basic Rorschach test factors. He indicated that Movement could validly be interpreted as an introversive trend in the sense of "an inner-creative activity in the healthy adult of superior intelligence." He also suggested that the color response probably has some relation to affect, described the organization response as having its greatest and least manifestations at the two ends of the intelligent scale, and contended that the clearly or "good" perceived form responses occur with the highest frequency in the healthy adult and most infrequently in the feeble-minded.

Beck's preference for the case study method was quite consistent with the time. It manifests an empirical approach wherein the basic demands were for test data, rather than clinical opinion. This approach is also, of course, found in the *Introduction to the Rorschach Method* wherein 59 cases were presented. In introducing these cases Beck pointed out:

"In making the selections, [of the cases included] two conditions were kept in mind. The first is, the material should in the main be representative of that which the clinician more commonly meets in his experience. Thus, for one thing, will be facilitated the early accumulation of new response records checking the validity of the present work and useful toward the further development of the test. For another, this work will be more helpful to the clinician insofar as it exemplifies the response pattern he most commonly encounters in his methods. The second condition has been that material be selected from those groups in which the writer's experience has left him reasonably satisfied as to the solidity of his ground. . . .In choosing the particular cases the effort was made to exemplify (a) the varieties of personalities found within any of the groups; (b) the different Rorschach features involved, and their utilization in interpreting as to psychological processes; and (c) when possible, to obtain approximately equal distribution between the sexes, and over a broad range of chronological age. . . .Validation, then, insofar as it enters into the present world is entirely by medium of external personality findings, and its validation of record with record, experimental with clinical. No effort is here made to treat the material statistically and establish measures of validity or reliability by the appropriate techniques. Such data would not fall within the scope of the present work. This, to repeat, is to offer a starting point for the collection of comparable material by different workers, and by the same workers at different times. . . .Until such a stable anchoring point is made available, Rorschach experimentation is in a state of chaos. It is such a stable anchoring point that is attempted in the present work, however much it may later be found necessary to re-shape the anchor, to correct the norms offered."

After 1937, Beck presented a series of papers designed to clarify the interpretive procedure. For example, in 1938 he published a monograph describing Rorschach Test results in schizophrenic and non-psychotic individuals. Using some 81 patients and 64 controls he found the psychological implications as related to schizophrenia were most clearly differentiated by a greater sensitivity to minor details, less orderliness of intellectual procedure, more impulsive affect, and less accuracy in interpretation on the part of the schizophrenics than the controls. In 1942, analyzing some 77 records, Beck elaborated on the effects of electroshock therapy on personality. By 1944, he had worked sufficiently with the technique to offer a description of the "character neuroses." By this time, from examination of Beck's writings, it would seem that he was thoroughly convinced of the discriminating capacity of the Rorschach for three basic groups, the healthy superior adult, the schizophrenic or psychotic, and the feebleminded or mentally retarded. Even after nearly 15 years of research, he was unwilling, or reluctant, to define Rorschach data on a more refined differential diagnostic basis. It should not be inferred, however, that Beck was unwilling to make such differential diagnoses prior to this time, for that is not the case. In both his teaching and practical work Beck became renowned for his own capacities for differential diagnosis while at the Michael Reese Hospital, Northwestern University, and the University of Chicago. It appears that he was simply unwilling to elaborate in writing on those Rorschach features most commonly characteristic to the variety of psychiatric nosologies. In part, of course, this manifests his basic orientation toward the use of the Rorschach and toward the problems of psychodiagnosis in general. That is, while using the nomethetic approach as much as possible, the final conclusions concerning a person are equally contingent on idiographic study.

The publication of *Rorschach's Test: Volume II*, in 1945, offered for the first time rather detailed suggestions for the interpretation of the scored test protocol. In the first chapter he dealt briefly with the concept of personality, although offering no new or modified personality theory as had been pointed out by Harriman in his critique of the text. Possibly the most important portion of this text was the second chapter pertaining to the psychologic significance of Rorschach Test factors. In that second chapter he offered some basic postulates for every one of the Rorschach scoring categories in his System to that time. Much like Klopfer, Beck suggested that the protocol should be approached from both the quantitative and qualitative aspects. Beck indicated that the W response is related to intellectual potential. The confabulatory W (DW) was interpreted as a reaction uncovering a process "that is not illogical but rather alogical. Its frequency in mental disease and in the feeble minded, its appearance notably less frequently in the more mildly disturbed, and its essential absence in the healthy, all converge to portray the infirmentalities that produce DW and DdW." At the same time, he indicated that some DW responses could be consistent with the healthy, even superior adult individual. He described the organization activity (Z score) as varying directly with the intelligence of the subject and cautioned that its interpretation would vary as personalities vary.

"The Z factor has certain virtues not inherent in W. For one thing, it takes account of much Z activity that W misses. Second, since it is not scored in discrete units, as is necessary in the case of W, it makes it possible to take account of intermediate values and continuous distributions, and is thus a more flexible measure. Third, it is an index of the intellectual energy as such, irrespective of the kind of intelligence that S uses, something that does not influence W. . . .Interpretation of W and Z varies with the total personality that produces them—a rule that holds for any Rorschach test factor. This is only to say that evaluation of an individual's W or Z score can be made only in light of what the test shows concerning his mental well-being or illness generally, the affective influences, the attitudes to reality, the fantasy living."

Beck also stressed the importance of considering the mode of approach, Rorschach's concept of *Erfassungstypus,* in interpretation. He advanced the notion that the relative amounts of W, D, and Dd indicate the style used by the person to deal with his problems, and the flexibility of that style as the problem situations change. He suggested that the average length protocol of 30 responses should contain a balance of 6W, 20D, and 4Dd. He also maintained that an understanding of intellectual adaptivity and orderliness of method are also relevant to a valid interpretation of mode of approach. He indicated that the Animal content and the number of Popular responses are the basic indices for understanding adaptive thinking. Beck's normative sample yielded a mean A per cent of 46.0 with a range from 30 to 65 per cent. He found high A percentages occurring in persons whose behaviors are marked by anxiety, depression and/or hysteriod features. He had also found a high A per cent in the defective, simple type schizophrenics. Correspondingly, he found a low A per cent in the estranged, extremely disordered schizophrenics. Beck's normative sample also revealed an average of about 7.0 Popular responses in a protocol of 30 responses. He suggested that the healthiest individuals give a slightly higher number, eight or nine, but expressed the caution that nine P's is "sufficiently at the high end of the normal range to be a sign of overconventionality." He also observed that an irregular sequence is not necessarily indicative of psychopathology, noting that, while common to clinical groups, especially the schizophrenic who presents a confused sequence, it does occur with regularity among the most superior and healthy adults.

Beck perceived the F+ per cent as the most reliable index of conscious control and respect for reality. In other words, ego functioning. He suggested that the highest F+ percentages are found in the depressed person whereas the lowest F+ percentages are manifest in manic excitements, feeble-minded, and schizophrenia. He described the critical minimum for the healthy person at 60 per cent with the upper limit falling somewhere between 90 and 95 per cent. In discussing the F+ per cent Beck clearly aligned himself with psychoanalytic theory as indicated by the use of phrases such as "regression in service of the ego," and "the extremely high F percentage in the depressed must mean that the ego has taken complete possession of the psyche."

Beck interpreted the M response much like Rorschach had some 20 years previously.

"In evaluating the significance of the separate M responses, it is necessary to note (a) the form quality of the percept . . . (b) how original or individualized the associational content is, (c) whether the M is seen in a Dd or in any very unusual portion of the figure, (d) whether the content is part human, . . . (e) whether there is any M in animal content, (f) the extensor or flector stance in the M, (g) most important, the response pattern as a whole—i.e., what kind of person is engaging in a fantasy."

He had found that the minus M response occurred "almost certainly" from a personal need reflected in an autistic creativity occurring most frequently in the schizophrenic. He was careful to indicate that such creativeness could also occur in the superior and healthy adult but cited a variety of criteria for this conclusion to be reached. He indicated that M when found in a Dd location is highly personalized, whereas M found in Hd content is of inferior quality. Following Rorschach's lead, he also suggested that the person giving many extensor M's is characteristic of the more active striving individual, whereas the person giving flector M's is a more submissive type of individual. Beck was careful to point out the necessity for a global evaluation rather than any rigid sign approach, a position taken by all of the Systematizers.

"Finally, the significance of M varies critically according to the personality that produces it. . . .Producing M is, genetically, a creative act. If then, an individual produces many M, it becomes important to know that his F+ percentage is high, but not excessively so, that it is, around the optimum, that Z and W are at comparable levels, that his color responses have certain nuances, and that findings for such factors as associational content, animal percepts, and popular responses, are consistent."

It is to Beck's great credit that, while demanding empirical data, he consistently has had the insights concerning the complexity of personality to recognize that no single test sign or score could be indicative of any single personalogic factor in and by itself. He has stressed the necessity for a comprehensive evaluation of the psychogram, in a global manner, including the integration of the qualitative or content evaluation of the protocol. Beck regards this approach as essential to an ultimate or final evaluation or description of personality. In this respect, he has become one of the champions of the idiographic method.

Beck interpreted the color responses as an index of affect, using Rorschach's hypotheses as the nucleus of his interpretation. He suggested that where the Pure C response occurs in the adult, it indicates the existence of 'ungovernable impulses and rages amounting in some instances to momentary psychotic episodes in which there is a schism between affect and intelligence." He had found that schizophrenics as a group produce a significantly larger number of Pure C responses than do normals or other clinical groups. He cautioned, however, that hysterics also frequently give one or more Pure C responses. He explained the CF type response as less impulsive than the Pure C but still marked by labile features wherein restraint, in the form of the F tendency exists, but does not always prevail. He described the CF dominated person as one easily irritated and suggested that other factors in the protocol, mainly those evincing signs of disintegration should be studied closely to determine the extent to which hypersensitivity and suggestibility dominate behavior. Inversely, Beck interpreted the FC answer as including affect but expressing it under ego concern for reality and with consideration for others. Beck found the FC response to be most frequent in the "healthiest adults.

Beck also commented in the 1945 text on the phenomenon of affect as dysphoria. He had found by this time that two Rorschach test phenomena project oppressive feeling experiences. These are manifest in the Y and V responses. He described the vista response as indicative of tendencies toward self appraisal, which could or could not be healthy depending upon the quality of V and its relationship to F. He suggested that where vista responses occur in quantity or free of form domination that an unpleasant, "morose feeling tone, depressing in effect, always overlies experience of the individual." He indicated that such Rorschach signs would be evident not only in the depressed but also in the inadequate or insecure individual where an abundance of ego consciousness is still in operation. He described the flat gray or Y response as stemming "from an anergic state, one in which the vigor has apparently been drawn out of the organism." He has found this prominent among persons listless or washed out. He indicated that a disquieting, oppressive affect essentially always accompanies Y as the emotional tone. He suggested that it is absent only in a few records, those of some schizophrenics and some brain-damaged persons. He denoted that Y could often express an absence of activity. Conversely, the FY response was perceived by Beck to be indicative of the same factors of thought found in the pure Y response but less extensively encompassing of the psychic life. The 1945 text offered little with regard to texture.*

"Texture associations have not received adequate study. They require it, first, because of their frequency, and second, because of the possibility that their source is in tactual experience, an interpretation that Klopfer offers. In view of the large place that touch has in the erotic life, and in view of the importance of erotic satisfaction of frustration in shaping the personality, this is a point that demands inquiry. Its validation would develop a factor of first importance, the more so since touch associations of other kinds are found."

The 1945 text offered interpretative commentary on both color-shock and gray-black shock. Beck offered some 14 signs of color-shock, interpretating the phenomenon much like Rorschach had, that is, as a manifestation of neurosis. Gray-black shock was interpreted as a manifestation of anxiety, "which, because its roots lie deep in the very early experiences of the individual, has become a central character force, diffusing his energies and paralyzing him in almost all of life's crises, even the minor ones. Gray-black shock lays this anxiety open."

Beck described the importance of associational content, white space, and oligophrenic details also similarly to that of Rorschach. His interpretation of the blend went considerably beyond Rorschach, and certainly differed significantly from Klopfer.

"Interpretation takes account of each determinant, in accordance with its usual significance. In addition, the blend as such has been found to signify activity of an especially vivid and intense mind. It is the more vibrant and creative among the healthy that produce it. When found in the disturbed and in the disordered, the blends tell of more poignant soul struggle or distress. It takes, after all, a complex psychic potential to issue in the response that is at once a fantasy and expression of

---

* Beck did not formally adopt a scoring for Texture responses until the 1949 revision of his Volume I of *Rorschach's Test*.

a high feeling state (M.CF) or of an inferiority consciousness overlayed with a dysphoric mood (FV.Y) or any of the blends. . . ."

Beck has been more reluctant to stress ratios or percentages than most of the other Systematizers. This is particularly true when compared with the Klopfer System. In the first two editions of *Rorschach's Test: Volume I* (1944, 1949), Beck suggested computing only the Z score total, the Erlebnistypus, an F+ percentage, an A per cent, the average time per response, and average time per first response. The publication of the third edition of *Volume I,* in 1961, brought the addition of the Experience Actual, the Affective Ratio, Lambda, and two ratios concerning fluctuation. In 1945, in *Volume II,* Beck suggested that concern also be given to the total of non-F responses, indicating that the percentage would be from 40 to 50 in superior adults and could exceed those figures in "severely conflicted neurotics," in some types of schizophrenia, and some patients in excitement. He suggested that this percentage would be low, less than 20, in the feeble-minded, the depressed, the anxious, the hysteric, some schizophrenics, and brain damaged patients.

"In the psychotic and in the neurotic, a large percentage of non-F determinants adds information as to the intensity of the inner experience. In the healthy, it stresses the fullness and richness of the known creativity and vibrancy of such persons. Underproduction of non-F associations is a less useful sign, since the sterility or restriction it reflects is clear without it."

Beck was also careful to point out in 1945 the importance of behavioral factors, such as qualifications, negations, general description, verbosity, self reference, attitude, card turning, and perseveration.

He was surprisingly brief in his interpretation of the Erlebnistypus, preferring to rely basically on Rorschach's original conception, that is, as an index of inner potential. He reaffirmed Rorschach's notion that it indicates the extent to which the individual is capable of responding and also the catuion that "it does not state how the individual lives in actuality. . . ." In fact, it would appear that Beck was uncertain of his own conception of the Erlebnistypus when writing the 1945 volume.

"From this language, Rorschach's Erlebnistypus becomes really a concept of the whole personality. It is truly that. Also, it is a hypothesis, as yet quite elusive, not representing any psychologic activity concerning which we have knowledge, and leaving much to the imagination in the effort to handle it. . . .The Erlebnistypus appears to be to Rorschach a psychologic medium or essence in which all the mental activities of the individual are suspended. To understand the Erlebnistypus is to him a prerequisite to understanding any aspect of a personality, its major forces and finer nuances. For all this, it still remains a vague concept not yet concrete enough to use as an interpretative test factor. It is safer to rest rather on its components M and C. Rorschach does essentially this, since he always identifies the Erlebnistypus in terms of dominance of M or C or of their equivalence, introversive or extratensive trends."

In 1952, Beck published *Rorschach's Test: Volume III* which follows essentially the same format as had *Volume II*, that is, the case study method. This volume, however, is at a considerably more advanced level in content and style than had been *Volume II*. One of the most basic changes in the format occurs in the presentation of the cases. Only four cases are presented, but exhaustively; some including more than one protocol on the same subject as well as clinical notes and therapy evaluation. The section on interpretation, Chapters I and II, is also considerably more advanced than in the 1945 volume. In part, this greater sophistication resulted from findings of two lengthy research projects in which Beck had been involved. He describes these in the Foreword.

"These advances are in part based on two research projects in which I have been engaged for the past five years. In part they result from continued exposure to clinical method. From these two sources have emerged the fresh insights into the significances of the psychologic operations projected by this particular instrument. . . .The data [from the research projects] have provided spheres of reference essential in any procedure that undertakes to measure. . . .The other area of advance, the one more characteristic of the clinical setting, has been of qualitative order. Many observations constantly force themselves in the use of the Rorschach test, observations that cannot be quantitatively defined or arranged in numerical rankings. They recur with a frequency such as to indicate some regularity behind their occurrence, given certain personality conditions. That is, they have validity. They also carry the pitfall of any qualitative judgment, that of being subjective. . . .The advances in interpretation are thus both quantitative and qualitative. . . .These interpretations are, therefore, a statement of where the Rorschach test, as I use it, is at the present time. The student will note that a great deal of quantitative analysis is possible in the Rorschach test. This is not to say that I am deceiving myself as to whether we have a measure of the whole human personality, in the strictly defined sense of the word measure. We do have a good test, one that uses a fixed set of stimuli, and that gives results useful to the clinic and to the practitioner. Within any range of error moderate for what it attempts, the test provides dependable diagnostic pictures, and guideposts for treatment."

Beck is also obviously more confident about the instrument in his 1952 text. That is not to say that at any time previously did he lack confidence in the Rorschach, for that was never the case, but, as has been noted, he was rather cautious in his evaluation and his willingness to extend the guidelines for interpretation. In 1952 the issue had shifted significantly. He notes that the test was being subjected to some "hard thinking" and considerable experimentation. He indicates that the majority of the experimental studies were designed to investigate single test variables and thereby are only partially applicable to "the problem of the whole personality conceived as a universe of interacting forces." He suggested that, for the most part, such studies would not contribute to the understanding of the validity of the test. He was more encouraging to those who would attempt investigations wherein the "global" test pattern would be considered.

"A very small number of students have taken up the challenge which the test is setting up. The issue is being squarely joined. It is from that quarter that I look for hypotheses and a logic that will advance the science of the whole human personality. Whether this will be with the Rorschach, or any other test, will not then matter. Meanwhile and in absence of research more convincing toward refuting the validities that have emerged, there are still the ten Swiss ink-blots."

Beck utilized the first 19 pages of his 1952 volume to present his conception of personality. It should be recalled that his 1945 volume was sharply criticized by Harriman for failing to do this. In these 19 pages comprising the first chapter, Beck clearly aligns himself with the theoretical constructs of three basic schools of thought. The first is that represented by Hughlings Jackson in the field of neurology. The second, is the Freudian psychoanalytic movement, and the third is the Gestalt psychology of Lewin. In using these three sets of constructs Beck presented an uncompromising position that he preferred to think of the human personality as a single functioning unit. In fact, he "took to task" some of the personality theorists striving to break personality down into a variety of functional or operational components whereby the total or integrated operation of the personality would be neglected. In clearly setting forth his notions of personality, Beck also was able to make clearer his approach to Rorschach.

"This is th only concept of personality with which I find it possible to understand any individual. It is a position inductively arrived at from study of clinical data concerning patients with mental disease, paralleling investigations with the Rorschach test. It is an interpretation of the observed data, clinical and Rorschach, which accounts for all of these behaviors, whether as part manifestations, or as wholes. The thesis enables us to understand: (a) why the patient has symptoms and (b) why he suffers any mental disturbance or illness at all. When enough of the facts are available, i.e., when we have knowledge concerning that whole person, this concept explains also (c) the choice of the symptoms and (d) the choice of the disease."

In pointing to the whole orientation toward personality Beck in turn described a variety of Rorschach characteristics which would be representative of the functioning of that personality. For example;

"The essence of my argument is: the Rorschach Test summary of the response scorings is a cross-section representing the present outcome of stresses between the higher activities and the lower ones (Jackson), or between ego and id (Freud). This interpretation is inherent in the quantitative ratios obtaining between F+, C-Y, M,

W-Z; all in press (Murray) against one another, in one multidimensional set of operations."

In suggesting such indices Beck was careful to point out that neither algebraic nor geometric summations of Rorschach factors could simply equal personality.

"The various clinical manifestations are all intelligible and explicable by this rationale. They are those activities specifically characteristic for each person in a mental hopsital, those unique sets of behaviors, attitudes and emotions which make each patient so distinct. . . .This logic explains too why the whole Rorschach test personality picture cannot be derived by any additive procedure: so much F+ and so much M and so much Z and the others. . . .The problem is always what does a person operating so as to produce his nF do to his nM; what does nM do to his nZ; and what do the interrelated activities nF, nM, do to nZ and to the inter-relation nF, nZ and to all the other variables, separately, and in interrelation."

Beck was also willing to set forth a considerable amount of material concerning the operation of the ego in the Rorschach. Some of the material on ego functioning is selected directly from Beck's 1948 paper concerning the relationship of the F+ per cent and the ego. In Chapter 2, however, he goes considerably beyond the 1948 findings, devoting much of the material to the operation of ego defenses as manifest in the Rorschach. In describing the task of the interpreter Beck set forth four specific goals toward which interpretation would be oriented.

"A test that undertakes to test the whole human personality should provide a cross section of at least three sets of data; and better still, also a fourth. The three are: (a) he psychologic structures; (b) the current functioning; (c) the adaptive solution by the person of his life's problems. The fourth, when available, would un-cover something of the psychodynamics preceding the present status."

Beck maintained his ever-present cautiousness concerning the fourth goal of uncovering the psychodynamics, but was nevertheless reasonably optimistic.

"The data of the fourth variety are information as to premorbid events. Whether it is the Rorschach test or any other method of investigating the personality, results such as the above report both its anatomy and the live tissues. That is, by any method the results must give us a valid picture of a live human being, one striving in the several dimensions, who feels, thinks, and who attempts to maintain his psychologic homeostasis constant. . . .The structural data (of the Rorschach) are a record of impersonal psychologic forces, and the cross section they give is that of the personality as it has jelled at the time of testing. The concept reports something of the social direction of the personality. The one tells us what the individual is; the other where he has been. The structural summary is the essence of the Rorschach test personality. It is the first approach to interpretation; but it does not highlight the details of the person's functioning from moment to moment. The high and low tones emerge only in a response-for-response inspection. . . .Scrutiny of the individual responses, and of their technical treatment, i.e., their scorings, is therefore essential toward the interpretation. There are the details which fill in and complete the picture of the personality."

The specifics for interpretation offered by Beck in *Volume III* are considerably more detailed than had been the case in Volume II. The nature of the $F+$ per cent, for example, is discussed in much greater depth with special notation that $F-$ responses should be considered as to whether personalized or impersonalized, the former being found most frequently in neurotics and in healthy subjects whereas the latter occur most frequently in brain damaged, feeble-minded, and schizophrenics. It is also noted where the $F+$ per cent is too high that this also could be indicative of ego insufficiency, denoting an excessive clinging to accuracy. W and Z are also elaborated on in more detail, wherein W is suggested as indicative of the conceptual activity of the subject, and Z denoting a grasp of relations between the stimuli and the perceptual field. A high A percentage is indicated as common to the person whose "too cautious adaptation and thus too fearful clinging to most familiar stimuli raises this percentage. It may also show loss of spontaneity or dullness in responding to the events of one's world."

Beck describes the basic defensive operations in terms of two major categories. One is that of withdrawal, the second being the self-reinforcing defensive maneuvers. Indications of self-reinforcing types of defense are listed as an excess of Dd responses, the distortion of the approach, extremely high or extremely low Z scores, an $F+$ per cent out of balance with the record as a whole, a high A per cent, a high lambda, and general inflexibility manifest in the record by the utilization of fixed or monotonous phrases. He specifies the characteristics of the withdrawal defects as falling most notably in the existence of M and Y. In this regard, M is considered to outweigh the total quantity of C, a low A per cent, a low number of popular responses, and generally a stereotyped or personalized approach in the responses. In addition to describing the two basic modes of defensive operation, Beck also concentrates on the specifics of other defenses such as displacement, projection, and most specifically anxiety. By publishing at length and systematically Beck not only offers a clear view of his Rorschach orientation but also emphasizes the depth of his own involvement in the study of psychopathology. He also expands considerably on the interpretative concept of affect, especially as manifest in Color (the lively affects) and in Shading (the painful affects), especially Y and V.

Considerable space is also allowed in the 1952 volume for discussion of the M response. Again, Beck reaffirms Rorschach's notions of movement, and is especially careful to underscore his disagreement with the scoring of

FM or m. He is particularly concerned with clarifying the emotional status of the M dominated person. He describes the "M person" as one moved by strong emotions, emotions which the person prefers to contain internally, thereby converting them in some manner. He indicates that the neurotic converts these emotions into daydreams, the psychotic into autistic living, and the healthy adult into more acceptable sublimations. Beck reports that his research to date had indicated that more than six Ms would be judged as "high." He also reaffirms that the M response is a "favorite technic for projecting paranoid thinking" and pointed to the fact that the actual type of movement requires evaluation for adequate interpretation. In this respect he emphasized the value of interpreting the content in the M associations so as to attain some indications concerning the fantasy activity of the subject.

Possibly one of the most interesting sections in *Volume III* is that dealing with the Erlebnistypus. It will be recalled that in *Volume II* there was considerable hesitancy on Beck's part to offer interpretations of the Erlebnistypus. This is not the case in *Volume III* although he does continue to emphasize the uniqueness of the concept and the difficulties in its interpretation.

"An element of the mystic has attached to this concept of Rorschach's. It is a unique concept, not only in the field of personality, but in all of psychology. In this uniqueness lies the difficulty. Other test techniques have not envisaged this perspective of personality, and hence have not directed thinking to such an idea. . . .[It] tells not how the person actually lives at any given moment but how he could experience. . . .The nub of the matter is in Rorschach's identifying as 'experience' that which, in more familiar language is called the "inner-resources of the individual The [inner-resources] are products of strong emotions, of high intellectual grasp, at the level of creative imagination. These are the two psychologic sources from which the experience balance is fashioned: feeling pressures and fantasy living, C and M. . . .All this should take the experience balance out of the realm of mystery in which it has so consistently been enveloped. It is just one more personality factor or, rather, cluster of two factors, the workings of which make sense only within the setting of the personality as a whole. A broad, restricted, ambiequal, extratensive, introversive experience balance—each as a mental activity of the organ of mind, the brain."

In describing the technical interpretations of the Erlebnistypus Beck cited previous findings such as, in the ambiequal an obsessive compulsive component may be found. The coarcted Erlebnistypus results from a rigid hold by the subject over himself, the constricted balance being likely found in patients intellectually restrained to change or in the passive-apprehensive individual. The extratensive balance is noted in neurotic patterns, especially indicative of a hysterical structure or in psychosomatic illness. The introversive balance, in turn, is to be interpreted to indicate that the fantasy life is dominating the subject's inner life and may even occur in the depressed, withdrawn individual.

Beck also expands on his interpretation of White Space responses. He indiactes that he now prefers to convert White Space responses to a percentage rather than to an actual number which had previously been the case. He offers the interpretation that a significantly high percentage of S responses must be interpreted in light of the Erlebnistypus; that is, when it is ambiequal it highlights the obsessive compulsive condition; when it is extratensive, the person is having difficulty in controlling his impulses. He perceives the White Space, in general, as a form of tenacity or stubborness, the healthiness or lack of which could only be interpreted in light of the entire record. He suggests that a low percentage of S responses are found in the passive or suggestible or even depressed individuals. Another highlight of the 1952 volume is a reasonably large amount of space devoted to the interpretation of content. Here he dealt specifically with different types of scorings for content and offered a variety of hypotheses concerning each.

In all respects *Volume III* presents a comprehensive Beck System, free of many of the cautious restrictions which Beck had imposed upon himself in his earlier writings. It is clear that by this time he was not only an expert in the Rorschach, but comfortable with his expertise, a comfort which had evolved, as he cited, from both his clinical work and the research which he had completed.

While the publication of *Rorschach's Test: Volume III* did, in a manner of speaking, bring completion to the development of the main body of the Beck System, Beck has continued to work toward further refinement. He also became deeply involved in the study of schizophrenia and in 1954 published his classic monograph, "The Six Schizophrenias," which, while adding important information on the psychotic process, also demonstrated the sophistication to which the Beck System of Rorschach had come, in that the data collected was done so in part to test out the Rorschach as a tool to detect schizophrenia. Consequently, the remainder of Beck's publications during the 1950's concentrated largely on the use of the technique as a research and diagnostic instrument for the study of psychosis, schizophrenia in particular.

In 1960, Beck strongly reafirms his "blind analysis" approach in Rorschach interpretation. This is done in his book, *The Rorschach Experiment: Ventures in Blind Diagnosis.* Once again he uses the case-study method elaborating in detail on his own interpretative reasoning. Eight cases are presented accompanied by lengthy discussion. Beck's purpose is stated quite clearly in the foreword.

"The objective of the present book is to demonstrate the processes entering into the interpretation of a Rorschach test protocol, the path the examiner travels from the raw data of the test—the patient's 'butterfly' or his 'two girls dancing an oopsie-daisy'—to the clinical report which he turns over to the therapist. In so doing, I also show the clinically meaningful material that can be obtained from an adequate set of test associations obtained, that is, while adhering strictly to the test data."

Beck sets forth his argument favoring the "blind" approach to test data by seizing upon, and elaborating about, Rorschach's original conception of the word "experiment." He is quick to point out that experimentation, if defined as a rigid application of laboratory-type experimental methodology, is inappropriate and impossible in dealing with the total human personality. He maintains, however, that, applying a broader criteria for experimentation, the whole human being can be studied effectively and with great accuracy.

"No more than any other psychiatrist was Rorschach interested in conducting controlled laboratory experiments on humans. He did not seek to vary his patients and observe what would happen under fixed conditions. But he did have varied groups of patients, and he invented an instrument which he could hold fixed. Far from subjecting his patients to any instrument, he subjected the instrument to his patients. The ten ink-blots constituted his dependent variable. The different groups of patients were his independent variables. . . .Rorschach then observed the varying behavior of his ink-blots under the different circumstances, the behavior which, for purposes of convenience, he labeled W, D, Dd, M, C, thought content, and the various other data of his test. This was Rorschach's experiment. . . .After observation the next step is reasoning. Rorschach could not but be intrigued by certain clusterings in his data. They showed a propensity for adhering in pattern, constant for each clinical condition and varying from one condition to another. This was still observation, but it went a step beyond—to what we are in the habit of calling experimental results. It is at this point in an experiment that thinking—interpretation is the word used technically—begins. Rorschach reasoned about his results in the light of his knowledge of psychopathology. . . .Translating these data into psychologic terms and converting his patterns into known diagnostic pictures, he arrived at his logic concerning the organization of the personality. . . .The bulk of his exposition is given over to this thinking and to the concept of the Erlebnistypus, of 'experience type.' "

Using this more broadly based definition of experimentation, Beck proceeds to describe his own eventual "settling on" a theoretical approach to Rorschach data, namely that which he had previously discussed in *Volume III* as the integration of the theoretical positions of Hughlings Jackson, Sigmund Freud, and Kurt Lewin.

Turning to the specifics of the "blind" approach Beck issues a strong warning to any who might be prone to the interpretation of Rorschach data with preconceived sets or with the naive assumption that only that which is quantified is interpretable. He emphasizes the use of all test data available which he defines as being, in addition to the structural findings manifest in the scorings, the array of "non-measurable, non-normative, and entirely qualitative observations" such as card turning, body shifts, and the variety of non-response vocalizations. He also stresses that the concept of "qualitative" data does not necessarily imply subjective data and should not include examiner opinion.

"The requirement behavior is paramount. The behavior recorded must be, like Caesar's wife, above suspicion is that of the subject. . . .On the question of 'blind' diagnosis and the test as clinical instrument, a confusion of issues persists. The issue and the confusion are those which exist between any technique as (a) an experiment and (b) its application to a practical situation in whatever field for which it has been invented, clinical or otherwise. The experimenter, to cite Bernard, puts certain questions to nature and is 'confronted with a real observation that he has induced and must note, like any other observation, without any preconceived idea.' The preconceived idea is the dog in the manger in much clinical psychology diagnosis, and it is an especial hazard in Rorschach test diagnosis. Information in the patient's clinical chart may provide clues to the condition and so channelize the psychologist's thinking, causing him to arrive at 'astounding' diagnostic formulations. These are not diagnoses from the test data, however, but from other behaviors. In 'blind' diagnosis, on the other hand, the examiner uses an instrument to ask his questions. From the answers obtained, as validated by the usual method of experiment and statistics he applies himself to the problem presented by his patient. At this point, reasoning intervenes . . . that is after he has read his instrument the psychologist asks for the clinical chart and studies his test findings, which have been obtained without preconceived idea, in light of the clinical problem. He steps out of the role of experimenter and into that of clinician."

Beck also strongly reaffirms in the 1960 text the same demands and expectancies for background and training for the user of the Rorschach that he had many years previously, namely, experience in psychopathology, personal analysis, experience using the test with many clinical groups, an orientation to the Rorschach-Oberholzer tradition, and a sound training in experimental psychology. He accents the need for a "rigorous self-discipline in objectivity" noting that the data obtained are those "of a field force constituted not of two variables only but of three: patient, test, and examiner."

While using the basic content of *The Rorschach Experiment* to demonstrate the process of test interpretation (as opposed to any attempt to validate the technique), Beck also uses the occasion to offer still further refined interpretation of the Erlebnistypus, the concept which, as has been previously noted, perplexed him for a number of years. In adding new substance to his interpretation of the Erlebnistypus, Beck included a chapter in the text on the "Experience Actual" which he cites as being drawn from Rorschach's concept of *Ambitendenz*. While he does not alter his previous conceptions of Erlebnistypus, he offers the Experience Actual as the key to interpretive understanding of the Erlebnistypus. In fact, he suggests that the Experience Actual represents the "total" Erlebnistypus.

"The M and C behaviors do not inform us as to the personal dynamics, but they are a means of entry and light up the psychologic processes as processes. They tell what the person is like in terms of process, or psychologic structure. Rorschach likes the term 'apparat.' The concept appears to be at one with Freud's 'psychologic economy.' . . .From the M and C we know the degree to which feelings play a role in the person's living pattern, but we do not yet know what the ideas are which they energize. . . .The Experience Actual indicates what we can expect of the subject in terms of emotional force, timber, depth, range. To know what he does with this emotional equipment, or what it does with him, we need to know all the rest of his test pattern, to have before us all the other data that contribuite to the in terpretation of a test record: the tabulations and qualitative structure and content. That is to say that we evaluate Experience Actual just as Rorschach evaluates Experience Balance. . . ."

In contending with the interpretative process of the Erlebnistypus and the Experience Actual Beck draws on the contributions of three philosophers, Dilthey, Husserl, and Spranger, for the concepts of understanding, purified phenomenology, and meaning, respectively. In doing so there is an obvious hint that he is more willing to moderate his traditional behavioristic orientation by injecting into Rorschach interpretation phenomenological characteristics thus possibly bringing him closer to Klopfer's orientation. But this is only a hint, and it is carefully delineated and qualified.

"Overt behaviors in the Rorschach test are M and C, while in life they would be the observable acts whereby we usually judge people. From acts we infer certain underlying personality activities in our friends, colleagues, or patients. How do we arrive at these inferences? We know from their words and actions the feelings and intents that accompany them because we have those feelings and intents when speaking and behaving similarly. . . .The essence of it is: we have lived or known the experience and related behaviors now being objectified in the subject's or patient's behavior and so can reason from his present behavior to his inner experience. Rorschach's M and C—always assuming validity—elicit these behaviors through the instrumentality of the fixed and controllable tool. Our understanding of others is always an inferential process. Phenomenologic though the data may be, they can only be known from some behavior—whether verbal or acted out behavior. The associations to the Rorschach tests are verbal behavior elicited under the standard microcosm which the ten ink-blots set up. It follows from the foregoing that one's understanding of the other has as its limits his own experience potential."

It would appear that while Beck is willing to concede the necessity for phenomenological interpretation between the examiner and the subject, using the test as the instrument of communication and experience, he does not temper his commitment to behavioristic requirements. Quite the contrary, there is the inference that phenomenological experience, as adequate interpretation, can only proceed if the basic demands of behavioristic objectivity are first fulfilled. Beck also offers in the first six chapters of the text interpretative material which previously he had not written on at any significant length. This involves the signs of prognosis, treatment recommendations, defenses, and transference. While none of these are discussed in great detail, each is considered in much more depth than may be found in earlier publications and in some instances, such as transference, his thinking on topics is offered for the first time.

In 1967, a long awaited revision of *Rorschach's Test: Volume II* was published in collaboration with Herman Molish. The revision follows the traditional Beck format, that is, utilization of the case study method. Here Beck offers 29 cases, the protocols of each analyzed exhaustively. Seventeen of these cases are taken from the 1945 volume but each with a fresh, more extensive interpretation. The first twenty pages of the text offer an exposition on the interpretive postulates. This exposition, for the most part, clarifies and extends hypotheses put forth in the 1952 *Volume III* and the 1960 text on blind analysis. Postulates concerning the relation of Color and Shading to affect are stated more clearly and consisely. A section on Movement answers gives greater emphasis to the fact that M is also emotion and discusses its adaptive nature, stressing again the necessity for evaluating M's in light of stance, psychological components, themes, and of course, in relation to the total protocol. The Erlebnistypus and Experience Actual are described in terms of the Freudian concept of "mental economics," accenting the understanding of the total emotional resources as applied to an understanding of overt behaviors. The characteristics of affective quality and intensity are portrayed more completely than in any previous discourse by Beck. He emphasizes the need to consider the Color and Shading components together as related to the total Form involvement. On this issue, he elaborates on a "pain-pleasure dimension," indicating how the Rorschach factors can be used to understand this dimension more fully. The last several chapters of the text, written by Molish, are devoted to an extensive review of the literature on the various components, intelligence, the ego and reality testing, affect, the Shading elements as subdued affects, and to content.

This then constitutes the development of the Beck System to this time. Unquestionably it is a total System, but it can also be said with great certainty that Beck himself would not consider it a "closed issue." Even after forty years of methodical investment in experimentation and practice with the Rorschach, Beck would be the first to proclaim that many questions are still unanswered or only partially answered. In fact, in the closing section of the revised *Volume II* he states, "Those younger persons who will be using the test will confirm what is sound. They will discard what they cannot confirm. They will go on from there. It is the way of all scientific flesh." Nevertheless, the Beck System, as such, constitutes a monumental achievement wherein the technique has been approached methodically and cautiously, maintaining the self-imposed traditions of behavioristic empiricism and all of its accompanying demands. In many respects the Beck System might be considered as the most inclusive developed by any of the Systematizers. Certainly this would be true if the base of nomothetic data is to be used as a judgmental criteria. It might well also be true if most any other judgmental approach is used. The question as to whether his failure to reconcile his Rorschach approach with that of the other Systematizers has been an asset or a liability in terms of the end product will be considered in a later chapter. But regardless of that issue, there is no question but that Beck has methodically and conscientiously pursued the "Rorschach-Oberholzer" tradition to the utmost, and therefore, quite probably represents a System of approaching the technique which would be highly compatible with, if not identical to, that which would have been purported by Rorschach himself were he to have lived for a longer period of time.

REFERENCES

Beck, S. J. Personality diagnosis by means of the Rorschach test. *Amer. J. Orthopsychiat.*, 1930, 1, 81-88.

Beck, S. J. The Rorschach test and personality diagnosis. I. The Feeble-minded. *Amer. J. Psychiat.*, 1930, 10, 19-52.

Beck, S. J. The Rorschach test in problem children. *Amer. J. Orthopsychiat.*, 1931, 1, 501-511.

Beck, S. J. The Rorschach test as applied to a feeble-minded group. *Arch. of Psychol.*, 1932, No. 136, Pp. 84.

Beck, S. J. Configurational tendencies in Rorschach responses. *Psychol. Bull.*, 1932, 29, 632.

Beck, S. J. The Rorschach method and personality organization. Balance in personality. *Amer. J. Psychiat.*, 1933, 13, 519-532.

Beck, S. J. The Rorschach method and the organization of personality. *Amer. J. Orthopsychiat.*, 1933, 3, 361-365.

Beck, S. J. Configurational tendencies in Rorschach responses. *Amer. J. Psychol.*, 1933, 45, 433-443.

Beck, S. J. The Rorschach method and personality organization. *Amer. J. Orthopsychiat.*, 1934, 4, 290-297.

Beck, S. J. Psychological processes, and traits, in Rorschach findings. *Psychol. Bull.*, 1935, 32, 683-684.

Beck, S. J. Problems of further research in the Rorschach test. *Amer. J. Orthopsychiat.*, 1935, 5, 100-115.

Beck, S. J. Autism in Rorschach scoring: a feeling comment. *Character & Pers.*, 1936, 5, 83-85.

Beck, S. J. Introduction to the Rorschach method: a manual of personality study. *Amer. Orthopsychiat Ass. Monogr.*, 1937, No. 1, Pp. XV + 278.

Beck, S. J. Some recent research problems. *Rorschach Res. Exch.*, 1937, 2, 15-22.

Beck, S. J. Psychological processes in Rorschach findings. *J. Abnorm. Soc. Psychol.*, 1937, 31, 482-488.

Beck, S. J. Personality structure in schizophrenia: a Rorschach investigation in 81 patients and 64 controls. *Nerv. Ment. Dis. Monogr.*, 1938, No. 63, Pp. ix + 88.

Beck, S. J. Thoughts on an impending anniversary. *Amer. J. Orthopsychiat.*, 1939, 9, 806-808.

Beck, S. J. Sources of error in Rorschach test procedures. *Psychol. Bull.*, 1940, 37, 517-518.

Beck, S. J. Error, symbol, and method in the Rorschach test. *J. Abnorm. Soc. Psychol.*, 1942, 37, 83-103.

Beck, S. J. Stability of the personality structure. *Psychol. Bull.*, 1942, 39, 512.

Beck, S. J. Effects of shock therapy on personality, as shown by the Rorschach test. *Arch. Neurol. Psychiat.*, Chicago, 1943, 50, 483-484.

Beck, S. J. The Rorschach test in psychopathology. *J. Consult. Psychol.*, 1943, 7, 103-111.

Beck, S. J. The Rorschach test in a case of character neurosis. *Amer. J. Orthopsychiat.*, 1944, 14, 230-236.

Beck, S. J. *Rorschach's Test I*: Basic processes. New York: Grune & Stratton, 1944, Pp. xiii + 223.

Beck, S. J. *Rorschach's Test II*: A variety of personality pictures. New York: Grune & Stratton, 1945, Pp. xii + 402.

Beck, S. J. The Rorschach experiment: progress and problems. *Amer. J. Orthopsychiat.*, 1945, 15, 520-524.

Beck, S. J. Trends in orthopsychiatric therapy. II. Rorschach F plus and the ego treatment. *Amer. J. Orthopsychiat.*, 1948, 18, 395-401.

Beck, S. J. *Rorschach's Test. I*. Basic processes. (2nd ed., rev.) New York: Grune & Stratton, 1949, xiii, 227 p.

Beck, S. J., Rabin, A. I., Thiesen, W. G., Molish, H. and Thetford, W. N. The normal personality as projected in the Rorschach test. *J. Psychol.*, 1950, 30, 241-298.

Beck, S. J. Emotional experience as a necessary constituent in knowing. In Reymert, M. L., *Feelings and Emotions*, N. Y.: McGraw-Hill, 1950, pp. 95-107.

Beck, .S J. The experimental validation of the Rorschach test. IV. Discussion and critical evaluation. *Amer. J. Orthopsychiat.*, 1952, 22, 771-775.

Beck, S. J. *Rorschach's Test. III*. Advances in interpretation. New York: Grune & Stratton, 1952, viii, 301 p.

Beck, S. J. and Nunally, J. C. Two researches in schizophrenia. *Amer. J. Orthopsychiat.*, 1953, 23, 222-237.

Beck, S. J. Tests of personality: Rorschach techniques: A Rorschach test. In Weider, A., *Contributions Toward Medical Psychology*. New York: Ronald Press, 1953, 2 vols., pp. 599-610.

Beck, S. J. The six schizophrenias. *Res. Monogr. Amer. Orthopsychiat. Ass.*, 1954, No. 6, 238 p.

Beck, S. J. Personality research and theories of personality structure: some convergences. *J. Proj. Tech.*, 1955, 19, 361-371.

Beck, S. J., Molish, H. B. and Sinclair, J. Current status of the Rorschach test. Symposium, 1955, 3. Concerning researchers' thinking in schizophrenia research. *Amer. J. Orthopsychiat.*, 1956, 26, 792-800.

Beck, S. J. The light-dark determinant in the Rorschach test. *Rorschachiana*, V, 1956, 179-193.

Beck, S. J. *The Rorschach Experiment*: Ventures in Blind Diagnosis. New York: Grune & Stratton, 1960, viii, 256 p.

Beck, S. J., Beck, A. G., Levitt, E. E. and Molish, H. B. *Rorschach's Test. I*. Basic processes. (3rd ed.) New York: Grune & Stratton, 1961, x, 237 p.

Beck, S. J. Rorschach's Erlebnistypus: An empiric datum. *Rorschachiana*, VIII, 1963, 8-25.

Beck, S. J. and Molish, H. *Rorschach's Test. II*. A variety of personality pictures. (2nd ed. rev.) New York: Grune & Stratton, 1967.

Levy, D. M. and Beck, S. J. The Rorschach test in manic-depressive psychosis. In *Manic-Depressive Psychosis*. Baltimore: Williams & Wilkins, 1931, Pp. 167-181.

Levy, D. M. and Beck, S. J. The Rorschach test in manic-depressive psychosis. *Amer. J. Orthopsychiat.*, 1934, 4, 31-42.

Molish, H. B. and Beck, S. J. Psychoanalytic concepts and principles discernible in projective personality tests: III. Mechanisms of defense in schizophrenic reaction types as evaluated by the Rorschach test. *Amer. J. Orthopsychiat.*, 1958, 28, 47-60.

Rabin, A. I. and Beck, S. J. Genetic aspects of some Rorschach factors. *Amer. J. Orthopsychiat.*, 1950, 20, 595-599.

Thetford, W. N., Molish, H. B. and Beck, S. J. Developmental aspects of personality structure in normal children. *J. Proj. Tech.*, 1951, 15, 58-78.

CHAPTER 6

THE PIOTROWSKI SYSTEM

Piotrowski's decision to use the Rorschach Method came nearly eight years after he had received his Doctorate in experimental psychology at the University of Poznan in Poland. He came to the United States in 1931 with the intention of returning to Europe in a year or, at best, two. But two years led to three, and three to four, and so on, and fortunately for American psychology, he eventually decided to make the United States his permanent residence. He had been aware of the existence of the Rorschach, having been a subject of the test as an undergraduate, but had given it no serious consideration during his years of graduate training nor even shortly thereafter. In fact, had it not been for the encouragement of Gladys Tallman who was among those responsible for organizing Klopfer's first seminar on the Rorschach, Piotrowski might well have continued to pursue other interests. Almost immediately after his introduction to the technique by Klopfer, Piotrowski became more and more enchanted with the possibilities for research especially in the area of psychodiagnostics and psychopathology.

Piotrowski's undergraduate training in mathematics and his subsequent strong commitment to "objectivity," plus his graduate training in experimental psychology, almost certainly predisposed the fact that he could not ultimately accept Klopfer's phenomenological orientation. Nevertheless, during his first four years of Rorschach involvement, he remained committed to the Klopfer orientation.

Piotrowski's early preoccupations with the Rorschach, as a diagnostic instrument, centered on organic disturbances. In 1936 he published three articles concerning the use of the instrument with organics. All three employed the case study method as was common for the time. In one of these articles, "On The Rorschach Method and its Application in Organic Disturbances of the Central Nervous System," Piotrowski presented data obtained from 33 protocols, taken from three clinical groups.* From these data he postulated the existence of what has come to be known as the 10 Piotrowski Rorschach signs of organic abnormality. He suggested that these signs could differentiate cortical and subcortical involvement from

---

* The sample was comprised of 18 organic cases with cerebral cortical involvement, 10 with non-cerebral disturbances of the central nervous system, and 5 of conversion hysteria.

non-cerebral involvement and also from the conversion hysteria neurosis. He noted that the differences between the cortically involved group and the other groups occurred in the quantitative data but not in the qualitative data. Thus, it is apparent that, as early as 1936, Piotrowski was seeking to obtain precise quantification of his data, and of differences which that data might reveal in differentiating diagnostic groups.

In 1937, one of Piotrowski's most widely cited articles was published. This was the article pertaining to the differentiation of Movement responses in the Rorschach. Klopfer had previously suggested scoring of FM for responses involving animal Movement. In the 1937 article Piotrowski suggested a third scoring category, that of m for responses involving Movement of inanimate objects. He offered a general hypothesis concerning the significance of FM and m responses as contrasted with human Movement responses. It was probably this article, more than any other characteristic of Piotrowski's writings, which precluded the possibility of his eventual alignment with the Beck System. It also laid the basic foundations for a schism between Piotrowski and Klopfer which was later to become much wider and unreconcilable. By 1938 Piotrowski was rapidly drawing away from the Klopfer group and by 1940 this withdrawal was essentially complete. As late as 1942, however, Piotrowski attempted to demonstrate that there was still considerable agreement between himself, Klopfer, Rorschach, Binder, and Beck. This was done through a publication of a comparative table of the main Rorschach symbols used by each.

One of the factors contributing to the differentiation between Piotrowski and Klopfer, and the other Systematizers, has been Piotrowski's unwillingness to devote himself to a personality theory as applicable to the Rorschach method. At some point in time between 1936 and 1942, Piotrowski became convinced that the Rorschach approach of the Systematizers was overly "theory oriented" at the expense of a more accurate description of the unique nature of the person. His objection to this orientation eventually led to the development of his System for the Rorschach, which he described as "Perceptanalysis." This position is expressed well in his book *Perceptanalysis* which appeared in 1957. He argues that, contrary to popular opinion, the validity of the method is not related to any theory of personality. Quite the contrary, he finds that the technique is compatible with any personality theory indicating that any characteristic found in the Rorschach can be interpreted psychoanalytically, sociologically, physiologically, educationally, or by any combination of concepts or orientations. He expresses the notion that a neutrality of orientation may, in fact, contribute to a greater flexibility of interpretation of the data as it is presented in the test.

Several factors probably were influential in causing Piotrowski to take a position different from the basic Klopfer orientation and into the development of a system of Perceptanalysis. First, having been trained as a mathematician in his undergraduate years and an experimental psychologist in his graduate work, he no doubt found it difficult to identify with the strongly phenomenological approach of Klopfer. Secondly, there was the fact that, at the time of learning the Rorschach from Klopfer and shortly thereafter, Piotrowski was concentrating much of his work energy to the study of organic conditions, which oriented him toward a somewhat different perspective with regard to pathology and patient populations. Third, and possibly most important, was his relationship with Kurt Goldstein. Goldstein had come to the United States as a refugee and beginning in early 1938 Piotrowski, while working one day a week at Mt. Sinai Hospital in New York City, formed a very close relationship with him. Goldstein had already made a significant "mark" and would continue to do so through his writings on the thought process and especially the areas of concept formation and abstraction. Goldstein gave Piotrowski strong encouragement to pursue the utilization of the Rorschach in the diagnosis of organic conditions and in fact, Piotrowski's ultimate "settling upon" his "ten signs" of organic involvement resulted from this work. Piotrowski had already begun to use Rorschach to study the projections of organically involved patients and had published on this in 1936. Goldstein now added much fuel to that fire in the form of encouragement and also through some conceptual postulates concerning the functioning of the organic patient. Fourth, due to his training in experimental psychology, Piotrowski must have found himself with an orientation toward the study of people lying somewhere between the comprehensive phenomenology of Klopfer and the behavioristic demands for objectivity of Beck. Some hint of this is found in the quotation from his first article in 1936.

"The use of statistics implies some arbitrary dogmatism; it always involves an attempt to force reality into discontinuous divisions. The aim of the Rorschach method is an adequate and as complete as possible qualitative description of real individuals and not of non-existent averages. The spirit of the method is empirical and not historical (statistical). However, statistics have their place and this is in diagnosis. When we try to make diagnostic suggestions with the aid of the Rorschach method we must have a good description of the patient's personality and additionally we must know what are the personality types found in the different diagnostic categories. This knowledge can be obtained only through statistical studies which, however, must be preceded by qualitative personality analysis."

Whatever the causes, it is quite clear that by 1939-40, Piotrowski had modified his approach to scoring Rorschach records in a manner somewhat different than that of Klopfer. In his 1942 article comparing his method of scoring with that of Rorschach, Binder, Beck, and Klopfer he concluded that except for the symbols for Shading determinants, animal Movement responses, and for Color naming, considerable agreement existed among the five scoring systems. In doing so, however, he failed to point out the rather significant differences which had evolved regarding interpretation, especially regarding Movement responses.

By 1947 his departure from the Klopfer System of scoring and interpretation was nearly complete. His publication, *A Rorschach Compendium*, was presented with the aim to consider the recent developments in his scoring symbols and their interpretative significance. He recommended in the *Compendium* that the beginning students of the technique should have clearly defined for them the assumptions and implications underlying the scoring symbols. He placed great emphasis on the interdependence of the scoring components, discussing inter-relationships of Movement, Color, Shading, and Form responses. He also reaffirmed in a more systematic manner his scoring scheme for Shading responses. Possibly of greatest significance in the *Compendium* was his stress on the idea that the Rorschach method, in and by itself, is not based on a specific theory of personality and that, to the contrary, could be applicable to almost any personality theory. In 1950 the *Compendium* was revised and enlarged, a publication which laid the basic groundwork for the text *Perceptanalysis*. The revised *Compendium* comprised what might be considered as the first crystallized manifestation of the Piotrowski System. Even though his independence from Klopfer had been expressed in earlier articles, it was here in a consolidated fashion that his differences with Klopfer and the other Systematizers could be fully perceived for the first time.

ADMINISTRATION

Piotrowski's suggested method of administration for the Rorschach is, in many respects, much more liberal than either that suggested by Beck or Klopfer.

"Rorschach gave a plate and asked, 'What might this be?' In the present era of intense psychological testing, it is prudent to add: 'You may turn it around any way you like,' to dispel any impression of procedural rigidity. This simple direction is satisfactory in most cases. Occasionally, when dealing with a very suspicious or greatly-inhibited individual, Rorschach explained the blots were accidental and tried to alleviate the testee's anxiety. This procedure is followed generally—with minor variations. It is advisable to adapt the verbal directions to the intelligence, education, and mood of the subject, as well as to the rapport existing between him and the examiner. When questions are asked about the purpose of the examination, it is best to evade them by a mute gesture or some equivocal words if this is feasible without increasing whatever tension the testee may have about the examination. As most subjects regard it as a test of imagination, the purpose of the examination may be described by saying, 'Well, I'd like you to see what you can say about this, what kind of imagination you have. All sorts of things can be seen in clouds and in this too,' or something to that effect. . . . Sometimes a person thinks he is expected to give only his first response, or the strangest, or the best. . . . should they ask questions about this, they ought to be instructed: 'Tell me all things this resembles, or makes you think of.' "

In essence then, Piotrowski uses an instructional set which goes beyond Klopfer but not quite as far as Beck. But then Piotrowski offers even more substance to the instructions, which appears to go even beyond Beck.

"It has been the writer's practice to keep silent during the first minute of each plate and start pressing for a response during the second if the subject fails to give any scorable response during the first minute. If the testee returns the plate before the first minute is up, the plate is given back and he is encouraged with, 'It looks like something, doesn't it?' or with similar words. . . . The seating arrangement should be the most natural one. Placing the subject in front of, and with his back toward the examiner may cause discomfort and therefore should be done only if better cooperation and greater freedom of association can thus be secured."

With these last suggestions, Piotrowski not only makes the role of the examiner somewhat more forceful, in that he nearly prohibits rejections of the cards, but also pointedly disagrees with both the Beck and Klopfer methods for seating arrangement. These same instructions are offered in the 1957 text, *Perceptanalysis* with the additional suggestion that, "When the subject does not turn Plate I around he is told in a casual tone that he may do so. Even when the subject has given a response but has not turned the plate, he is encouraged to turn the plate."

In both the 1947 *Compendium* and in the 1957 text Piotrowski refers to a "Beck-like" Inquiry, wherein the principle aim is to elucidate the scoring of the responses. To this he adds a second aim.

"The second aim of the inquiry is to collect additional data. These are of three kinds: (1) percepts which have occurred to the subject during the original examination but which he failed to communicate; (2) new percepts which the subject produces during the inquiry and which are treated as genuine responses; and (3) elaborations upon the original percepts, which the subject is invited and encouraged to give whenever the examiner believes that a full and unequivocal interpretation of the subject's percept is impossible without additional clarification."

Piotrowski also stresses the importance of examining Movement responses carefully to determine whether they are really Movement of a kinesthetic nature or whether the percept is really static. He suggests that the Klopfer method of Testing the Limits is advisable "when the subject is certain not to be retested," but he points out that "Testing the Limits, however, complicates the interpretation of a repeat Rorschach examination if the repeat record comprises percepts which were proposed by the examiner during the early examination."

Piotrowski is also firm in the 1957 text on his point that there is no differentiation between the Free Association responses and the material elicited from the Inquiry in terms of personality evaluation. This point had been raised previously by Beck and had been discussed specifically by Levin (1953) who had suggested that really two different psychological tests are involved, one occurring in Free Association, the second in the Inquiry. In response to Levin's argument Piotrowski offers the following:

"According to Levin, the important motives and the more personal attitudes are much more likely to be expressed frankly and without modifications, caused by fear of what others might think, during the performance proper than during the inquiry; the latter is likely to reveal ego defenses and the 'icing of rationality.' . . . it is based on the assumption that the conscious and the unconscious can be separated temporally and that the unconscious appears first, in the performance proper, while the conscious waits until the inquiry to make itself felt. This assumption seems hardly tenable. Theoretically, the conscious and the unconscious are believed to be intertwined so intimately that one cannot appear without the other in any overt action of a person . . . in fact, the 'ego defenses' usually are more prominent during the performance proper than during the inquiry . . . experience has shown that frequently the most disturbing, unpleasant, and malignant responses are obtained during the inquiry."

SCORING

Piotrowski describes his conception of scoring as one in which the symbols serve a function of a dictionary by which the examinee's responses may be translated into a description of his attitudes and tendencies pertaining to interpersonal relationships. The symbol system used is oriented toward the notion that the record would provide a most reliable and valid summary of the individual's personality. He argues that the most reliable test conclusions concerning the structure of personality are those derived from the "formal" characteristics of the percepts, i.e., size, location, determinants, content, etc. He maintains that, assuming a scoring method which is easily applied, the formal features of the percepts are more reliable than analysis of the verbalizations of the responses. He also points out that the formal perceptual characteristics, especially the determinants, are beyond the conscious control of the subject. In other words, a subject may consciously withhold sexual, aggressive, or other seemingly derogatory or undesirable content, but he cannot withhold responses deliberately because they are determined by Movement, or Color, or Shading unless he is well trained in the principles of the Rorschach and decides to attempt deception. Piotrowski also suggests that these more formal features of the percepts are not influenced by transient and superficial environmental changes as is specific content. In the 1957 text Piotrowski offered some clarification concerning his orientation toward simplicity in scoring.

"The more elaborate the classification system, the more difficult it is to apply and to interpret it. The simpler it is, the easier it is to apply and to interpret it, but the more data are left out of it. The ideal system is one which is elaborate enough to encompass the most important data needed for a satisfactory personality analysis and simple enough to permit valid generalizations about the significance of the whole scoring system and each of its parts."

Piotrowski's scheme for scoring Location is shown in Table 5 as it has evolved from his 1942 article through the 1957 text, and as it compares with Rorschach's original suggestions for scoring Location. Until 1957 Piotrowski was prone to agree with the basic Klopfer scores for Location but did not adopt Klopfer's suggestions that rare or unusual detail responses be further subdivided beyond the use of the small d symbol. In addition, he did not incorporate the use of the cut-off whole (W̶), nor of the scoring of "additional" Location symbols. In regard to the latter, he utilizes the traditional Rorschach method of combining symbols such as Ws or Ds. It is also of interest to note that he continues the utilization of the Do response as suggested by Rorschach although both Beck and Klopfer had discarded or modified this in their own Systems.

DETERMINANTS

Piotrowski's approach to the scoring for Determinants is closely related to his overall conception of the test, that is, as one based on perception. In 1957 he clarified his position concerning the importance of the Determinant component of the response by suggesting that it reveals the manner in which the person relates to his world. He contrasts the Determinant factor with the Location element, which he describes as the "scope of the tasks the individual is willing to tackle actively and the efficiency with which he solves problems." He cautions that the Determinant is often ascertained less reliably than is the Location element but concedes that their analysis offers valid data concerning the experiences and "action tendencies" that are of the greatest importance and deepest intensity for the subject. Table 6 indicates the transition of scoring Determinants in the Piotrowski System from 1942 through 1957, and as contrasted with those suggested by Rorschach.

From examination of Table 6 it will be noted that the Piotrowski System, as early as 1942, manifests several distinct differences from that purported by Rorschach, as well as that suggested by the other Systematizers. These differences are most notable with regard to Movement and Shading responses. Piotrowski sets forth three basic requirements for the

TABLE 5

A Comparison of the Piotrowski Method of Scoring Location
from 1942 to 1957 with that Originally Suggested by Rorschach

Symbol	Rorschach	Piotrowski—1942	Piotrowski—1947-50	Piotrowski—1957
W	Plate interpreted as a whole	Same	Same	Same (Includes responses to Card III which encompass only the main gray areas)
DW	Plate interpreted as a whole secondarily, the answer based primarily on a detail	Same	Not mentioned but scored in records during this period	Same but specifically reserved for the confabulated response. Always scored –
D	A normal detail of the plate	Same	Same (Based on blot areas frequently selected by healthy subjects)	Same (Definition slightly modified as "the normal or large-detail" frequently selected by healthy subjects)
Dr	Not used	Not used	Not used	A rare version of a normal detail where a percept includes a D area plus some adjacent area(s) or where 2 or more D are combined
d	Not used	Small or rare detail (For responses to areas rarely selected by healthy subjects)	Same	Same (Clarified as any response which is not scorable as W, D, or Dr)
S	White intermediate figures (space detail)	Same	Same	Same (Suggested that when several space responses occur in a record they should be sub-divided by size using S for large areas, s for small areas)
Do	A detail is interpreted in place of a whole	Not used	Not mentioned but scored in records during this period	Defined as same as Rorschach

scoring of the human Movement response (M). First, it must be accompanied by a feeling of muscular tension; second it must describe humans or animals behaving like humans, and third; a requirement which Piotrowski describes as "technical," "the blot itself should be so ambiguous as to make percepts of any type of movement or posture about equally plausible." This same prerequisite has been set forth and elaborated upon in greater detail in the 1957 text. In fact, it will be evident in the section on interpretation that the existence and interpretation of M responses forms the cornerstone of the Piotrowski System. Thus, he became very cautious in his elaboration on the existence of M and the matter of its interpretation without neglecting color and shading.

In the 1957 text Piotrowski points out that he considers the scoring for M to be one of the "thorniest" problems.

"The reason for these difficulties in scoring seems to lie in the incompleteness of Rorschach's technical definition of the M. He started out by saying that movement responses are those interpretations of the blots which are determined by a perception of form plus kinesthetic additions; the subject imagines that the object is in motion. According to him, it is the felt movement, not the movement rationally inferred, which changes the form responses into movement responses. . . . From the manner in which Rorschach scored cases in his book and in the Appendix, it is clear that he knew this (M occurring in stationary figures) very well for he himself classified as M not only overt movements but all kinds of posture as well. Thus, we can disregard his statement that the object must be imagined in motion for a response to be scored as M. . . . There seems to be no deliberate intention on the part of anyone using Rorschach's Perceptanalysis to score the M in any way other than that suggested by Rorschach. In practice the actual differences stem from the difficulty of deciding whether or not the movement or pose 'perceived' in the blot was accompanied by felt sensations in the muscles of the subject's body. . . . Since it is often difficult to determine the presence or absence of the kinesthetic innervation, it is imperative to pay attention to the other conditions of scoring the M."

Statements such as these demonstrate that Piotrowski painstakingly has considered Rorschach's intentions with regard to M. The inference is that if Rorschach's conception for scoring M is valid, Piotrowski's prerequisites for scoring M therefore also become valid. Thus, the antecedents of the three prerequisites for scoring M as outlined in the 1950 *Compendium* are reaffirmed in the 1957 textbook. He is quite careful to include in his description of the scoreable M those "perceived" conditions which infer the existence of kinesthesis.

"One need not inquire about kinesthetic sensation. Rorschach doubted that many overt movement responses were genuine M. He thought they were not accompanied by autokinetic sensations. His doubts seem unjustified on the basis of the high percentage of correct deductions made when overt movements are scored as M. Rorschach may have felt that speaking openly of overt movements was but a step

TABLE 6

A Comparison of the Piotrowski Method of Scoring Determinants from 1942 to 1957 wth that Originally Suggested by Rorschach

Symbol	Rorschach	Piotrowski—1942	Piotrowski—1957	Piotrowski—1947-50
F	Form Answers (Scoring of + or − based on frequently recurring answers, allowing for subjective evaluation where statistical data insufficient)	Same	Same (F produced by at least one-third of healthy subjects represents the standard of the quality of fit which is satisfactory for the lowest quality F+. The ± symbol to be used for objects not having permanent shape. The percentage of sharply perceived forms is to be used as a guide for evaluation of rare or original responses)	Same
M	Movement answers involving kinesthetic influences (restricted to humans or human behaviors)	Same	Same (Must occur to an area sufficiently ambiguous as to make any type of Movement or posture equally plausible)	Same
FM	Not used (In Rorschach's 1923 paper reference is given to Form tending toward Movement which could involve either human or animal figures)	Animal Movement	Same	Same

m	Not used	Inanimate Movement (Defined as percepts which are accompanied by a feeling of muscular tension and describing an inanimate object or natural forces in Movement)	Same	Inanimate Movement which must (1) describe an inanimate, inorganic, and insensate object, solid, liquid or gaseous, moving or in a state where the Movement is actively prevented; (2) the source of the Movement must be outside the object; (3) must be accompanied by a feeling of muscular tension
C	Color answer, interpretation based on the Color of the blot alone	Same	Same	
Cn	Not used (In Rorschach's record #17 he used the symbol CC to denote Color naming and counted it as a C response)	Color naming	Same (Defined as merely naming or describing a chromatic Color area where the subject makes it known that he has not given thought to any meaningful interpretation of that area	Same
Cp	Not used	Color Projection (Where chromatic color is projected into an area containing only varieties of gray)	Same	
Cd	Not used	Color denial (Where the influence of color is explicitly denied when it is obviously present)	Same	Same (Clarified that the denial must be spontaneous and unsolicited)

TABLE 6 (*Continued*)

A Comparison of the Piotrowski Method of Scoring Determinants from 1942 to 1957 with that Originally Suggested by Rorschach

Symbol	Rorschach	Piotrowski—1942	Piotrowski—1947-50	Piotrowski—1957
CF	Color-Form answer determined primarily by the Color, secondarily by the Form	Same	Same	Same
FC	Form-Color answer determined primarily by the Form, secondarily by the Color	Same	Same	Same
(C)	Chiaroscuro responses	Not used	Not used	Not used
c'	Not used	Interpretations of the very dark nuances of the blots in which Form is disregarded and a direct reference is made to the dark or black aspect, or a dysphoric mood is expressed	Same	Same (Clarified as usually responses in which the dark and the black are used as colors—". . . in which the darkest gray or black areas are interpreted meanginfully, the conscious perception of the dark or black having contributed to the content")
Fc'	Not used	Responses determined by Form but which include reference to the dark or black aspect of the area or are qualified in mood by the unpleasant impressions created by the darkness of the area	Same	Same

c	Not used	Shading responses in which Form is disregarded and the interpretation of a dysphoric mood is absent (Formless texture responses are also included here)	Same	Same (Clarified as being prompted by the light shades of gray—"...the coexistence of many gradations of gray is of essence")
Fc	Not used	Shading responses in which Form is primary and shading is secondary but "enriching" to the interpretation (Form-dominated texture responses are included here)	Same	Same
Cw	Not used	Not used	White-Color responses (Where white space is actually used as the color white. To be scored with respect to the use of Form, i.e. Cw=formless, CwF=form secondary, FCw=form primary)	Same
Cg	Not used	Not used	Not used	Gray-Color responses (Where the gray is actually used as the color gray. To be scored with respect to the use of Form, i.e. Cg=formless, CgF=form secondary, FCg=form primary)

from acting out and, therefore, could not qualify as M; for according to him, the M reflected only repressed action tendencies. The third requirement (the response should be accompanied by a kinesthetic innervation in the subject) is met also by indications that the overt movement is being hampered or frustrated, i.e., someone standing tensely, or holding on to a cliff. As long as some tension is needed to maintain these immobile poses, they should be scored as M. . . . Any act showing awareness of the postural stance, regardless of whether the percept implies an increase or a decrease in muscular activity qualifies the response as an M provided the other two requirements likewise are met."

Piotrowski describes the FM symbol to be used for the scoring of animal movement in responses as first, it must be accompanied by a feeling of muscular tension, and second, it must describe animals in a movement or in a pose that is impossible, or at the very best difficult or a human being to perform. The scoring definition for m is given as, "(1) it must be accompanied by a feeling of muscular tension, and (2) it must describe an inanimate object with natural forces and movement."*

It will be noted from examination of Table 6 that Piotrowski's basic scoring for color does not, in essence, differ significantly from that scored by Rorschach nor, in fact, that scored by the other Systematizers, at least with regard to the three basic scorings of C, CF, and FC. However their interpretive meanings are significantly different from the others. In the main, he regards color responses not as an "acting-out tendency" but rather as indicators of desire. He does require that color naming responses be scored Cn, and interprets them separately from the regular color response. He also offers the concept of "color projection," to be scored Cp.

"Another distinct color reaction likewise merits a symbol of its own. Some people project chromatic colors into blots which display only a number of shades of gray. They may interpret plate V as 'a brilliantly colored butterfly,' or VI, as 'a yellow rug.' Although there is no color to respond to, the person gives a color response. According to this writer's experience, such a projection of non-existent color, symbolized by the letters Cp, is a sign that the patient . . . endeavors to appear serene and cheerful when in reality he feels thoroughly dejected and depressingly hopeless."

Piotrowski also offered the symbol for color denial, Cd, for the scoring of those instances "when the subject explicitly denies the influence of color—which is actually present—upon his percepts."

Second only to his concern for adequate interpretation for the scoring of Movement responses is Piotrowski's concern for the Shading response. He points out that it is in this sphere that the greatest discrepancy among Systematizers seemed to have occurred.

---

* This definition differs considerably in meaning and scope from that offered by Klopfer.

"Both the symbols and the psychological implications vary from author to author. This variance of opinions concerning the shading responses may be accounted for by the fact that they are of utmost importance in deducing the degree to which personality traits are manifested directly in overt motor behavior, and by the fact that Rorschach introduced them after he had completed the presentation of other symbols. . . . He himself used only one symbol, $F(C)$, for all the qualities of light and shadow. . . . A simplified scoring scheme for the shading percepts is offered here. It is believed that it consolidates the principle ideas of various authors about the psychological significance of shading responses, and that it furthers the usefulness of chiaroscuro percepts."

In conjunction with this notion, Piotrowski offers four symbols: c', Fc', Fc, and c. In 1957 he notes that his scheme for scoring chiaroscuro responses could be further sub-divided into six symbols by adding c'F and cF, but prefers to use only four for purposes of simplicity and to minimize error. Additionally, like Klopfer, he uses special symbols for scoring responses wherein white or gray is used. In the instance of white, the symbol Cw is included with or without F depending upon the degree of form involvement. Similarly, the letter g is also included, such as FCg for a response on top of card X of "gray animals." The c' symbol is used for those responses involving the black color.

The symbol F is used for the scoring of form responses, as had been suggested by Rorschach. Piotrowski, like the other Systematizers, also has been concerned with the goodness or poorness of the form as it fits the blot and, consistent with Rorschach, endorses the use of + or − signs. In 1947 he made the following statement regarding good and poor form, and provides clarity about his willingness, or lack thereof, to score on the basis of verbalizations.

"If the new percept fits its respective area in the blot as well as, or better than, the frequently-used percepts, then it is classified as a 'good form'; otherwise, it is a 'poor form.' In estimating the quality of the F it is imperative to make certain what type of image the subject meant by his F response. The emphasis should always be placed on the percept, the image, and not on the words which convey the image. . . . In case of an unusual response of doubtful fit, Rorschach advised comparing the F of doubtful quality with the same subject's unquestionably good and unquestionably poor F; such a comparison would facilitate the decision as to whether the doubtful F ought to be scored good F (F+), or poor F (F−). There are F, which following Oberholzer's example, should be scored F±. These responses refer to objects which do not have a permanent or invariable shape though they are not formless. For instance, islands, flowers, clouds, etc., occur in a variety of forms; no exact fit is possible and, on the other hand, the fit cannot be completely poor.

"The F produced by at least one-third of healthy subjects provide the empirical data from which we extract the standard for the quality of fit which is satisfactory for the lowest quality F+. The quality of every F is then measured against this F extracted standard. A list of popular responses, i.e., responses given by at least one-third of healthy subjects, does not—by itself—suffice in view of the existence of rare or original responses and of superior quality responses. If the standard of frequency alone were used, the superior and original responses would be scored F–, implying an unrealistic and inferior type of thinking, while actually those responses reflect a realistic and superior intellect."

This latter statement clearly places Piotrowski in a position of disagreement with the Beck notion concerning goodness and poorness of form based on frequency data. This is especially important when it is noted that Piotrowski regards the percentage of good form to be one of the most important single diagnostic factors in the test.

In the 1957 text Piotrowski is more specific concerning his rejection of frequency tables as criteria for scoring good or poor form.

"Consequently, the principle that the classification of an F as F+ or F– depends on the frequency of the response must be either rejected altogether or corrected and modified. It would be most desirable to have a long list of responses indicating most, if not all, of the F+ and of the F–. Scoring would be objective. Endeavors to create such lists beginning with the first by Ovsiankina are understandable. Unfortunately, such an objective and automatic procedure is logically inadequate. For this reason, Beck's list of good and poor quality responses cannot be used as an ultimate criterion. Moreover, Beck made up his list not according to the visual images contained in the responses, but according to words used. This led to some unusual results. The response 'insect,' pertaining to all of Plate V, was classified as F+ because it was given frequently. On the other hand, the response 'beetles' to the same Plate V was declared an F– because it was not given with sufficient frequency. Now, from the relevant standpoint of the visual correspondence between the shape of the imagined object and its respective area, the image of a beetle fits Plate V no worse than does the image of an insect. . . . There remains then but one procedure to ascertain the quality of forms: a comparison with the form quality of the popular responses."

Piotrowski uses symbols for the scoring of response content which are essentially similar to those prescribed by Klopfer. Some minor alterations have occured, basically on the use of lower case letters rather than capitals or slightly different abbreviations such as Anat. for anatomy versus Klopfer's At. Otherwise, however, the procedure has remained the same as that suggested by Klopfer.

Up to, and including, the 1950 revision of the *Rorschach Compendium*, Piotrowski did not concern himself with the issues of Popular responses, nor Original responses except, as has been previously noted, to suggest that the evaluation of the adequacy or goodness of fit of Form responses should be contrasted with that existent in Popular responses. To this point, however, he preferred to use the Klopfer listing of Populars rather than one of his own. In the 1957 text he lists thirteen Popular responses based on protocols obtained from a sample of 200 adults described as "normal, or mildly neurotic." Like Beck (to that time) and unlike Klopfer, he lists at least one Popular for each of the blots with the exception of Plate IX. His criterion for defining Popular responses is consistent with that suggested by Rorschach, as those given by approximately one-third of the normal population. On the issue of Original responses, Piotrowski adopts Rorschach's criteria that they be defined as responses which occur not more frequently than once in a hundred records of healthy subjects. Piotrowski elaborates on this concept to the extent of pointing out that many unique and sometimes highly bizarre responses occur with considerably less frequency and thus must be considered as Original, and that their subsequent interpretation should be contingent upon the quality of form used, together with the content associated with a response.

As early as 1942 Piotrowski committed himself to following Rorschach's suggestion for the scoring of multiple determinants in a single response, i.e., using the symbols in combination, such as MC, or Mc', and preferring not to separate the Determinants with a dot or period as exists in the Beck System to specify "blends."

INTERPRETATION

Piotrowski's basic orientation to the interpretive process for the Rorschach consistently has emphasized the necessity for perceiving the globalness of the personality rather than as a composite of semi-independent traits. As early as 1937 he described the potentials of the Rorschach as being such to reflect the structure of the total personality more conveniently than through direct observation. He perceived the technique as a "short cut" to the systematic collection of data necessary for diagnostic and prognostic operations.

In 1942, in his Presidential Address to the *Rorschach Institute,* he approached the problem of interpretation by discussing the matter of re-examination of the subject. In discussing this problem he offered considerable information on his own interpretive approach.

"Personality has many aspects. Those aspects which are acceptable to the Rorschach method refer chiefly to an individual's action upon other members of his social environment, to the part which he plays in the interaction of his environment and himself; in Rorschach's words, the method reveals 'the manner in which the individual experiences the world'!. . . A personality analysis performed with the Rorschach method does not furnish a compound quantity, a unitary product of many different personality traits; it does not furnish a cross-section of a manifest personality of an indivdual at the time of the examination. It describes rather the latent personality traits together with their interactions on one another. . . . The differentiation between latent and manifest personality is a fundamental one in the Rorschach method. Hence the problem of the modifiability of latent personality should be differentiated from that of the modifiability of the manifest personality."

With such statements Piotrowski was, in effect, reaffirming many of the constructs offered by Rorschach concerning interpretation of the test data. In the 1947 *Rorschach Compendium* and the subsequent 1950 revision Piotrowski again affirmed his approach to the technique as a test rather than manifestations of a personality theory.

"Theorists occupy themselves with the origin and causal relationships of objects and processes. Theorists of personality are concerned more with the personality in the making than with the personality made. The Rorschach method reveals the present state of the personality. It does not reveal, by itself or directly, the causes which made the individual what he is. For this reason, the validity of the Rorschach method does not rest on any specific theory of personality. The purpose of the method is description and not theoretical explanations."

In 1966, Piotrowski offered some of his thinking on the theory of the Rorschach.

"The concept 'projection' as used in these tests should be taken in its basic psychological meaning. The tests are concerned with visual images, elicited by and externalized on the test stimuli—and thus made objects in space, as it were; for convenience let us call these images, projected on the test stimuli, 'percepts.' It is a frequent error to believe that the concept 'projection' is to be taken in its specific Freudian meaning which limits the process of psychological projection to traits (action-tendencies, emotional attitudes, instinctual drives, intellectual processes, etc.) which the projecting individual represses in himself because they cause him anxiety when he becomes aware of them—and which he, denying them in himself, unconsciously ascribes (or projects) to others when he cannot repress them completely. The fact that every single examination with a projective test also reveals traits which the tested subject does not hide, of which he is aware, and of which he approves— as well as some which cause him anxiety and of which he is unaware—proves that Freudian 'projection' and psychoanalysis are too narrow a base for the modern projective tests of personality. . . .

Projective test conclusions result from an analysis of visual images (percepts). Remove a person's visual imagery and you render him almost mindless. The eye is embryologically derived from the brain, the only part of the nervous system exposed to the outer world. It is man's most precious sense organ because, through it, reality is more comprehensively perceived than through any other sense organ. The sense of vision originates very early in the phyletic scale. Even protozoa possess rudimentary vision, an eye spot, which cannot be said for the sense of hearing. Our visual images are trial actions on a low level of intensity; they foreshadow the future."

By the late 1930's it was clear that Piotrowski interpreted Rorschach's intentions for the use of the technique as being based on the study of the subject's perceptions, in other words, the visual images which were elicited by the blot, and how those images corresponded to the subject's interactions with his environment. It is upon this premise that his use of the term "perceptanalysis" developed as the descriptive term for his intrepretive process. He expressed considerable disagreement with the method of training which required the student to learn a system of scoring symbols before learning the assumptions and implications related to particular types of responses.

"The differences between the definition of certain symbols by various percept-analysts loom large in the mind of a beginner if he starts to learn the Rorschach method with the scoring of responses. At this stage of learning the decision as to whose symbol is to be used and why it should be selected in preference to others is difficult. However, if training begins with an elucidation of the psychological assumptions and implications underlying the symbols, the differences existing among authors dwindle to relative insignificance. . . . Every symbol has a basic or constant, and a conditional or variable, meaning. If properly defined, each symbol always has the same basic meaning regardless of the quality and quantity of all other symbols occurring with it in the same Rorschach record. The conditional meaning is an addition to the basic meaning with which it cannot be incompatible; it specifies the basic meaning, adding useful information about the subject's personality."

Piotrowski suggests the Principle of Interdependence of Components (PIC), refering to the interpretive process, in which no single factor such as color or movement, etc., can be accurately interpreted unless related to a variety of other components such as the existence or lack thereof of color shock, the number and type of shading responses, the use of wholes versus parts, the type of movement responses, etc. In other words, while advocating that each symbol has a reasonably specific meaning, that meaning cannot be uniformly applied to all protocols in which the components exists unless it exists in specific relationship with a variety of other components. In this respect he agrees with all of the other Systematizers on the necessity for "global approach" and, while not discarding the importance of "signs" research, makes it clear that such research can only be profitable if the Principle of Interdependence of Components is fully applied.*

In the 1957 text Piotrowski elaborates in much greater detail on the Principle of Interdependence of Components but in no way changes his earlier conclusions. In fact, his ultimate certainty concerning the validity of this principle led him, in turn, to the use of the computer in an effort to find the "key" to a consistent synthesis of components. The problem, which he later attacked with a computer, is clearly stated in the 1957 text.

"Theoretically, every component qualifies in some manner and to some extent

---

* In personal correspondence (1968) he indicates, "I have come to the conclusion that the more you know about the meaning of specific test reactions, the less you are in need of the principle of the interdependence of components. It is true, however, that we will probably never reach a level at which we would have no need of qualifying the significance of test reactions by the presence or absence of other test reactions in the same test record."

all the other components appearing with it in the same record, and in turn is qualified by them. However, a complete, systematic, and valid synthesis that gives proper consideration to every component in a record is most difficult. At present, we have not tried out formal rules for this kind of comprehensive synthesis. The simultaneous consideration of even more than two components is intricate and hard to deal with. . . . The most difficult part of perceptanalysis is such an application of the PIC that the conclusion be valid and that the resultant picture of personality be lifelike. The skill in handling the PIC determines the scientific status of the perceptanalyst. The very difficult problem of inferring from the test data the degree and manner in which the various tendencies revealed in the data are manifested in overt behavior cannot be solved without the PIC, although even then it is far from a perfect solution. The PIC makes great demands upon one's experience and reasoning power because it requires thinking in terms of component patterns and not in terms of single components."

Using the Principle of Interdependence of Components as a base, Piotrowski is willing to offer a variety of hypotheses concerning the significance of the nature of the Rorschach components and many of their interrelationships. In the 1947-1950 *Compendium* he put forth these hypotheses in an orderly manner for the first time.

Like the other Systematizers, Piotrowski accepts Rorschach's postulate that the W response is directly related to intellectual capacity. To this, he adds the notion that the structural differentiation of the W, as well as frequency, is related to general motivation tendencies, especially the degree to which one would be willing to exert himself in order to accomplish difficult or complex tasks. He also points out that W is not the only factor contributing to the understanding of intelligence, citing the fact that the degree of correspondence to the form and the area, the number of human movement responses, and the originality of the content are the other major components indicative of intellectual operation. He suggests that the D response should ordinarily be interpreted as "an inclination to tackle the immediate problems of life as one encounters them one by one," and that the d response provides an indication of the tendency to occupy oneself with minute and frequently inconsequential details. He also expresses agreement with Rorschach's definition of the S response, that is, as indicative of oppositional tendencies. He is quick to point out, however, that the occurrence of S responses in a protocol should not be regarded as unfavorably as Rorschach suggested. Instead, he points to the fact that they may simply manifest a need for independence rather than obstinacy for the sake of obstinacy. He is quick to point out that the strong S reaction (more than two S) characterizes a person who reacts to a difficulty or challenge with a feeling of certitude whether it is a matter of making up one's mind about an abstract or a practical question, or whether it is a matter of deciding upon a course of action which involves no disagreement with others or one which causes friction and disagreement. The strong S person reaches his definite decisions rapidly and confidently and, possibly for this reason, changes them easily, each change being accompanied by the same feeling of certitude, decisiveness, and finality. The changes are made with a free heart and in the belief that the last decision is the final and best possible choice. The difference between the strong S type and the obsessive doubter and procrastinator is great. The latter never does anything with a feeling of finality, self-confidence, and certitude. He doubts his strength and his ability, and worries excessively about the opinions and actions of others. The S type trusts his strength and his individuality, but he acts like a person who feels that he must defend himself against bad environmental influences even when no one actually is influencing him deliberately. He likes to exert influence himself.

Piotrowski suggests that in the record of average length (20 to 40 responses) an anticipated distribution of Location scores will approximate 25 per cent W, 65 per cent D, 6 per cent d, and 4 per cent S. The distribution is essentially the same as that indicated by Rorschach.

In the 1957 text he elaborates considerably on the Location of responses. W is defined as the indication of "the ability to organize, synthesize, plan, and carry out plans. . . ." In amplifying that definition he cautions that an evaluation of the quality of the W is equally important as the frequency if not more so. He suggests the use of W + percentage calculated by taking the number of good W, and WS, and dividing it by the sum of all the Whole responses, suggesting that the higher the W percentage, the greater efficiency and consistency of planning of the individual. DW is interpreted as a tendency to jump to unwarranted conclusions or to evaluate a situation on insignificant evidence. While admitting that normal children may produce DW responses because of their immaturity of reasoning, he expresses considerable skepticism that such a response would occur in the healthy adult, thus differing considerably from Beck in this interpretation. While not modifying his conception of the D response he offers some slight modification for the interpretation of the d response by indicating that the d tendency can be socially useful, even though the individual manifesting it might not obtain gratification. He points out that many social and occupational skills require attention to minor details and, provided they are relatively free from anxiety, contain much secondary gain from this type of behavior. He cautions, however, that protocols containing few W and many d are indicative of passivity and a lack of direction. He points out that the signs of pathology often manifest themselves in the content and selection of area in the d response. In elaborating on the S response in 1957 he suggests that one of the best indicators of how tendencies toward unconventionality might be expressed is found in the ratio of M to sum C with special regard to the type of color responses involved. If the protocol is CF dominated, the person is more likely to manifest delinquent behavior or inappropriate suggestability whereas, if the color responses are FC dominated, this might not be the case.

In the 1947-1950 *Compendium* Piotrowski cites Rorschach's explanation of Form responses as "unsurpassed in perceptanalytic literature." By this he refers to the interpretation that F responses represent activities or behaviors which are provoked or controlled by the intellectual or rational processes.

"They [Form Responses] reflect the least unique personality traits, and the most frequent types of Rorschach reactions, and indicate the most conventional and socialized part of human personality. . . . F contains not only the image of an area limited in space and shape like some known object, but it also represents the result of a positive and constructive arrangement of space which is associated with the individual's work habits and with spheres of activity in which he is spontaneously interested. . . . The F significantly contribute to our knowledge of the individual's degree of conscious control over his thought process."

This same concept is affirmed and elaborated upon in the 1957 text. Piotrowski notes that either too much F or too little F in a record is indicative of mental disturbance. He emphasizes the fact that ,interrelated with the existence of F, the evaluation of the goodness or poorness of the fit is relevant to understanding the method and degree to which an individual tests reality effectively. He finds that the adequate range of F+ should fall between 85 per cent and 95 per cent and suggests that where this percentage falls below 70 it should be regarded as probably indicative of psychopathology. Conversely, F+ percentages of 100, although occasionally produced by healthy but pedantic people somewhat limited in imagination, are most frequently found in persons concerned about their self control. This sign, provided other components also exist, may even manifest destructively critical attitudes, having an undesirable inhibitory effect on the subject's overall behavior.

One of Piotrowski's greatest concerns in his System of interpretation is that appropriate consideration be given to the Movement responses. In the 1947-1950 *Compendium* he cites the M response as among the most important to the "perceptanalyst." He indicates that the M responses can be utilized interpretively more so than can any other Determinant. He suggests that this evolves when the M symbol is sufficiently elaborated and understood by redefining the meaning of M, increasing the means by which M can be understood in the PIC, and comparing the M's with other types of movement occurring in a protocol. Piotrowski maintains that the M response always reveals something of the subject's "role-in-life" which is defined as definite tendencies that are basic characteristics of the personality. He suggests that the quality of M does not change readily and seems to be the least modifiable feature of Rorschach performance as indicated by re-examinations over the years.

In the *Compendium*, Piotrowski elaborates on Rorschach's conception of the human movement response as indicating the tendencies of thinking to take precedence over feeling. He quotes Rorschach's concept of introversion, as manifest in the M response, as "a psychological mechanism which selects and limits the subject's awareness of environmental, mainly social, stimulants." He suggests that three main roles can be distinguished in the varieties of M responses, self-assertion, compliance, and indecisiveness. He offers a strong caution that the type of movement perceived should be considered as well as the content involved. He also emphasizes the necessity for interpreting the ratio of M to color responses, in much the same way that Rorschach had emphasized this ratio (Erlebnistypus).

In the 1957 text Piotrowski presents a considerably expanded discussion of the human movement response. It is here that he takes issue with Rorschach's conception of this component.

"Rorschach's lengthy and comprehensive exposition of his ideas about the human-movement responses supports the inference that to him the M were indicators of a tendency to withdraw into one's fantasy life, to be intellectually creative, to deal with reality on an imaginative level both intellectually and emotionally, and not deal with it directly, concretely and forcefully. . . . According to him (Rorschach), the varieties of M determined not the direct relationships with others but the subject's attitude toward his inner life, i.e., his fantasies and daydreams. . . . The definition of M as indicators of conception of role in external and active social life is plainly inconsistent with Rorschach's explicit and comprehensive theory of the M. . . . Rorschach was not inconsistent in his exposition of the psychological significance of the human-movement responses, but he related them to mental activities dissociated from overt mode of conduct."

This was not the first time that Piotrowski had seriously questioned Rorschach's interpretation of M. As early as 1937 he had raised the issue, but had not attacked the problem in as much length nor depth at any time as he did in 1957.

"My view of the psychological basic meaning of the human-movement response differs from that of Rorschach in several respects and particularly in one, i.e., in regard to the relation between the M and overt behavior. Rorschach stressed the idea that there is a negative correlation between the M and overt motor behavior. Since 1937, I have emphasized the opposite view, viz, that the correlation between M and overt behavior is positive: 'The M represents the conception of life according to which the individual makes his adjustment to reality. The M stand for the most individual and integrated strivings which dominate the individual's life. Thus the M indicate traits stabilizing the relation between the individual and his environment.' This change in meaning is fundamental; it influences the procedures needed to validate the meaning of the M and markedly enhances the theoretical, practical, and prognostic significance of the M. . . . One cannot develop a fundamental attitude like a life role without stirring experiences and without some notion of what reality is like. On the other hand, it is not necessary to be fully aware of one's life role in order to have one and to be directly influenced by it. . . . By way of definition, the M indicate prototypal roles in life, i.e., definite tendencies, deeply embedded in the subject and not easily modified, to assume repeatedly the same attitude or attitudes in dealing with others when matters felt to be important and personal are involved."

In his elaboration on this definition, Piotrowski suggests that M always implies interest in people, an awareness of the self, and concern with the future. It is associated with emotions which are quite definite, and reveals an organized system of movement and social interactions.

Piotrowski had, of course, become quite well known in the Rorschach world for his 1937 paper on movement responses. In that paper, he devoted most of the space to the animal movement responses (FM) and to the development of the new scoring category (m) for responses involving movement of inanimate objects. At that time, he described the meaningfulness of the FM response in light of Klopfer's notion that, "it indicates a normal stage in the growth of inner life not yet fully developed," and interpreted the m response as "tendencies which are not expressed outwardly and constructively." It is interesting to note (as a side light) that Piotrowski in the 1937 article, suggested that the FM type response should be interpreted as meaning a drive state less integrated with the total personality; "tendencies which originated early in life but which have not fully matured," inferring no significant stabilizing value to the subject's relation with his environment. This is quite different than Klopfer had purported. He also noted that the m responses often manifest thoughts and tendencies incompatible with the predominant attitudes or orientations of the personality, thereby inferring their destructive tendency to the total personality. In the 1947-1950 *Compendium,* Piotrowski describes the FM response as revealing "past conceptions of role in life . . . and are an approximate measure of vitality." In this respect, he disagrees with Klopfer's interpretation. He also disagrees with Klopfer on the interpretation of m. For Piotrowski, m is reaffirmed as "a conception of role in life which the individual feels to be very desirable but which he considers unattainable because of external difficulties or because of personal incapacity." He is also careful to point out that his actual scoring requirements for m differs considerably from those used by Klopfer.

In the 1957 text, Piotrowski emphasizes that FM and m responses should be evaluated in terms of the total M.* He notes that the FM responses should be appraised with consideration to the subdivision recommended for M responses, that is, assertive, compliant, and inhibited. He suggests that the FM response may be indicative of subcortically controlled activity patterns in which there is little or no cortical participation, noticing that FM may be indicative of the role in life which, at one time, influenced overt social behavior, "probably up to about the sixth or eighth year of life." He also reaffirms, in the 1957 volume, that m responses signify thoughts or drives which are less well integrated into the subject's personality than those thoughts or drives manifest by either of the other types of movement responses. The m is elaborated as a manifestation of two basic personality characteristics, the tendency to habitual psychological introspection, and superior intellect.

Through the years Piotrowski's interpretation of color responses has differed significantly from that offered by Rorschach. He has differentiated color response in terms of positive and negative emotions and manifests some disagreement with the postulate that Color responses relate to overt behaviors. He has also pointed out that where color occurs in a response having poor form, the protocol must be interpreted in light of the limited intellectual or rational capacity adequate for necessary adjustments. Like Rorschach, he has emphasized the value of the sum of the color responses which, taken alone, may be interpreted as "an approximate measure of the ease with which the individual responds emotionally to environmental stimulation. . . ." The only differences between Piotrowski and Rorschach concerning the interpretation of Color responses occurs in the areas of Color naming, Color projection, and Color denial, none of which Rorschach had really mentioned in any detail. Piotrowski suggests, in the 1947-1950 *Compendium*, that Cn is found in personalities impoverished and prone to sudden mood changes, especially psychotics or brain damaged individuals. This same interpretation is included in the 1957 text and elaborated upon as "a measure of a very superficial affectivity characterized by sudden mood changes and shallow transient emotions . . . produced by confused schizophrenics, epileptics, and sometimes by intellectually inferior adults having no demonstrable lesions of the central nervous system." He characterizes individuals giving Cp responses as "seriously disturbed people" who ordinarily endeavor to appear calm and cheerful but

---

* Piotrowski had inferred this in a number of earlier statements regarding the importance of Movement responses especially in the 1937 paper and the 1947 *Compendium*, but had not argued this need with as much firmness or directness as in 1957.

who, in reality, feel quite dejected or depressed. In the 1957 text he adds to this concept by indicating that the Cp response is but a superficial facade, "a self-imposed serenity to dispel depression caused by deeply felt frustrations."

Color denial is described in the 1947-1950 *Compendium* as a sign of color shock, that is, related to neurotic anxiety of an unconscious but deliberate attempt to repress feelings. In the 1957 volume, Piotrowski admits to some doubt existing in his own thinking as to whether the same interpretation of color shock should be routinely applied to instances of color denial. He suggests that the Cd response is probably an indication of "a wish to feel and act out other emotions more pleasant than the ones being experienced at the time . . . it reflects a certain superficiality of emotion, a partial dissatisfaction with the present and a wish for more genuine and intense emotional experiences."

Piotrowski has strongly advocated that color responses alone cannot be translated directly into indications of the individual's action. Quite the contrary, he offers the notion in both the 1947-1950 *Compendium* and the 1957 text that a most necessary, and the most important single test component to understanding color responses is the shading response.

"The emotional attitudes revealed by the color responses are not only subjective feelings but also thoughts of objective deeds. The desire is parent to the thought of action but the wheel of causality does not always roll easily between them. There are desires gratified immediately and fully, but many of them are disguised and inhibited in varying degrees. It is the primary role of the shading responses to shed light on the ways in which desires are translated into actions."

In the 1947-1950 *Compendium* the shading responses are described as, "signs of anxiety, of uncertainty, of a feeling of being exposed to danger, of considering the environment hostile, and of doubt concerning the most suitable method of restoring security." It is suggested that the shading response gives the implication that the need or desire to act in a spontaneous or impulsive manner has been somehow delayed. In accounting for the differences between his method of scoring shading responses as contrasted with others, Piotrowski points to considerable agreement with Binder.

"The main psychological difference between the dark shading responses, the c' and Fc', on the one hand, and the light shading responses, Fc and c, on the other hand, seems to consist in the type of concession which the subject makes in order to stabilize as well as possible his relationships with the world. The Fc and c suggest that the subject tries to sacrifice his important goals of external achievement in order to appear less assertive and thus more acceptable to the world; the individual then is set to value his relations with the environment too much to jeopardize the respect, affection, and protection which the environment can give; . . . thus the Fc and c point to a submissive and conscientious adaptation to the environment. Contrariwise, the c' and Fc', appear to be indications of a readiness to give up, if necessary, many emotional gratifications which the environment can give, but to save the subjectively important ideals and individual goals. They imply a certain lack of flexibility, a rather assertive although painful form of adaptation to the environment, accompanied by a decreased regard for consequences."

In general then Piotrowski suggests that responses to the dark areas of the blot may be interpreted as the need for some active behavior to alleviate or decrease anxiety, whereas responses to the lighter grays of the blot suggest a tendency to a reduction of activity and a restrained attitude whenever anxiety becomes reasonably intense. This same basic interpretation is given in the 1957 text and expanded in considerable detail. In 1947, however, his more detailed explanation of the shading response includes emphasis on the relation of shading responses to color and the interrelationship of the types of shading responses to each other. He points to the fact that the actual frequency of cR and c'R require careful consideration before conclusions can be derived and, that the actual content of the shading responses also requires evaluation prior to any conclusions. He is also prone to agree with Binder concerning the instance of white and gray color responses, that is, as indicating a state of euphoria. In this respect he differs from Beck, Klopfer and Rorschach, all of whom had interpreted the white space response as indicative of unconventionality or feelings of negativism. In offering justification for this difference, Piotrowski notes that white Color responses are quite variable from record to record and "do not seem to last from one examination to another."

In 1947-1950, Piotrowski suggests interpretation of relatively few frequencies, percentages, and ratios (total responses, average time per response, initial reaction time, F+ per cent, sum c, sum c', M to sum C). In 1957, he expands on this orientation to interpretation considerably. In addition to those basic frequencies, ratios, and percentages listed in the 1947-1950 *Compendium,* the 1957 text also calls for consideration of a variety of indices of shock (Color shock, Shading shock, Movement shock), an 8-9-10 per cent (similar to that of Klopfer), investigation of rejections or refusals, approach and sequence, and offers considerable space to the interpretation of specific content categories. He also indicates the necessity for interpreting the symbolic significance of single responses.

COMPUTERIZATION

By the mid-1950's Piotrowski had considered the phenomenon in his Principle of Interdependence of Components to the extent of postulating that the professional diagnostician, with all his assets and experience, would still be prone to subjectiveness and other limitations which, possibly, the computer could alleviate. He began drawing up an interpretive program consisting of as many possible test components and rules which were readily available to him. By 1963, the program had been completed to the extent of including some 343 parameters and 620 rules with the ultimate goal of inclusion of over 500 components and a minimum of 1,000 rules. The revised program was completed in 1968 comprising 323 parameters and 937 rules. In describing this approach to Rorschach interpretation he notes:

"Many considerations entered into the decision to prepare ink-blot perceptanalytic test data for digital computer interpretation. . . . Among the nonessential reasons are convenience, speed, facilitation of the process of interpretation, and reduction of personal responsibility for the test interpretation. . . . The essential conditions responsible for the computer program relate to functions which no human being can perform even under optimal conditions, but which a digital computer can easily perform well. These functions are necessary if interpretation of the ink-blot test data is to be raised to a high level of objectivity and validity, and if there is to be a continuous improvement in the scope and meaningfulness of the information provided by the ink-blot personality test." (1964)

To undertake the programming of Rorschach components for interpretive processes Piotrowski selected 100 patients, schizophrenics, neurotics, and some organics, all of whom had been rediagnosed on follow-up studies. His basic goal is to increase the power of the diagnostician enabling the quick and meaningful use of limited amounts of data leaving more time for the difficult task of synthesizing all of the information and thereby raising the predictive value of the overall professional contribution. The same case of a 22 year old female, interpreted by the 1963 computer program and by the revised 1968 computer program is shown here to demonstrate the nature of the process and its revisions.

FEMALE. CA.=22   IQ=103   Case#4024   (1963)
Computer interpretation of 17 responses Rorschach of psychoneurotic woman who improved greatly 7 years later

050   Is hesitant and neurotically ambivalent about handling personally vital matters in accordance with own life roles.

055   Has an immature outlook on life. Is mentally or intellectually dependent. Has an underdeveloped personal scale of values, and a meager inner life. Is a much greater conformist than would be expected or found in persons of similar intelligence and education.

063   Unimaginative. Inhibited fantasy. Down-to-earth type. Only practical problems arouse subject's interest. Motivation limited chiefly to gratification of basic needs for food, shelter and security. Has an uncomplicated outlook on human motives, human nature and interhuman relations.

071   As a child felt rejected and neglected by parents and incapable of influencing parents' (especially mother's) attitudes toward self. Has an infantile or immature outlook on life.

146   Needs a long warming up period before responding emotionally to others.

147 Is capable of making an easy and adequate social adjustment of a conventional kind in new but non-challenging social situations.

155 Now and then experiences an urge to behave in an impulsive and inconsiderate manner, oblivious of consequences.

228 Displays about average amount of emotional interest in others.

231 Emotionally lively; feelings easily aroused.

240 Spontaneous emotional interest in people is about average.

264 Makes adequate adjustment to others in conventional social situations.

1026 Apparently has had no conflict over attitude to any authoritarian male figure.

1030 Weak personality structure. Frequently at a loss on how to handle situations. Largely ineffectual.

1031 Has intermittent depressive moods which are not conspicuous in overt social behavior. However, once in a while makes a sudden move which in the eyes of others looks unnecessarily hostile and aggressive. When feeling anxious is strongly inclined to actively do something to lower anxiety, even if this might incur the opposition of hostility of others. Feels increase in energy when anxiety increases and answers challenges better than when in a state of relaxation. Avoids pain less than others do.

1047 Very much preoccupied with personality growth. In fact too much so. Apparently fears to be left behind in the competitive world.

1071 Obsessive-compulsive.

1136 Neurotic ambivalence regarding the manner of relating to others in personally vital matters. Avoids thinking about interhuman relations. Feels increase in anxiety when has to face a serious life situation invloving those who are close to him or her. It is possible that rather strong latent homosexual tendencies are in part responsible for this ambivalence.

1139 Reaction formations against anxiety are pleasantly toned.

1147 May feel that he is losing conscious control over his thought processes.

1169 Normal, average amount of interest in what makes others tick, in their motives and goals, and in the possible effects of the actions of others upon his own life and future.

1170 A model pupil type.

1175 Possesses a high degree of conscious and voluntary control over conscious thought processes and overt manifestation of action tendencies. Can control self well even in very irritating situations at least for a limited time. General behavior in usual social situations is adequate.

1177 Alert, adaptable, capable of steady and good but routine work.

1184 Systematic, disciplined thinking, good capacity for prolonged voluntary attention. Methodical approach to problems.

1271 There is keen awareness of anxiety whenever a genuine feeling (positive or negative) is aroused. The patient has the habit of deliberately controlling the strength and the outward manifestations of this anxiety.

FEMALE. CA.=22   IQ=103   Case #4024   (1968)

Computer interpretation of 17 responses Rorschach record. Diagnosis=Psychoneurotic

27 About average intelligence.

37 "A model pupil" type.

40 Unimaginative; inhibited fantasy. Down-to-earth type. Only practical

problems arouse subject's interest. Motivation limited chiefly to gratification of basic needs for food, shelter, and security. Has an uncomplicated but not necessarily consistent outlook on human motives, human nature and interhuman relations.

40   Has a narrow outlook on life. Intellectually dependent. Has an underdeveloped scale of values, and a meager inner life. Is much more a conformist than would be expected in persons of similar intelligence and education.

41   No constructive original thinking. Not an intellectual. No interest in or insight into psychosocial relations. Does not deal with interhuman relations on an imaginative level and as a preparation for real situations.

1045   Unimaginative. Does not have original ideas.

49   Lacks creative imagination; is intellectually sterile and uninteresting. Has no inner goal toward which he strives in his endeavors. Interests and ambitions are exclusively environmentally determined. Survival is his main motive rather than realization of aesthetic, scientific or social goals. Interested only in things that are close at hand. Takes advantage of what exists. Uses reality as it is for his concrete, material needs.

58   Some tendency to withdrawal from intellectual competition. Does not like to be challenged or to challenge.

1084   Feels somewhat defensive and in need of strengthening his position by adducing additional evidence lest his judgment be questioned.

94   Occasionally jumps to unwarranted conclusions. Attempts to size up situations on insufficient evidence. At such times does not think matters through carefully. Tries to make reality conform with expectations to a degree which unfavorably affects judgments.

1122   Alert, adaptable. Capable of steady and good but routine work.

124   Expends a moderate (average) amount of effort in planning for future success and recognition, relative to his intelligence.

1127   Subject is striving beyond his inner resources. Has higher goals than are justified on the basis of past achievement. Tries to compensate for feelings of insecurity and inadequacy.

130   Has very little capacity for starting new undertakings and displays very little initiative in anything. Feels he should be more creative but is unable to do so.

141   Needs external stimulation and continuous encouragement to perform satisfactorily on a job which is more than simple routine.

1142   Prefers comfort to exertion in the intellectual sphere. Is likely to neglect essentials due to inertia. Likes routine work.

1147   Incapable of initiative. Cannot cooperate as an equal or start activities which would raise his position in life. Circumstances determine his work and success more than his own effort.

1227   Well proportioned affect. Emotions are tempered by intellect.

233   Normal, average amount of interest in what makes others tick, in their motives and goals, and in the possible effects of the actions of others upon his own life.

235   Makes superficially adequate adjustment to others in conventional social situations.

237   Is capable of making an easy and adequate social adjustment to conventional and non-challenging social situations.

239 Has a limited genuine interest in sharing emotional experiences with others. Both positive and negative emotions are weak.

1240 Avoids both positive and negative emotional attitudes. Shows perseverence at work.

277 Controls his overt behavior well, even in challenging situations, at least for a limited time. Behavior in conventional, non-challenging, situations is adequate. Accurate.

1392 Takes a stand on all issues but tends to adhere to his original view and changes only with difficulty. Functions below his potential without being deeply depressed.

1301 Accepted parental dominance.

400 Seems to have had no conflict over attitude to any authoritarian male figure.

492 There is moderate anxiety whenever a genuine emotion ,positive or negative, is aroused. Subject attempts to alleviate the anxiety by intellectual analysis of the situation.

443 Makes a deliberate effort to hide depression by forcing self to be and appear serene. Can stand a good deal of strain associated with depressions. Does not despair. Carries on in spite of obstacles.

522 Too much preoccupation with personality growth. Apparently fears being left behind in the competitive world because of slow personal development and limited alertness.

615 Feels rebellious against male authority. Very anxious about sexual intercourse.

624 Coprophilic interests.

It is difficult, if not impossible, to predict the ultimate value of computerization of Rorschach variables as Piotrowski has now undertaken. Certainly, if the Piotrowski System of approach and interpretation to the Rorschach is a valid one, and assuming that the programming of Rorschach components and computer rules is adequate, then the subsequent "print outs" describing the subject should likewise be valid. Another important question which remains to be answered in light of computerization is that concerning the extent to which such a System, based on Piotrowski methods of scoring and interpretation, might be applicable to the methodologies suggested by other Systematizers. For the moment, however, it would appear that the Piotrowski System is at least as contemporary, in terms of basic psychological methodology, as of any of the other Systematizers, if not more so.

In reviewing the sources from which Piotrowski's System has been derived, it is clear that there remains some alignment with Klopfer, but much more to Rorschach. For this reason the Piotrowski System is more like, at least in the basics, that of Beck than Klopfer. Nevertheless, there are many areas which differ quite significantly from Beck, and thus the System must be judged for its own merits.

REFERENCES

Levin, M. M. The two tests in the Rorschach. *J. Proj. Techn.*, 1953, 17, 471-473.

Piotrowski, Z. The Rorschach method of personality analysis in organic psychoses. *Psychol. Bull.*, 1936, 33, 795.

Piotrowski, Z. On the Rorschach method and its application in organic disturbances of the central nervous system. *Rorschach Res. Exch.*, 1936-1937, 1, 23-40.

Piotrowski, Z. Personality studies of cases with lesions of the frontal lobes: II. Rorschach study of a Pick's disease case. *Rorschach Res. Exch.*, 1936-1937, 1, 65-77.

Piotrowski, Z. The M, FM, and m responses as indicators of changes in personality. *Rorschach Res. Exch.*, 1936-1937, 1, 148-157.

Piotrowski, Z. The methodological aspects of the Rorschach personality method. *Kwart. Psychol.*, 1937, 9, 29-41.

Piotrowski, Z. "Some recent Rorschach problems." *Rorschach Res. Exch.*, 2, 1937, 68-69.

Piotrowski, Z. The fallacy of measuring personality by the same methods as intelligence. *Psychol. Bull.*, 1937, 34, 546-547.

Piotrowski, Z. Rorschach studies of cases with lesions of the frontal lobes. *Brit. J. Med. Psychol.*, 1937, 17, 105-118.

Piotrowski, Z. A comparison of congenitally defective children with schizophrenic children in regard to personality structure and intelligence type. *Proc. Amer. Ass. Ment. Def.*, 1937, 42, 78-90.

Piotrowski, Z. The reliability of Rorschach's Erlebnistypus. *J. Abnorm. Soc. Psychol.*, 1937, 32, 439-445.

Piotrowski, Z. The Rorschach inkblot method in organic disturbances of the central nervous system. *J. Nerv. Ment. Dis.*, 1937, 86, 525-537.

Piotrowski, Z. Blind analysis of a case of compulsion neurosis. *Rorschach Res. Exch.*, 1937-1938, 2, 89-111.

Piotrowski, Z. Recent Rorschach literature. *Rorschach Res. Exch.*, 1937-1938, 2, 172-175.

Piotrowski, Z. The prognostic possibilities of the Rorschach method in insulin treatment. *Psychiat. Quart.*, 1938, 12, 679-689.

Piotrowski, Z. A Rorschach blind analysis of a compulsive neurotic. *Kwart. Psychol.*, 1939, 11, 231-264.

Piotrowski, Z. Rorschach manifestations of improvement in insulin treated schizophrenics. *Psychosom. Med.*, 1939, 1, 508-526.

Piotrowski, Z. and Kelly, D. M. Application of the Rorschach method in an epileptic case with psychoneurotic manifestations. *J. Nerv. Ment. Dis.*, 1940, 92, 743-751.

Piotrowski, Z. A simple experimental device for the prediction of outcome of insulin treatment in schizophrenia. *Psychiat. Quart.*, 1940, 14, 267-273.

Piotrowski, Z. Positive and negative Rorschach organic reactions. *Rorschach Res. Exch.*, 1940, 4, 147-151.

Piotrowski, Z. The Rorschach method as a prognostic aid in the insulin shock treatment of schizophrenics. *Psychiat. Quart.*, 1941, 15, 807-822.

Piotrowski, Z. A comparative table of the main Rorschach symbols. *Psychiat. Quart.*, 1942, 16, 30-37.

Piotrowski, Z. On the Rorschach method of personality analysis. *Psychiat. Quart.*, 1942, 16, 480-490.

Piotrowski, Z. The modifiability of personality as revealed by the Rorschach method: methodological considerations. *Rorschach Res. Exch.*, 1942, 6, 160-167.

Piotrowski, Z. Tentative Rorschach formulae for educational and vocational guidance in adolescence. *Rorschach Res. Exch.*, 1943, 7, 16-27.

Piotrowski, Z. Use of the Rorschach in vocational selection. *J. Consult. Psychol.*, 1943, 7, 97-102.

Piotrowski, Z. A note on the "Graphic Rorschach" and the "scoring samples." *Rorschach Res. Exch.*, 1943, 7, 182-184.

Piotrowski, Z., Candee, B., Balinsky, B., Holtzberg, S., and Von Arnold, B. Rorschach signs in the selection of outstanding young male mechanical workers. *J. Psychol.*, 1944, 18, 131-150.

Piotrowski, Z. Experimental psychological diagnosis of mild forms of schizophrenia. *Rorschach Res. Exch.*, 1945, 9, 189-200.

Piotrowski, Z. Rorschach records of children with a tic syndrome. *Nerv. Child.*, 1945, 4, 342-352.

Piotrowski, Z. Differences between cases giving valid and invalid personality inventory responses. *Ann. N. Y. Acad. Sci.*, 1946, 46, 633-638.

Piotrowski, Z. The personality of the epileptic. *Proc. Amer. Psychopath. Ass.*, 1947, 36, 89-108.

Piotrowski, Z. A Rorschach compendium. *Psychiat. Quart.*, 1947, 21, 79-101.

Piotrowski, Z. The personality of the epileptic. In Hoch, P. H. and Knight, R. P. *Epilepsy*. New York: Grune & Stratton, 1947, p. 89-108.

Piotrowski, Z. A Rorschach compendium: revised and enlarged. In Brussel, J. A., et al. *A Rorschach Training Manual*. Utica, N. Y.: State Hospitals Press, 1950, p. 33-86.

Piotrowski, Z. Principles underlying the projective technics of personality measurement. *Arch. Neurol. Psychiat.*, Chicago, 1950, 64, 478-479.

Piotrowski, Z. and Lewis, N. D. C. An experimental Rorschach diagnostic aid for some forms of schizophrenia. *Amer. J. Psychiat.*, 1950, 107, 360-366.

Piotrowski, Z. A case of stationary schizophrenia beginning in early childhood with remarks on certain aspects of children's Rorschach records. *Quart. J. Child Behavior*, 1950, 2, 115-139.

Piotrowski, Z. A Rorschach compendium: revised and enlarged. *Psychiat. Quart.*, 1950, 24, 543-596.

Piotrowski, Z. and Abrahamsen, D. Sexual crime, alcohol, and the Rorschach test. *Psychiat. Quart. Suppl.*, 1952, 26, 248-260.

Piotrowski, Z. and Lewis, N. D. C. An experimental criterion for the prognostication of the status of schizophrenics after a three-year-interval based on Rorschach data. In Hoch, P. H. and Zubin, J. *Relation of Psychological Tests to Psychiatry*. New York: Grune & Stratton, 1952, pp. 51-72.

Piotrowski, Z. Tendances actuelles du Rorschach. (The present trends of the Rorschach.) *Bull. Group. Franc. Rorschach,* 1953, No. 3, 2-4.

Piotrowski, Z. and Berg, D. A. Verification of the Rorschach alpha diagnostic formula for underactive schizophrenics. *Amer. J. Psychiat.*, 1955, 112, 443-450.

Piotrowski, Z. A defense attitude associated with improvement in schizophrenia and measurable with a modified Rorschach test. *J. Nerv. Ment. Dis.*, 1955, 122, 36-41.

Piotrowski, Z. Rorschach method in review. In Brower, D. and Abt, L. E. *Progress in Clinical Psychology*, II. New York: Grune & Stratton, 1956, 16-31.

Piotrowski, Z. *Perceptanalysis.* New York: Macmillan Co., 1957.

Piotrowski, Z. (Chm.) Psychoanalytic concepts and principles discernible in projective personality tests: I. Freud's psychoanalysis and Rorschach's perceptanalysis. *Amer. J. Orthopsychiat.,* 1958, 28, 36-41.

Piotrowski, Z. and Bricklin, B. A long term prognastic criterion for schizophrenics based on Rorschach data. *Psychiat. Quart. Suppl.,* 1958, 32, 315-329.

Piotrowski, Z. and Levine, D. A case illustrating the concept of the alpha schizophrenic. *J. Proj. Tech.,* 1959, 23, 223-236.

Piotrowski, Z. A. and Bricklin, B. A. A second validation of a long-term Rorschach prognostic index for schizophrenic patients. *J. Consult. Psychol.,* 1961, 25, 123-128.

Piotrowski, Z. A. and Rock, M. R. *The Perceptanalytic Executive Scale: A Tool for the Selection of Top Managers.* New York: Grune & Stratton, 1963, iv, 220 p.

Piotrowski, Z. Digital-Computer Interpretation of Ink-blot Test Data. *Psychiat. Quart.,* 1964, 38, 1-26.

Piotrowski, Z. The use of projective personality tests in the study of mental disturbances. *The Friends-Jefferson Newsletter,* 1966, 1, 3-4.

CHAPTER 7

THE HERTZ SYSTEM

Marguerite Hertz might well be described as the "grand dame" of the Rorschach. Her involvement with the technique traces back as early as 1930 when she became coincidentally interested in it when reviewing possible techniques for use with children while working as a research associate at the Brush Foundation in Cleveland, Ohio. In 1930, during a visit to New York City, she discussed the technique in detail with David Levy and, on his encouragement, very much like that given to Samuel Beck some three years earlier, she began considering the practical and research aspects of the Rorschach. As has been mentioned previously, it was actually Samuel Beck who first showed her the Rorschach plates and shortly thereafter she embarked on what has become a long and productive career in Rorschach psychodiagnostics. Although her first research with Rorschach, encouraged by her thesis chairman, L. Dewey Anderson, was undertaken with the notion that the technique was of little value, she quickly became impressed with its many diagnostic possibilities. Almost immediately on completion of her dissertation, she began a long series of Rorschach investigations which have resulted in more than fifty publications. As one of the early American pioneers of the Rorschach method, it was inevitable that her publications would become widely reviewed and that her findings and ideas would have a significant impact on others.

Klopfer's encouragement to her has played no small role in her subsequent commitment to the use and investigation to the technique. At times she has disagreed with the Klopfer System, but she has also leaned heavily on many of his opinions. In a 1967 interview with Dr. Hertz, when she was asked to recall some of her early Rorschach experiences, she frequently referred with superlatives to Klopfer's influence and contribution, both to herself, and to the Rorschach world in general. To her great credit is the fact that, while she has frequently been prone to assume a subjective theoretical position concerning the Rorschach, her training and general orientation in psychology, has frequently caused her to disagree with subjective opinions and align herself more closely with the standards of objectivity. In fact, during the early discussions in the *Rorschach Research Exchange* on the issue of standardization, she was among those strongly advocating standardization of those aspects of the technique amenable to such treatment. In doing so, she assumed a relatively unpopular position but never veered from her opinion.

Hertz began her work with the Rorschach using a psychometric "set" wherein she emphasized a nomothetic approach to the study of the individual. Her continuing involvement with the technique as a teacher, researcher, and practitioner gradually altered her orientation toward greater emphasis with idiographic concerns. Her work and orientation demonstrate the adoption of a strong psychoanalytic commitment by the middle or late 1940's. She attributes the causes for this transition to many factors, including her admiration for Klopfer and his work. Another highly significant element which contributed to her shift in orientation was an article written by Lee J. Cronbach. Cronbach (1949) pointed to many of the fallacies in normative and standardization data compiled on the Rorschach and used several of Hertz's studies as examples. Hertz reports in the 1967 interview that this caused her to re-evaluate the overall usefulness of the nomothetic approach and the statistical procedures employed, ultimately concluding that a much more sophisticated research methodology would be required to study the technique realistically. It was about this time that she decided to abandon the score-centered approach in both research and practical application. In personal correspondence (1968) she explains this in greater detail.

"I was willing to admit that some Rorschach categories in their broadest sense permit this type of approach, that with appropriate statistical procedures such as factor analysis, some common factors may emerge. I soon realized however that we had to consider the many qualitative differentiations of the scores, that research has to take proper cognizance of the intricacies of patterns and the qualitative features of the total record, and that 'signs' just could not be productive."

This professional introspection led her to de-emphasize the score oriented research and become more deeply involved with the qualitative aspects of Rorschach methodology.

Hertz has never worked with the specific intention of creating a unique Rorschach System. At the same time, she has not found herself to be in complete agreement with any of the other Systems. Instead, she has attempted to glean from each those features which are most compatible with her own thinking and research and incorporate them into her Rorschach methodology. Thus, one finds the Hertz approach marked by such features as the Binder treatment of vista, the Klopfer identification of texture, and the Rapaport orientation toward analysis of content. But the bulk of the approach is Hertz. Its total composite forms a Rorschach methodology which is different than any of the other Systems and consequently becomes a System in itself. It is also important to note that many of Hertz's ideas and findings have been adopted by other Systematizers. For example, she was among the first to develop a coding scheme for recording the location of responses and also was among the earliest to work with personality "configurations" in the test rather than concentrate on scores per se. This occurred in her work on suicidal tendencies which continues to be a classic in Rorschach literature. She was also among the first to publish frequency tables for use in scoring normal details, form quality, Populars and Originals.

In her early work with the test, Hertz devoted much effort to the study of young children, adolescents, and "normal healthy" subjects as contrasted to the emphasis on pathological groups found in the work of the other Systematizers. This focus of research afforded her the opportunity to view the test from a different perspective and no doubt influenced some of her decisions concerning methodology and interpretation. Many of her findings, especially those concerning adolescents which were published in a series of papers in 1942 and 1943, provided a substantial format which could be used by others for the study of similar groups. Quite possibly, had her manuscript not been destroyed through a tragic error, as has been previously noted in Chapter 2, the overall impact of her thinking and research on the Rorschach world would have been still greater than has been the case.* But even without such a book, her impact as a teacher, and researcher, has been highly significant. Among her greatest contributions has been that in the role of the "evaluator" of progress or lack thereof with the technique. Her continuing evaluation of the status of the Rorschach has, more than once, placed in the appropriate perspective the continuing research needs, methodological gains, and interpretive understandings. Many of her publications have either attempted to synthesize the work of others, or pointed markedly to the shortcomings and needs in Rorschach research. During this same period, the nature of her occasional disagreements, or orientation differences, with other Systematizers has led her to continue to develop her own System of scoring and her own approach toward interpretation. In the 1967 interview, Hertz argued the position

---

* The data included in that manuscript had been derived from an enormous normative study involving several thousand subjects. In personal correspondence (1968) she describes the incident. "One day it was decided to dispose of the material which was no longer in use and which the authorities felt was worthless. I was called and told that I may *have* my material. I went over at once with graduate students and a truck, but to my dismay, I learned that my material had already been burned 'by mistake.' It had been 'confused' with all other data which had been discarded. All the Rorschach records, all the psychological data, all the worksheets, plus my manuscript went up in smoke. Of course the loss was irreparable."

that, although different scoring methods may have evolved, there remains only one Rorschach System and that differences between Rorschach authorities are minor and have not really confused issues or retarded progress. She maintains that the ultimate success or failure of the Rorschach lies in the conclusions of the examiner, and it is on this point that she believes "inter-System" differences to be negligible.

ADMINISTRATION

As early as 1936, Hertz expressed concern for the failure of many users of the Rorschach to approach the administration of the technique with a standardized procedure. She pointed out that while most examiners during that time administered the test in general accord with Rorschach's directions, those directions were frequently vague and permitted excessive variability. In an effort to resolve some of the aspects of variability she formulated a detailed method of administration and investigated its usefulness with some 150 subjects of which 70 were considered normal and 80 were selected from a patient population.

"The subject and the examiner were alone in the room, seated before a desk, the subject to the side and a little in front of the examiner, facing away from the desk. The examiner could look over the subject's shoulder and could watch him as he pointed to different parts of the blots. . . . Uniform directions, prepared and memorized by the examiner, were given: 'I am going to show you some cards one by one. The cards have designs made on them make up of ink blots. I want you to take each card in your hand, look at it carefully, and tell me what you think it could be, what it looks like to you. You may hold the card any way you wish, but be sure to tell me everything you see in the design. When you have finished with the card you may give it to me and I'll give you the next card. If you do not understand, ask me any further questions. . . .' "

One of the most interesting features of this investigation and procedure was that a trial blot was used.

"While these directions were given, the examiner showed the trial blot and turned it on all sides to indicate it may be viewed from all angles. . . . When the subjects gave answers he was encouraged by such remarks as 'yes, it does look like that,' or 'that's what I said too,' 'so many people say that,' or 'why, that's an interesting answer'. . . . If the subject hesitated still the examiner said: 'There is no right or wrong answer to these blots. They are just inkblots. All I want you to tell me is what you think of.' . . . After the subject gave all the responses he could to the trial blot and when it was certain that he understood the nature of the test, the test proper was begun. . . ."*

A time limit of two minutes for each card was imposed on the subject in this experiment. After the time limit had elapsed a brief Inquiry was initiated, following in effect, the procedure endorsed by Oberholzer and

---

* The trial blot is still used in the Hertz System.

later adopted by Rapaport. The Inquiry questions were indirect and cautious but followed the basic Inquiry intentions of clarifying the response location and discovering the elements of the blot, form, movement, color, or shading, which determined the response. Inquiry was performed only for those responses about which the examiner "felt doubtful." Subsequent to the 1936 investigation Hertz eliminated the two-minute time limit for the Free Association period.

Hertz's 1939 paper "On the Standardization of the Rorschach Method" again pointed to the fact that a variety of techniques of administration still existed. She acknowledged that her own method was different from that suggested by either Beck or Klopfer and called for the establishment of "some standardized procedure." Although calling for standardization of a procedure, Hertz gave no inference in her 1939 paper that she was willing to modify her 1936 method in accordance with techniques of administration suggested by the other Systematizers even though she noted that Klopfer, in particular, called for an Inquiry at the end of the test rather than after each card as she had suggested in 1936. In 1941, in her classic paper, "Rorschach: Twenty Years After," presented as her presidential address to the Rorschach Institute, she indicated:

"A desire for a systematic form of questioning to elicit essential information has led to the development of the 'systematic inquiry' which embraces a discussion of responses, conspicuous omissions of details and determinants of responses, and includes a procedure of 'probing' or what Klopfer calls 'testing the limits' by provoking additional responses to determinants not used in the performance proper. It should be noted that at no time have questions themselves been rigidly standardized. Along with a minimum of uniformity, emphasis has been placed on natural conversation and flexibility of approach."

By this time Hertz had discontinued the procedure of Inquiry after each card, instead, adopting the original Rorschach approach of Inquiry after the Free Association period. Her revised procedure for administration closely follows the Klopfer format but uses more detailed pre-test instructions and does not endorse some of the more "direct" questions in the Inquiry such as Klopfer permits. In several later publications she describes the Analogy Period and Testing the Limits (called the Probing in the Hertz System) as being useful in some instances.

As recently as 1963 Hertz restated her recommendation for a standardized method of instructions and procedures.

"It appears wise for us to direct our attention to a scientific program which will include both in the clinic and in research orderly, systematized and standardized methods of administering the test, objectified scoring, more careful definition of concepts and principles used in scoring and interpretation, and more extensive use of the subjective variables, making them explicit, defining them operationally, and studying them systematically according to the rules of scientific procedure. In our judgment, the Rorschach test situation should be controlled. The method of administration should be standardized by uniform instructions. As many situational, dispositional, and motivational variables as possible should be identified. Rorschach workers should agree upon developing a systematic inquiry to elicit essential information. Although emphasis must be placed on natural conversation and flexibility of approach, a minimum of uniformity in procedure must follow."

The fact that after some nearly 30 years Hertz was still making the same pleas for uniformity of administration, says something about the Systematizers themselves and of their disagreements.

SCORING

The Hertz approach to scoring Rorschach responses has changed markedly from the mid 1930's through the mid 1950's. The method for the scoring of Location in the Hertz System from 1938 to the present is shown in Table 7. It will be noted that the 1938 orientation used by Hertz for scoring Location was remarkably similar to that suggested by Rorschach. It will be noted from examination of Table 7 that, as years passed, she included the Klopfer scoring for the cut-off Whole response but otherwise made few changes in her original format. It is also of interest to note that her utilization of the symbols S, and s and her symbols for detailed responses are very much like those of Piotrowski.

While Hertz has not altered significantly her scoring for Location since 1942, like the other Systematizers, her scoring for Determinants has been expanded and modified considerably, especially in the areas of color and shading responses. A comparison of the various stages of scoring for Determinants in the Hertz System as contrasted with that originally suggested by Rorschach is shown in Table 8. Ultimately, as it will be seen, the Hertz method of scoring Rorschach Determinants has evolved into a composite which utilizes some of Rorschach's original symbols, some of the scoring symbols suggested by Klopfer, and many comparable to those used in the Rapaport-Schafer System. While the criteria for the use of some of these symbols is different than other Systematizers, and different from Rorschach in some instances, the similarity of the Hertz symbols and those of the other Systematizers is nevertheless striking.

An examination of Table 8 reveals that the 1938 Hertz method used three symbols for Form, two for Movement, three for Color, and one for Shading. The scoring system had been expanded by 1942 to include special symbols for Animal Movement, inanimate Movement, Color Naming, Color Description, and Color Symbolism,* plus some thirteen separate symbols to

---

* Even though Hertz did not list scoring symbols for Color naming, Color description, and Color symbolism in 1938, she did score for these components at that time.

TABLE 7
A Comparison of the Hertz Method for Scoring Location from 1938 to 1951 with that Originally Suggested by Rorschach

Symbol	Rorschach	Hertz—1938	Hertz—1942	Hertz—1951
W	Plate interpreted as a whole	Same	Same	Same
W	Not used	Not used	Response to the whole blot with one or two small parts omitted	Same
DW	Plate interpreted as a whole secondarily, the answer based primarily on a detail	Same	Same as 1938 plus use of symbol DW for scoring responses defined as "combinatory" (several details successfully combined into a whole); or "contaminated" (response to the whole blot but two interpretations combined into a confused or absurd whole)	Same as 1942
D	A normal detail of the plate	A normal detail (based on norms established in 1935 and 1936 studies)	Same as 1938 (norm group expanded)	Same as 1942
Dd	An unusual or small detail	Not used	Not used	Not used
Dr	Not used	A detail infrequently perceived	Same	Same
Do	A detail is interpreted in place of a whole	Same	Same	Same (Subsequently changed symbol to DF or Drf)
S	White intermediate figures (space detail)	Same	A white space detail which is frequently perceived	Same
s	Not used	Not used	A white space detail which is rarely perceived	Same

TABLE 8

A Comparison of the Hertz Method for Scoring Determinants from 1938 to 1951 with that Originally Suggested by Rorschach

Symbol	Rorschach	Hertz–1938	Hertz–1942	Hertz–1951
F	Form answers (Scoring of + or – based on frequently recurring answers, allowing for subjective evaluation where statistical data insufficient)	Form answers (Scoring of + to be reserved for "good" Form, scoring of – for "poor" Form: Where frequency data or clear qualitative criteria are inadequate, scoring of F with no + or – signs will be used)	Same	Same (Use of F without + or – eliminated by defining + responses as (1) given frequently by normals or, (2) responses resembling an established F+, or (3) responses quite unlike any in lists, but subjectively judged to fit the blot area
M	Movement answers involving kinesthetic influences (restricted to humans or human behaviors)	Same but made provisions for the scoring of movement in animals, natural Forms, or objects if kinesthetic influences are revealed in inquiry	Same as Rorschach	Same as Rorschach
(M)	Not used	Not used	Responses determined for the most part by Form but having a feeling of impending human movement, strain or tension	Not used
$\underline{M}$	Not used	Not used	Animal movement	Not used
$\underline{(M)}$	Not used	Not used	Tendencies toward animal movement	Not used
FM	Not used	Not used	Not used	Animal movement

m	Not used	Inanimate movement, including movement of natural forms and artificial happenings, where Form is not involved (Included scorings of Fm and mF to be used for inanimate movement where Form is involved)	Same
C	Color answer based on the Color of the blot alone	Same	Same
CF	Color-Form answer, interpretation based primarily on Color, secondarily on Form	Same	Same
FC	Form-Color answer, interpretation based primarily on Form, secondarily on Color	Same	Same
Cn	Not used (In Rorschach's record #17 he used the symbol CC to denote Color naming and counted it as a C response	Color denomination where Color is enumerated and no effort made at interpretation	Same but scored only when an interpretation is intended
Cdes	Not used	Color description, where colors are described but no interpretation intended	Same but scored only when an interpretation is intended
C denom	Not used	Not used	Color referred to specifically
C sym	Not used	Response in which Color is used to stand for an abstract idea	Same

TABLE 8 (*Continued*)

A Comparison of the Hertz Method for Scoring Determinants
from 1938 to 1951 with that Originally Suggested by Rorschach

Symbol	Rorschach	Hertz—1938	Hertz—1942	Hertz—1951
C/F	Not used	Not used	Color-Form response where Color is used artificially (as in maps): F/C used where response is determined primarily by Form	Same as 1942
FC Arbit	Not used	Not used	Response in which Color is arbitrarily assigned to a Form without noting it to be artificial	Same as 1942
Cdet	Not used	Not used	Crude Color response involving deterioration, disintegration, disease, etc.	Same as 1942
FC denial	Not used	Not used	Not used	Color is referred to but denied or negated
F(C)	Chiaroscuro response	Defined as response which include reference to the gray-black areas	Responses determined by the differentiated gray black areas, where Form and light-dark values play a part	Same (defined to include vista or perspective)
(C)F	Not used	Not used	Not used	Responses having three-dimensional effects where shading dominates Form

(C)	Not used	Not used	Not used	Responses having three-dimensional effect with no Form involved
c	Not used	Not used	Responses determined by the surface texture (scorings provided of cF and Fc depending on the extent of Form involvement)	Same
Ch	Not used	Not used	Chiaroscuro responses determined by the general shading, diffusion or haziness with no Form involved (scorings provided of ChF and FCh depending on the extent of Form involvement)	Same
Ch'	Not used	Not used	Responses in which gray or white are actually used as colors (scoring provided of Ch'F and FCh' depending on the extent of Form involvement)	Same
Ch"	Not used	Not used	Responses determined by black as a Color value (scoring provided of Ch"F and FCh" depending on the extent of Form involvement)	Same

be used for Shading responses or when the gray black characteristics of the blot are noted.

It is also interesting to note that while Hertz established her own System for scoring for Location and Determinants, she consistently pointed to the fact that differences between the Systematizers existed, and on numerous occasions continued to call for more standardized agreement. This was, for example, true in her 1939 paper on standardization problems, her 1941 presidential address, and even in her 1963 paper which had been presented to the International Rorschach Congress, although by this time she appeared less convinced of the necessity for standardizing scoring symbols, instead concentrating more on the principles of scoring than the symbol to be used. In fact, with regard to scoring symbols she stated:

"In the area of scoring, further development of scores and more consistent procedures are needed for the objectification of the method. A common scoring system would of course hasten progress in this direction. Differing codes or symbols, however, do not create the difficulty. Rather it is consistency in scoring principles and in the psychological assumptions underlying the scores which is important."

It is evident from examination of Table 8 that the Hertz approach to scoring has been marked by numerous changes as the System has developed. In fact, probably more changes have occurred in the Hertz scoring methodology than has been the case in any of the other Systems. This seems to characterize her constant search for greater sophistication of the test and her willingness to test out new ideas as well as those which she had previously adopted. Some of the symbols were changed for very simple reasons. For example, the 1942 symbol $\underline{M}$ for animal Movement was replaced in 1951 by the symbol FM because a publisher indicated that it was complicated to reproduce. In other instances a symbol was replaced or added to provide a more appropriate coding of certain response characteristics.

While she had been somewhat critical of Beck's criteria for the scoring of F+ and F− in her 1937 paper, she did ultimately use a similar format, that is, being concerned with the Form fitness and operationally defining this as those forms given with a certain frequency by a "healthy group." She has continuously rejected the more subjective Klopfer method for using a Form Level Rating. In 1938, her criteria for scoring Form plus or minus was as follows:

"1. All forms which received a frequency of 13 or more were considered good forms and scored F+.

2. All forms which received a low frequency but which belong to a similar group or class were scored as that group was scored.

3. All forms of low numerical frequency, where there was no basis of comparison with the same or similar forms, were scored according to the concurrent estimates of from 3 to 5 judges."

By 1942 her collection of frequency data was such that very few responses required a scoring of F without a plus or minus sign. In 1951 she indicates that the published lists of plus and minus are highly desirable and useful as guides for decision making, but that where the response does not occur on such a list the subjective evaluation of the examiner must be accepted, suggesting that, provided the examiner is adequately trained, the use of "Form Level Scoring" becomes reasonably objective.

Hertz has also been concerned with the development of some scheme for the identification of the organizational activity occurring in a response. In 1940 she proposed the use of the symbol "g" for this purpose. This symbol had been used previously by Vernon but with different criteria. She had decided on the letter "g" about the same time that Beck was publishing his work on Z. Although the symbols are different, the criteria and interpretation are essentially the same.*

It is also useful to the understanding of the Hertz System to note that she has never endorsed a method of scoring based exclusively on the verbalizations of the subject. Quite the contrary, she has continually insisted that scoring must be, in the final analysis, a "subjective" process, but has always emphasized the necessity for "trained examiners." As early as 1933, in her work at the Brush Foundation she began to employ a method of Inquiry designed to circumvent some of the problems of scoring verbalizations. This method utilizes a supplementary set of cards showing the basic Form of the blot but with changes in Color, Shading and some figure-ground characteristics. Thus, if a subject gives a response of "flower" to a colored area but does not verbalize Color, he is shown the modified blot during the probing which is accompanied by an indirect probing to see if he remarks on the absence of Color as in some way altering his original impression. Neither does she endorse the rule adopted by some of the Systems that recommends the scoring of Form as primary when the object perceived has definite class characteristics. In a 1968 personal communication she indicates that "a priori rules make a false kind of objectivity." She points to the fact that a "pansy" response to Card VIII, which is ordinarily scored FC in most Systems can be a CF and that a "flower" response given to the same area, which is ordinarily scored CF in most Systems can be FC.

Hertz also provides in her System for both the scoring of Popular and Original responses. In 1938, "all forms given approximately 50 times were scored Popular" (out of 300 records). Originality was defined by the

---

* Although the Hertz criteria for "g" is the same as Beck's Z, she does not employ a Table of Weights, postulating that the simpler g scale provides the same interpretation.

frequency of 1 in 100. Hertz has continued to use the ratios wherein responses given by 1 in 100 normal subjects are scored Original.

INTERPRETATION

The process of interpretation in the Hertz System is by no means as clearly defined as in the Systems of Beck, Klopfer, or Piotrowski. Originally Hertz was concerned with typological factors as defined by Rorschach scoring patterns of "psychograms." Her initial training and orientation to the Rorschach required that she explore the test using a nomothetic approach. At no time, however, did she neglect the importance of the qualitative aspects of the protocol. Through the years of development of the Hertz System she has become even more convinced of the importance of seeking out interpretive patterns rather than attempting to concentrate on any seeming relationships between a Rorschach factor and behavior. Her current approach to the technique calls for interpretation to ensue not only in terms of personality configurations as exist in the test but requires that these be understood in relation to the total life situation and life style of the subject as historically presented through case history data. She has, like all of the other Systematizers, adopted many of the interpretive suggestions of Klopfer and Binder, and on the matter of color, those purported by Schactel. But all of these are marked by the Hertz signature in that they are interwoven with occasional modifications and additions in a manner that calls for continuing emphasis on the total pattern of development. There has been a gradual shift in her approach to interpretation. When contrasted with her original conceptions of the technique, which sought the typological factors as defined by Rorschach patterns, her contemporary approach which seeks to integrate Rorschach configurations with life history and life style configurations is markedly different. She calls this the "interactionist approach" and has as its ultimate goal some form of objectively defining those socio-educational-situational-life style variables into a configurational pattern in which Rorschach data can also be included.

The nature of this transition from a relatively firm commitment to normative typological factors to a global clinical approach is probably best represented by quotations from her 1942 article, "The Rorschach Method: Science or Mystery," her 1952 article, "The Rorschach: 30 Years After," and her 1963 paper to the International Rorschach Congress, "Objectifying the Subjective." In the 1942 article Hertz wrote:

"Thus the Rorschach method offers an instrument of unique promise in that it permits both quantitative and qualitative evaluation of personality. It is quantitative in that many traits of the subject are compared to those of his peers, and qualitative in that many facets are viewed for their special and idiosyncratic significance in that unique configuration which we call the individual's personality. . . . Despite the rapid progress in the field, the impressiveness of research and the accumulation of valuable data, the scientific validity of the method is still open to challenge. Many of the limitations have already been discussed—over-generalization, conclusions drawn from small groups and from preliminary observations, the uncritical lumping of Rorschach data, lack of statistical treatment of statistical problems. More may be said. Research has not kept up with therapeutic usage; subjective interpretation has outrun scientific judgment. Doctrinaire inflexibility has characterized much of the work on the refinement and development of the method and much of its clinical validation. These shortcomings are serious because they surround the method with an aura of mystery. Much that has been offered has not been or cannot be explained, or can be applied only by a chosen few. Therefore, even at the risk of over-emphasis and reiteration, mention should be made of those features which deter scientific acceptance of the method. . . . One must keep in mind, however (speaking mainly about the Klopfer and Kelly book), that there is a subtle distinction between the validity of a method and the skill of the interpreter. All too often success in diagnosis and prognosis may be due to the intuitive deductions of the expert which need not necessarily be based on the method in use. Further, one must not forget that subjective interpretation is only one type of validation, a type which depends on personal concept, personal theories and personal experiences. . . . Most important, experience may dictate various refinements of method but such refinements contribute nothing to the validity of the method. They may make the method more objective and more sensitive, perhaps, but not more valid. Validity still has to be established. Thus, although much has been done in the field of the Rorschach method, much remains. Despite the clinical acceptance and usefulness of the Rorschach method, it has not yet acquired the full dignity and status of a science. Unless objectivity and validity are obtained and established, it must become inevitably the discipline of a chosen few. . . ."

This quotation seems to clearly indicate that Hertz, at that time, was un-accepting of the Klopfer-type "clinical approach" without a similar commitment to psychometric standards which would breed adequate data for reliability and validity of the technique. In 1952, however, she lessened these demands somewhat. In fact, it might appear that her orientation to Rorschach had changed directions considerably. She pointed to the fact that, even though evoking controversy, the basic elements of Rorschach interpretation are subjective. She also emphasized that interpretation had gradually drawn away from the "diagnosis in terms of the traditional clinical entities" and had become more oriented toward the dynamic features of the subject thereby requiring greater emphasis to be given to the total history of the subject. She cautioned that the validity of the method depends largely on the skill of the examiner, his objectivity, his competence, his clinical judgment, and the breadth of his training in theoretical, experimental, and clinical psychology. The summary of that article provides an almost complete reversal of her earlier demand for statistical procedures.

"In viewing the working of the last few years, we have seen that many negative results have been reported in research studies. Basic theoretical issues are still unresolved. In the interpretation of records there is still too much servitude to subjectivity and insights. There is still a serious dearth of basic research. Studies are sporadic and uncoordinated. Statistical procedures have been grossly overemphasized and have often been erroneous. Many Rorschach hypotheses have been challenged. Considerable doubt has been cast upon the validity of many basic Rorschach concepts. Few studies have been replicated. Results of research are thus far tentative and suggestive, but not definitive. . . . Too many investigators have been absorbed in statistical procedure and have forgotten the dynamic aspects of the method. Too many have attempted to make clinical deductions from isolated patterns without considering the global nature of the method. . . . More attention must be given to the qualitative aspects of the method which lend themselves less readily to statistical manipulation, to the subject's definition of the test situation, for example, or to ego strength as it is expressed in the individual record, or to content of thought which is personal and meaningful to the individual. . . . No strict mathematical formulas can be devised for any aspects of a configuration. No precise and exhaustive criteria can be furnished for every trend. In the last analysis, decisions are made on a strictly individual basis in terms of the subtle aspects of the record, perhaps more so than the formal test indications. . . . It is our belief that qualitative features and clinical intuitions can be made explicit, but the differentiating criteria on which inferences are made can be delineated and systematically studied and that clinical intuitions, if used by clinicians with adequate training and experience, can attain a practical degree of objectivity."

In her 1963 presentation to the International Rorschach Congress Hertz follows essentially the same line of reasoning that she had in 1952, possibly somewhat stronger, but never really giving up the words "objectivity" or "standardization." To a large extent, it would appear that her transition in Rorschach orientation, especially as applied to interpretation, was much like the transition of Piotrowski, except almost in opposite directions. That is, while Piotrowski has attempted to computerize Rorschach data, and thus ultimately treat it statistically, Hertz argues that much data cannot be treated statistically and that acceptance of the "global-clinical" approach is inevitable to the ultimate validation of the technique.

"Inherently, the process of interpretation is a highly subjective procedure. It depends upon the personality theory embraced and upon knowledge of the personality trends Rorschach data reflect as a result of experimental background and experimental and empirical studies. Hence our approach, our inferential processes and our emphasis may differ. Despite such subjective elements, the ultimate interpretation of a record should embrace the same salient dimensions of personality and the same dynamically active problem for all who interpret the Rorschach record regardless of orientation. Unfortunately this is not always accomplished. . . . Today, there are many workers who fail to utilize the formal scores. . . . This procedure certainly does not contribute to the objectivity or validity of the interpretation. Then there are many workers who utilize scores but fail to summarize them. . . . On the other hand, there are interpreters who use detailed summaries and restrict their analyses rigidly and mechanically to numerical data, failing to take into account the qualitative features of the record. This procedure may appear to be an objective system of interpretation, but the resulting interpretation has little validity. . . . Again, many examiners fail to make explicit the bases upon which they make their inferences. As a result, they are apt to overlook configurational relationships and patterning. Thus, some interpreters tend to over-emphasize pathological tendencies, fail to weigh them against adaptive strength, and fail to consider them in terms of the degree of resiliance manifested in the record. . . . Many interpreters restrict themselves to the Rorschach response record apart from life context. They favor 'blind interpretation.' This may be a good teaching and training device. It may be one of the procedures to be used in research to determine the validity of certain general inferences on personality structure and dynamics, or to test relative skills in interpreters. But in the clinic and even in research, where diagnoses, full descriptions of the dynamically functioning individual and prediction are required, a dynamic synthesis of the findings of personality structure cannot be considered apart from its historical, social and cultural context. . . . In our judgment, there would be significant improvement in our interpretations and in our research if life history data were more appropriately utilized. There is a strong possibility that our failures in validating many of the Rorschach hypotheses is due to the use of 'blind' data alone rather than to the inherent limitations of the method or even of clinical judgment of itself."

In summarizing her 1963 presentation Hertz again makes a plea for objectification of the technique but with a much different approach than she emphasized in the late 1930's or the early 1940's or even in her 1952 article. Here she stresses the "interactionist" approach, that is, the methodical and total integration of the clinicians' intuitive judgments, the Rorschach scoring data, behavior descriptions of the individual at the present, and, possibly most important, the life history data of the individual. She suggests that with newer and refined statistical procedures that the goal of objectification may be closer for Rorschach than ever before.

It is quite clear that for more than 35 years of Rorschach experience Hertz has consistently, and even sternly at times, pointed a demanding finger at the Rorschach. The firmness with which she has done so has varied considerably from the days of her earliest psychometric involvement wherein the words "standardization" and "objectification" could in no way be compromised, to more recent years where she has conceded the subjectiveness of interpretation and the necessity for integrating not only a clinical approach to interpretation but also data from outside of the Rorschach before achieving desired levels of reliability and validation.

To the historian of the Rorschach Systems, it would seem that Hertz has, for years, been saying many of the same things as Beck, yet has never clearly aligned herself with Beck on many issues. Quite the contrary, she has adopted a System of scoring and an orientation towards interpretation considerably more like that of Klopfer, a much more subjective and phenomenologically oriented system. It would also appear that she has experienced a transition in her Rorschach orientation not unlike that of Piotrowski and yet has never really "sided with" Piotrowski. Quite possibly the difficulty in judging the total impact of the Hertz System is due to the fact that her thinking and research has never been totally integrated into a single manuscript and that, many of her articles are marked by the fact that they review the works of others rather than present her own thinking. The ultimate relevance of this approach to Rorschach can only be judged in the appropriate time perspective. Whatever that impact, Hertz has clearly been a figure with which to contend, no matter what orientation one might take.

REFERENCES

Cronbach, L. J. Statistical methods applied to Rorschach scores: a review. *Psychol. Bull.,* 1949, 46, 393-429.

Hertz, M. R. The reliability of the Rorschach ink-blot test. *J. Appl. Psychol.,* 1934, 18, 461-477.

Hertz, M. R. Rorschach norms for an adolescent age group. *Child Develpm.,* 1935, 6, 69-76.

Hertz, M. R. The Rorschach ink-blot test: historical summary. *Psychol. Bull.,* 1935, 32, 33-66.

Hertz, M. R. The method of administration of the Rorschach ink-blot test. *Child Develpm.,* 1936, 7, 237-254.

Hertz, M. R. *Frequency tables to be used in scoring the Rorschach ink-blot test.* Brush Foundation, Western Reserve Univ., Cleveland, Ohio, 1936.

Hertz, M. R. The normal details in the Rorschach ink-blot test. *Rorschach Res. Exch.,* 1936-1937, 1, 104-121.

Hertz, M. R. Discussion on "Some recent Rorschach problems." *Rorschach Res. Exch.,* 1937-1938, 2, 53-65.

Hertz, M. R. *Code charts for recording Rorschach responses.* Brush Foundation and the Department of Psychology, Western Reserve University, Cleveland, Ohio, 1938.

Hertz, M. R. Scoring the Rorschach test with specific reference to "normal detail" category. *Amer. J. Orthopsychiat.,* 1938, 8, 100-121.

Hertz, M. R. Scoring the Rorschach ink-blot test. *J. Genet. Psychol.,* 1938, 52, 15-64.

Hertz, M. R. The "popular" response factor in the Rorschach scoring. *J. Psychol.,* 1938, 6, 3-31.

Hertz, M. R. and Rubenstein, B. B. A comparison of three "blind" Rorschach analyses. *Amer. J. Orthopsychiat.,* 1939, 9, 295-315.

Hertz, M. R. On the standardization of the Rorschach method. *Rorschach Res. Exch.,* 1939, 3, 120-133.

Hertz, M. R. and Wolfson, R. A Rorschach comparison between best and least adjusted girls in a training school. *Rorschach Res. Exch.,* 1939, 3, 134-150.

Hertz, M. R. Some personality changes in adolescence as revealed by the Rorschach method. *Psychol. Bull.,* 1940, 37, 515-516.

Hertz, M. R. The shading response in the Rorschach ink-blot test: a review of its scoring and interpretation. *J. Gen. Psychol.*, 1940, 23, 123-167.

Hertz, M. R. *Summary sheet: The Rorschach psychogram.* The Brush Foundation and the Department of Psychology, Western Reserve University, 1940, 1942.

Hertz, M. R. *Percentage charts for use in computing Rorschach scores.* Brush Foundation and the Department of Psychology, Western Reserve University, 1940.

Hertz, M. R. and Kennedy, S. The M factor in estimating intelligence. *Rorschach Res., Exch.,* 1940, 4, 105-160.

Hertz, M. R. and Baker, E. Personality changes in adolescence. *Rorschach Res. Exch.,* 1941, 5, 30.

Hertz, M. R. Rorschach: twenty years after. *Rorschach Res. Exch.,* 1941, 5, 90-129.

Hertz, M. R. Validity of the Rorschach method. *Amer. J. Orthopsychiat.,* 1941, 11, 515-520.

Hertz, M. R. Pubescence and personality. *Psychol. Bull.,* 1941, 38, 598.

Hertz, M. R. Personality changes in 35 girls in various stages of pubescent development based on the Rorschach method. *Psychol. Bull.,* 1941, 38, 705.

Hertz, M. R. Evaluation of the Rorschach method and its application to normal childhood and adolescence. *Character & Pers.,* 1941, 10, 151-162.

Hertz, M. R. The validity of the Rorschach group method. *Psychol. Bull.,* 1942, 39, 514.

Hertz, M. R. The scoring of the Rorschach ink-blot method as developed by the Brush Foundation. *Rorschach Res. Exch.,* 1942, 6, 16-27.

Hertz, M. R. Personality patterns in adolescence as portrayed by the Rorschach ink-blot method: I. The movement factors. *J. Gen. Psychol.,* 1942, 27, 119-188.

Hertz, M. R. Rorschach: twenty years after. *Psychol. Bull.,* 1942, 39, 529-572.

Hertz, M. R. Comments on the standardization of the Rorschach group method. *Rorschach Res. Exch.,* 1942, 6, 153-159.

Hertz, M. R. and Baker, E. Personality patterns in adolescence as portrayed by the Rorschach ink-blot method: II. The color factors. *J. Gen. Psychol.,* 1943, 28, 3-61.

Hertz, M. R. The Rorschach method: science or mystery. *J. Consult. Psychol.,* 1943, 7, 67-79.

Hertz, M. R. Personality patterns in adolescence as portrayed by the Rorschach ink-blot method: III. The "Erlebnistypus" (a normative study). *J. Gen. Psychol.,* 1943, 28, 225-276.

Hertz, M. R. Modification of the Rorschach ink-blot test for large scale application. *Amer. J. Orthopsychiat.,* 1943, 13, 191-212.

Hertz, M. R. Personality patterns in adolescence as portrayed by the Rorschach method: IV. The "Erlebnistypus" (a typological study). *J. Gen. Psychol.,* 1943, 29, 3-45.

Hertz, M. R. and Elbert, E. H. The mental procedure of 6 and 8 year old children as revealed by the Rorschach ink-blot method. *Rorschach Res. Exch.,* 1944, 8, 10-30.

Hertz, M. R. Review of M. R. Harrower-Erickson and M. E. Steiner's "Large scale Rorschach techniques." *Rorschach Res. Exch.,* 9, 1, 1945, 46-53.

Hertz, M. R. The role of the Rorschach method in planning for treatment. *Rorschach Res. Exch.,* 1945, 9, 134-146.

Hertz, M. R., Ellis, A. and Symonds, P. M. Rorschach methods and other projective techniques. *Rev. Educ. Res.,* 1947, 17, 78-100.

Hertz, M. R. Further study of suicidal configurations in Rorschach records. *Amer. Psychologist*, 1948, 3, 283-284.

Hertz, M. R. Suicidal configurations in Rorschach records. *Rorschach Res. Exch.*, 1948, 12, 3-58.

Hertz, M. R. Further study of "suicidal" configurations in Rorschach records. *Rorschach Res. Exch.*, 1949, 13, 44-73.

Hertz, M. R. The first International Rorschach Conference. *J. Proj. Tech.*, 1950, 14, 39-51.

Hertz, M. R. Current problems in Rorschach theory and technique. *J. Proj. Tech.*, 1951, 15, 307-338.

Hertz, M. R. *Frequency tables for scoring responses to the Rorschach ink-blot test.* (3rd Ed.) Cleveland, Ohio: Western Reserve University Press, 1951; ii, 240 pp.

Hertz, M. R. Evaluating adjustment in terms of the Rorschach: Reliability of different test interpreters. *J. Proj. Tech.*, 1951, 15, 416-417.

Hertz, M. R. The Rorschach: thirty years after. In Brower, D. and Abt, L. E., *Progress in clinical psychology*. N.Y.: Grune & Stratton, 1952, 108-148.

Hertz, M. R. and Loehrke, L. M. The application of the Piotrowski and the Hughes signs of organic defect to a group of patients suffering from past-traumatic encephalopathy. *J. Proj. Tech.*, 1954, 18, 183-196.

Hertz, M. R. and Loehrke, L. M. An evaluation of the Rorschach method for the study of brain injury. *J. Proj. Tech.*, 1955, 19, 416-430.

Hertz, M. R. The use and misuse of the Rorschach method: I. Variations in Rorschach procedure. *J. Proj. Tech.*, 1959, 23, 33-48.

Hertz, M. R. and Paolino, A. F. Rorschach indices of preceptual and conceptual disorganization. *J. Proj. Tech.*, 1960, 24, 370-388.

Hertz, M. R. The Rorschach in Adolescence. In Rabin, A. and Haworth, M. (Eds.) *Projective Techniques with Children*. N.Y.: Grune & Stratton, 1960.

Hertz, M. R. The organization activity. In Rickers-Ovsiankina, Maria (Ed.) *Rorschach Psychology*. N.Y.: Wiley & Sons, 1960.

Hertz, M. R. *Frequency tables for Rorschach scoring*. Western Reserve University Press. Re-editions with revisions, 1961, 1966.

Hertz, M. R. Objectifying the subjective. *Rorschachiana*, 1963, 8, 25-54.

Hertz, M. R. The need to objectify the subjective in the Rorschach. *Rorschachiana Japonica*, 1965, VIII, 1-25.

Hertz, M. R. Detection of suicidal risks with the Rorschach. In Abt, L. and Weissman, S. (Eds.) *Acting Out*. New York: Grune & Stratton, 1965.

CHAPTER 8

THE RAPAPORT-SCHAFER SYSTEM

Unlike the other Systematizers, neither David Rapaport nor Roy Schafer have devoted a major share of their professional involvement exclusively to the Rorschach. Working together and separately, however, they have made significant contributions to the understanding and application of the Rorschach. In doing so they have developed an approach to the technique which is an organized and documented System. It differs considerably on a number of issues from any of the other Rorschach systems, including that of Rorschach himself.

David Rapaport was born in 1911. He received his Ph.D. in 1938 from the Royal Hungarian Petrus, Pazmany. He died at the age of 49, in 1960. In the 22 years encompassing his professional lifetime, he achieved a distinction of brilliance in both the theoretical and applied aspects of clinical psychology that comes to few men. Those who knew David Rapaport well never ceased to be awed by his endless amount of energy. He was very strongly psychoanalytically oriented, having trained under Paul von Schiller, and had considerable Rorschach experience before immigrating to the United States in 1938 after completion of his degree. His first position was at Mt. Siani Hospital in New York City. This was at the same time that Kurt Goldstein assumed a position there, and that Piotrowski was working there one day a week.

After a year at Mt. Sinai, Rapaport accepted a position at the Kansas State Hospital at Oswatomi, Kansas, which in turn, in 1940, led to his affiliation with the Menninger Foundation. He remained at the Menninger Foundation through 1948 and subsequently accepted a position as a Research Associate at the Austen Riggs Center, where he remained until his death. It was while at the Menninger Foundation that the basic crystalization of the Rapaport-Schafer System occurred. This System became manifest in the publication of the two volumes, *Diagnostic Psychological Testing*, which was done in collaboration with Merton Gill and Roy Schafer.*

---

* The two volumes of *Diagnostic Psychological Testing* which were published in 1946 went out of print about 1960. In 1968, a condensed version of *Diagnostic Psychological Testing* appeared as a result of the skillful editing of Robert R. Holt. The 1968 version has deleted the mass of graphs and statistical tables and some of the quantitative analyses which had provided some difficulties in continuity in the original, thus leaving the reader free to focus on the procedures and rationale which have characterized the Rapaport approach to psychodiagnostics.

Those two volumes represent an extensive accumulation of test data on 217 clinical cases and 54 control cases. The basic purpose of the investigation was to demonstrate the diagnostic usefulness of the test battery. Eight tests were used and attempts made to validate each in the general clinical sense, to demonstrate useful interrelationships of the test materials and the tests themselves, and to develop a psychological rationale for each of the tests. The Rorschach, of course, was included in the battery.*

Earlier Rapaport had published four papers dealing directly with the Rorschach. The first of these was the brief 1939 article presented at the Symposium on Standardization Problems and the second, his previously mentioned 1942 article, concerning general principles of projective techniques. The third was a collaborative work with Gill, Lozoff and Knight in which a test battery, of the sort used in the investigation published in *Diagnostic Psychological Testing* was demonstrated on a sample of three clinical cases. The fourth article appearing prior to 1946 was done in collaboration with Roy Schafer concerning the diagnostic value of the Rorschach itself.

Schafer's involvement with the Rorschach came somewhat directly as a result of his contact with David Rapaport. Schafer received his Bachelor's Degree in 1943 at City College of New York in the department chaired by Gardner Murphy. From 1943 to 1945 he served his internship at the Menninger Foundation under Rapaport's direction. It was in this role that he became a collaborator with Rapaport and Gill on *Diagnostic Psychological Testing*. His Master's Degree was awarded in 1947 from the University of Kansas and his Ph.D. from Clark University in 1950. In 1948 he published a text, which he described as a sequel to *Diagnostic Psychological Testing*. This is, *The Clinical Application of Psychological Tests: Diagnostic Summaries and Case Studies*. In 1947 he accepted a position as a staff psychologist at the Austen Riggs Center. In 1953 he moved to Yale University as a clinical professor in Psychology. He has remained there to the present, working chiefly in the Division of Student Mental Hygiene. In addition to *The Clinical Application of Psychological Tests*, he has made a major contribution through the publication of *Psychoanalytic Interpretation in Rorschach Testing*, which appeared in 1954. It has become a classic in the literature. In 1967, a collection of Schafer's papers on projective methodology was published in *Projective Testing and Psychoanalysis*.

---

* The tests included in the battery used were the Wechsler-Bellevue Adult and Adolescence Intelligence Scale, the Babcock Deterioration Test, the Sorting Test, the Rorschach Test, the Thematic Apperception Test, the Word-Association Test, and the Szondi Test.

Both Rapaport and Schafer have also contributed largely to the literature on psychoanalytic theory and particularly ego psychology. The Rorschach System of Rapaport-Schafer is clearly based on dynamic psychology. In the 1945 article, "The Rorschach Test: A Clinical Evaluation," Rapaport and Schafer describe the Rorschach as "the most efficient single diagnostic tool we possess." The basic theoretical construct underlying the Rapaport-Schafer approach to the Rorschach is essentially the same as most of the other Systematizers, that of the projective hypothesis; but they have been considerably less convinced of the "unstructured" nature of the blots themselves. In the second volume of *Psychological Diagnostic Testing* it is argued that the superficial impression that the inkblots represent "unstructured" perceptual material is deceptive. It is emphasized that no sensory stimulation "falls on a passive-receptive organ" but instead occurs in relation to a complex system for receiving sensory imputs. The needs, interests, experiences and "sets" of the individual all contribute to the complexity of the receiving system and thus, "invalidates any sharp distinction between 'structured' and 'unstructured' perceptual raw material." Accordingly, the organizational activity of the perceptual process becomes more extensive and/or more conspicuous as the sensory inputs achieve a greater degree of ambiguity. Familiar stimuli provoke swift recognition but unfamiliar stimuli produce a variety of memory activity and concept formation so as to distinguish stimulus similarities, organize the material at hand, and ultimately produce some interpretation. Rapaport maintains that the organizational and interpretive processes are significantly influenced by the "subject's own anticipations" which will vary situationally. The inkblot, because of its relative ambiguity, forces a more active organizing perceptual process than occurs under the familiar stimulus, thereby providing the examiner with "a treasure of insight into hidden aspects of an individual's adjustment or maladjustment" as the subject must identify the stimulus mainly from internal images, ideas and relations. The focal point of Rapaport's postulate concerning the response process is that, because the response content is not provided by the inkblot stimulus, an association process must evolve. In other words, by 1946, and the publication of *Diagnostic Psychological Testing,* Rapaport felt somewhat convinced that he had successfully contended with one of the validation issues that he had raised in 1939, i.e., to investigate how a Rorschach response is "born" and why it has significance. Quoting from the 1946 Volume II:

"At this point, we see three prominent phases in the process of the coming about of a Rorschach response: in the first phase, the salient perceptual features of the blot initiate the association process; in the second, this process pushes beyond these partial perceptual impressions and effects a more or less intensive organizational elaboration of the inkblot; in the third, the perceptual potentialities and limitations of the inkblot act as a regulating reality for the association process itself. Clearly then it would not be correct to reason that the Rorschach response is to be considered mainly either a perceptual product or one of free association. Either view would fail to reflect the cogwheeling of the process of perceptual organization with associative processes.

In Schafer's 1954 *Psychoanalytic Interpretation in Rorschach Testing* he reaffirms, in effect, Rapaport's postulate concerning the birth of a response and adds to it considerably by dealing at length with the interpersonal dynamics of the test situation. In doing so, he points to the intricacies of the interpersonal relationship between examiner and subject.

"Analyzing the interpersonal relationship and the real test situation may take us out to, or beyond, the borders of 'objective' test interpretation—in the narrow and, I believe, superficial sense of 'objective' test interpretation. But if we mean, as we should, to track down the origins and vicissitudes of the patients test responses, we must deal with the total situation in which the responses occur. The inkblot alone, the digit span sequence alone, the picture of a boy and a violin alone, do not totally define the stimulus situation existing at any moment. There are many other more or less uncontrolled but more or less identifiable stimuli in the situation. There are larger situational and interpersonal meanings that surround and invade the simple test stimuli."

It is on this broad premise that Schafer proceeds to consider the problems and needs of the examiner. He approaches this by citing the importance of the personal situations, the testing situation and interpersonal relationship, the psychological situation of the patient being tested, and consequently, the implications of these processes on the analysis of the data collected.

ADMINISTRATION

The Rapaport-Schafer technique of administration is, in several ways, quite different from that of the other Systematizers. First, the subject is seated facing the examiner. The rationale for this approach rather than the approach used by Rorschach or the other Systematizers of sitting side by side or behind the subject relates to the total testing situation. It is important to review again the fact, that for Rapaport and Schafer, the Rorschach is only one of several instruments in a battery of tests. In this context they find it important to present the Rorschach in a manner consistent with all other testing, i.e., face to face. This technique dispels any special significance which the subject might attribute to the test were it administered in a unique procedure. In addition, Rapaport and Schafer find it important for the examiner to be in a position where he can observe facial expressions and other significant movements, especially for the purpose of contending with any appearance of negativism by the subject.

The examiner comments introducing the test are considerably more limited in the Rorschach-Schafer System than in other Systems.

"The test is usually not given as the first in the battery. No explanation of the test is offered. Our aim is to leave the subject with as few bearings as possible. . . . The patient, seated facing the examiner, is shown the first card and asked: 'Tell me, please, what could this be? What might it be?'"

In the 1954 text Schafer indicates that the subject is usually told that it is a personality test designed to help understand the subject better and that the ultimate purpose is to derive the best possible recommendations on the subject's behalf.

"With no further orientation, with nothing at all said about the specific nature of the test stimuli or about how people usually respond to these stimuli, the patient is then confronted with card I and asked, 'What could this be? What might it look like?'"

In both the 1946 and 1954 texts it is recommended that, on card I, when the subject gives only one response, he is encouraged to give more. There is no notable difference in the comment to the subject subsequent to card I in the 1946 *Diagnostic Psychological Testing* and the 1954 *Psychoanalytic Interpretation in Rorschach Testing*. In each, the post-Card I instructions are as follows:

"Once the subject is finished and the card removed, the examiner explains, 'You see how it goes; it will be the same with all the rest of the cards. You will take your time, you will tell me everything you think they might be, or could be, and when you are finished, tell me and I will take the card away.' Thus, the subject has not been told that people see all kinds of possibilities in each card, his own inclination to productivity becomes usually quite clear on the first card. The brief explanation about the rest of the cards also leaves the subject on his own; he has no idea what the rest of the population does and is not put to task to meet their producivity; the entire problem is posed as one specific to him, and his idea of what others would do reflects his own expectations."

In the 1954 text, Schafer points out that these instructions are designed for four basic purposes. First, the instructions indicate that the responses should fit the configurations of the blots; second, they imply that the resemblance or approximation required is not necessarily an exact one; third, they implicitly request that the subject utilize his imagery of things; and fourthly, they emphasize self expression rather than some basic standard of achievement.

Rapaport apparently had been trained in a manner consistent with the Oberholzer tradition of inquiry, that is, doing inquiry after each card rather than after the entire Free Association has been completed. He defends this unique approach in the 1946 Volume II.

"The usual procedure described in the literature is to conduct inquiry into the subject's responses only after all ten cards have been interpreted by the subject. We do not follow this procedure: for purposes of diagnostic testing, it has proved expedient to do the bulk of inquiry after each card is finished. One might object that inquiry in the course of the test administration prejudices the rest of the test results by revealing to the subject not only those aspects of the inkblot in which we are particularly interested, but also his poor responses. We shall discuss the validity of this objection below. Furthermore, we found it necessary to conduct the inquiry as far as possible with the inkblot removed from the sight of the subject; and under this condition, to delay inquiry until the end of testing makes it so dependent on memory that the inquiry becomes unreliable. If the subject's response has been determined by a color or a shading in the inkblot, it will be easily discovered in this 'blind-folded' inquiry which throws the subject back upon images of the inkblot which he has retained; in such inquiry only those determinants which were most influential in the coming-about of the response will be conspicuous. But if the card is kept before the subject during inquiry, such questions as, 'Was there anything else that suggested the response to you?' might intimate that aspects of the inkblot were neglected; and subjects who were not influenced by color or shading might re-examine the inkblot and discover these or other aspects which are compatible with their response. This danger is present even when the inkblot has been removed, but much less so. It must be understood that we all can perceive what there is on a card, and the issue is not what is perceptable, but what is spontaneously perceived—that is, what features of the perceptual mass initiate association processes spontaneously and influence their course."

It is implicit in this method of Inquiry that the number of questions asked by the examiner be kept to the absolute minimum and that questions always be indirect so as to avoid the possibility of giving clues to the subject. Rapaport also infers, in the 1946 Volume II, that Inquiry need not be done for all responses, pointing to the fact that minimal Inquiry keeps the record free from speculation, rationalization, and elaboration, provides greater freedom of response by the subject and saves time. These same procedures for Inquiry are reaffirmd by Schafer in the 1954 text.

Thus, the Rapaport-Schafer System deviates considerably from any of the other Rorschach Systems with regard to general instructions and procedure of administration. Possibly the most striking difference occurs in the lack of formalized Inquiry and in the fact that the Inquiry is accomplished after each card. In such a system, scoring is accomplished primarily on the Free Association and has the potential for more subjectivity entering into the scoring than has been endorsed by any of the other Systematizers. Rapaport, in the 1946 Volume II, was adament concerning the scoring procedures and their significance.

". . . first we must acknowledge the fact that the individual scores refer to psychological functions of the subject, and that just as all of his functions are inter-related and in constant interplay so of necessity are the Rorschach scores; and secondly, the inter-relationships of these scores—i.e., the psychological functions they refer to—

must be clarified. Validation and standardization of the single scores do not make the Rorschach test a machine to be used by examiners ignorant of the psychology and pathology of personality. Personality is not compartmental, but consists of continua of a great variety in extent and shading. Standardized diagnostic indicators and validated score-significances in themselves will therefore be useful for only the crudest and most obvious diagnostic problems, where any or all of the test can be unequivocal."

Here, Rapaport not only supports the necessity for a global approach to Rorschach interpretation but also, in effect, provides for minor scoring errors which, when not approached as individual scores, can have no major impact on the ultimate interpretation.

Scoring

The Rapaport-Schafer System, like the other Rorschach Systems, provides for the scoring of Location, Determinants, Content, From-Level, plus indications of whether the response is Popular or Original. The System is rather specific concerning what actually constitutes a response, "A scoreable response is one which lends itself to scoring in the first four major scoring categories—that is to say, if it refers to a definite area of the ink-blot, has a definite conceptual content, reveals its determinants either spontaneously or in inquiry, and can be evaluated as to a form-level if form is involved as a determinant." Thus, responses sometimes scored in other systems such as Color Naming or Color Abstraction or Color Description, or even responses which might, in some systems, be scored as Movement, such as "It seems to have an upward thrusting quality," would not be scored in the Rapaport-Schafer System.

Table 9 shows the procedure for scoring Location in 1946 Rapaport-Schafer Volume II of *Diagnostic Psychological Testing* and the 1954 Schafer text, *Psychoanalytic Interpretation in Rorschach Testing*, as compared with Rorschach's suggestions for scoring. The 1954 Schafer procedure is, in essence, identical to that recommended in 1946, The apparent difference between the 1946 and 1954 scoring for W is more artificial than real. The subdivision of the W response into W+, Wo, Wv, and W— had been used for research purposes in the study on which the 1946 volume is based. Subsequently, it did not become a routine part of the scoring scheme although the concept has been encouraged for use whenever evaluating W's. It should also b noted that Schafer emphasized in the 1954 volume that his concern with scoring, in writing that book, was at best secndary.

"While my attention will be paid in the case studies to the scores, test attitudes and imagery, the scores will often be relatively under-emphasized. This is because I hope to show how much we can understand the Rorschach record without referring to scores. This is not for the purpose of a tour de force. I believe that the

TABLE 9

A Comparison of the Rapaport-Schafer System for Scoring Location as Suggested in 1946 and 1954 with that Originally Recommended by Rorschach

Symbol	Rorschach	Rapaport-Gill-Schafer—1946	Schafer—1954
W	Plate interpreted as a whole	Same, but subdivided into W+= sharply and intensely differentiated W's; Wo=average good W responses; Wv=responses based on a vague general impression; and W-= involving considerable arbitrariness in the percept showing little congruence with the blot (Specifically rejects "cut-off" W concept)	All or nearly all of the blot (This infers agreement with Rorschach and also some incorporation of Klopfer's "cut-off" W) — (No inclusion is made of W+, Wo, Wv, or W— as described by Rapaport)
DW	Plate interpreted as a whole secondarily, the answer based primarily on a detail	Same as Rorschach	Same
D	A normal detail of the blot	Same; defined as a part of the card, conspicuous by its size, its location and the frequency of responses which it draws	Same
Dd	An unusual or small detail	Small but not tiny areas which stand out by reason of their clarity	Same
Dr	Not used	Very small or perceptually unbalanced areas	Same; defined as tiny areas or relatively large areas which are neither clearly set off nor frequently interpreted
De	Not used	Interpretation only of the contour of the blot without really using an area	Same
Do	A detail is interpreted in place of a whole	Same	Same
S	White Intermediate figures (Space detail)	A relatively large white area in or around the blot (May be used separately or in combination with W, D, Dd or Dr)	Same
s	Not used	A relatively small space detail (May be used separately or in combination with W, D, Dd, or Dr)	Same

development of Rorschach technique has tended to restrict attention to scores and their sequences to the point where scores often become barriers between the tester and the patient. Theory and interpretation suffer as a result, becoming mechanical and jargonistic. Rapaport's emphasis on analysis of verbalization represents an important break with the score-oriented tradition. . . . Another reason for my relative neglect of scores in what follows is that the standard principles for interpreting scores, score sequences and score patterns have been set forth in detail by a number of writers. . . . Despite this didactically required de-emphasis of scores, a brief summary of the scoring system is necessary. This is because the scoring system, which is virtually identical with that set forth by Rapaport, is not widely used."

It will be noted from examination of Table 9 that the similarity between the Rapaport-Schafer method for scoring Location and that recommended by Rorschach is high. It is only with the inclusion of separate scorings for rare details, edge details and the use of a second symbol for white space responses that any differences of significance occur.

Table 10 shows the method of scoring Determinants as recommended in the 1946 volume, and in Schafer's 1954 text, as compared with Rorschach's conceptions for Determinant scoring. Considerable agreement exists between the 1946 and 1954 recommendations for scoring Determinants. In only two instances, that is, the definitions of scoring criteria for FM and (C)F, are any differences noted. In the latter, Rapaport used the scoring symbol (C) to denote those responses where texture and color associations are combined somehow. His scoring is C(C)F. Schafer also uses the (C) to encompass such responses but relegates the symbol (C) primarily for responses in which shading components are used to specify outline or details. This symbol is combined with F depending on the degree of Form involvement in the percept.

It is also important to mention that the Rapaport-Schafer System includes a formal notation in the scoring whenever the response includes some notably deviant feature. The 1946 volume lists twelve such notation categories: fabulizations, fabulized combinations, confabulations, contaminations, autistic logic, peculiar or queer verbalizations, confused or incoherent verbalizations, preoccupation with symmetry, deteriorated responses, and affective-reactive responses. The 1954 text lists essentially the same notions with added clarification concerning the definition of each.

It will be noted from examination of Table 10 that the Rapaport-Schafer System is somewhat unique from the other Systems in that, not only is the criteria for scoring M consistent with that of Rorschach, but also the scoring of FM as a tendency toward movement and specifically excluding animal movement, is consistent with the Rorschach tradition. Unlike other Systems using the FM Symbol, the Rapaport-Schafer method also calls for such responses to be included in the computation of the Erlebnistyp, giving each

TABLE 10

A Comparison of the Rapaport-Schafer System for Scoring Location as Suggested in 1946 and 1954 with that Originally Recommended by Rorschach

Symbol	Rorschach	Rapaport-Gill-Schafer—1946	Schafer—1954
F	Form Answers (Scoring of $+$ or $-$ based on frequency of recurring answers, allowing for subjective evaluation where statistical data insufficient)	Form Answers (Uses criteria similar to Rorschach's for evaluating $+$ or $-$ Form level qualities but also includes Form level scoring of $\pm$ to denote responses of essentially good Form with some poor Form features and $\mp$ to denote responses of essentially poor Form with some good Form Features. Also recommends that Form responses be evaluated qualitatively into four categories; Special F+=sharp and definitive; Fv=vague; Fo=mediocre but acceptable; Special F– definite but arbitrary and unconvincing)	Same (But makes no mention of Special F+, Fv, Fo, or Special F–)
M	Movement answers involving kinesthetic influences (restricted to humans or human behaviors)	Same criteria but restricted to complete or nearly complete human figures	Same
Ms	Not used	M responses given to areas of small size	Same
FM	Not used (In Rorschach's 1923 paper reference is given to Form tending toward Movement which could involve either human or animal figures)	Weak Movement Tendency (Not used for animal movements except where animal Forms in human-like motion are seen where human Forms are ordinarily seen; also to be used where part-human figures are large and the movement tendency clear. Used in computation of Erlebnistyp)	Essentially the same; definition modified as "an M response with weak emphasis on motion or tension, with animal-like features stressed, or with animals in human-like activity"

C	Color answers, interpretation based on the Color of the blot alone	Same	Same
CF	Color-Form answer, determined primarily by the Color, secondarily by the Form	Same	Same
FC	Form-Color answer, determined primarily by the Form, secondarily by the Color	Same	Same
F/C	Not used	Form-Color answers where the Color is used to distinguish content with definite form, i.e. specific anatomical drawings	Same
C/F	Not used	Color-Form answers where the use of Color is artificial, i.e. colored map	Same
C Det	Not used	Deterioration Pure Color Response (Interpretation is gory, uncanny, or gives the impression of extreme haphazardness of association)	Not included
Color Symbolism	Not used	Color symbolically used to represent an abstract idea (no scoring abreviation used)	Not included
Color Naming	Rorschach used symbol CC for Color naming	Where colors are named in a manner implying compliance with the test instructions (no scoring abreviation used)	Not included
Color Denomination	Not used	Where colors are named but not the intention of a response (no scoring abreviation used)	Not included
Color Description	Not used	Reference to the beauty or colorfulness of the cards with no response intended (no scoring abreviation used)	Not included

TABLE 10 (*Continued*)

A Comparison of the Rapaport-Schafer System for Scoring Location as Suggested in 1946 and 1954 with that Originally Recommended by Rorschach

Symbol	Rorschach	Rapaport-Gill-Schafer—1946	Schafer—1954
FC	Not used	Form-Color Answer by Denial; defined as a negation of the Color of the area chosen; i.e. "a bear, but it's the wrong Color"	Not used
FC arb	Not used	Arbitrary Form-Color response where Color used is incompatible to the content with no effort to rationalize it as artificial	Same
F(C)	Chiaroscuro Answers, Form primary	Form responses in which shading components are used to specify the outline or important inner details. Also used to specify the use of texture in Form-Color answers	Same
(C)F	Chiaroscuro Answers, Chiaroscuro features primary	Color-Form responses with texture, i.e. "lumps of strawberry ice cream" to lower Card VIII (restricted only to Color responses). The scoring here is C(C)F.	Defined to include the 1946 definition but also used for responses which are a vague F(C) type, i.e. can be used for achromatic responses
Ch	Not used	As recommended by Binder to denote chiaroscuro responses; defined to include FCh, ChF or Ch depending on the degree of Form involvement	Same
C'	Not used	Achromatic Color used as a Color. Defined to include FC', C'F, or C' depending on the degree of Form involvement in the response	Same

FM response a value of 0.5. Like the other Systematizers, Rapaport-Schafer have added symbols for scoring types of responses not considered by Rorschach. In the area of olor this occurs with the adoption of Klopfer's symbols F/C and C/F for the scoring of Color when artificially used. Symbols are also included to denote Color denial and arbitrary use of Color. Several symbols are used for chiaroscuro responses. The pattern for scoring chiaroscuro responses is very similar to that recommended by Binder, that is, using the symbol Ch for the basic scoring of Shading responses. In addition to the adoption of Binder's method of scoring Shading, Rapaport and Schafer have also encompassed Klopfer's score of C' to denote instances where achromatic Color is used as a Color and have also incorporated Rorschach's use of the symbol (C) to denote instances where the Shading characteristics of the blot are either used as contour, or as texture components in colored responses. Where differences seem to exist between the 1946 and 1954 texts, these differences may simply be of omission rather than commission in that Schafer devotes only four pages to problems of scoring and quantitative summary. At no time is there any reference to a disagreement with the procedures originally recommended in the 1946 text.

The scoring of Content in the 1946 text lists 15 symbols reasonably consistent with those used in the other systems ranging from H for human to N for nature scenes. It is recommended in the 1946 text that responses not fitting into those specific categories be registered individually. A slightly different list of 14 content scoring symbols is offered in the 1954 text with a similar implication that responses not fitting those categories be registered individually. The 1946 text calls for 19 different responses qualifying as Populars. In addition, the concept of a "conditional" Popular is offered. This is scored as (P) and used for responses in which the area chosen is identical with that of a Popular response but the content of the response is less common and therefore disqualifies it for a scoring of an ordinary Popular. An example of this would be on Card V wherein the common responses of bat or butterfly would be scored P and responses such as bug or bird would be scored (P). Rapaport was also concerned that a second kind of response be considered together with Populars, although they are not scored as Populars. These are responses which tend toward popularity but do not completely meet the criteria to be scored P or (P), yet occur with sufficient frequency to be interpreted as indicating some leanings toward conventionality. Original responses, to be scored O, are defined in the 1946 text as those occurring once or twice in 100 records. In the 1954 volume Schafer provides identical definitions for scoring of both Popular and Original responses as well as tendency toward Popular responses.

The 1946 and 1954 volumes both offer agreement with Rorschach concerning responses in which more than one Determinant is obviously present and is given spontaneously by the subject. In these instances the Determinants are combined into a single scoring such as MC' or CC'F. This is similar to the Piotrowski System as well as the Beck method of distinguishing "Blend" responses. The Rapaport-Schafer method of combining Determinants should not be confused with their notation "Comb." The notation Comb is used in the System to denote those unique situations where two or more interpretations are scored separately but meaningfully related by the subject. The 1946 text does not indicate how combined Determinant scores are to be treated in the quantitative summary. Schafer makes this quite clear in the 1954 text in which he notes, "Scores listed after the first will be tallied 'additional' in the score summary." Thus a consistency with Klopfer's basic concept of Main and Additional scores seems to exist.

It is important to the understanding of the Rapaport-Schafer System to emphasize that, while it has encompassed a broad scheme for coding or scoring almost all kinds of responses, it is predicated on the requirement that quantitative summarization of Rorschach responses causes neither loss of the qualitative wealth nor distortion of the interpretation of the protocol. In the 1946 volume, Rapaport offers some of his thinking concerning the problem of scoring.

"The 'refinements' (referring to the increased number of determinants scored) make sense insofar as they call attention to qualitative features of the record not thus far systematized, but only if the psychological significance of these new determinants and a reasonable frequency of occurrence can be established. . . . Furthermore, too much refinement of scoring gives the impression that interpretation can be achieved by consulting a handbook of scores and without genuine understanding of the theory of personality and psychopathology. The use of the text in this manner becomes mechanical and out of touch with clinical reality; and the psychologically meaningful relations of the scores become reduced to echoing magic words, 'Rorschach record is a configuration (or gestalt) in which the meaning of the different scores are interdependent.' "

INTERPRETATION

In 1946 Rapaport set forth a variety of interpretive hypotheses pertaining to individual scores and score patterns. He was highly insistent that these postulates, some having been obtained from the quantitative profiles of the sample, and some from qualitative inference, cannot be indiscriminately applied to all protocols. Instead, he forcefully maintains that each protocol must be interpreted in light of the overall or global pattern obtained. He recommends that interpretations be formulated using four different, yet overlapping, sources of data; the quantitative record, the qualitative record, the Form level of the record, and the verbalization of the record. He suggests that the quantitative aspect of the record offers an impression concerning the subject's output, the scope of his environment, and the degree of rigidity or flexibility available. In turn, qualitative evaluation aids in clarifying the dynamic interplay of the subject's quantitative productivity and his ideational and affective operations. Form level evaluation is used mainly to clarify the extent to which the subject's responsiveness adequately meets the realities of the stimulus situation and the extent to which subsequent judgments concerning these stimulus situations are effective. Finally, the verbalization analysis provides those highly idiographic bits of information which portray the unique features of the individual in his interplay with perceptual, affective, and associative processes. Rapaport notes that while these verbalizations do not always provide direct manifestations of the idiographic phenomenon, there are frequently cues given off, especially among instances of psychopathology, which provide considerable understanding of the intrapsychic conflict structure.

Providing such a format for interpretation and insisting upon the ever present awareness of global interpretation, Rapaport thus proceeded with the diagnostic postulates which might be relevant to particular scores or score patterns. The W response is interpreted as representing the abstracting, surveying, and integrating abilities of the subject. Going beyond this hypothesis for W interpretation, which is quite similar to Rorschach's W hypothesis, Rapaport interprets the W in terms of his four basic scoring subdivisions. The W+ is perceived as the highest form of integration or abstraction encompassing a whole blot. Wo responses are interpreted as those in which the abstraction itself implies validity to the percept but with little impressiveness, imagination, or importance to overall adaptivity. Wv is interpreted as a response made too quickly with a "restricted grasp of the perceptual material, as well as the possible limitations of the underlying associative processes. . . ." W− is interpreted as arbitrary articulation in which the overall judgment of the individual is significantly lacking.

D responses are suggested to indicate a grasp of "the obvious" with the notation that the expected D percentage is largely dependent upon the length of the record (40 to 50 per cent in short records; 50 to 60 per cent in longer records). Interpretatively, the importance of D is not so much its existence but the lack thereof or an overemphasis on this kind of response.

The interpretation for other location scores is relatively consistent with Beck and/or Klopfer. The Dd response is perceived as ordinarily portraying a sharp perception of articulation, thus being relatively high in form level. A small percentage of Dd type responses are implied to be relevant in most records of well adjusted people. Such responses become excessive in number in highly productive groups such as over-ideational pre-schizophenics or obsessives or become lowered when inhibition becomes too strong or when perceptual capacities become "sluggish." The Do response is interpreted as being due either to "fragmentary perceptual organization or to a failure of the associational process to pave the way for integrations. . . ." Responses utilizing rare details or edge details are suggested as quantitatively unimportant when occurring with very small frequency. Whenever a high frequency occurs, however, the accumulation of such responses is probably indicative of significant pathology. Rapaport was not prone to disagree with Rorschach's concept of space responses, as indicative of negative tendencies, but was quick to point out that he could not offer validating information from his sample for this postulate. He indicates that space responses could easily occur in a variety of protocols and seem highly correlated with the rare detail response. He suggests that where such responses occur in abundance with rare detail responses, the protocol is probably one of a "doubt-ridden character suggestive of the presence of a paranoid condition."

Unlike some of the other Systematizers, Rapaport has been careful to emphasize that the inter-relationship of the location scores would change depending upon the length of the record. Thus a 1:2 relationship should occur between the W and D responses in an average size record (25 to 30 responses). He adds, however, that in larger records the prevalence of D could increase making the ratio as great as 1:3 or in shorter records the prevalence of W could increase thus making the ratio of 1:1. He implies that other types of location scores (rare detail, space detail, etc.) will ordinarily not exceed 10 per cent of the record.

As had been noted in a previous chapter, Rapaport tended to be critical of those seeking to increase the number of Determinants scored in a protocol. Yet, as will be noted from examination of Table 10 the number of Determinants used in a Rapaport-Schafer System is not significantly different from that used in most of the other Systems. At the same time, he maintained his criticism of undue increases in symbols used in the 1946 volume.

"The 'refinements' make sense in so far as they call attention to qualitative features of the record not thus far systematized, but only if the psychological significance of these new determinants and a reasonable frequency of occurrence can be established. However, the psychological meaning of the majority of the added scores that have been promulgated has been even less validly established than those of the scores originally produced by Rorschach; they refer mainly to features by no means as conspicuous as those the original scores refer to; and their relation to major characteristics of adjustment and maladjustments is harder to assess by experience or to capture by statistics. Furthermore, too much refinement of scoring gives the impression that interpretation can be achieved by consulting a handbook of scores, and without genuine understanding of the theory of personality and psychopathology. . . . Many investigators have been concerned with this difficulty. Several answers to it have been proffered."

At this point in his discussion Rapaport severely criticizes both those Systematizers who have attempted to extend the scoring system to the point where "finer nuances of responses" are codified and the formal psychogram developed and weighed heavily for interpretation and those, especially Klopfer, who extended the inquiry technique so as to avoid a "paucity" of Determinants.

"This method (Testing of Limits) obviously aims to unearth 'subliminal' determinants. Upon the disadvantages of too extensive inquiry we have already commented. It is possible by means of it to collect more material concerning the subject: but it is inadvisable because it disrupts the unity, internal consistency, and objectivity of the test, and makes it a cumbersome and time-consuming tool. . . . the relationship between spontaneous and forced productivity is not well understood. We have some evidence that certain kinds of responses cannot be elicited even under pressure but this is by no means true for all; the total number of responses, or the use of color and shading as determinants, can be so increased. Thus, a new unknown is introduced by this 'testing of limits' into a test already abounding in unknowns."

Thus, with his intellectual guns blazing away, Rapaport sternly reinforced his oft-stated concept that the qualitative aspects and the verbalizations of a protocol must be interpreted as well as the quantitative aspects and the form level. Rapaport indicates that nearly two thirds of all responses in most protocols are pure Form responses. This is interpreted as the individual striving for objectivity manifesting a process of "formal reasoning" or, in the ego psychology concept, the conflict-free sphere of ego operation. It is Rapaport's contention that the Form response represents a "capacity for delay of discharge of impulses" wherein the utilization of vague forms indicates that the subject cannot perceptually articulate the area with which he is dealing and offers "only a few partial perceptual impressions and a few associative contents which are diluted . . ."; the F+ type response indicates that the delay in itself has reached a peak of productivity; the Fo response indicates that the delay "has allowed only for sufficient ideation for the association process to integrate the necessary minimum for perceptual impressions . . ."; and F– responses indicate instances where the subject has abandoned his strivings for equilibrium between the perceptual and associative process and instead creates a percept haphazardly or arbitrarily manifesting considerable poor judgment. Rapaport finds that the general plus percentage of Form responses should fall between 65, as the minimum, and 80, as the maximum, in the relatively "healthy" individual.

The Rapaport-Schafer interpretation of Movement responses starts with the general acceptance of Rorschach's postulate that M is a manifestation of the inner tendencies and indicates the degree of associative wealth available. The System goes well beyond that basic interpretation and offers considerable modification to the concept of "introversion" as had been postulated by Rorschach. The difference concerning the issue of introversion might best be described as a reinterpretation rather than outright disagreement. Rapaport agrees that M responses are preponderant among people who are inclined to "think things out" versus those who are more prone to follow their impulses and act out more immediately. Thus, M indicates a tendency of the individual to delay his responses and generally denotes "a readiness to make anticipations, and a versatility and flexibility of perceptual and associative processes in general." M is seen as representing a resistance to spontaneity but *not* a tendency toward internalization, although the possibility exists for more intense "ideational activity." Rapaport suggests, in the 1946 volume, that the number of M responses should be relatively equal to the number of color responses in the most well adjusted individuals. It is also suggested that "within the normal range, therefore, we should expect M's to be more abundant in subjects who show cultural interests and less so where these are absent and where 'normal' inhibition increases."

Prefacing the interpretation of Color responses, the 1946 volume stresses the problem of inquiry.

"The real issues of inquiry are: (a) when not to make it and still be safe in scoring; (b) how to make it without arousing the critical awareness of the patient, and thereby disrupting the homogeneity of the record; (c) how to use its results not merely to give a score but also—and mainly—to assess the quality of the response behind the score. . . . In connection with the color responses, inquiry should be made only if one of two basic requirements is met: when the subject's spontaneous verbalization indicates that color has played a role in his response, without indicating the strength of this role; or when the content of the response given appears congruous with the color of the area chosen, although the subject has not specifically mentioned color."

After attaching this conservative warning concerning the scoring of Color responses, the Rapaport-Schafer System adopts, in principle, the basic Color interpretations offered by Rorschach with some variation on the concept of extroversion or extratensive tendencies. Pure Color responses are noted to represent an absence of impulse delay and a general disruption of the harmonious perceptual and associative process; Color-Form responses are interpreted as representing attempted delays in which the perceptual reorganization of the blot results in a weak or indefinite integration of Form and Color; and where the Form-Color response indicates that the impact of both Form and Color of the area chosen "were worked through in the course of the associative process." It is also noted, regarding interpretation of Color responses, that the F/C response indicates regulating attempts to affect whereas C/F represents similar attempts but lacking integration. Color denial responses are interpreted as a weakness of ability to integrate colors in the course of the associative process. The arbitrary use of Color is suggested as an unsuccessful attempt at emotional adaptation creating disharmony and inappropriate affective discharge. The symbolic Color responses and deterioration Color responses are interpreted as having continuity with the pure Color response, that is, lacking perceptual organization and being indicative of tendencies toward liability. Color naming is described as, "no associative departure" from the Color impression itself, and indicate—by the misunderstanding of the test instructions—that the subject's anticipatory abilities are impaired." The use of so-called "Color descriptions" or denominations are equated somewhat with Color naming responses but also cited as indicative of the fact that colors have had some impact, but not such as to be included in the evaluation of the associative process.

Discussion is also provided, in the 1946 volume, to the relationship of Color to affect. It is noted that much speculation concerning this relationship had preceded the writing of the volume. It is accepted that there is a direct relationship but admission that the validation of the existence of such a relationship is "still forthcoming." There is no question, however, that, like the other Systematizers, the Rapaport-Schafer interpretation of Color is contingent upon the assumption that Color responses are directly related to affect and, subsequently, the relation of Form to Color is indicative of the extent to which the control of delay of impulse occurs within the individual.

"The smoother the control of the delay and satisfaction of the instinctual impulses, the more varied and rich their derivatives become. If the delay cannot be achieved smoothly, repressive measures become necessary, with a consequent impoverishment of the derivatives. But their repressive measures are not always successful and do not always result in smooth control, and their inability for achieving delay will be indicated by the appearance of affects in spite of the repression: in this case, the affects will not manifest themselves in mild, smooth, and richly variable form, but rather in spasmodic and explosive forms, with little variation of modulation of feeling tones."

It is also important to note that Rapaport has been concerned with a card by card evaluation of the "stimulus pull" for the incidence of Color responses. It is suggested that the occurrence of Form-Color responses is derived most easily on cards VIII and X and with greatest difficulty on cards II, III, and IX. The implication is clear that the type of Color response must not only be evaluated in and for itself, as it occurs, but also with regard to the card and even the area of the card to which it occurs. It is suggested, in the 1946 volume, that the average length record will ordinarily contain two FC and one CF responses. It is also postulated that, regardless of the ultimate length of a record, the number of FC responses should generally exceed that of all other Color responses except in instances of serious pathology.

Rapaport's interpretation of the Shading response is closely aligned with his interpretation of Color responses, that is, a manifestation of affect. In general, Shading responses are perceived as indicative of some form of anxiety within the subject.

". . . The presence of pure Ch response is—in our experience—usually referable to a relatively steady, free-floating anxiety; and accumulation of ChF responses usually refers to paralyzing anxieties, more directly related to specific situations and ideas; the FCh scores appear to refer mainly to anxieties which are relatively well controlled and/or bound up in bodily symptom formation."

The F(C) type response and the C' type of response are interpreted by Rapaport as indicating anxious or cautious adaptation and/or conscious control of or defense against affective discharge. This interpretation is relatively consistent with that provided in the Rorschach-Oberholzer paper. Rapaport emphasizes that the significance of the shading response is the least thoroughly explored of any of the Determinants. He also points out that manifestations of anxiety can appear in Rorschach protocols having a complete absence of shading responses, such as would be manifest in excessive emphasis on small details or excessive utilization of Fo type responses. It is postulated that wherever Shading-type responses, especially of the F(C) or (C)F variety occur in colored areas, that this be interpreted as a "mingling of affect and anxiety."

The Rapaport-Schafer interpretation of scored content is quite similar to interpretations given by the other Systematizers. It is perceived as indicating the breadth of interest both in things and in people, the existence of any specific preoccupations as manifest in overemphasis on a particular content, and also analytically, as a manifestation of specific affects. The latter is revealed in responses such as blood, being indicative of aggressive affects, plants, being indicative of sensitive or delicate affects, or cloud responses which are indicative of anxiety and feelings of vagueness.

Popular and Original responses are also interpreted similarly to the other Systematizers. Popular responses are indicated as a representation of compliance with the thinking of a community, with the suggestion that the average size record should contain four or five P responses. The Original response is interpreted as representing tendencies toward freedom of thought, indicating that where the Original occurs with good Form the native endowment of the individual is expected to be higher than the average. It is also stated that where the Original response encompasses areas where the Form level is vague or inadequate, pathological features are probably influencing the creation of the response.

In addition to providing interpretive postulates for all of the location factors, determinants, and content scores, the Rapaport-Schafer System gives emphasis to a few ratios and percentages, some of which have already been mentioned. The Erlebnistypus, or Experience Balance, is calculated in a slightly different manner than in the other Systems. The Movement side of the ratio includes the FM responses, giving each a value of 0.5. The Rapaport-Schafer interpretation of the Experience Balance is similar to that offered by Rorschach, as representing some indication of the balance between impulses and affects on one side and delay in ideation developing on the other side. Rapaport also suggests two additional measures dealing with Movement and Color responses to supplement or clarify the interpretation of the Experience Balance.

"We have already indicated that the Experience Balance (EB) may be approached from the point of view of its general dilation and coarctation, or from the point of view of which side of it (movement or color) is more heavily weighted. In order to represent statistically the former aspect of qualitative wealth, we shall employ the measure: sum M + sum C. Obviously this measures does not take account of the direction of the EB, and for this we shall employ a second measure: $\frac{\text{sum M}}{\text{sum M} + \text{sum C}}$ x 100. The latter gives the percentage of sum M in the total of sum M + sum C. Thus, any record in which there is an equal weight of movement and color responses, this measure equals 50 per cent; and one with no colors and only movement, it equals 100 per cent.

The first of these two measures (sum M + sum C) is very similar to the criteria for Beck's Experience Actual. It should also be noted that the interpretation of this measure, which was not given a name by Rapaport, is nearly identical to the early interpretation given by Beck of the Experience Actual. The second measure was defined as a "M%." The interpretation of the M% is somewhat vague in the 1946 volume except to indicate:

". . . M prevalence in a psychotic protocol points mainly to the presence of an acute delusional conditioning; in a pre-schizophrenic setting it points to the over-ideational type; in a depressive setting it usually indicates some obsessive or schizoid trends accompanying the depression; in the neurotic range it always points to the presence of obsessive pathology; and in the normal range, it is most regulraly associated with a better—more sublimated—mode of adjustment.

The Rapaport-Schafer System also calls for the computation of the F+ percentage and F percentage, a W to D ratio, a Dr percentage, and other percentages, where appropriately high or low, and "substantially important" to the overall interpretation of the protocol.

The 1946 volume gives considerable emphasis to the analysis of the subject's verbalization. Fifteen separate categories concerning the verbalization of the subject are discussed in this text. Many of these had been previously discussed or implied as important by earlier writers on Rorschach interpretation. But none had systematically categorized them as was done here. It is Rapaport's argument that the actual verbalizations of the subject can be viewed as highly idiographic and are among the most relevant data pertinent to the understanding of the individual. It is also stressed that verbalizations elicited from a "too direct" type of inquiry would confuse the ultimate analysis of the verbalizations.

'The questions asked by the examiner should remain as vague as possible; they should give the subject no clue as to the examiner's intent or the specific aspect of the response he is concerned with. The examiner should never ask, 'What is there about the card or on the card that makes you think so?' Instead, relatively ambiguous questions such as, 'What makes it look like this?' or 'What makes you think this?' are preferable."

It is emphasized that verbalizations are especially important to the understanding of pathological conditions. Therefore, most of the section on interpretation of verbalizations deals with pathological conditions. The basic categories into which analysis of verbalization are considered are, (1) the reality of the testing situation, (2) the DW response, (3) the absurd response. This latter category is subdivided into twleve types of deviant verbalizations according to the scoring notations employed: fabulized responses; fabulized combinations; confabulations; contaminations; autistic logic; peculiar and queer verbalizations; vague, confused, or incoherent verbalizations; symmetry verbalizations; deteriorated verbalizations; affective-reactive verbalizations. The symbolic verbalization is also emphasized, but with the caution that the examiner should not attempt to infer unconscious ideas or feelings without a firm base.

"The hazards of wild symbolic interpretations are overwhelming, and the examiner will only discredit himself in the eyes of responsible psychiatrists by speculations not based on an intimate knowledge of the patient himself. However, symbolic responses can be interpreted in their formal aspects as indications of psychotically artistic thinking, or as reflexive normal or obsessive neurotic indications."

Schafer's 1954 text is, in many ways, an extension of the 1946 concept of analyzing verbalizations and content. Schafer suggests this in his statement:

"From what has been said so far, we may now formulate a major characteristic of the Rorschach response: by virtue of its spread along the dreaming-perceiving continuum, the Rorschach response may and often does simultaneously bear the imprint of primitive, unrealistic, unconscious processes and articulated, realistic conscious processes. . . . Rorschach responses, on the other hand, ordinarily constitute a set of isolated, static, generalized images that do not explicitly express specific content drawn from the patient's real life. . . . The Rorschach communications, when they are not confabulated, are more abstract and fragmentary than the typical dream communication. They often state problems but cannot articulate them, at least not to any significant degree."

The 1954 Schafer volume, as has been previously pointed out, was designed to integrate the variety of previously published psychoanalytic conceptualizations concerning the Rorschach response process, and to extend these conceptualizations into a practicable, interpretive scheme. Like Rapaport, Schafer is firm to caution that the content categories typically used in the various systems, although demonstrating some generalized interpretive value, are really idiosyncratically inadequate, mainly because they are static categories.

"The psychology of personality has long since abandoned strict adherence to such class concepts and has shifted emphasis to functional or dynamic concepts. For example, a lamb, a sleeping infant, and a cradle have much in common thematically, although they represent three different static content categories, i.e., animal, human and object respectively. They may be said to deal with theme of infantile innocence, or perhaps the need for care and protection, or both."

Schafer is particularly critical of the approach to content as had been recommended previously by Lindner, Brown, and Phillips and Smith. He sets forth six basic criteria for judging the adequacy of interpretation: (1) There must be sufficient evidence for interpretation; (2) the depth of the interpretation should be appropriate to the material available; (3) the manifest form of the interpreted tendency should be specified; (4) the intensity of the interpreted trend should be estimated; (5) the interpreted tendency should be given a hierarchic position in the total personality pattern; (6) the adaptive and pathalogical aspects of the interpreted tendencies should both be specified. Using these criteria as a basic format, Schafer describes the fundamental analytic approach for interpreting Rorschach responses, especially in light of the defensive mechanisms of the ego. It should not be inferred that the Schafer approach concentrates only on verbalizations and content and neglects scoring or score patterns. Quite the contrary, like Rapaport, Schafer insists on the routine scoring for a protocol and uses scores plentifully in interpretation. His approach to analytic interpretation of the Rorschach, which stresses an understanding of the defense mechanisms as they are manifest in the protocol, provides a thorough integration of quantitative and qualitative data. Schafer offers a variety of nomothetic speculations concerning score relationships as they are apparent in different defensive maneuvers. For instance, where repression is evident he anticipates a low numbr of R, , M, and Dr and a relative high emphasis on color and shading responses whereas in the incidence of isolation he expects to find a high Dr, F%, extended F%, F+%, extended F+%, and M and a relatively low number of color and shading responses. It is important to re-emphasize however, that Schafer does not simply offer potential psychograms to be interpreted in a cookbook fashion for that is definitely not the case. All factors of the test and the test situation are stressed, ranging from the examiner-subject relationship to the structural and symbolic representations of the responses. In doing so, Schafer is able to extend the material in the 1946 and 1948 volumes in a manner to provide a greater wealth of interpretive understanding, especially as relevant to the processes of repression, regression, denial, projection, isolation, intellectualization, reaction formation and undoing.

Schafer has also contributed a number of important papers on the Rorschach, as well as on other diagnostic methods. Several of these have been assembled in the volume *Projective Testing and Psychoanalysis* (1967). These represent, for the most part, his continuing commitment to the psychoanalytic model of interpretation. His goal, in terms of the understanding of the individual, continues to be the goal of Rapaport. Schafer states this goal succinctly in personal communication: "the point being to avoid a Rorschach psychology and to approach Rorschach data, or any other data, from a psychological point of view that draws heavily, though not exclusively, on Freudian psychoanalysis" (1968). The fact that a Rorschach System has developed as work toward this goal has ensued is somewhat coincidental, although not surprising. Rapaport and Schafer have consistently endorsed the use of many sources of data, i.e., testing, observations and history. In this scheme the Rorschach has almost always taken a nuclear role and thus, much time and energy has been devoted to its understanding. In some respects, the resulting Rorschach System is not as fully crystalized as other Rorschach Systems but when viewed in terms of specific aspects, such as examiner-subject relationships or depth of psychoanalytic interpretation, it is more fully developed.

The totality of the Rapaport-Schafer System has clearly achieved a level of organization wherein it can be applied as a System in itself, different from the other Rorschach Systems. It is sufficiently elucidated to be contrasted with the other Systems. In such a contrast it is found to be radical in some ways, such as the method of Inquiry or the approach to verbalizations, and quite traditional in other respects. It is probable that it is the least researched System in that it is heavily oriented toward analysis via the psychoanalytic model which requires more complex research designs. The extent of its use is probably more similar to the Piotrowski and Hertz Systems as compared with the more widely expounded Beck and Klopfer Systems. Regardless of its past or future impact on Rorschach, this System represents a dimension of Rorschach use significantly important to any evaluation of Rorschach methodologies.

REFERENCES

Binder, H. Die Helldunkeldeutungen im psychodiagnostischen Experiment von Rorschach. *Schweizer Archiv für Neurologie und Psychiatrie*, 1933, 30, 1-67, and 233-286.

Brown, J. F., Rapaport, D., Tillman, C. G. and Dubin, S. S. An analysis of scatter in a test battery used in clinical diagnosis. *Psychol. Bull.*, 1941, 38, 715.

Kenyon, V. B., Rapaport, D. and Lozoff, M. Note on metrazol in general paresis. *Psychiatry*, 1941, 4, 165-176.

Knight, R. P., Gill, M., Lozoff, M. and Rapaport, D. Comparison of clinical findings and psychological tests in three cases bearing upon military personnel selection. *Bull. Menninger Clin.*, 1943, 7, 114-128.

Miale, Florence. The Rorschach Forum at the Sixteenth Annual Meeting of the American Orthopsychiatric Association, February 23, 1939, in New York City, *Ror. Res. Exch.*, 1939, 3, 106-119.

Pilot, M. L., Lenkoski, L. D., Spiro, H. M. and Schafer, R. Duodenal ulcer in one of identical twins. *Psychosom. Med.*, 1957, 19, 221-227.

Rapaport, D. Principles underlying projective techniques. *Character & Pers.*, 1942, 10, 213-219.

Rapaport, D. Manual of diagnostic psychological testing. I. Diagnostic testing of intelligence and concept formation. *Publ. Josiah Macy Jr. Found.*, 1944, 2, No. 2, Pp. xiii, 239.

Rapaport, D. Diagnostic testing in psychiatric practice. *Bull. N.Y. Acad. Med.*, 1950, 26, 115-125.

Rapaport, D. and Brown, J. F. Concept formation tests and personality research. *Psychol. Bull.*, 1941, 38, 597-598.

Rapaport, D., Gill, M. and Schafer R. *Diagnostic Psychological Testing*; the theory, statistical evaluation, and diagnostic application of a battery of tests. Vol. II. Chicago: Year Book Publishers, 1946, Pp. xi + 516.

Rapaport, D. and Schafer, R. The Rorschach test: a clinical evaluation. *Bull. Menninger Clinic*, 1945, 9, 73-77.

Rapaport, D., Schafer, R. and Gill, M. Manual of diagnostic testing. II. Diagnostic testing of personality and ideational content. *Publ. Josiah Macy Jr. Found, Rev. Ser.*, 1946, 3, No. 1, Pp. 100.

Rapaport, D., Gill, M. and Schafer, R. *Diagnostic Psychological Testing.* Revised Edition, Holt, Robert R. Editor. New York: International Universities Press, 1968.

Robb, R. W., Kovitz, B. and Rapaport, D. Histamine in the treatment of psychosis; a psychiatric and objective psychological study. *Amer. J. Psychiat.*, 1940, 97, 601-610.

Schafer, R. Some problems in clinical psychological testing. *Amer. Psychologist*, 1947, 2, 424.

Schafer, R. *The Clinical Application of Psychological tests*: *Diagnostic Summaries and Case Studies.* New York: International Universities Press, 1948, 346p.

Schafer, R. Content analysis of the Rorschach test. *J. Proj. Tech.*, 1953, 17, 335-339.

Schafer, R. *Psychoanalytic Interpretation in Rorschach Testing*: *Theory and Application.* New York: Grune & Stratton, 1954, xiv, 446p.

Schafer, R. Some applications of contemporary psychoanalytic theory to projective testing. *J. Proj. Tech.*, 1954, 18, 441-447.

Schafer, R. Transference in the patient's reaction to the tester. *J. Proj. Tech.*, 1956, 20, 26-32.

Schafer, R. On the psychoanalytic study of retest results. *J. Proj. Tech.*, 1958, 22, 102-109.

Schafer, R. Bodies in schizophrenic Rorschach responses. *J. Proj. Tech.*, 1960, 24, 267-281.

Schafer, R. Representations of perceiving and acting in psychological test responses. In J. G. Peatman and E. L. Hartley (Eds.) *Festschrift for Gardner Murphy.* New York: Harper, 1960, 291-312.

Schafer, R. *Projective Testing and Psychoanalysis.* New York: International Universities Press, 1967.

CHAPTER 9

THE SYSTEMS: PROCEDURES AND SCORINGS

Hopefully, it will have been made clear in the preceding chapters that the American Rorschach Systems which have developed subsequent to Rorschach have neither adhered to Rorschach's original System of the test nor have they developed in a manner compatible with each other. To be sure, considerable overlap exists, but most of that overlap appears to be that provided through the potency of Rorschach's suggestions. In other words, those factors, such as the criteria for scoring the human movement response, the color response, or the whole response, about which Rorschach seemed uncompromisingly certain, have not been altered significantly. But in other areas, where Rorschach was more suggestive than certain, or seemingly incomplete in his thinking, the Systematizers have injected their own orientations and findings in such a manner as to magnify the divergence between each other, and from Rorschach. What follows is an attempt to compare the similarities and the differences of the Systems, with regard to procedure of administration, and method of scoring.

INSTRUCTIONS AND ADMINISTRATIVE PROCEDURES

The first point of comparison should be the basic administrative procedures. This includes seating arrangement, pre-test instructions, comments during the Free-Association, method of Inquiry, and post-Inquiry procedures.

Table 11 offers a brief comparison of the methods of administration recommended in the five Systems as contrasted with that recommended by Rorschach. It will be evident from examination of Table 11 that the differences between the Systematizers are considerable. First, with regard to seating arrangement, it will be noted that only Beck rigidly adheres to Rorschach's recommendation that the examiner sit behind the subject. Both Klopfer and Hertz indicate that the examiner should sit slightly behind the subject but also give indication that the examiner may sit next to the subject. Piotrowski stresses the use of the "most natural position," indicating that the examiner should sit behind the subject only when it provides better cooperatin or greater freedom of association. The Rapaport-Schafer System emphasizes the necessity for the examiner and subject to be

TABLE 11

A Comparison of Methods of Administration as Recommended by Rorschach, Beck, Klopfer, Piotrowski, Hertz, and Rapaport-Schafer

	Rorschach	Beck	Klopfer	Piotrowski	Hertz	Rapaport-Schafer
Seating Arrangement	E behind S	E behind S	E behind or to the side of S	Variable; stresses the "most natural position"; E behind S only when it provides greater cooperation and greater freedom of association occurs	E next to and slightly behind S	E in front of S
Instructions	E handed card and asked, "What might this be?" (In some instances S is told how ink-blots are prepared)	S told he will be given card and may keep as long as he wants and should tell everything he sees on the card (permits paraphrasing)	Essentially the same as Rorschach	Essentially the same as Rorschach but adds that it is permissible to turn card (Also, when S is reluctant, E comments about the test as one of immagination)	Similar to Beck	Same as Rorschach (Schafer suggests introducing the test to S as one designed to study personality)

Comments during Free Association	None specified (indicates that an attempt is made to obtain at least one response to each card)	None specified	None specified	After one minute if no response is given S is encouraged	None during Free Association but during trial blot gives encouragement by by comments such as "it does look like that," or if no response is given by indicating that there are no right or wrong answers	Uses reinforcement after first card plus instruction at that time to "tell me everything they might be"
Inquiry	After Free Association to all cards. Variable as needed to determine location and determinants	After Free Association to all cards. Each response is inquired non-directively*	After Free Association to all cards. Each response is inquired non-directively*	After Free Association to all cards. Each response is inquired non-directively*	Originally inquired after each card but later adopted Klopfer format of inquiry	After Free Association to each card but not to all responses. (Only those in which Location and/or determinant unclear)
Post-Inquiry Procedure	None	None (for mental defectives permits asking, "What else do you see?"	Testing of Limits and/or Analogy Period	None (although advises Testing of Limits when S is sure not to be tested again)	Probing and/or Analogy Period useful only "in some special instances"	None

* Although all of the Systematizers recommend that the inquiry be conducted "non-directively," there is considerable difference beteen them concerning the limits of "non-directive" questioning and the type of questions which may be employed.

in a "face-to-face" situation. Thus, even before the "test proper" is begun, potentially significant differences are noted between the Systems.

Next, turning to the test instructions, similar significant differences are found. Rorschach merely specified handing the subject the card and asking, "What might this be?" He further indicated that in some instances the subject might be told how the inkblots are prepared if this would enhance his cooperativeness or alleviate his anxiety. The Klopfer System follows this same procedure. The Rapaport-Schafer System follows this procedure but Schafer also suggests that the test be introduced by describing it as one designed to study personality, thereby deviating slightly from the Rorschach suggestions. Piotrowski also uses the same instructions as Rorschach but then emphasizes the importance of adding that it is permissible to turn the card, and, in instances where a subject might be reluctant to participate, to comment concerning the test to be one basically of imagination. Beck and Hertz deviate most significantly from Rorschach's instructions. Each suggests that the subject is to be given the card and told that he may keep the card as long as he wishes but emphasizes that the subject should "tell everything" he sees on the card. As has been noted in Chapter 8, Rapaport is highly critical of this procedure suggesting that it provokes an orientation toward the test which is not in keeping with the basic concepts of the projection hypothesis.

While Rorschach specified that an attempt is made to obtain at least one response to each card he did not indicate the manner in which this might be done. Thus, some of the Systematizers have seen fit to suggest that encouraging comments be given during the Free Association period. Neither Beck nor Klopfer do this. In the Piotrowski System, if the subject does not respond in the first minute he is encouraged. In the Hertz System nothing is said during the Free Association but during the Trial Blot continuous encouragement is suggested, even to the extent of indicating there are no right or wrong answers. In the Rapaport-Schafer System, reinforcement is given after the first card plus the added Beck-Hertz type instruction of "Tell me everything they might be." Beck suggests that encouragement may be employed through the administration of the first five cards.

These differences become even greater when the Systems are compared for the method of Inquiry. Rorschach did not write specifically about a "technique" of Inquiry although he clearly implied that there is need to determine the Location of the response to the blot, and also, to determine where Movement and/or Color might be involved versus simply the use of Form. These suggestions have generally been interpreted by the Systematizers to mean that a comprehensive method of Inquiry should be established. Beck, Klopfer, Piotrowski, and Hertz all follow a reasonably standard method of undertaking Inquiry; that is, after the Free Association Period is completed, each response is Inquired. All four of these Systematizers emphasize the fact that the Inquiry is to be done "non-directively" but the definitions, or at least the examples, of non-directive Inquiry vary considerably. Beck and Hertz are prone to ask questions such as, "Is there anything else?," whereas Klopfer is prone to be more directively "non-directive" by asking such questions as "Did the color help?," or "Which side of the skin is up?," or "Did you use the upper part?" While the Hertz questioning is similar to that of Beck, her requirement for maximizing the Inquiry goes well beyond Beck. The Rapaport-Schafer System deviates sharply, both from Rorschach's suggestions and those recommended by the other Systematizers. The Rapaport-Schafer System calls for an Inquiry after each card but not to all responses. Inquiry is recommended for only those responses in which Location or Determinants are left unclear by the Free Association. In general practice, this means that approximately 65 to 75 per cent of the responses will be Inquired in the average length record.

Differences between the Systematizers are also striking concerning the utilization of a "post-Inquiry procedure." Rorschach called for none. Beck suggests following Rorschach's recommendation with the exception of mental defectives wherein questions such as "What else do you see?" might be asked. The Rapaport-Schafer System provides for no post-Inquiry procedure. Klopfer, Piotrowski, and Hertz all endorse some form of post-Inquiry. Klopfer's is the most elaborate. Here the technique of "Testing of Limits" and/or the use of Analogy Period is recommended. Hertz endorses the Klopfer procedure, but cautions that it should only be used in "special instances." Piotrowski advises Testing of Limits, but only in instances where the subject is not to be tested again.

As the test has developed subsequent to Rorschach's death, it would appear that highly significant differences in administrative procedures have evolved between the Systematizers. In fact, it might be realistic to suggest that the data collected by one of the Systems cannot truly be compared statistically or qualitatively with that collected under a different methodology. Certainly data collected under different experimental procedures would not be compared in such a manner, yet the history of Rorschach shows that such comparisons are routinely made and that little consideration has been given in the literature to the possible effects of these differences. The magnitude of the differences might be emphasized even more in light of the many research publications concerning "set," "examiner influence" and "social desirability factors."

SCORING SYMBOLS AND CRITERIA
Location

While the differences between the Systems in method of administration may seem remarkable, the differences between them concerning the method of scoring Rorschach responses is even more so. Table 12 offers a comparison of Location Scoring recommended by Rorschach with that suggested in the five other Systems. Fifteen different location scores have been suggested by the various Systematizers. Rorschach suggested six of these.

While differences in scoring might be predicted, some are quite unexpected. For example, there is no single location score which is completely agreed upon by all five of the Systematizers. This fact is truly surprising as one reasonably sophisticated to Rorschach methodology might think that at least the location score for the Whole response, W, would be consistent, but this is not the case. It is true that Rorschach used the symbol W for responses wherein the plate was interpreted as a whole, and this procedure was endorsed subsequently by Beck, Klopfer and Hertz. Piotrowski, however, uses this score for responses to Card III where only the gray areas are included.

It also would seem reasonable to speculate that the simplicity of the D response would be endorsed by all Systematizers but this is not the case. Rorschach's basic concept, that the symbol D be used when a normal detail of the plate is responded to, has generally been adhered to in all the Systems, but deviations have occurred. Beck has established an elaborate frequency distribution and defines the D response in terms of frequency. Hertz has established a similar distribution but not the same as Beck's. Klopfer has not established such a distribution leaving that judgment in the hands of the examiner and defining D as a large usual detail. Piotrowski defines the D area as one frequently selected by healthy subjects but offers no distribution for this. Rapaport and Schafer probably align themselves most closely with Rorschach by defining the D area as one conspicuous by its size and isolation and the frequency of response which it draws, but like Klopfer leaving the ultimate decision to the examiner. Klopfer and Piotrowski have also included a second symbol, d, to provide a differentiation of size of commonly responded-to areas.

Beyond this point the differences become even greater. The use of the cut-off Whole (W) is endorsed only by Klopfer and Hertz and not used by the others. The DW response is defined essentially the same as Rorschach by all Systematizers but qualified by Klopfer, Piotrowski and Hertz as always being a poor form level response. The symbol Dd which was prescribed by Rorschach for scoring an unusual or small detail response has been perpetuated only in the Beck and the Rapaport-Schafer Systems. Beck defines this as a detail area infrequently used (as per his frquency distribution), whereas the Rapaport-Schafer scheme suggests that the scoring be used for small but not tiny areas which stand out by reason of their clarity. Klopfer and Piotrowski use the symbol d for small, commonly responded to areas. Most of these areas would be scored by Beck and Hertz as D, and by Rapaport-Schafer as Dd. An even wider variety of symbols exists in the Systems for the scoring of unusual or rare detail responses. Beck scores all of these as Dd. Piotrowski, Hertz, and Rapaport-Schafer use the symbol Dr. Klopfer offers four symbols, dr, dd, di, de, all of which pertain to unusual detail responses but each with a different criteria.

Thus, it would not be uncommon, if one were to score responses across all Systems, to find a single response being scored W by the Piotrowski System, W by the Klopfer System, D by the Beck and Hertz Systems, and Dd by the Rapaport-Schafer System. Another response could feasibly be scored Dd by the Beck method, di by the Klopfer method, and Dr by the other three Systems.

The Do response is one which Rorschach described as an interpretation of the plate as a whole based on a detail. This same criteria and symbol has been adopted by two of the Systematizers, Piotrowski, and Rapaport-Schafer. Hertz uses the location symbol Df or Drf. Both Beck and Klopfer have evolved different methods by handling such responses in content symbols.

The symbol S, like the symbol W, is one about which some agreement between the Systematizers and Rorschach is approached. Rorschach used this symbol to denote the use of white space in a response. Beck agrees with this, but indicates that it should always be combined with some other location symbol. Klopfer and Piotrowski endorse Rorschach's recommendation while Hertz and Rapaport modify the recommendation to the extent that the symbol S be used for space details either frequently perceived, or for a large white area. Piotrowski, Hertz, and Rapaport-Schafer have added the symbol s, to refer to white areas used in responses which are small in size. Hertz mentions these as "rarely perceived," whereas Piotrowski and the Rapaport-Schafer Systems indicate that they are merely small space detail areas on the blot.

Thus, the differences between the Systematizers, including Rorschach, become magnified as the location of the response is scored. As is true concerning differences in method of administration, it is difficult to conceive that the research which has been done on location scoring, wherein the definition or utilization of symbols is so grossly different could be ap-

TABLE 12

A Comparison of Symbols Used for Scoring Location as Recommended by Rorschach, Beck, Klopfer, Piotrowski, Hertz, and Rapaport-Schafer

Symbol	Rorschach	Beck	Klopfer	Piotrowski	Hertz	Rapaport-Schafer
W	Plate interpreted as a whole	Same as Rorschach	Same as Rorschach	Same (Also includes responses to Card III using only the gray areas)	Same as Rorschach	Same as Rorschach (Subdivided into W+, W₀, Wv, and W− for research purposes)
W̃	Not used	Not used	When at least 2/3 of the blot is used with the intention of using as much as possible	Not used	Response to the whole blot with one or two small parts missing	Not used
DW	Plate interpreted as a whole secondarily; the answer being based primarily on a detail	Same as Rorschach	Same as Rorschach (Always involves minus Form level)	Same as Rorschach (Always involves minus Form level)	Same as Rorschach (Always involves minus Form level)	Same as Rorschach
D	A normal detail of the plate	A frequently selected detail as defined by a frequency distribution	A large usual detail	A large detail area frequently selected by healthy S's	Same as Beck but defined by a different frequency distribution	Similar to Rorschach but defined as conspicuous by size, isolation, and frequency of responses which it draws
d	Not used	Not used	A small usual detail	Same as Klopfer	Not used	Not used

Dd	A usual or small detail	Rare detail as defined by infrequent use	Not used	Not used	Not used	Small but not tiny areas which stand out by reason of their clarity
Dr	Not used	Not used	Not used	A rare version of a normal detail	An infrequently perceived detail	Very small or perceptually unbalanced areas
dr	Not used	Not used	A rare detail	Not used	Not used	Not used
dd	Not used	Not used	A tiny detail	Not used	Not used	Not used
de	Not used	Not used	An edge detail	Not used	Not used	Not used
De	Not used	Not used	Not used	Not used	Not used	An edge detail
di	Not used	Not used	An inside detail	Not used	Not used	Not used
Do	A detail is interpreted in place of the whole	Not used	Not used	Same as Rorschach	Same as Rorschach	Same as Rorschach
Df	Not used	Not used	Not used	Not used	Same as Rorschach's Do	Not used
S	Space detail	Same as Rorschach (Always combined with W, D, or Dd)	Same as Rorschach	Same as Rorschach	A frequently perceived white space detail	A relatively large white space detail (May be used separately or with other location scores)
s	Not used	Not used	Not used	Small space details	Space details rarely perceived	A relatively small space detail

plicable across Systems. As one reviews basic literature on location scoring, an impression is conveyed that considerable agreement exists between investigators concerning the meaningfulness of the Whole and Large Detail responses. There is also a reasonable semblance of agreement between investigators concerning the Space response, but this agreement is less clear than with Whole or Large Detail responses. Data collected concerning small detail responses is, indeed, limited, and at this point it is difficult if not impossible to suggest whether the Klopfer-like breakdown of the small detailed responses into sub-categories of Location scores is interpretively meaningful.

DETERMINANTS

Whereas the differences between the Systematizers and Rorschach's suggestions for scoring Location are striking, the differences between Rorschach and the other Systematizers for scoring Determinants are even more so, in fact, in some instances almost unbelievably different. Tables 13 through 16 offer a comparison of the various symbols used for scoring Determinants as recommended by Rorschach and the five Systems.

Form

Table 13 deals with the comparison of the Form scoring. It will be noted from examination of the table that the symbol F is agreed upon by Rorschach and all five of the Systematizers for the scoring of pure Form responses. It will also be noted however, that the qualification of the Form answer varies considerably from System to System. Rorschach recommended a scoring of plus or minus of all Form answers to be based on a frequency of recurring answers. In that his experiment was based on a relatively small sample, he also allowed for the subjective evaluation of the examiner where the statistical data might be insufficient, but implied that ultimately statistical data should be the deciding factor in all but a very few instances. As has been noted previously in Chapters 2, 3, 4, and 5, the qualification of Form answer as "good" or "poor" Form was to become a major point of contention in the early days of the development of Beck and Klopfer Systems. Beck has persisted in allegiance to Rorschach's original recommendation and has continued to establish frequency tables for the scoring of plus or minus Form answers. He continues to allow, as did Rorschach, for the use of the symbol F with no plus or minus qualification where statistical data is insufficient. Hertz has also continued to endorse Rorschach's philosophy and has established her own frequency distribution for the scoring of plus or minus for Form answers. She also perseverates Rorschach's suggestions by recommending that where responses

TABLE 13

A Comparison of the Methods Recommended for the Scoring of Form Responses
by Rorschach, Beck, Klopfer, Piotrowski, Hertz, and Rapaport-Schafer

Symbol	Rorschach	Beck	Klopfer	Piotrowski	Hertz	Rapaport-Schafer
F	Form answers (Scoring of + or − based on the frequency of recurring answers allowing for subjective evaluation where statistical data insufficient)	Same as Rorschach (+ and − scorings determined by established frequency distribution. Whenever data from frequency distribution inadequate response to be scored F with no + or − evaluation)	Form answers (Only symbols F or F− to be used. All responses to be judged on Form Level Rating from + 5.0 to − 2.0 depending on the accuracy, organization, and specification)	Form answers (Those produced by at least 1/3 of healthy subjects establish the standard for scoring + or −. The scoring ± to be used for objects not having permanent shape)	Same as Rorschach (+ and − scoring determined by established frequency distribution different than that used by Beck. Also permits subjective evaluation where a response cannot be judged from the frequency tables)	Form answers (Uses a criteria similar to that of Rorschach for the scoring of + and − but also includes the scoring of ± and ∓ where the response evaluation is not clear. Also provides for a sub-division of the category into Special F+, Fo, Fv and Special F−)

occur infrequently, a subjective evaluation of the examiner should be the deciding factor. Klopfer, Piotrowski, and Rapaport-Schafer have not established frequency tables for plus and minus evaluation as such. Klopfer has, in essence, discarded the basic plus or minus criteria of Rorschach and instead established the Form Level Rating as discussed in Chapter 5. This system calls for all Form answers to be evaluated either as F or F− and judged on a Form Level Rating from +5.0 to −2.0 depending upon accuracy, organization, and specification factors as verbalized by the subject. In doing so, Klopfer has taken an orientation much more closely aligned with his 1936-1939 arguments in favor of examiner subjective evaluation of Form Rating. Piotrowski has established a criteria in which any response produced by at least "one third of healthy subjects" could be scored F+. He does not, however, provide a Beck-like distribution of such responses so that, like Klopfer, he endorses the ultimate subjective evaluation of the examiner. Piotrowski also includes the ± symbol, to be used for objects which do not have permanent shape, thus deviating even more from Rorschach's original intention. The Rapaport-Schafer System specifies a criteria for evaluating Form answers similar to that of Rorschach's, but then includes the evaluative symbols ± and ∓ which are to be used for responses in which there is no clear indication as to whether the response falls into a plus or minus category. Rapaport-Schafer also go one step beyond this by creating four separate sub-categories for scoring Form responses.

Movement

Whereas differences between the Systematizers and Rorschach are reasonably comprehensive in scoring for Location and the scoring for Form answers, an almost complete divergence is noted in a comparison of the scoring of Movement responses. One basic thread of agreement exists, that pertaining to the scoring of the Human Movement response. The Human Movement response was described by Rorschach as involving kinesthetic influences which would be restricted to humans or human behaviors. Beck, Klopfer and Hertz all continue to offer this definition for the scoring of M. Piotrowski and Rapaport-Schafer also give the same definition but with qualification. Piotrowski restricts such scoring to responses which are given to areas sufficiently ambiguous as to make any kind of Movement or posture equally plausible. The Rapaport-Schafer System restricts such scoring to responses which contain complete or nearly complete human figures. The Rapaport-Schafer System also calls for the use of the symbol, Ms, to denote instances where such responses are given to areas of relatively small size. Table 14 contrasts the scoring of Movement responses of all categories in the five Systems with that originally proposed by Rorschach.

It will be noted from examination of Table 14 that, in addition to the basic symbol of M, and the Rapaport-Schafer version of the symbol Ms, four other symbols have been used by various Systematizers. Klopfer has introduced the "tendency" symbol (→) for all types of movement as well as for other Determinants. Several Systematizers, including Klopfer have also developed symbols for animal Movement and/or inanimate Movement. As has been previously described, it was upon this point that Beck broke most sharply with Klopfer and Piotrowski during the 1930's. It is interesting to note that only the Rapaport-Schafer System has perpetuated Rorschach's 1923 notion of Form tending to Movement.* It is also interesting to note that only Beck has failed to provide some aspect of scoring for responses involving animal Movement. Rapaport-Schafer restricts such scoring to animals in human-like activity, similar to Beck and to Rorschach. But Klopfer, Piotrowski, and Hertz all use the symbol FM for the scoring of animal movement. Hertz has also adopted Klopfer's basic definition for the use of the symbol m for the scoring of responses involving inanimate Movement but does not extend the criteria as much as does Klopfer. Piotrowski uses the same symbol but with a different definition for its use. In fact, it will be noted that the Klopfer definition has grown closer and closer to that provided by Piotrowski as the Klopfer System has evolved.

Thus, as with the scoring for Location, a single response scored across the five Systems, could be F by Beck and Hertz, FM by Rappaport-Schafer, →M by Klopfer, and m by Piotrowski. Another response could be scored M by Beck, Ms by Rapaport-Schafer, and m by Klopfer, Piotrowski, and Hertz. A third sample response could be scored M by Beck, FM by Rapaport-Schafer, m by Klopfer and Hertz, and F by Piotrowski.

Color

No less than 16 different symbols for the scoring of color responses are recommended by Rorschach and the five Systems. Table 15 provides a comparison of the respective scoring symbols for color and the criteria for their use as recommended by Rorschach and the five Systems.

It will be noted from examination of Table 15 that there are instances where the same symbol is used in all Systems but criteria differences create a lack of unanimity about when the smybol is to be used. This occurs most notably in the basic Rorschach scorings for the color response, C, CF,

---

* Rorschach used no specific symbol for Form tending toward Movement. Rapaport-Schafer adopted the symbol FM for such a purpose.

TABLE 14
A Comparison of the Symbols and Criteria Recommended for the Scoring of Movement by Rorschach, Beck, Klopfer, Piotrowski, Hertz, and Rapaport-Schafer

Symbol	Rorschach	Beck	Klopfer	Piotrowski	Hertz	Rapaport-Schafer
M	Movement answer involving kinesthetic influences (restricted to humans or human-like behaviors)	Same as Rorschach	Same as Rorschach	Essentially the same as Rorschach but restricted to responses occuring to an area sufficiently ambiguous as to make any type of Movement or posture equally plausible	Same as Rorschach	Essentially the same as Rorschach but restricted to complete or nearly complete human figures
Ms	Not used	Not used	Not used	Not used	Not used	Movement responses given to areas of small size
FM	Not used (reference given in 1923 to Form tending to Movement which could involve either human or animal figures)	Not used	Animal Movement	Animal Movement	Animal Movement	Similar to Rorschach's concept of Form tending to Movement. Defined as an M response with weak emphasis on motion or tension, with animal-like features stressed, or with animals in human-like activity

→M	Not used	Not used	A tendency toward M, elicited only under fairly direct questioning	Not used	Not used	Not used
→FM	Not used	Not used	A tendency toward Animal Movement; acknowledged reluctantly or with considerable inquiry	Not used	Not used	Not used
m	Not used	Not used	Inanimate Movement involving expressive descriptions, natural forces, or ambiguous dynamic terms (Also includes facial expressions, phallic forces, and human abstracts)	Inanimate Movement which must (1) describe an inanimate, inorganic, and insensate object moving or in a state where Movement is actively prevented, (2) the source of the Movement must be outside of the object, (3) must be accompanied by a feeling of muscular tension	Same basic criteria as Klopfer but excludes facial expressions, phallic forces, and human abstracts	Not used

TABLE 15

A Comparison of the Symbols and Criteria Recommended for the Scoring of Color by Rorschach, Beck, Klopfer, Piotrowski, Hertz, and Rapaport-Schafer

Symbol	Rorschach	Beck	Klopfer	Piotrowski	Hertz	Rapaport-Schafer
C	Color answer, interpretation based on the Color of the blot alone	Same as Rorschach	Similar to Rorschach but defined as totally undifferentiated, without any organizational relationship to any other percept, and is repetitive	Same as Rorschach	Same as Rorschach	Same as Rorschach
Cp	Not used	Not used	Not used	Color projection (Where chromatic Color is projected into areas containing varieties of grey)	Same as Piotrowski	Not used
Cd	Not used	Not used	Not used	Color denial (Where influence of Color is explicitly denied when it is obviously present)	Criteria similar to Piotrowski but symbol not used	Not used
C det	Not used	Not used	Not used	Not used	Crude color response involving deterioration, disease or disintegration	Deterioration color response (Where interpretation is gory, uncanny, or gives the impression of haphazardness of association)

C denom	Not used	Not used	Not used	Not used	Color denomination (Where colors are referred to specifically)	Symbol not used but concept included in the 1946 volume (to be used only where no response is intended)
Cn	Not used (Symbol CC was used to denote Color naming in Rorschach's record #17)	Not used	Color naming (Used only where S makes it known that he has not given thought to any meaningful interpretation to that area of the blot)	Color naming (Used only where an interpretation is not intended)	Color naming	Symbol not used but concept included in the 1946 volume (to be used only when a response is intended)
C des	Not used	Not used	Color description (used only when an interpretation is intended)	Not used	Same as Klopfer	Symbol not used but concept included in the 1946 volume (to be used only when no response is intended)
C sym	Not used	Not used	Color symbolism (used only when Color represents an abstract association. May be scored as CFsym or FCsym depending on Form involvement)	Not used	Same as Klopfer	Symbol not used but concept included in the 1946 volume (criteria same as Klopfer)
CF	Color Form answer determined primarily by Color, secondarily by the Form	Same as Rorschach	Similar to Rorschach but would include some responses which Rorschach would score C	Same as Rorschach	Same as Rorschach	Same as Rorschach

TABLE 15 (Continued)

A Comparison of the Symbols and Criteria Recommended for the Scoring of Color by Rorschach, Beck, Klopfer, Piotrowski, Hertz, and Rapaport-Schafer

Symbol	Rorschach	Beck	Klopfer	Piotrowski	Hertz	Rapaport-Schafer
FC	Form Color answer determined primarily by Form, secondarily by the Color	Same as Rorschach	Form Color response where the object has definite Form and is specific	Same as Rorschach	Same as Rorschach	Same as Rorschach
C/F & F/C	Not used	Not used	Arbitrary or artificial use of Color (symbol used dependent on degree of Form involvement)	Not used	Same as Klopfer but must include inference that use of Color is artificial	Same as Klopfer but must include inference that use of Color is artificial
C↔F & F↔C	Not used	Not used	Forced use of Color (symbol dependent on degree of Form involvement)	Not used	Not used	Not used
FC arb	Not used	Not used	Not used	Not used	Artificial use of Color without indicating it is being used artificially (Symbol used is FC arbit)	Arbitrary use of Color with no effort made to rationalize it as artificial
FC̄	Not used	Not used	Not used	Not used	Symbol used is "FC denial" with same definition as Rapaport-Schafer	Color denial where the Color of the area chosen is negated or denied

and FC. The symbol C was recommended by Rorschach for the pure color answer, where the interpretation is based exclusively on the Color of the blot. This criteria has been adopted by all of the Systematizers with the exception of Klopfer who has defined the criteria for the use of C only for responses which are totally undifferentiated, and without any organizational relationship to any other percept, and which are repetitive. It is this latter point which makes the Klopfer criteria different from the others and provides for a more stringent, conservative scoring of pure Color. Simliarly then, the scoring of Color-Form responses, CF, as recommended by Rorschach is consistent throughout all systems except Klopfer's wherein some responses Rorschach or the other Systems would score pure C, would be scored CF in the Klopfer System. The Klopfer criteria for scoring CF and FC are also different from Rorschach and the other four Systems. FC is scored where the object has definite form and is specific. CF is scored whenever a vague indefinite form occurs pertaining to genus or class, and by color.

The other Systems, and Rorschach, recommend determination of the use of CF or FC depending on whether Color is of primary or secondary importance in the formulation of the percept. Going beyond the three basic scorings for Color responses, C, CF, and FC, the differences become more extreme. Piotrowski and Hertz use scoring symbols for Color Projection, and Color Denial (Cp and Cd), which are not included in any of the other Systems. Hertz and Rapaport-Schafer use special notations for responses involving Color Deterioration and Color Denomination plus special designations where Color is used arbitrarily, but where the arbitrariness is not mentioned, or where Color is mention but later negated or denied. All of the Systems, except the Beck System but including Rorschach's, use some notation for Color Naming but then disagree on whether the verbalization should be intended as a response. Piotrowski and Hertz suggests that Color Naming should be scored only when the subject does not intend meaningful interpretation while Rapaport-Schafer use a Color Naming notation when the subject does intend an interpretation. The intention of the subject further becomes an issue with regard to the scoring of Color Descriptions or Color Symbolisms as the Klopfer, Hertz, and Rapaport-Schafer Systems are evaluated. Special symbols are provided in the Klopfer System for the arbitrary and forced use of Color. The symbol for the arbitrary use of color is adopted in the Hertz and Rapaport-Schafer Systems but the symbol for forced use of Color is not.

Thus where Rorschach began with four basic scorings for Color, sixteen have evolved which fragment the Systems considerably. Therefore, a response might be scored CF by the Klopfer System and C by all of the other Systems. Another response could be scored F by Beck and Piotrowski, FC arb by Hertz and Rapaport-Schafer, and F/C by Klopfer. Another type of response could be scored Cn by Piotrowski and Klopfer, C denon by Hertz, C des by Rapaport-Schafer, and not scored at all by Beck. Thus, once the Systems are compared beyond the two basic scoring of FC and CF, any semblence of agreement dissipates rapidly.

Shading and Achromatic Color

The most complete absence of agreement between the Systems occurs with regard to the scoring of Shading and achromatic Color responses. This might be expected in that Rorschach gave no attention to shading responses in his monograph, *Psychodiagnostik,* and only passing attention to it in the posthumously published 1923 paper. In that paper Rorschach used the symbol (C) to denote the existence of any chiaroscuro response, that is, one involving a light-dark determinant. None of the Systematizers have actually perpetuated Rorschach's use of the symbol (C) to denote the Shading response although the symbol is included in both the Hertz and Rapaport-Schafer Systems but with a significantly modified criteria.

The actual methods of scoring Shading responses vary greatly from System to System with only minor overlap. Most agreement appears to occur between the Hertz and Rapaport-Schafer Systems in that they have adopted some of the basic recommendations of Binder (1928). However, even between these two there is considerable disagreement with Hertz also adding Klopfer's symbol for scoring texture and separate symbols for the scoring of achromatic Color. While Rapaport and Schafer adopted some of the Klopfer System for scoring Color, they give little attention to the scoring of texture responses except where they occur in chromatically colored areas. From examination of Table 16, which offers a comparison of the Systems for scoring Shading and Achromatic Color with that suggested by Rorschach, it will be noted that the scoring symbols used by Beck, Klopfer, and Piotrowski are almost entirely different. Beck uses symbols Y, V, and T; Klopfer uses symbols K, k, and c; and Piotrowski uses symbols c (different from Klopfer's c) and c'. The Hertz and Rapaport-Schafer System have included the use of the symbol Ch, consistent with Binder's recommendations but with limited agreement between each other. Not only do the symbols differ, but the definition of areas to be covered differ so significantly that it is almost impossible to compare one System with another. For instance, the Beck symbol for the light-dark determined response (Y) overlaps with both of Klopfer's symbols K and k, the Piotrowski symbols of c and c', and the Hertz and Rapaport-Schafer symbol Ch. This same Beck symbol, Y, also overlaps with the Klopfer symbol, C'.

Two of the Systems, Piotrowski and Rapaport-Schafer, offer no specific symbol for the scoring of texture responses. Neither of these Systems offers any specific symbols for the scoring of vista or perspective responses. The fact is that the differences for scoring of light-dark determined type responses are so great that no agreement occurs across all Systems, and in only two instances is there agreement on any single scoring between two Systems. The symbol C' is used by the Klopfer System and the Rapaport-Schafer System for the scoring of achromatic Color responses when used as a Color, and the Klopfer and Hertz Systems both use the scoring of c for texture responses. Beyond these two points, however, there is no identical agreement between any two of the Systems.

Almost any light-dark determined responses, scored across the five Systems would yield at least three, more commonly four, and in some instances, five different scorings. For example, a response could be scored T by Beck, c by Klopfer and Hertz, c' by Piotrowski, and Ch by Rapaport-Schafer. Another type response might be scored Y by Beck, C' by Klopfer and Rapaport-Schafer, Cg by Piotrowski, and Ch" by Hertz. Thus, it should not be surprising to note that the least amount of definitive research has been accomplished in the area of the light-dark determined responses and that, of all the Determinants, this area continues to provide the greatest mystery for the Rorschach interpreter.

The widespread differences between the Systems regarding criteria and symbols for scoring carries over into the quantitative summarization of the protocol. There are only two instances of agreement among all Systems concerning what data should be converted into ratios or percentages. One of these is the Rorschach Erlebnistypus which is the ratio of all Movement responses to the Sum of the Color responses. But even here some slight deviation occurs in that Rapaport-Schafer include FM responses, with a value of 0.5, in the Movement side of the ratio. This does not occur in any of the other Systems. A percentage of all animal responses is computed in all of the Systems. Beyond these two points, the extent of agreement becomes less and less as the quantitative summaries of the various Systems are compared. In some instances, there is agreement across two or more Systems concerning a structural concept to be quantified, but then differences occur in the method of computation. For example, most of the Systems recommend concern be given to the proportion of pure Form responses in the record. Klopfer and Hertz compute a percentage based on the number of F responses to the total number of responses. Beck computes the number of F responses to the number of non-F responses; Rapaport-Schafer use the same procedure as Klopfer and Hertz but add a second percentage which includes all responses which demon-

TABLE 16

A Comparison of the Symbols and Criteria Recommended for the Scoring of Shading, Texture, and Achromatic Color by Rorschach, Beck, Klopfer, Piotrowski, Hertz, and Rapaport-Schafer

Symbol	Rorschach	Beck	Klopfer	Piotrowski	Hertz	Rapaport-Schafer
(C)	All chiaroscuro responses	Not used	Not used	Not used	Not used as defined by Rorschach (see (C)F & F(C))	Not used as defined by Rorschach (see (C)F & F(C))
(C)F & F(C)	Not used	Not used (see V for similarities)	Not used (see FK for similarities)	Not used	Responses having 3-dimensional effect. Scored (C), (C)F, or F(C) depending on the degree of effect of the light-dark values	Chiroscuro responses in which shading components specify important inner details; or for Color Form responses which include texture (Scored (C)F or F(C) depending on the degree of Form involvement)
Y	Not used	Ligtt-dark determined responses not including reference to texture or vista (scored Y, YF, or FY depending on Form involvement)	Not used (see K and k for similarities)	Not used (see c and c' for similarities)	Not used (see Ch for similarities)	Not used (see Ch for similarities)

V	Not used	Vista responses where shading creates the impression of depth or distance (scored V, VF, or FV depending on Form involvement)	Not used (see FK for similarities)	Not used	Not used (see (C)F for similarities)	Not used
T	Not used	Texture responses where shading creates the impression of texture (scored T, TF, or FT depending on Form involvement)	Not used (see c for similarities)	Not used (see c for similarities)	Not used (see c for similarities)	Not used (see (C)F for similarities)
K	Not used	Not used (see Y and V for similarities)	Shading as depth or diffusion; FK scored for vista, linear perspective, reflections and landscapes; KF and K scored for diffusion of darkness responses	Not used (see c and c' for similarities)	Not used (see (C)F and Ch for similarities)	Not used (see Ch for similarities)
k	Not used	Not used (see Y for similarities)	Responses in which a 3-dimensional effect is projected on a 2-dimensional plane (scored k, kF, or Fk depending on Form involvement)	Not used (see c for similarities)	Not used	Not used

Table 16 (*Continued*)

A Comparison of the Symbols and Criteria Recommended for the Scoring of Shading, Texture, and Achromatic Color by Rorschach, Beck, Klopfer, Piotrowski, Hertz, and Rapaport-Schafer

Symbol	Rorschach	Beck	Klopfer	Piotrowski	Hertz	Rapaport-Schafer
c	Not used	Not used (see T for similarities to Klopfer; Y for similarities to Piotrowski)	Responses in which a textural, surface, or reflective quality occurs (scored c, cF, or Fc depending on Form involvement)	Shading and/or texture response in which interpretation of a dysphoric mood is absent (scored c or Fc depending on whether Form is involved)	Same as Klopfer	Not used (see (C)F for similarities)
c'	Not used	Not used (see Y for similarities)	Not used (see K, k, and c for similarities)	Interpretation of the very dark nuances of the blot or where a dysphoric mood is expressed (scored c' or Fc' depending on whether Form is involved)	Not used (see Ch and c for similarities)	Not used (see Ch for similarities)
Ch	Not used	Not used	Not used	Not used	Chiaroscuro responses (scored Ch, ChF or FCh depending on Form involvement)	Chiaroscuro responses (scored Ch, ChF, or FCh depending on degree of Form involvement)

C'	Not used	Not used (see Y for similarities)	Use of achromatic color as a color (scored C' C'F, or FC' depending on degree of Form involvement)	Not used (see Cw and Cg for similarities)	Not used (see Ch' and Ch" for similarities)	Same as Klopfer
Cw	Not used	Not used (see Y for similarities)	Not used (see C' for similarities)	Where white space is actually used as a color (scored as Cw, CwF, or FCw depending on degree of Form involvement)	Not used (see Ch' for similarities)	Not used (see C' for similarities)
Cg	Not used	Not used (see Y for similarities)	Not used (see C' for similarities)	Where grey is actually used as a color (scored Cg, CgF, FCg depending on degree of Form involvement)	Not used (see Ch' for similarities)	Not used (see C' for similarities)
Ch'	Not used	Not used (see Y for similarities)	Not used (see C' for similarities)	Not used (see Cg and Cw for similarities)	Where grey or white are actually used as colors (scored Ch', Ch'F, or FCh' depending on Form involvement)	Not used (see C' for similarities)
Ch"	Not used	Not used (see Y for similarities)	Not used (see C' for similarities)	Not used (see Cg for similarities)	Where black is actually used as a color value (scored as Ch", Ch"F, or FCh" depending on Form involvement)	Not used (see C' for similarities)

strate "strong form." Piotrowski does not include such a percentage in his System. Similar differences occur when most any of the other ratios or percentages are examined. For example, the number of Popular responses which can be scored varies considerably across the Systems. Beck lists the greatest number of Popular responses, 15, while the Klopfer System endorses the fewest, 9. Only 3 of the 5 Systems score Original responses (Beck and Piotrowski do not). The Klopfer System calls for the routine computation of the largest number of ratios and percentages, 17, whereas the Rapaport-Schafer System calls for the smallest number, 5.

Content

The scoring for content brings the five Systems into closer agreement than any other area. Certain basic symbols suggested by Rorschach such as H for human, Hd for human detail, and A for animal, prevail throughout all the Systems. Beyond these points of congruence, however, once again varying levels of disagreement occur. In some instances these disagreements can be simplified to the utilization of the scoring abreviation, such as Klopfer's use of the symbol At for anatomy versus Beck's use of the symbol An. In other instances the disagreement becomes greater, where abreviation or scoring symbol lists vary in length. The list provided by Beck is the longest, 39, as contrasted with the list provided by Klopfer which is the shortest, 23. Many items which Klopfer would include in his category Obj (object) would be differently categorized among the other Systems. In the Rapaport-Schafer System, for example, a caution is given against excessive use of the category Obj with the notation that such contents that are unique should be fully spelled out rather than lumped into a single category.

It should be obvious, even to the most naive, that the differences which exist between the Systems are not minor or unimportant. Quite the contrary, in most areas of comparison the differences appear quite significant. Even beginning with the method of administration, differences erupt which raise questions concerning the validity of comparing the data collected by different Systems. Seating arrangements differ, as do instructions, participation by the examiner during the Free-Association, technique of Inquiry, and post-Inquiry procedures.

Even if it can be assumed that the procedural differences in administration do not create differences in the data ultimately collected, it is difficult to comprehend how valid comparisons of that data can be made when methods and criteria for scoring differ in such magnitude. Interestingly, it will be found in the next chapter that differences in interpretation do not seem to occur with such frequency or breadth as do those pointed to here.

REFERENCES

Beck, S. J., Beck, A. G., Levitt, E. E. and Molish, H. B. *Rorschach's Test: Vol. I. Basic Processes.* 3rd Ed. New York: Grune & Stratton, 1961.

Beck, S. J. and Molish, H. B. *Rorschach's Test: Vol. II. A Variety of Personality Pictures.* 2nd Ed. New York: Grune & Stratton, 1967.

Hertz, M. R. *Frequency Tables for Scoring Responses to the Rorschach Ink-Blot test.* 3rd Ed. Cleveland, Ohio: Western Reserve University Press, 1951.

Hertz, M. R. The use and misuse of the Rorschach method: I. Variations in Rorschach procedure. *J. Proj. Tech.,* 1951, 23, 33-48.

Klopfer, B., Ainsworth, M. D., Klopfer, W. G. and Holt, R. R. *Developments in the Rorschach Technique. Vol. I. Technique and Theory.* Yonkers-on-Hudson, N.Y.: World Book Co., 1954.

Klopfer, B., et al. *Developments in the Rorschach Technique. Vol. II. Fields of Application.* Yonkers-on-Hudson, N.Y.: World Book. Co., 1957.

Klopfer, B. and Davidson, H. H. *The Rorschach Technique.* New York: Harcourt, Brace & World, 1962.

Piotrowski, Z. *Perceptanalysis.* New York: Macmillan, 1957.

Piotrowski, Z. Digital-Computor interpretation of inkblot test data. *Psychiat. Quart.,* 1964, 38, 1-26.

Rapaport, D., Gill, M. and Schafer, R. *Diagnostic Psychological Testing. Vol. II.* Chicago: Yearbook Publishers, 1946.

Rorschach, H. *Psychodiagnostics.* Bern: Bircher, 1921, (Transl. Hans Huber Verlag, 1942).

Schafer, R. *Psychoanalytic Interpretation in Rorschach Testing: Theory and Application.* New York: Grune & Stratton, 1954.

CHAPTER 10

THE SYSTEMS: INTERPRETATION

It is an onerous and sometimes impossible task to provide a realistic comparison of the interpretive approaches and hypotheses offered by the five Systems. There are several factors which make for this difficulty. First, there are the differences in general theoretical orientations between the Systematizers. Such differences in orientation toward the concept of personality, its organization, and its description, frequently give rise to different professional languages. On occasion, translation is thwarted because of a lack of equivalent concepts. Beck's Experience Actual, Piotrowski's Principle of Interdependent Components, Hertz Interactionist Approach, and the Rapaport-Schafer M per cent are all exclusive to their respective Systems thereby defying translation. In other instances concepts are similar but different, sometimes deceptively so, in that the same language may be employed in several of the Systems, but each having a different meaning. This has already been demonstrated in the section concerning scoring criteria, but it becomes even more apparent when interpretive hypotheses are contrasted. For example, the concept of introversion has found a place in all of the Systems and all use the M response as a basis for interpretation of the concept. But there is a considerable lack of agreement across the Systems regarding the definition of introversion. Beck, agreeing with Rorschach, views introversion as an internalizing process. Rorschach had specifically denied congruency between his ideas and those of Jung concerning introversion. Klopfer and Hertz employ the concept in a form very similar to Jung. Piotrowski suggests that introversion, as predominantly defined by the M response, has a positive correlation with overt behavior. In doing so, he deemphasizes the internalization process. Rapaport-Schafer use the concept to imply a resistance to spontaneity wherein internalization may or may not occur. The word used, introversion, is the same in all of the Systems, but the definitions, although not completely exclusive, differ markedly.

A second problem to an inter-System comparison develops from scoring differences. Each System has scoring categories and corresponding interpretive postulates which are unique to that System. These unique features, such as the Klopfer dd, the Rapaport-Schafer Ms, or the Piotrowski c' have been noted in previous chapters. Any attempt to compare these components could cause more misunderstanding that clarification. In other instances, like language, the same scoring category is used in two or more of the Systems but the criteria for its application and interpretation are defined in a manner so as to make it unique to a particular System. The Klopfer criteria for the Pure C response and the Piotrowski restrictions for M are among the most obvious examples of this problem.

Another difficulty to inter-System comparison is created by the differences in interpretive approach suggested in the respective Systems. There is complete agreement between the Systems that Rorschach data is interpreted adequately *only* if a "global" approach is employed. The fundamental requirement to the "global" interpretation is that all Rorschach data be considered, and more specifically, that each bit of Rorschach data be evaluated with respect to all other Rorschach data. Consequently, where a specific hypothesis is offered in a System, for example, concerning Color responses, the word *if* must always be injected as a qualification to the hypothesis. Therefore, a Sum C equal to a Sum M in a protocol where Shading components are high and W answers few would be interpreted differently than the same Sum C and Sum M in a protocol where Shading components are absent and W answers frequent. In each instance the Color responses would be interpreted in the general framework of the basic Color hypothesis, that is, Color relates to affect. The more specific description of how the affect relates to the personality and to behavior would, however, be determined by the presence or absence of many other factors such as Shading, Location answers, Content, Form accuracy, and an all encompassing evaluation of the verbalizations of the subject. This variable is even more difficult to compare across Systems because the number and length of intra-protocol comparisons recommended by each differs considerably. As has been previously indicated, only two elements of the quantitative data, the Erlebnistypus and the Animal per cent, are recommended for computation by all five Systems. Beyond these two, much variability occurs. The Klopfer System calls for computation of some seventeen ratios and percentages whereas the Rapaport-Schafer System calls for computation of only five. The Rapaport-Schafer System is the only one providing lengthy discourse on content analysis and analytic interpretation of verbalizations. But the complexities posed by differences in interpretive approach go well beyond this point. In the early days of the Rorschach the common procedure was to interpret the protocol "blindly." The philosophy of that era was consistent with that recommended by Rorschach, that it, the test data should be treated independent of extraneous factors. This methodology was congruous with the characteristics of his experiments with the technique. The development of the technique and the five Systems has generated differing opinions concerning the worthiness of the "blind approach."

All of the Systems endorse the blind approach but not to the same degree nor for the same purpose. Beck has maintained that the blind approach is the only valid interpretive method for Rorschach data. Piotrowski also follows the tradition of the blind approach, more recently even to the extent of using the computer as the "analyzer," comparing protocols with programmed interpretation inputs. The other Systems do not give an unqualified endorsement to the blind method. Instead, its use is specifically restricted to particular conditions of interpretation, mainly for teaching purposes. Beck and Piotrowski argue that the Rorschach dat ashould be interpreted independently from other data except for minimum information such as age, sex, and marital status. They prefer to interpret the data from the Rorschach and then integrate it, *without changing the interpretations,* with data from other test materials, or with the social-developmental history. They believe that the test data is accurately representative of the personality, even though some of the responses represent the most deeply unconscious feelings, needs, and thoughts. Therefore, all of the data is applicable to the understanding of the individual, and blind analysis avoids the problems of bias or set.

The Rapaport-Schafer System offers only partial agreement with the Beck-Piotrowski argument for blind analysis. Neither Rapaport nor Schafer have ever given unqualified endorsement to the use of the Rorschach as a complete diagnostic tool. They have stated that the Rorschach is probably the most valuable of the diagnostic instruments available, but they have also emphasized the use of the test battery in which several instruments are employed. According to this System, such a battery should include a variety of tests, ranging from an intelligence test to the Rorschach, all of the data from which should be interpreted blindly, but with an integration of the interpretive patterns revealed. Thus, the total data pattern could feasibly alter a Rorschach derived conclusion, or conversely, the interpretive pattern could support a Rorschach conclusion while rejecting one derived from a different test. In this System all data must be interrelated and ultimately, the test data should be integrated with the history and observational data.

Klopfer and Hertz disagree most with the Beck-Piotrowski position concerning blind analysis. Both advocate the method for teaching purposes but suggest that its use in the real diagnostic situation has limited value. Interestingly, both Klopfer and Hertz were early advocates of the blind technique and published on the method during the 1930's. Klopfer was the first to change his position. It was not an abrupt change but rather a gradual alteration to the view that Rorschach data can be used most profitably when interpreted with respect to other data available, such as social-developmental history, observations, interviews, and other test data.

Klopfer assumes a position similar to that of Rapaport-Schafer, that is, all Rorschach data should be utilized, but some Rorschach derived conclusions may be modified or omitted if other data sources provide clearly different conclusions. Klopfer suggests that interpretation should start with Rorschach data and as many hypotheses as possible formulated. Subsequently, these hypotheses should be tested against other data sources and altered where necessary. Where Beck and Piotrowski are quite reluctant to alter Rorschach conclusions, Klopfer is more willing to do so when alternate conclusions appear to be more valid. The Hertz position regarding blind analysis seems to differ most with that offered by Beck and Piotrowski. She advocates the use of the blind technique for teaching purposes but not for use in the clinical situation. Her interactionist approach views Rorschach data much like Rapaport and Schafer view the test battery, namely that each bit of data offers some clue to the understanding of personality, but the clue can be interpreted accurately only if studied in light of data from other sources. Hertz maintains that the symbolic and sometimes fragmentary data of the Rorschach should be interpreted with respect to the socio-edu-cational-developmental history so as to gain full appreciation for the idiosyncratic nature of the personality.

The differences in approach to interpretation do not create a complete diversification between the Systems but do make for comparative diffi-culties. It will be found that many interpretive postulates are the same across all Systems, but a diversity does exist concerning the application of a given postulate. This factor, when combined with differences in theoretical approach, operational language, and methods of scoring creates a situation in which inter-System comparisons are possible only on a limited scale. In some instances, it is as if apples were compared to apples. In other instances, it is as if apples were compared to tangerines, and in a few instances, it is as if apples were compared to a distant planet. What follows then is a somewhat limited inter-System comparison. Comparisons will be made where the data is so amenable and not attempted where interpretive postulates are incomparable. It also seems important to re-emphasize the fact that none of the Systems endorse an interpretive ap-proach based exclusively on nomothetic data. At times, interpretive hypo-these are stated in a manner as to seemingly imply only nomothetic consi-derations. But this is never the case in any System. All of the Systems do require the scoring and summarization of all responses, usually as the be-ginning step interpretation. All of the Systems are also specific concerning the requirement of a qualitative evaluation of the protocol. None of the Systems endorse, neither explicitly nor implicitly, a "cookbook" approach with regard to either quantitative or qualitative data which would, in any manner, circumvent the global methodology which always has as its object the idiographic features of the personality.

The format that follows is an attempt to provide a realistic comparison of the Systems with regard to interpretation. It is somewhat restrictive in the sense that only those interpretive hypotheses which are comparable (apples with apples) are included. Those interpretive hypotheses which are unique to a System are not included so as to avoid confusion and/or misunderstanding.

INTERPRETATION OF LOCATION COMPONENTS

A substantial thread of agreement exists between the Systems concerning the broader interpretations of Location scores. All of the Systems include Rorschach's postulate as a nucleus for the interpretation of the W answer. He had suggested that W has some direct relationship to intellectual operations and to the ability to organize and synthesize the components of one's environment into a meaningful concept. All of the Systems call for evaluation of the type of W response given, combinatory, ordinary, spontaneous, vauge, etc. All of the Systems also recommend that the W component should be evaluated in relation to other location scores and more particularly with respect to the quality of the Form responses. Beck and Hertz offer a special method for evaluation of the organizational activity in the protocol (Beck's Z and Hertz's g), which, among other uses, is relevant to the interpretation of W. There is some minor disagreement among the Systems concerning the percentage of W responses to be expected in the average length protocol. Estimates range from 25 to 35 per cent but appear to be created by the differences in the scoring criteria for W rather than by differences in interpretative set. For example, both Klopfer and Hertz include Cut-off W's in this estimate, which would be scored as D in the other Systems.

There is considerable agreement across the Systems concerning the meaning of the Large Detail response. All of the Systems have accepted Rorschach's hypothesis that such responses indicate an ability to perceive and to react to the obvious characteristics in the environment. Differences do appear in the Systems concerning D, but are based more on expected percentage in the average length protocol of the healthy subject rather than the meaning. Beck and Piotrowski hold that approximately two-thirds of the protocol should ordinarily be comprised of D responses. Klopfer and Hertz suggest that between 45 and 55 per cent should be D, and Rapaport-Schafer anticipate 40 to 60 per cent D. There is also some variability across the Systems concerning the optimal proportion of W to D, ranging from one to two, to one to three. Most of these differences, like in the instance of the W response, are created by differences in the criteria for scoring D. A D response in the Rapaport-Schafer System could be W for Klopfer and Hertz, D for Piotrowski, and Dd for Beck.

There are no significant differences concerning the interpretive meaning of the rare or unusual detail response. Rorschach hypothesized that such responses are produced as a result of an undue preoccupation for reality. He suggested that such a process can be highly impairing to one's ability to respond effectively to the environment when it dominates a protocol. Rorschach also implied that most normal subjects "overlook" the rare or unusual detail. None of the Systematizers agree with this finding. Quite the contrary, all Systems cite the fact that most records of healthy subjects include a small number of such responses and interpret this to be indicative of the capacity for making such responses when necessary or meaningful to the need system of the person.

Four of the five Systems offer a similar interpretation for the confabulatory type response, DW. It is perceived as indicating a highly unique thought operation in which ego controls are lacking. The fifth System, that of Beck, offers a similar hypothesis but qualifies it by suggesting that these types of responses may also be given by the healthy adult, especially those of superior endowment. This point has not been found acceptable to the other Systematizers.

The greatest disagreement across the Systems concerning the meaning of Location scores occurs regarding the Space response. Rorschach had postulated that such responses represent some form of oppositional or negative tendency. The Rapaport-Schafer System endorses this postulate but with the caution that little validity has been demonstrated for it. Similarly, Beck also uses the Rorschach hypothesis in his System but includes the qualification that, quite commonly, such responses may simply represent a form of stubbornness and that the final interpretation must be made in relation to the entire protocol. Piotrowski, Hertz, and Klopfer all offer interpretive hypotheses for the Space response which are more positive. Piotrowski, in effect, agrees with Beck and adds that such responses can also be a manifestation of strivings for independence. Klopfer and Hertz both point to the fact that the Space response frequently represents a healthy and intelligent kind of opposition which should be interpreted as a tendency to question or challenge rather than blandly accept the rules and regulations of the environment.

Accordingly then, there is considerable agreement between the Systems regarding the meaning of the various Location scores. This is clearly the case for the three primary types of Location responses, Wholes, Large Details, and Unusual or Rare Details. Where variability exists concerning the interpretation of these three elements, it is typically in the form of additional material, as for instance the Beck and Hertz organizational scoring, or is created by differences in scoring criteria. It is important to note that this interpretive homogeneity occurs mainly because Rorschach's hypotheses have been accepted. He was reasonably specific on these three elements. He was less specific concerning the Space response, and it is here that some divergence does exist.

INTERPRETATION OF DETERMINANTS
Form Responses

An examination of the Systems concerning the suggested meaning of Form responses yields substantial agreement. Each of the Systems includes Rorschach's postulate that Form responses are indicative of the ability to perceive things conventionally and respond to them in a manner relatively free of affective domination. In all Systems then, Form responses are regarded as an ego operation wherein the capacity of the ego to function free of emotion, and with regard to reality, is manifest. Beyond this basic interpretive agreement some inter-System differences do occur, but as in the instance of Location scores, the differences arise from the heterogeneity of approaches used in the Systems to score Form responses and to evaluate the accuracy of "fit" of the response. The number of responses which are considered pure Form varies considerably from System to System. For example, the Beck and Rapaport-Schafer Systems regard most responses as pure Form which would be scored and interpreted as Animal or Inanimate Movement in the other three Systems. Similarly, some types of responses which might be scored Color by Hertz would be scored as Form by the Beck and Rapaport-Schafer methods. Some responses which might be scored as Texture by Klopfer and Beck would also be scored as pure Form by the Rapaport-Schafer System.

The differences become even greater when the techniques for evaluating the quality of "fit" of the percept are examined. All of the Systems interpret the lack of good quality of Form to be suggestive of some malfunction in reality testing. Beck and Hertz use frequency tables to evaluate this quality, but the frequency tables are different for the two Systems. Piotrowski uses a criteria based on one-third of responses given by healthy subjects but does not list this distribution, thus leaving the final evaluation to the examiner's experience. Rapaport-Schafer endorse the concept of a frequency distribution, consistent with Rorschach, but offer no data from which to make comparisons. They also provide special scorings for ambiguous responses. Klopfer uses the Form Level Rating which is considerably more ambiguous than the frequency distribution method. All of the Systems except Klopfer compute an F+ per cent to represent the quality of the Form responses but, as is obvious, the data comprising that computation can vary considerably, and thus the interpretations concerning reality testing can also vary. It is important to note that the Systems also differ with regard to the method of evaluating the predominance and/or quality of Form in those responses which are not pure Form. The Rapaport-Schafer System, for example, includes the computation of the extended F+ per cent referring to all responses, including pure F, where Form is dominant. All of the Systems follow a similar procedure, either quantitatively or qualitatively but differences still exist, created by the scoring criteria for the various Determinants and the degree to which scoring is based on the subject's verbalizations. For example, as has been previously noted, Hertz will score some responses CF which, because of the nature of the verbalization, Beck and Klopfer would score FC. Subsequently, while all Systems postulate that too much or too little Form in a record constitutes some manifestation of inadequate personality functioning mainly of the ego, a substantial lack of agreement exists concerning the optimal proportion of Form in a protocol. All Systems except that of Klopfer use a general percentage for anticipated Form quality. Various ranges are suggested which extend as low as 60 per cent to an upper limit of between 90 and 95 per cent. Klopfer, of course, uses a Form Level Rating which is applicable to most all responses in a record. There is agreement across the Systems that, when the percentage of adequate Form fit falls below the specified level, some disintegrating element is impinging on the ego functioning. Conversely, it is agreed that when the Form fitness is excessive (usually 100 per cent), there is some undue preoccupation with reality which probably causes the individual a loss of uniqueness.

Movement Responses

The interpretation of the Movement type response has probably stimulated more written material by the Systematizers than any other single test factor. Historically, it was one of the critical elements leading to the early divergence among Rorschach authorities. There is probably greatest disagreement between the Systems concerning the scoring and meaning of Movement. Only one of the Systems, that of Beck, has steadfastly given endorsement to Rorschach's hypothesis concerning the human Movement response. The Beck System is the only one of the five Systems which has not included some formal method for noting and evaluating responses demonstrating a tendency toward Movement. The Beck and Rapaport-Schafer Systems do not give special consideration to responses manifesting Animal or Inanimate Movement.

Rorschach suggested that the human Movement response represents an internalization phenomenon. His notions of introversion imply that M is a manifestation of the inner life denoting tendencies to use internal experiences in an affectively adaptive manner. Beck uses this hypothesis as the nucleus for his interpretation of M. Not all of the other Systems reject this hypothesis. In fact, only Piotrowski has done so. But the other three Systems, Klopfer, Hertz, and Rapaport-Schafer, have all modified or extended Rorschach's hypothesis considerably more than has Beck. Klopfer and Hertz have both been prone to interpret the M response as a psychological process representing a functional relationship between the fantasy of the individual and his external orientations to reality and object relationships. Klopfer has also implied that the Rorschach concept of introversion is essentially the same as the Jungian concept of introversion.* While Beck rejects the Jungian concept of introversion he does not completely disagree with the Klopfer or Hertz interpretations. Instead, he states very similar ideas but uses a different descriptive emphasis. Beck postulates that good Form M's are an indication of one's awareness of the external world. In doing so, he gives considerably more emphasis to the internalization of this awareness than do either Klopfer or Hertz. For Beck then, the M represents a clear vestiture of energy internally wherein a private fantasy world permits displacement or sublimation of pent-up needs or affects.

"M is emotion. A person has wishes or fears which he cannot act out. Social roles, which is to say his ego, prevent. M is his substitute for action. He lives his wishes and fears where others cannot observe them, in his imagination. The very fact that they must conceal them from outward show is evidence of the force he exerts on him."

Piotrowski's interpretation of the human Movement response differs most significantly from the other Systems and from Rorschach. As early as 1937 Piotrowski adopted the position that the correlation between M and overt behavior is positive. Thus, the M response in a Rorschach protocol provides revelation concerning the traits which are the mainstay of behavior for the individual in his environment.

". . . The M indicates prototypal roles in life, i.e., definite tendencies, deeply embedded in the subject and not easily modified, to assume repeatedly the same attitude or attitudes in dealing with others when matters felt to be important and personal are involved."

While Piotrowski's position is different from that of Beck, Klopfer, and Hertz, it is not completely opposite. There is at least a fragment of agreement between Piotrowski, Klopfer and Hertz in that the latter do regard the Movement response as bridging inner resources with external reality.

---

* Rorschach had specifically rejected the idea that his concept of introversion is identical to that of Jung.

Agreement with Beck is more fragmentary in that Beck assumes the M response to be adaptive for the individual in the sense of providing displacement or sublimations. Subsequent behaviors, therefore, are somewhat consistent as derived from these sublimations, and on this basis one could state a case for a positive correlation between M and overt behavior. But overall, the Piotrowski interpretation of the human Movement response does differ significantly from these other three Systems. The Rapaport-Schafer interpretation of the human Movement response poses some acceptance of Rorschach's hypothesis but with distinct modification through the rejection of the concept of introversion. The Rapaport-Schafer System regards the M response as indicating a delay in overt behaviors. There is agreement with Beck concerning a readiness to make anticipations, but unlike Beck, Klopfer and Hertz, the Rapaport-Schafer System does not interpret M as a tendency toward internalization. Rapaport-Schafer argue that internalization may occur but this is not always a consequence of the type of psychological process involved in M. Instead, that process is perceived as a resistance to spontaneous behavior from which some responses may be internalized but others may give rise to overt behavior. To some extent, the Rapaport-Schafer interpretation appears to have integrated some of the concepts of the other Systems into a single, more liberal interpretation.

All of the Systems call for interpretation of the M response in relation to the quality of the response as well as the stance or posture of the movement itself. On this latter point, considerable agreement exists across all Systems. There is also unanimous agreement across the Systems that M, in effect, provides much information concerning the self-concept of the individual including his internal stability and degree of self-acceptance.

The interpretation of Animal Movement responses is relevant to only three Systems, Klopfer, Piotrowski, and Hertz. Klopfer and Hertz describe the Animal Movement response as rising from the most primitive aspects of personality, having an instinctual basis or having been acquired very early in life. These responses manifest an awareness of such impulses striving for immediate gratification. Klopfer and Hertz both indicate that immediate discharge in overt behavior does not always ensue and is dependent upon the total configuration of the personality. Piotrowski appears to agree partially on this issue by suggesting that the FM response is probably indicative of the subcortically controlled activity patterns. Piotrowski disagrees with Kloper and Hertz concerning the archaic nature of the impulses revealed in the Animal Movement response. He suggests they are simply past conceptions of one's role in life and remain as indications of one's vitality. Such responses, therefore, indicate a once normal thought pattern which never reached complete maturity. He also rejects Klopfer's hypothesis that these impulses are striving for complete gratification, indicating that while energy is available, its discharge will be determined by a variety of personality factors.

As with the Animal Movement response, only three Systems deal with the Inanimate Movement response. Again, these are the Klopfer, Piotrowski, and Hertz Systems. Klopfer interprets the Inanimate Movement response as an awareness of forces or impulses beyond the control of the subject which threaten the overall stability or organization of the personality. Piotrowski and Hertz do not interpret these responses as a threat, but instead, as thought or drive merely less well integrated with the total personality which in turn create a tendency toward habitual introspection. They, unlike Klopfer, also suggest that Inanimate Movement responses occur very commonly in the records of subjects with superior intellect.

Color Responses

Unlike the differences which exist across the Systems for the interpretation of Movement responses, there is considerable inter-System agreement concerning the meaning of Color responses. All of the Systems have incorporated Rorschach's hypothesis that Color responses are indicative of affect as related somewhat directly to the external world. There is clear agreement between all Systems that healthier subjects demonstrate affect in the Rorschach by Form dominated Color responses, FC, but offer the qualification that in even the most well adjusted, some instances of Color dominated responses will occur. The suggested ratios of CF to FC vary slightly across the Systems, ranging from one to three to one to four. It is also suggested in all Systems that the pure Color response is rare and that its presence in a record manifests a liable discharge of affect in which the thought operations are overwhelmed and become functionally ineffective. Klopfer, because of his more stringent requirements for the scoring of pure C, goes beyond this interpretation to suggest that when such responses occur a psychotic process is active. The other four Systems, using the less stringent criteria for scoring pure C, are not this specific but clearly imply that the possibility of a psychotic process is not unlikely. Nevertheless, all Systems do agree that the FC type response is usually a healthy, controlled emotional discharge whereas the CF type response is a more impulsive, inappropriately controlled representation of affect.

It is impractical to attempt any comparison of the other types of Color responses that are formally included in some of the Systems such as Color Naming, Color Description, Color Denial, Arbitrary or Forced use of Color and the like. The definitions of these types of responses vary significantly and it is unusual where the same criteria occur in more than two Systems. It is important, however, to emphasize that all Systems call for interpretive evaluation of any mention or use of color in the protocol. In some instances this occurs through formal scoring and interpretation whereas in other instances, the evaluation will be predominantly qualitative. An example of this is the Color Naming response which is formally scored and interpreted in two of the Systems, Klopfer and Hertz, when it occurs as a response. Although not formally scored in the Rapaport-Schafer System it is mentioned as important interpretive material. Piotrowski scores this when no response is intended by the subject. Beck does not score it under any circumstances but undoubtably includes its occurrence in the qualitative evaluation of the record. Similarly, the occurrence of denial of color is formally scored and interpreted in only one System, that of Piotrowski. But all Systems consider the phenomenon in one form or another, through a qualitative evaluation of responses to the colored stimuli, or through the more formal procedure of examining for color-shock, or both. The variety of approaches to the scoring and evaluation of Color responses seem to represent differences in the manner by which Rorschach's hypothesis concerning color has been extended rather than significant interpretive differences between the Systems.

Shading Responses

A comparison of the interpretive approaches to the Shading responses is probably the most difficult to make of all the Determinants. This is created by the great variability which exists across the Systems in defining the Shading responses. It is made more complex by the fact that Rorschach gave no mention to these responses in his monograph, referring to them only in the 1923 paper. Piotrowski indicates that this is because Rorschach's original blots contained no shading, that instead they were uniform in hue. Apparently a printer's error produced shading effects at the time the monograph *Psychodiagnostik* was being published. Rorschach suggested that Shading responses have a relation to difficulties in affective adaptability and postulated that they represent a timid and cautious approach, possibly correlated with a feeling of "insufficiency." This hypothesis is endorsed in all of the Systems wherein general postulates concerning Shading imply cautiousness, fearfulness, and definitely a feeling of discomfort. This feeling of discomfort is usually described as a subdued or contained affect, the product of which is anxiety and restrained relations with the environment. All of the Systems, as in the instance of the Color responses, place great importance on the degree of Form involvement in the Shading answer. It is speculated that the intensity and disruptiveness of the discomforting or painful affect are contingent on the degree of reality testing and effective adaptation of the individual. Thus, where Form dominates the response, the affect is seen as controlled whereas in responses where Form is secondary or non-existent, the affect is interpreted as being diffuse and destructive.

It has been noted in the preceding chapter that the subdivision of Shading responses into specific categories is quite diversified. This diversification can be described by four general categories, Depth or Vista responses, Texture responses, achromatic Color responses, and the more general type of Shading or Chiaroscuro responses. All of the Systems do not include these four categories, but instead subsume two or more into a single category and depend on qualitative evaluation to make the appropriate distinctions. For example, Beck does not use a separate category for achromatic Color responses, the Rapaport-Schafer System makes no formal provision for Texture responses, and Piotrowski differentiates Shading responses by the lightness or darkness of the area and by the mood expressed in the response.

Three of the Systems, Beck, Klopfer and Hertz, offer specific interpretive hypotheses for responses which include reference to texture. Beck describes the texture answer as indicating an affective hunger which has as its roots, the infantile erotic needs. The Klopfer and Hertz texture interpretations are quite similar to Beck's. They suggest that such responses relate to an awareness of needs for affection and dependency. All three Systems caution that the strength and relevance of the need must be judged with regard to the degree of Form involvement in the response as well as other characteristics of the record in which affect is displayed. Klopfer specifically indicates that the Form dominated texture responses indicate awareness, sensitivity, and tactfulness whereas the responses with limited or no Form involvement manifest a cruder, more immature striving for affective closeness.

The vista or perspective type response is also formally included in only three Systems, Beck, Klopfer and Hertz. The Piotrowski and Rapaport-Schafer Systems mention such responses but do not deal with them as specifically as do the other three Systems. The more general interpretation offered for such responses centers about reflectiveness or introspction. Klopfer suggests that these responses represent an effort to tolerate and understand anxiety. He indicates that they are a positive therapeutic sign. Hertz generally concurs with this notion and follows Binder's suggestion that they represent positively toned affects. Beck's interpretation of the vista response focuses on the postulate that it is a manifestation of feelings of inferiority that can be taken positively but more often is a liability. He suggests that they occur commonly in the pre-depressive or depressive states. Piotrowski, although not formalizing consideration of the vista response, suggests that they occur most frequently in more intelligent people. He indicates that these responses imply the tendency to express anxieties indirectly in aesthetics in an active or passive manner and thus avoid direct verbalizations about personal anxieties. While the focal points for interpretation of the vista responses differ somewhat across the Systems, there is an obvious agreement by all Systematizers that the self-appraisal process is involved.

Four of the Systems, all but Beck, make special note of those instances where achromatic Color is used as a Color. The Klopfer, Rapaport-Schafer, and Hertz interpretations all include mention of a "toning down" of affect. It is implied that this represents an attempt to be more adaptive in affective discharge. Piotrowski offers some agreement with this hypothesis but stresses the importance of considering the lightness or darkness used in the percept. He concludes that the use of the lighter achromatic colors relate to feelings of euphoria whereas the darker color projections manifest depressive feelings.

It is important to note that Piotrowski's exposition concerning Shading responses probably offers greatest divergence from the other Systems. In part this is created by his deliberate restriction of the categories for such responses, using only c and c', but more importantly is the assumption for the evaluation of Shading which underpins those categories. He maintains that Shading responses are directly related to overt motor behavior and that the subjective experience of anxiety is not simply manifest by the number of shading responses but by the relation of light Shading responses to dark Shading responses and by the relation of either to Color responses. He rejects the notion that Shading responses *per se* are potential Color responses, thereby differing to some degree with the other Systematizers. Piotrowski postulates a fundamental psychological difference between responses to light and dark colored areas of the cards, the former indicating a need to alleviate anxiety by a decrease in overt motor behavior in the "spheres of life which cause fears or anxiety," the latter indicating the opposite, i.e., an increase in overt motor activity in the "spheres of life" which provoke fear and/or anxiety.

The Shading response, somewhat like the Movement response, yields a number of interpretations across the Systems. These interpretations are quite similar in some respects, but very different in others, with Piotrowski generating the most divergent view in all of the Systems. All Systems appear to agree on certain general hypotheses but, as elaboration ensues, differences evolve and become greater as a System becomes more specific. It is important to note that the basic substance of agreement between the Systems concerning the Shading response occurs, as in several other instances, due to agreement with Rorschach's hypotheses on the issue.

Popular and Original Responses

There is some disagreement across the Systems concerning the criteria necessary for a response to be described as Popular. Rorschach had suggested that Popular (Vulgar) responses be defined as those occurring once in every three records. Beck and Hertz have endorsed Rorschach's criteria and offer lists of Populars accordingly. Rapaport-Schafer define the Popular to be a response occurring "once in every four or five" records but provide no specific listing. Klopfer and Piotrowski recognize the general requirement that a Popular is one which occurs frequently in a large number of records but do not specify a given proportion. Each offers a diffent listing of Popular responses. Although the lists of Populars, where they are given, vary considerably across the Systems there is considerable agreement concerning the Popularity of certain responses such as the "Bat" to Card I. There is also considerable agreement concerning the meaning of the Popular response. Following Rorschach's suggestion, all Systems have included the postulate that the Popular indicates an awareness of conventionality and an ability to respond in light of it. All Systems regard an excess of Popular responses as a serious preoccupation with conformity or conventionality. Conversely, it is held that the record offering a low number of Popular responses is indicative of the atypical, unconventional person.

The Original response was defined by Rorschach as those occurring once in 100 records. All Systems except Beck employ a formal consideration of Original responses.* Where the Original response is formally endorsed it is interpreted in two respects. First, it is noted that Original responses can be an index of the highly intelligent, very creative person who is willing to express his uniqueness in his thought operation. More commonly however, it is noted that Original responses occur in the protocols of the preoccupied, wherein the nature of the response typifies the nature of the deprived need state or conflict situation. Piotrowski and Rapaport-Schafer note that most Original responses are given to unusual or rare detail areas of the blots and suggest that the final interpretation must be given with respect to the Total record, especially the use of Location.

---

* Beck suggests that the concept of the Original is difficult to teach and that the frequency tabulation required is too cumbersome. He adds, however, that careful evaluation should be given to highly "unique" responses offering a general interpretation for these similar to that prescribed by the other Systematizers for the Original response.

Content Scores

There is nearly unanimous agreement between the Systems concerning the general interpretation of the Content of responses. These are perceived as indicating the breadth and depth of interest, in the self and in the environment. All of the Systems suggest that the highest proportion of Content will be comprised of the Animal-type response. It is also expected that a significant number of Human-type responses will occur. All of the Systems indicate that it is important to compare the proportion of Human to Animal responses suggesting ratios which vary from one to two, to one to three depending on the length of the record. It is also cautioned in all of the Systems, following Rorschach's lead, that an unusually high proportion of A responses is representative of the restricted, stereotyped person. The proportion of Human responses is regarded as the need and/or willingness to interact with people. The Systems also call for special attention to be given to the breadth of Content as being indicative of the variety of interests and the scope of one's environmental and personal interactions. Conversely, the Systems caution the necessity for attention to excessive frequency of a single Content category representing preoccupation, and/or with a restriction of Content, representing a narrowing of one's interactive patterns.

Verbalizations

The five Systems all emphasize the importance of evaluating the subject's verbalizations. It is agreed across the Systems that while critically important data is revealed by the structural and/or formalized aspects of the protocol, many of the important idiographic features are revealed by the verbalizations. Rapaport and Schafer have possibly written more concerning verbalizations than have any of the other Systematizers but this should not be interpreted as a significantly greater emphasis in that System. The "global analysis" demanded by each of the Systematizers includes a careful qualitative evaluation of all verbal and non-verbal material offered in the testing situation. The fact that the general interpretive framework for each of the Systems rests within the broad boundries of the psychoanalytic model makes for considerable similarity in qualitative interpretation of the verbal material. In some instances, vocabulary differences do occur but they are relatively minor when the overall interpretation is considered.

It is important to reaffirm that the comparisons presented here are those generally applicable to all five Systems. A much more substantial discourse could ensue comparing any two or three of the Systems and, of course, would reveal both more similarities and more differences. But such an onerous task would not fall within the immediate scope of this work. It seems more important at this time to contrast all five Systems in as much depth as possible. And that contrast appears to clearly denote major differences between the Systems concerning the meaning of a significant portion of Rorschach data. This seems especially true in the instance of the Movement and Shading responses and, to a lesser extent, in some of the aspects of Location, Form, and Color. The interpretive impact of these differences may be even greater when the general method of approach to interpretation is included, i.e., blind versus non-blind, although that must be left to speculation as there are no records which have been interpreted by several of the Systematizers using the contemporary status of their respective Systems as the interpretative base. In that such data is not available to consider the inter-System reliability for interpretation, it is necessary to rely more on the limited type of contrast offered here.

Finally, it seems important to underscore the fact that, for the most part, the similarities and agreements which occur across the Systems are agreements with Rorschach. It is that series of interpretive hypotheses offered by Rorschach which constitute the substantial linkages between the Systems. Whether this is caused by validity or loyalty, or both, is not always clear. The inter-System interpretive agreements, as in the instance of the scoring criteria and scoring symbols, seem to occur most where Rorschach was most definitive. Differences between the Systems occur most on matters where Rorschach was less definitive or offered no hypotheses. Naturally, this is not true for all cases but one is hard-pressed to find an example where all of the Systematizers have "agreed to disagree' with Rorschach. More frequently than not, the differences have arisen on issues involving an extension of a Rorschach hypothesis. This is probably a positive sign as it can be interpreted as an important consistency factor which has survived the rigorous evaluation of a variety of significant investigators, each working within the context of relatively broad differences in training, experience, and theoretical orientations.

REFERENCES

Beck, S. J., Beck, A. G., Levitt, E. E. and Molish, H. B. *Rorschach's Test. Vol. I. Basic Processes*. 3rd Ed. New York: Grune & Stratton, 1961.

Beck, S. J. and Molish, H. B. *Rorschach's Test. Vol. II. A Variety of Personality Pictures*. 2nd Ed. New York: Grune & Stratton, 1967.

Hertz, M. R. *Frequency Tables for Scoring Responses to the Rorschach Ink-Blot Test*. 3rd Ed. Cleveland, Ohio: Western Reserve University Press, 1951.

Hertz, M. R. The use and misuse of the Rorschach method: I. Variations in Rorschach procedure. *J. Proj. Tech.*, 1951, 23, 33-48.

Hertz, M. R. The organization activity. In Rickers-Ovsiankina, Maria (Ed.). *Rorschach Psychology*. New York: Wiley and Sons, 1960.

Klopfer, B., Ainsworth, M. D., Klopfer, W. G. and Holt, R. R. *Developments in the Rorschach Technique. Vol. I. Technique and Theory*. Yonkers-on-Hudson, N. Y.: World Book Co., 1954.

Klopfer, B., et al. *Developments in the Rorschach Technique. Vol. II. Fields of Application*. Yonkers-on-Hudson, N. Y.: World Book Co., 1957.

Klopfer, B. and Davidson, H. H. *The Rorschach Technique*. New York: Harcourt, Brace & World, 1962.

Piotrowski, Z. *Perceptanalysis*. New York: Macmillan, 1957.

Piotrowski, Z. Digital-Computor interpretation of inkblot test data. *Psychiat. Quart.*, 1964, 38, 1-26.

Rapaport, D., Gill, M. and Schafer, R. *Diagnostic Psychological Testing. Vol. II*. Chicago: Yearbook Publishers, 1946.

Rorschach, H. *Psychodiagnostik*. Bern: Bircher, 1921, (Trans. Hans Huber Verlag, 1942).

Schafer, R. *Psychoanalytic Interpretation in Rorschach Testing: Theory and Application*. New York: Grune & Stratton, 1954.

CHAPTER 11

AN OVERVIEW

The American history of the ten Swiss Inkblots has been marked by the rise of clear and often unequivocal differences among those closest to its development. These differences are impressive and have stimulated the evolution of five Rorschach Systems. The Systems are not completely different from one another. Quite the contrary, many identical or nearly identical features are found when each is compared with the others. But the Systems are different and, on certain points, so much so that they defy comparison. It would be truly unjust, however, to criticize the Systematizers because of their divergence. Controversy breeds interest. Without question, some of the differences in theoretical orientation and clinical opinion which existed between the Systematizers during the mid-1930's and early 1940s' stimulated much interest. Almost two full decades of seemingly healthy and productive research ensued which otherwise might not have occurred with such scope or magnitude. One might reasonably hypothesize that had the divergence not evolved, much of the early strength of the instrument, necessary to keep it alive in clinical practice and current in research thinking, might not have occurred. Therefore, it is easy to conclude, without reservation, that the six people involved in the development of the five respective Systems, Beck, Klopfer, Piotrowski, Hertz, Rapaport, and Schafer have all made major contributions to the development of the technique and its psychodiagnostic usefulness.

The total impact of the divergence is difficult to assess. Thirty-five years constitutes a long developmental history for any instrument. To be sure, each of the Systems has developed to a point of sophistication significantly greater than had been provided by Rorschach. But questions remain, and are being asked with even greater frequency by contemporary psychology, concerning the overall worth of the technique when contrasted with the often laborious complexities of its administration and interpretation. Literally thousands of books and articles have appeared regarding the technique and its clinical application .There have been consistent validity demands voiced concerning the Rorschach which have not always been answered to the satisfaction of the test and measurement "purist," and even the more simple demands concerning standardization have not always been responded to adequately. Has the divergence and subsequent multi-system development contributed measurably to the onset of grounds for criticism? To some, it has appeared that the instrument has been maintained in an almost "fixated-like" state of perpetual adolescence after having "lost its father" at a very early age and having been subjected to the whims, orientations, and opinions of a variety of foster parents. Such critics suggest that a lack of "demonstrated validity" and the issue of differences between the Systems has achieved such a disproportionate stage that the instrument itself is no longer worthy of investigation and has far too many complications for continued clinical use.

A reasonable understanding of the Rorschach and particularly, of its American history, would suggest that, while some of these criticisms have a valid base, any recommendations for discarding the technique or discontinuing research on it would be naive and premature. In fact ,an opposite position seems more realistic and justifiable. Research should be increased but possibly some of the goals of the research altered. But before discussing the specific research requirements, there are two other factors which require consideration. These are the more generalized issues of psychodiagnostics, and "clinical validity."

The role of the clinical psychologist has changed rather markedly since Hermann Rorschach selected the ten cards which comprise the test today. During the 1930's and 1940's when the era of divergence was occurring, the role of the clinician was seen primarily as a psychodiagnostician. Strong commitments were made by psychologists through testing. Subsequent to World War II some of these commitments began to wane and a much greater emphasis has evolved to the role of the clinician as a psychotherapist. The sometimes unpalatable concepts of "mental health" and "diagnostic labeling" have caused clinical psychology to move further away from archaic psychiatric nosology and undertake a stern review of the "medical model." Beginning with the 1946 Boulder Conference and the most recently having been reaffirmed in the 1966 Chicago Conference, clinical psychologists have been questioning their own roles as professionals. Yet, few are willing to endorse the suggestion that the clinician should completely relinquish his diagnostic skills. Instead, it remains generally agreed that the fundamentals of clinical psychology are based on the intricate knowledge of personality and psychopathology. If the psychologist is to devote his greater efforts to the modification of ineffective, unproductive, or destructive behaviors it seems clear that some understandings of the individual manifesting these behaviors is relevant as a starting point. It would also seem that to assume that such information can be derived using only nomothetic criteria is professionally unsound and even ethically incompatible with the commitment of the professional to the patient. Thus, some means of identifying the idiographic features of the individual becomes vitally important to the whole process. Rapaport and Schafer, more than any of the other Systematizers, have devoted themselves to a variety of tests. They suggested in 1948 that the Rorschach seems to be the most useful technique for the understanding of idiographic characteristics. This position has been directly and/or indirectly endorsed by all of the other Systematizers. It also seems worthwhile to point out the fact that critics of the Rorschach have not, in general, criticized other projective techniques. In fact, many outstanding pieces of research have been accomplished using other types of projective methodology, mainly the sentence completion test and the Thematic Apperception type test. It seems also naive to assume that the projective approach provided by the Rorschach is of little use if other instruments such as these have such significant value when all are based on the same assumptions. In fact, the Rorschach, when appropriately used according to any one of the recommended Systems, is probably less prone to the subjective errors of the interpreter than are other projective methods. Consequently, it seems realistic to purport the notion that if the clinician is to be a psychodiagnostician, he will be concerned with idiographic features. If so, of all instruments available to the clinician today, the Rorschach seems most appropriately designed for an "in depth" understanding of personality and psychopathology.

The second issue at hand concerning the future of the Rorschach involves the concept of validation. It is probably true, as many critics proclaim, that a true statistical validity has not been demonstrated for the Rorschach regardless of the fact that more than 3,000 books and articles concerning the instrument have been published. It is easy to suggest that statistical techniques, as devised thus far, are not sufficiently sophisticated nor oriented toward the type of instrument that the Rorschach represents. It could be argued that these statistical techniques are more specifically oriented toward nomothetic procedures which become, at best, only partially applicable to the Rorschach or for that matter, to any other projective method. And these arguments may well be true. But such statements only serve to oversimplify the Rorschach problem and do little to provide a solution for the problem. The concept of validity as generally accepted today in psychology ordinarily refers to any one of at least three types of validation; predictive validity, concurrent validity, and construct validity. If one is to examine data presented on most test instruments, it will be found that the latter, construct validity, is demonstrated with least frequency. Construct validity in itself is a knotty problem requiring rigorous guidelines and procedures which are often impossible to apply. Bechtold (1959) has pointed to the fact that the implementation of the criteria for construct validity frequently creates a narrowing of interpretation of operational criteria and a tendency to avoid or reduce specific terminology. Concurrent validity is that which is probably most frequently demonstrated in that the requirements may be reduced to agreement with the results of other instruments or similar data concerning the element to be measured. Since 1935 a number of Rorschach studies have been published suggesting that test-derived descriptions do indeed coincide with descriptions obtained from other sources. Most of these have been discounted by critics on the premise that measured agreement is too limited or, more commonly, on the premise that interpretations have not occurred under the truly "naive" situations necessary for comparison. Most frequently, studies of a concurrent nature have been concerned with specific Rorschach variables, i.e., Color, Movement, Shading, etc., and thus, have not met the plea for "global" analysis manifest by the various Rorschach authorities. Beck, for example, indicates that such studies have little merit for the understanding of the full personality, especially its idiographic features, and at the same time place the test in the position of being viewed negatively whenever the results are not strongly positive.

The third type of validation, common to the area of tests and measurements, is that dealing with predictive accuracy. This type of validity is possibly the most difficult with which to contend by Rorschach enthusiasts. Rorschach data has been frequently demonstrated to be of little apparent use in predicting such behaviors as success in graduate school, pilot training, job satisfaction, job competency, and the like. Correspondingly, these failures are frequently cited by critics of the test as evidence of its worthlessness. Such critics fail to mention that the technique was not designed for such predictive purposes nor is it used commonly in those respects. To be sure, Rorschach, and all of the Systematizers have offered postulates concerning test performance and behavior, but these are not necessarily meant to provide elaborate predictions concerning future behaviors except in the most gross terms. The technique is not purported to include elements which will predict the environmental circumstances of any person in the future. When predictions are made, it is always with the provision that "under specific circumstances" a behavior such as a suicidal gesture, acting out, or the like, is highly probable. The fact that these predicted behaviors do or do not occur does not necessarily reflect on the accuracy of the description. And it would be indeed foolish for anyone, be he pro- or anti-Rorschach to suggest a specific behavioral correlate to a specific test response or type of response. Any of the Systematizers, and Rorschach, would regard this as extremely inappropriate.

Harris (1960) provides a very competent review of the problems of Rorschach validation. He points out that Rorschach enthusiasts have placed themselves in the precarious position of permitting the instrument to be evaluated by orthodox tests and measurements standards even though the test is neither designed nor interpreted along such standard lines. He indicates that such variables as the language of the subject and/or examiner and/or interpreter must all be considered in any questions of Rorschach validity. He also emphasizes that problems such as identifying the responses as a reasonable sample of the individual's personality and problems of validating criterion have not been approached directly or sufficiently in Rorschach research. Cronbach (1949) had raised many of these same questions earlier leaving the clear implication that current statistical methodology and the validity problems of the Rorschach are far from compatible. Wyatt (1968 focused his presidential address to the Society of Projective Techniques on the problem of objectivity in projective methods, and most specifically as applicable to the Rorschach. He accents the impracticality of relinguishing "large portions of human experience as a legitimate subject matter for psychology" simply because it is difficult to demonstrate their existence using the contemporary statistical and research methodology. He cites the gross inadequacy of attempts at "Trait isolation" and condemns studies in which the investigator's method defines the subject matter. Unfortunately, it would appear that much Rorschach research has followed the very format which Wyatt strongly rejects. In some research, criteria has been dictated by methodology. In other research, criteria has been narrowed or an issue even confused through the utilization of definitions and/or methods from a single Rorschach System in a manner to imply applicability to "Rorschach" as if only one System exists. Such studies may yield data which is relevant to a single System but not necessarily to all Systems. The probability of such an error occurring is significantly increased whenever research is structured to seek behavioral correlates for specific scoring categories in a given System ignoring either the "global evaluation" or the intra-System uniqueness of the scoring category being studied. A relatively small number of studies have been reported which seem to be applicable to all Systems but their importance is seemingly less clear when appraised in the myriad of publications following more restrictive research designs.

The foregoing should not be interpreted as an attempt to minimize or excuse the Rorschach problem, for that is not the case. It is important however, to provide an appropriate perspective of the conditions and problems which have existed through the era of divergence, the development of the five American Rorschach Systems, and the attempts to study the validity of the instrument. Wyatt also notes that Koch (1964) has implored the importance of a "language community," i.e., a precise semantic understanding among investigators concerned with the study of the same phenomenon. In such a context, the ramifications of the Inter-System differences can be more fully appreciated for the language community of the Rorschach has become extremely limited through the inter-System divergence. It would, of course, be unrealistic to suggest that inter-System differences are a singular cause of the Rorschach problem for that is obviously not the case. But these differences have contributed in more than a passing manner to the problem and quite probably have rendered its solution to be more difficult. The lack of agreement does exist in all three areas basic to the test: administration, scoring, and interpretation. It might not be inaccurate to suggest that there is not one Rorschach test, but rather five, or even six if Rorschach's own System were to be included. To be sure, there are similarities between these Systems including the use of the same stimulus figures, but the differences occur with such depth and frequency that each has become quite unique. The substantial thread of agreement that does exist across all Systems is mainly in the form of acceptance of many of Rorschach's procedures and hypotheses, but this thread is embelished in a unique fashion by each of the Systematizers.

This then constitutes something of the magnitude of the Rorschach problem. And it does extend beyond the simple inadequacies of statistical procedures and research methodology. It extends to the "language community" discussed by Koch. It is quite difficult to conceive of productive Rorschach research of any of the major test variables until the problems posed by the inter-System differences are brought to some resolution, The only viable alternative, and it is probably not a good one, is to undertake and/or evaluate research as applicable to one of the Systems. Such an alternative, in effect, provides for recognition of the differences in language and methods. The adoption of this alternative would seem to be premature. It seems more realistic to approach the Rorschach problem through a research integration of the Systems if the test is to survive and flourish in psychodiagnostic work. It should not be inferred that such an integration, if that be the proper term, could be accomplished with ease. Quite the contrary, the task would be difficult and have as prerequisite a re-evaluation of previous research concerning test methods used and research design followed. This could provide for a composite summary of past research as applicable to each of the Systems, therein pointing to a potential direction for the settlement of disagreements concerning methods and interpretive hypotheses. New research should also be designed in which the language community problem is recognized and methodology employed which circumvents this problem as much as possible. Optimally, the Rorschach future should encompass progress and hopefully resolution in the four areas basic to the test: (1) procedure of administration, (2) method of scoring, (3) interpretation, (4) teaching standards. The confusion in each of these areas contributes in some manner to the overall Rorschach problem. Problems in these areas are not new to anyone familiar with Rorschach history. It has been indicated in several preceding chapters that many Rorschach authorities, including the Systematizers, have noted the presence of such problems and have made suggestions, as early as 1935, concerning their resolution. Unfortunately, and for a variety of reasons mentioned previously, these suggestions were not followed with any degree of consistency. It might be futile to point to these needs again but but possibly the wisdoms which have accumulated concerning the test over the past three decades may have created a different atmosphere for its study and growth.

ADMINISTRATIVE PROCEDURES

It is not known which of the variety of procedures is the most appropriate to the Rorschach, or for that matter, if the different methods do provoke different results. It has not been demonstrated whether the basic substance of the test data changes if the examiner sits in front of a subject, or next to a subject, rather than behind the subject. There is considerable information in contemporary psychology referring to instructional sets and the "social desirability" phenomenon but this has not been made applicable to Rorschach. That data does lead to the speculation that differences in test productivity will probably ensue under different instructions or different administrative conditions. Conversely, it may be true that the nature of projection, especially to an inkblot, is such that these factors have little influence. Certainly the Systematizers, all of whom permit variability in instructions, imply that the true nature of personality will be projected in the responses even though collected under a variety of conditions. This should be investigated. There is also no consistent information to indicate what form of encouragement, if any, is appropriate to the Free-Association segment of the test. Should a subject be encouraged after one response, one minute, several responses, some cards, all cards, or never? And more importantly, do such variations create substantial differences in the record which would change the description of the personality?

The matter of Inquiry also requires concern. Should there be an Inquiry, and if so to what extent should it progress? Should all responses be Inquired and what restrictions should be placed on the types of questions? Do differences arise if Inquiry follows each card rather than after the entire Free-Association? Is there a value to post-Inquiry procedures such as Testing of Limits, or the use of an Analogy Period? More importantly, what weight should be attributed to material collected in the Inquiry versus the material given in the Free-Association? Seemingly, many research hours can be devoted to these relatively simple areas if for no other reason than to be assured that data collected in other Rorschach studies can be legitimately compared.

METHOD OF SCORING

The word *score* has probably contributed greatly to the misunderstanding and misuse of the Rorschach in practice and/or research. The traditional concept of a score implies some nomothetic basis in which the "right or wrong," "true or false" notions are applicable. It also implies the potential for summation, the establishment of normative data and, in the area of personality evaluation, the development of the psychogram. These traditional measurement concepts and procedures are, of course, amenable to contemporary statistical evaluation. This is true for the Rorschach in only the most limited sense. Rorschach responses, rather than being scorable in the customary measurement routine, are really coded. This coding is much like the coding of data which takes place in the use of the computer. It is a type of *scoring* very unlike that applied to tests of intelligence, achievement, interest, or personality questionnaires and inventories. Frequency tabulations are maintained and some generalized normative standards have evolved but not for the purpose of constructing a psychogram of the personality. The use of the psychogram endorses a scheme of interpretation which is exactly the opposite of the interpretive approach argued for by the Systematizers and by Rorschach. Wherever the psychogram is used, it subverts the goal of understanding the personality on the idiographic dimension. But even if the coding of Rorschach responses were not treated by some as a measurement score and even if no Rorschach psychograms were constructed, the inter-System differences that exist for scoring Rorschach responses would still provide confusion. It has been demonstrated in Chapter 9 that there are a few points of total agreement among all Systems concerning the utilization of particular symbols and their criteria. But more commonly, there is only limited inter-System agreement on either symbol or criteria and in many instances the symbol and/or criteria is unique to only a single System.

The scoring methodology for each of the Systems appears to have considerable merit and the differences that have evolved appear to have resulted from justifiable differences of opinion. Each of the Systems offers the method of scoring or coding which, in the framework of the particular System, seems to best exemplify the true characteristics of the response given. All of the Systematizers have warned against over-extension of the number of scoring categories which might in some manner deplete the meaningfulness of the data. It seems important to suggest that each such category be studied with respect to clinical agreements and research findings. Where a category is of demonstrated positive value it should be retained but where possible it might be integrated in some way with like categories of other Systems. If the symbol and/or criteria is of dubious value it should be researched further, or if the findings warrant, be discarded. It is also necessary to give due consideration to the phenomenon of multiplicity as appears to occur in some responses. Some of the Systems currently score for all factors occurring in the response while other Systems relegate a single factor to a primary role and assume all others to be secondary and provide for a somewhat different interpretation. Naturally, all such studies should proceed under the more general postulate that all data will ultimately be integrated but the actual process of weighing and integrating must be justly considered before any final determinations concerning scoring methodology occur.

INTERPRETATION

The actual proof of the instrument, or of any instrument, lies in the effectiveness with which the task for which it has been designed is accomplished. It has been noted in Chapter 10, and in other chapters, that a substantial thread of agreement appears across all Systems concerning interpretive postulates. For the most part, differences occur when the System provides an extension or modification of a general hypothesis. Almost all of Rorschach's early hypotheses have been incorporated into the five Systems and have formed the nucleus for their development. Most of the inter-System differences occur in the elaboration to the hypothesis provided by the Systematizer and frequently it is a difference in emphasis rather than an actual disagreement. Thus, one step which seems necessary is the integration of the interpretive statements and the completion of more definitive "global" interpretive studies to determine the circumstances under which certain conclusions are justified and the circumstances under which the same conclusions are not justified.

This is not to intimate that all which is important will easily fall into place. Were it so simple! But these types of studies can establish the appropriate base from which a greater understanding of the interpretive process can evolve and can give more specific direction to the requirements of future research. Some issues will be very difficult to resolve but many appear reducable to the more thorough expositions in which an acceptable language community is utilized. For example, the apparent differences between Beck and Piotrowski concerning the meaning of Movement responses may well be more semantic than theoretical. The obvious differences in approach to Shading interpretation may be reduced in much the same way. The end product of semantic integration could be two-fold. First, the inter-System differences which now appear to exist could be substantially reduced. Second, and more important, greater clarity of real differences could evolve thereby accenting areas in which further research would be critical. It is important to caution however, that any attempts at integration of interpretive hypotheses must be accompanied by a similar integration of those test features and criteria which define a class of response, i.e., scoring categories. It is the definition by class which determines which responses are amenable to particular interpretations. Consequently, any integration and/or reconciliation of the Systems must occur "across the board" and not merely in restricted areas or categories.

TEACHING RORSCHACH

Many years ago, the *Rorschach Research Exchange* set forth a meaningful criterion for Rorschach proficiency. That criterion was very similar to recommendations made by other Rorschach authorities, including all of the Systematizers. The generally agreed upon criterion specified training by a competent instructor, considerable depth of supervised Rorschach experience, and a reasonable knowledge in the areas of personality and psychopathology. Some, such as Beck, also recommended personal psychoanalysis. While this latter point may be less practical in training in clinical psychology today, the other requirements are not. Yet, a cursory examination of Rorschach teaching methodology in programs throughout the country indicates that the extent of training is considerably more limited than desirable. In fact, Rorschach courses at some institutions are reduced to reviewing of research literature with little or no practicuum experience. Too frequently the task of providing the Rorschach practicuum is relegated to the internship installation which is seldom capable of providing these experiences within the limited space of time available and the vast array of subject matter which must be presented. This is a regrettable situation for it only contributes to the Rorschach problem by placing the instrument in the hands of the novice of limited experience and/or understanding of the technique.

SUMMARY

There seems to be little doubt that the Rorschach test has experienced a stormy history. The controversies which have been attached to it have been provoked by both its proponents and its antagonists. Its survival is indeed remarkable when considered amidst the chronic disparaging calls for abandonment from without and fragmentation into separate Systems which has occurred from within. Even more remarkable than its mere survival is the fact that it flourishes in a perennial fashion, not simply as a test, but as a mainstay in psychodiagnostic methodology. It has been described in the most negative terms which range from accusations of being invalid, unreliable, cumbersome, and overly complex, to the more affectively dominated charges of subjectivity, which, not infrequently, carry with them the implication of some artistic mysticism. These descriptions have had little apparent influence on those who know and use the test.

Quite probably the success of the technique can be largely attributed to two elements. First, it seems to work well in the clinical setting. Second, and possibly more important, there has been the long and deep commitment of those responsible for the development of the test. A listing of such people would number into the hundreds or even thousands and quite obviously would include the six Systematizers whose work has been the major focus here. Through their teaching, research, writing, and stimulation to others, the Rorschach has gained an important position in the clinical world.

Few, if any, would suggest that there is no Rorschach problem. Certainly, the Systematizers would not do so, for anytime information is incomplete some form of problem exists, and the Rorschach is no exception. So long as such a Rorschach problem exists, the Rorschacher cannot afford to ignore it for, most certainly, others will not. Wyatt (1968) indicates, "It will be a happy day when we are finally released from having to defend our position and instead can summon our energies for attending to our work." The achievement of that goal is probably difficult but not insurmountable and, at least in part, it would seem more easily attainable if the Rorschach community is able to define with greater precision the subject matter with which it works. To this end the matter of System clarification and integration should not be avoided.

REFERENCES

Bechtold, H. P. Construct validity: a critique. *Amer. Psychol.*, 1959, 14, 619-629.

Cronbach, L. J. Statistical methods applied to Rorschach scores: a review. *Psychol. Bull.*, 1949, 46, 393-429.

Harris, J. G. Validity: The search for a constant in a universe of variables. In Rickers-Ovsiankina, Maria (Ed.) *Rorschach Psychology.* New York: Wiley & Sons, 1960.

Koch, S. Psychology and emerging conceptions of knowledge as unitary. In Wann, T. W. (Ed.) *Behaviorism and Phenomenology.* Chicago: Univ. of Chicago Press, 1964.

Wyatt, F. How objective is objectivity? *J. Proj. Tech.*, 1968, 31, 3-19.

APPENDIX

Possibly one of the best techniques for demonstrating any given Rorschach System is the Case Study Method. It not only manifests the formal structural features of a System as evidenced by the formal scoring and summarization of responses but also provides amplification and clarification of the interpretive approaches used in each System. Most importantly, it demonstrates the "globalness" of the interpretive procedures used in each System.

What follows herein are five case studies, one each representing the respective five American Rorschach Systems. The cases have been selected by the Systematizers either from previously published material or from material especially prepared for this text. The Klopfer Interpretation, the Case of A.S., has been reproduced from the 1962 Klopfer and Davidson book, *The Rorschach Technique.* The Beck Interpretation, G.A., pathologic gambler, has been selected from the 1967 revision of *Rorschach's Test: Volume II.* The Piotrowski Interpretation, the Case of Delia, has been especially prepared by Dr. Piotrowski for this text. The Rapaport-Schafer Interpretation has been selected by Dr. Schafer from his 1954 text, *Psychoanalytic Interpretation in Rorschach Testing.* The analysis of this particular case is not as lengthy as the others, nor as inclusive as the typical Rapaport-Schafer Interpretation might be. It is Dr. Schafer's desire however, to offer material which most specifically represents the interpretive approach used by Dr. Rapaport. This particular case has been used by Dr. Schafer to represent the phenomenon of repression as it may occur in the Rorschach. The Hertz Interpretation offers a case especially prepared by Dr. Hertz for inclusion here.

In reviewing these case interpretations it is vitally important to exercise those cautions necessary whenever small sample material is offered. While each case is representative of a System, it remains an N of one. Thus, while the interpretive format presented in an interpretation does represent a specific System, there would be nevertheless subtle alterations in interpretation if a different protocol were analyzed. Naturally these characteristics of a System can be best understood by referring directly to primary source material.

A KLOPFER INTERPRETATION

Autobiographical Sketch of A.S.

I am 32 years old. My mother is a housewife, 62, and my father is a construction contractor and is 73. My relationship with my parents is very good, so long as I am not living with them. We think differently, are all very dogmatic, and therefore quarrel if we are together for more than two days. But, it's always good to see them again, and I do see them quite frequently.

I have two brothers: Freddie, who's 36, and Joseph, who is 26. Freddie is married, with two children. I'm not close to Freddie. When we were home together, he considered me a kid sister and a nuisance. Joseph is away at school studying physics. Although we do not spend a great deal of time together, our relationship is good.

I lived at home until ten years ago. My youthful days were very happy ones for me as I remember them. Although I was extremely overweight, I never lacked friends, and was always a popular member of the group.

Until high school years, the weight problem never concerned me. However, throughout this period, although I remained popular I did not have "dates" of the romantic type—naturally a great calamity to any teenager. I would diet sporadically, but remained very much overweight until I went to a small New England college.

I was always a good student, though not particularly interested in intellectual life. I was attending college as most other girls do—with the intention of marrying and raising a family shortly after graduation. Therefore, I spent a great deal of time having a good time during the college years. I met my first real boyfriend here and had my first tragedy in this area. After two years of courtship with plans for the future together, he broke off our relationship just before I graduated.

Upon graduation from college, I held a succession of jobs in the editorial field for three years. During the period I spent a two-month vacation in Europe with a girl with whom I had grown up. Upon our return, we decided to live in New York City, sharing an apartment together. When she married, less than a year later, I returned home to live with the family.

After giving up our jobs because we were simply "sick of it all," I and a fellow worker traveled around the United States for about one year. We spent the winter working as maids, waitresses, etc., in an elite hotel in Florida in return for room, board, a very small salary, and free time every afternoon which we spent water skiing. Here I had my second big romance, with a water-skiing instructor attached to the same hotel. This young man was everything that a girl's middle-class parents would *not* want to have for a son-in-law: not well-educated, a water bum, and, as I found out, an alcoholic. However, he was *very* masculine. When I informed my parents of the marriage plans, they came scooting down to Florida to "size up" the situation. The resort season having come to an end, I returned home with my parents. I expected to marry my water-skiing instructor when he came to New York, but he never came, although his letters kept saying "in a few weeks." After working at a temporary clerical job for awhile, I returned to Florida to see him, and it was then that I learned about his alcoholism and a few other unsavory facts.

I returned home very much disheartened, and in a state of confusion as to what to do next. I decided to go to graduate school so that I could prepare myself for some profession. Being unsure of my motivation and my interest in chemistry (which had been my undergraduate major), I entered the science department. In the meantime I continued working as a secretary, and also continued living at home. I became extremely interested in my studies, and with the help of one of my professors, I was able to give up full-time working and give more time to being a student.

Again I was a good student, but now I was working hard to maintain that status. I had been out of school so long, and had forgotten most of what I knew about chemistry. I was therefore very unsure of my own abilities. This uncertainty concerning myself and my abilities still remains today.

Shortly after beginning studies again, I met a young professor at the university. We fell in love. But because he was of a different faith and, perhaps even more important, because he had some serious psychological problems, and he had some sexual difficulties, we never married. The objections have never been mine. We go through periods of not seeing one another, and at present I have not seen him for several months (the longest period yet). I suspect, however, that I am still "carrying the torch."

I have been living alone in New York with no intention of ever returning home to live.

I finished my course work for the Ph.D. in chemistry, and have been working on my doctoral dissertation. I started teaching, and am now an assistant professor at a junior college in New Jersey.

A.S. DESCRIBED BY TWO COLLEAGUES WHO HAVE KNOWN HER PROFESSIONALLY AND SOCIALLY FOR ABOUT THREE YEARS

A.S. is a person of superior intelligence. She dresses modestly and makes a very neat appearance. A.S. is a hard, conscientious worker, though not particularly creative. She is a loyal and dependable person, who is friendly and generous (gives gladly of herself in terms of time and energy).

She frequently expresses feelings of unworthiness, and has little confidence in herself. Her outlook regarding social, political, and moral issues is very conventional and uncompromising. A.S. is prone to hysterical outbursts, is verbally aggressive toward men, and apparently enjoys arguing vehemently with them. She is a very tense person (smokes incessantly, likes to consume liquor, and finds it difficult to control intake when at parties).

Other descriptive adjectives: good-natured to the point of being gullible, distrustful of men, argumentative.

RORSCHACH PROTOCOL, CASE OF A.S.

Card I
Performance
3″

| Inquiry |

1. This looks like some family shield of two heads, some sort of animal. The whole thing looks like a crest of some sort. Shall I elaborate? Here are the heads of the animals. I don't know what would be in the center.

1. Location: W
S: The whole thing is a family crest.
E: Show me the animal's head.
S: Here is the nose, ears, the thing in the middle is just something decorative to hold the whole thing together. I like that—that is very good.

Score: W   F   *Emblem*   1.5
Comment: The whole blot was included in the response, the shape being the sole determinant used. The basal rating of 1.0 was given for the concept "shield," which adequately fit the blot area, and additional credit was given for the specification of the animal heads.

Card II
Performance
Inquiry

Good God! Is this the right way? May I turn? (E. answered that she may do so, if she wants to.) It does not matter which way I turn? V∧V∧ This will take me a little while. V∧
45″
I can't possibly tell you what the whole thing looks like. I can only tell you about this part.

1. V This looks like some kind of bug with antennae sticking out.

1. Location: D_1
S: Instead of a bug, I think it is some kind of sea animal—in the crab

family but not dangerous—it doesn't bite.

E: What makes it look more like a sea animal?

S: Bigger than a bug and it is broad this way and bugs usually are not.

Analogy Period:

E: When you said this part looked like a crab did you think of the color?

S: When I changed it to crab it was partially because it was red and because it was too broad for a bug.

Score: D   F,FC   A   1.0

Comment: This is a popular-level response to a large usual detail; therefore, a form-level rating of 1.0 was given. Although the subject said the response was changed to "crab" partially because of the color, this was elicited only after the analogy period; therefore an additional FC was scored.

2. These other two red things would be bugs—unicellular animals, very strange, nothing I have seen. I just can't make anything out of the black.

2. *Location: D_2*

S: It is something you would see under a microscope, like amoeba or paramecium.

E: What is it about this part that makes it seem as if it is under a microscope?

S: Because of these darker portions, looks like structure of a cell, looks magnified. This larger siphon would take food in and smaller ones like excretory organs.

E: You said these "red things"—tell me what you meant by red things.

S: Looks like it is stained under a microscope.

Score: D   Fc,FC   A.At   1.5

Comment: The shading appears to be the primary determinant. Although the subject specified "red," this has been scored as an arbitrary use of color, as almost any color may be used for staining. The basal form-level rating of O.5 was assigned to a response that is semidefinite in form. To this was added an additional credit of 0.5 for the use of the shading determinant, and another 0.5 for the specific organs named.

Add. Location: $D_2's + d_1$

S: (turned card and said spontaneously) I wish I could do something with this part (the black areas)—

it is some sort of medical-book diagram of a male pelvic bone and this
(small d) his—you know what. (E.
supplied the word "penis.") Yes, his
penis.

Score: W   F   Sex   1.0
Comment: The concept seems to fulfill the minimal requirements for
accuracy of fit to justify a basal rating of 1.0.

Card III

Performance	Inquiry

He! He!
    7″

1. These are two people playing a
   game together, involving this
   gadget (center red area). I'll say
   it is a ball; it gives the impression of motion.

   1. *Location*: W
E: Tell me more about how you see
   the ball and the people?
S: It is one ball, going back and forth
   between them, very unrealistic,
   doesn't really look like that.
E: Do these people look like men or
   women?
S: Neither; such a rough drawing, I
   couldn't possibly tell.
E: What about this part (the leg area)?
S: I can only see one leg because it is
   only a profile.
E: What about this part (lower center
   detail)?
S: Could be their hands and playing
   this game with some kind of racket,
   this part is the shadow.

Score: W   M,Fm   H,Obj   P→O   1.5
Comment: These are the popular human figures usually seen on this card.
An additional Fm has been scored for the ball in motion. To the basal
form-level rating of 1.0 normally given for the popular response, 0.5 has
been added for the organization involved in seeing them "playing a game."
No additional credit has been given for the rackets, the ball in motion, or
the shadow, since these concepts are too vague as far as form is concerned. Credit has already been given for the organizational element.
Notice that the sexual specification of the figure has been avoided as well.

2. Two monkeys hanging from its
   tail—raccoons or monkeys.

   2. *Location*: D_2's
S: Whichever it is which hangs from
   their tails.
E: Can you describe the monkeys for
   me?
S: Here are their tails, the heads.

Score: D   FM   A   1.5

Comment: The determinant FM has been used, as the hanging is not an involuntary action, but one that is attributable to monkeys. The basal rating of 1.0 was given for the concept of the monkeys, and additional credit of 0.5 was added for the specification of "hanging by their tails." If the subject had left "raccoons" as the response, this would have resulted in a minus form-level rating, because the action would be inaccurate for a raccoon.

Card IV

Performance	*Inquiry*
5″	

1. Amphibious animal, if you call them that; it has wings, it can fly, also crawls along the ground, a prehistoric animal.	*1. Location: W* S: Walking or crawling, the animal is on land now. E: Tell me about these parts (pointing to the lower extensions)? S: It does not have ordinary kind of legs, maybe it's asleep, it has closed eyes, sleeping position, got ears, too. E: Tell me what else about this gives you the impression of an amphibious animal? S: It has tough scaly skin—it's horny and horrible.

Score: W   FM,Fc   A   1.5

Comment: Stress has been placed on what the animal was doing, the texture of the skin having been mentioned only after some questioning; therefore, Fc is scored as additional. To the basal rating of 1.0 for prehistoric animal, which is general enough to be conceivable for this blot area, an additional credit of 0.5 was added for the specifications of eyes and ears. However, no credit was added for the wings because of the poor fit to the blot area, and poor proportion in relation to the size of the animal. The wings are irrelevant specifications.

Card V

Performance	*Inquiry*
1″	

1. This is a bat but I don't know what these are (upper extensions). I don't think bats have things like that. I did not know it was split up the back either (pointing to the lower extensions).	*1. Location: W* S: I am not awfully sure that bats have these things. E: Can you tell me more of how you see it? S: He's in motion, flying, because wings are outspread.

Score: W   FM   A   P   1.0

Comment: In spite of the subject's criticism of the fit, the response remains the popular one for this card. No credit is added for the "flying," since it is part of the basic concept in this card and is an irrelevant for the form level as is the split up the back.

Card VI

Performance	*Inquiry*

Oh, dear! My goodness! O.K.
    8″

1. Just this part (upper D) is a bug. Something like an ant— one of the social group which is a worker, trying to pull something. I think, this is some kind of food for rest of ants. It's a bee because it has wings, a worker bee bringing up something edible for the rest of clan.	1. *Location:* $D_1 + D_2$ E: Tell me about the bee. S: Here is the bee, the mouth and the wings. I don't think bees eat leaves but it looks like a leaf or a piece of lettuce. E: What makes it look like a piece of lettuce? S: It's the shape and it has a vein up the middle. It is definitely a bee.

Score: $\left. \begin{array}{l} D \\ D \end{array} \right\}$ $\begin{array}{ccc} & FM & A \\ W- & Fc & P1 \end{array}$ $\left. \begin{array}{l} \text{Add. 1.0} \\ O- \quad 1.0 \end{array} \right\}$

Comment: Since the subject apparently first saw each of the D's separately and then combined them, the bee and the lettuce leaf have each been scored separately, and an additional W scored for the combination. The basal form-level rating for the bee is 1.0, since this is a popular level response for this area. The lettuce leaf would receive a basal form-level rating of 0.5 as semidefinite in form, to which would be added 0.5 for the specification of the vein. The far-fetched combination does not raise or lower the form level. However, it deserves an additional O–. The subject is quite definite in making the upper D a bee, yet is just as definite about the lower part being some sort of food that it is pulling—an act of which the subject is critical but which she is unable to improve.

CARD VII

Performance	*Inquiry*
6″	

1. Two dogs standing on their heads.	1. *Location:* D_4 S: They look like poodles. E: What makes them look like poodles? S: The hair seems to be curly, not clipped yet.

Score: D   FM,Fc   A   2.0

Comment: The location has been scored D because the concept "two dogs" is merely a function of the symmetry of the blot and does not suggest any attempt to organize the two areas. Had any sort of relationship between the dogs been indicated, the scoring would have been W. The chief determinant appears to be the action of the dogs, but an additional Fc was given for the curly hair, a differentiated texture response. In this connection, it should be noted that the inquiry did not go far enough to establish whether or not the shading actually determined the curly hair. An additional question, such as "What makes the hair seem curly?" would probably have elicited the additional information. However, the subject has previously given some indication of the use of shading, and it has been assumed that the determinant in this case is Fc. A basal form-level rating of 1.5 was given for the specific concept "poodle," and additional credit of 0.5 was added for the position of "standing on their heads," which increases the accuracy of the match to the blot. It has been assumed that these are trick dogs and that this is not a bizarre response. Again, there should have been additional questioning during the analogy period to determine this fact.

2. ∨ And this is a butterfly. Let me see if I can make something of the whole. (long pause)

2. *Location*: D_1
S: Here is the body and here the wings, the butterfly is on top of the flower, he's getting his pollen from the flower.

Score: D   FM,FK   A   1.5

Comment: The concept "butterfly" requires little imagination and was therefore given a basal rating of 1.0, to which was added 0.5 for the constructive organization. The "flower" was seen in the light gray portion of the central area in the middle of the card, so that the body of the butterfly was seen on top of the flower. The difference in shading was therefore used to see two different objects at a different distance from the eyes—therefore the additional FK.

3. This part looks like the Western Hemisphere, North America, South America, Central America, here the Pacific and Atlantic Ocean (white areas) just on the one side though. I can't make anything out of the whole.

3. *Location*: D_4
S: It is a little distorted here, but this part looks like North America, etc.

Score: D,S   F   Geo   1.0

Comment: Although the two oceans are implied in the concept "Western

Hemisphere," and usually would therefore not be scored separately, an additional S score has been given in this case because the subject specifically pointed out and labeled these areas. A basal rating of 1.0 is indicated because the concept was specific and is a reasonably accurate match to the blot area. Had the subject merely indicated a continent, or given some similar reply, this would have been a semidefinite concept and been rated 0.5.

Card VIII
Performance   *Inquiry*

That's very pretty.
   4″
1. These two are polar bears—pink   *1. Location: D₁*
   ones.   E: Tell me about the bears; you said
                                   pink ones, what do you mean?
                                  S: No, not pink, just painted pink,
                                  looks like a drawing by some kinder-
                                  garten child.
                                  E: How do you see the bears?
                                  S: They are looking down at the water,
                                  sort of standing there.
                                  E: Do you see the water?
                                  S: No.

Score: D   F←→C,FM   A   P   1.0
Comment: Although the subject offered an explanation for the pinkness of the bears, this is still considered a forced use of color, since any attempt to explain the color of these animals is considered forced. Color has been given precedence in the scoring of this response because the movement was mentioned only after some questioning in the inquiry. The basal rating of 1.0 was given to a popular response.

2. This is a crab.   *2. Location: D₃*
                                  S: I used this whole part but it's a
                                  very rough idea, something like a
                                  horseshoe crab, but these things are
                                  too long.

Score: D   F   A   1.0
Comment: The concept is considered accurate enough to warrant a basal rating of 1.0. The remark "but these things are too long" is a criticism of the card which, however, does not improve the form level and therefore is used as an irrelevant specification.

3. Some undersea growth—algae or   *3. Location: D₄*
   something.   S: Food for the crab but the crab is

going away from it, not toward it.
E: What made it look like algae?
S: Just an association with crab.

Score: D   F   P1   0.5
Comment: This is a vague F response suggested by the previous concept and has therefore been given a basal rating of 0.5, which is reserved for concepts that are vague or semidefinite in form.

4. V This way a vase of flowers, this is the vase and these the flowers.

4. *Location: W*
S: A decorated vase, the outline is a little off. Not all here, the vase is painted, the rest is all flowers or could be one flower with petals (usual animal) ready to fall off.

Score: W,S   FC,CF,mF   Obj,P1   1.5
Comment: The vase appears to be the dominant concept of this response, with the principal determinant score of FC, because it is painted. The additional CF was given for the flower, no specific flower having been mentioned, and the mF score was included to account for the falling petals. Although the subject made some effort to reconcile the concept with the blot area, the response is not convincing since the vase is unable to stand on its base but must hang. However, the organizational detail of the falling petals justifies raising the total concept from 1.0 to 1.5.

5. Right here is an iris.

5. *Location: D_2*
S: The shape and the color.

Score: D   FC   P1   1.0
Comment: The scoring in this case is FC because a specific flower is mentioned which matches the blot area fairly accurately.

Card IX

Performance
6″

Inquiry

1. V This right here is a carnation, the pink thing with a green stem. ΛVΛ (long pause) I don't know, I can't see anything. V

1. *Location: D_5+extension of D,S*
E: Tell me more about the carnation, how many do you see?
S: Just one, it's very rough. I really can't see anything.

Score: D   FC   P1   1.0
Comment: A specific flower has been mentioned, and it matches the blot area adequately; therefore, the score is FC rather than CF and the form level is 1.0.

Card X

Performance	Inquiry

Oh!
5″

1. Little rabbit's face and he's cry-   1. *Location:* D_5
ing, I guess.

    E: What makes you think he is crying?
    S: To account for this business.
    E: What about this business?
    S: Green tears, modern art or some-
      thing.

Score: D   FM,CF,mF   Ad   P,O−   1.0

Comment: The green tears warrant additional CF and mF scores but do not add to the form accuracy; therefore, the basal form-level rating of 1.0 for a popular response remains. An additional O− is given for the far-fetched combination.

2. Wishbone, a turkey wishbone.   2. *Location:* D_{12}
    S: Just an association, whenever I think
      of a wishbone, I think of a turkey.

Score: D   F   Aobj   1.0

Comment: The scoring needs no explanation.

3. These are some kind of odd   3. *Location:* D_3
animals sniffing up a tree, I
don't know what kind, though. Let   S: They are yelling at each other, tails
me see, they have tails and horns   here, hind legs, standing up on hind
and they don't like each other   feet.
very well, they both want the
same thing up at the top. V∧

Score: D   FM→M   A   2.5

Comment: Although the response depicts animals in animal-like action, the subject has used the word "yelling" in the inquiry, suggesting that she is possibly ascribing some human-like activity in these animals; therefore, the tendency to M has been indicated in the scoring. To the basal rating of 1.0 for the animals, credits have been added as follows: 0.5 for the additional specification of horns and tails on the animals; 0.5 for the organization of the concept, around the tree; and 0.5 for the animals "standing up on hind feet," which adds to the fit to the blot area.

4. These are two mountain goats,   4. *Location:* D_6 + *portion of* D_{15}
moving very rapidly, gracefully,
galloping off in opposite directions.   S: On top of their heads there is dark-
      er hair, front legs out here, and back
      legs way out here.

Score: dr   FM,Fc   A   2.0

Comment: The location score dr has been assigned because the response combines the usual detail D_6 with a part of another usual detail, D_{15}. The additional Fc score is for the use of shading indicated in "darker hair." The basal form-level rating of 1.5 for the specific animal includes the determinant specification of galloping. Were these seen as mountain goats merely standing still, the form-level rating would be minus, since the concept would be a poor match for the blot area. An additional credit of 0.5 was given for the darker hair.

5. These blue things are octopi.   5. *Location:* D_1
   (long pause)   S: The shape only.
   Let me see, what are these things?

Score: D   F   A   P   1.0
Comment: This is the usual popular response for this area. The color was used only to identify the specific area and was not part of the response.

6. These are just islands in the mid-   6. *Location:* D_3
   dle of the lake, connected by a   S: Simply the shape, the color is all off.
   strip of land.

Score: D   F   Geo   0.5
Comment: This, again, is a large usual detail, to which a basal rating of 0.5 was given for a response that is semidefinite in form.

> *Add. Location:* D_{11}
> S: I didn't say anything to this part—
> two collie dogs sitting down at their
> master's feet.
> E: Tell me more about it, what makes
> it look like a collie dog?
> S: The shape and color, the color is
> right too. I didn't say anything
> about these parts, either.

Score: D   FM,FC   A   2.0
Comment: This score was assigned a basal form-level rating of 1.0 and additional credits of 0.5 each were added for the specification that the dogs are sitting, and for the use of color.

Total Time: 22 minutes
Testing the Limits
M: *Card* II—could not see people.
   E: Why?
   S: I couldn't see why they should have red feet and red hats, and
      rest black; it's out of proportion.
   Then, spontaneously:
   S: I can see two animal heads here; they have their snouts together;
      why I don't know.

Card VI-v

S: Two people walking arm in arm, and one arm sticking out, two legs close together—it's a possibility.

Card VII-v

S: Little girls because heads are so large for their bodies, doing a dance, heads are thrown back, touching, here are their legs and arms, and their fannies stick out.

Card X—the red area

S: Some kind of ghosts holding, shaking hands, facing each other.

Subject could not find M's in Card I or IX.

Fc: Subject could easily see Card VI as a fur rug—only the bottom part.

Cards Liked Most and Least

Likes Cards III, VII, VIII most—"I like the pattern in Card III, found interesting things in Card VII, and I liked the color in VIII."

Likes Card IX least—"I couldn't see much."

I. Basic Relationships: Main Responses Only

Total Responses	R24
Total Time	T1320 sec.
Average Time per Response	T/R55 sec.
Average Reaction Time: Achromatic Cards (I, IV, V, VI, VII)	4½ sec.
Chromatic Cards (II, III, VIII, IX, X)	13 sec.
$\dfrac{F}{R}$	33F%
$\dfrac{FK + F + Fc}{R}$	42%
$\dfrac{A + Ad}{R}$	54A%
(H + A): (Hd + Ad)	13:1
Popular Responses	p 5
Original Responses	O 0 + 3
$\dfrac{FC + 2CF + 3C}{2}$	sum C 2.0
M: sum C	1:2.0
(FM + m): (Fc + c + C')	9:2
$\dfrac{\text{Responses to Cards VIII} + \text{IX} + \text{X}}{R}$	50%
W : M	5:1

II. Supplementary Relationships: Main + ½ add.

M : FM	1½:10
M : (FM + m)	1½:11½
(FK + Fc): F	4:8½
(Fc + cF + c + C' + C'F + FC'): (FC + CF + C)	3½: 6½
(FK + Fc + Fk): (K + KF + k + kF + c + cF)	4 : 0
FC: (CF + C)	5½: 1

III. Manner of Approach

Main Responses

	No.	Actual %	Expect %	No. Add. Scores
W	5	21	20-30	2
D	18	75	45-55	1
d	0	0	5-15	0
Dd+S	1	4	< 10	2

IV. Estimate of Intellectual Level

Capacity *Approaching superior*
Efficiency *Average to above average*

V. Succession:

Rigid
Orderly
Loose √
Confused

VI. Form Level Summary:
Average Unweighed FLR 1.3
Average Weighted FLR 1.4

QUANTITATIVE ANALYSIS, CASE OF A.S.

The Psychogram

The initial examination of the psychogram reveals an unusual combination for an adult record, of extraordinarily few M responses (1 + 1) together with a high number of FM responses (9 + 2). (About three M responses are expected in a "normal" record.) Since there are so few M responses, the relationship of M to FM, and the M: (FM + m) ratio, cannot be discussed in this case. However ,other hypotheses may be tentatively applied.

The low M score suggests that A.S. may have some difficulty in interpersonal relations, perhaps because of a lack of empathy. It suggests also that in stress situations the subject can have little recourse to inner resources, that there may be an absence of a strong value system, and that, finally, there has been some difficulty in self-acceptance. It should be noted that, in spite of the paucity of M responses, low intelligence is contraindicated because of the additional M response indicating that potential capacity is not being used, perhaps owing to inhibition; also because of the additional m responses which may mean that tensions exist which are too strong to allow A.S. to utilize her inner resources constructively. Furthermore, the form-level rating of 2.5, achieved for the third response on Card X, must be taken into account in this connection.

The large number of FM responses suggests that A.S. has an awareness of her impulses to immediate gratification. However, it is quite likely that she has little insight, understanding, or acceptance of these impulses. Moreover, in view of the inadequate number of M responses, and the presence of only two additional CF responses, it seems reasonable to assume that frustration feelings may result both from the failure to act out these impulses and from lack of self-acceptance.

The over-all pattern of the psychogram shows that the responses bulk in the left half and in the center, with relatively few responses in the color area. This suggests that, although for the most part A.S. does not react freely to her environment, and her view of the world and her responsiveness are largely determined by her own needs, she does have the ability to view the world in a more impersonal, matter-of-fact way.

The proportion (FK + Fc): F of 4:8½ indicates that the affectional needs are well-developed and are satisfactorily integrated in the personality organization. Therefore, they serve as a sensitive control function, permitting a healthy response to people without a vulnerable overdependence on them. The Fc score relates to an individual's recognition of his affectional needs of approval, belongingness, and response from others. A.S. shows a tendency to some emphasis on the Fc score, as indicated by the three additional Fc responses. It should be borne in mind, therefore, that there is possibly some sensitivity in this area, perhaps to the needs of others or to hurt from others. However, the proportion of differentiated to undifferentiated shading responses of 4:0, counting additionals as $\frac{1}{2}$, again supports the hypothesis that, on the whole, the affectional needs are adequately integrated within the personality organization.

The relationship of the achromatic surface responses with the chromatic surface responses, (Fc + c + C'): (FC + CF + C), which yields the proportion $3\frac{1}{2}$: $6\frac{1}{2}$, suggests that A.S. has the ability to interact and respond positively in emotional situations. However, the forced FC response (F←→C), suggesting some tension in social relationships, and the use of the two CF responses as additionals only, suggesting some hesitancy about actually expressing emotional responsiveness, indicate that A.S. may not fully utilize her ability. In this connection, the presence of the additional F/C score suggests that A.S. may modify her reactions by responding in a more superficial, behavior way. The ratio of FC: (CF + C), $5\frac{1}{2}$:1, tends to confirm the conclusion that A.S. may have possibly excessive control over her impulsive expression of emotionality, and that her socialized responses may have a superficial flavor. The Sum C of only two (three is expected "normal" Sum C) indicates, again, that there is apparently too little overt responsiveness to environmental influence.

Introversive-Extratensive Balance

The three pertinent proportions to consider are: M:Sum C of 1:2, (FM + m): (Fc + c + C') of 9:2, and the percentage of responses to the last three cards (VIII, IX, X) of 50.

The M:Sum C ratio of 1:2 suggests an extratensive balance, but interpretation of this ratio is necessarily qualified by the presence of only one M response. However, the indication is that this individual is most responsive to environmental factors. This may be an adjustment by a flight into reality in order to protect herself from the threat which the inner impulse life may present.

On the other hand, the second ratio, (FM + m): (Fc + c + C'), shows marked introversive tendencies. The apparent contradiction in orientation indicated by the two ratios may mean that A.S. is in a state of transition between introversion and extratension. It is also possible that the second ratio represents the direction in which A.S. is retreating. Another feasible supposition is that there exists a persistent secondary organization which has not been realized, but which remains as a source of conflict. In any case, such a discrepancy represents a conflict in tendencies within the personality, but the specific significance cannot be explained at this point.

Since half of the responses in this record occurred to the last three cards, it is indicated again that A.S. is stimulated to greater productiveness by environmental impact. However, this conclusion must be modified by the fact that six of the twelve responses were given to Card X, which lends itself to greater responsiveness because of its structure. It should also be noted that the relatively small amount of color actually used in the responses suggests that there is inhibition of overt expression to emotional reaction.

Control

In discussing the implications of the movement, shading, and color proportions, it has already been indicated that A.S. may be said to have "outer control," that is, control of emotional expression. The two additional factors to be considered in this area are the form responses of 33 per cent and the total of form plus differentiated shading responses (FK + F + Fc) of 42 per cent.

The 33 per cent of F responses (which is within the normal expected range of 20-50 per cent) suggests an ability to view the world in an impersonal, matter-of-fact way, which should help A.S. to achieve a controlled adjustment. It suggests, also, that she has retained the ability to be responsive to her own needs and to react to emotional impact from outside. This hypothesis is substantiated by the FK + F + Fc percentage of 42 per cent. However, the tendency to suppress Fc responses shown by the three additionals suggests that there may be some difficulty in making close and warm affectional contacts, and that there may be some restraint in dealing with people.

Intellectual Estimate and Manner of Approach

The initial over-all impression with regard to intellectual estimate is that A.S. has average to above average capacity. However, the average unweighted form level of 1.3 and the weighted form level of 1.4, as well as the autobiographical materials, clearly indicate that A.S. is actually functioning on a better than average level. That her real capacity is in fact above average and approaches the superior is suggested by the fact that she achieves a form-level rating of 2.5 for one response, and a rating of 2.0 in three others, one of these an additional. Since it can be assumed that the presence of even one response of form level 2.5 is indicative of capacity between above average and superior (in the absence of any overtly contradictory material in the record), it seems likely that there are factors in personality organization that keep A.S. from realizing her full intellectual potential.

The combination of 21 per cent W, 75 per cent D, 0 per cent d, and 4 per cent Dd + S shows an overemphasis of D responses. The presence of 75 per cent D shows an interest and an ability to differentiate perceptively, but relatively little interest in integration and organization. This common-sense approach may be an indication that A.S. feels insecure and may have some fear of losing her bearings if she does not stick close to the obvious. While A.S. has the ability to be intellectually critical, as indicated by her critical (mostly self-critical) remarks in her record, the presence of W, the 0 per cent d, and the ratio of 13:1 for (H + A): (Hd + Ad) show that on the whole her attitude is not a very critical one. The presence of 50 per cent A responses reinforces the impression that A.S. tends to take a rather stereotyped view of the world, and that the range of interest is limited, perhaps because of disturbed adjustment.

The five popular responses, which is the expected average, indicate that the ties to reality are quite adequate; but the absence of main original responses and the presence of only three additionals suggests again that there is an inadequate use of capacity as well as some timidity. The W:M ratio of 5:1 (2:1 is the expected proportion) suggests a level of aspiration that is unrealistic and probably leads to feelings of frustration. However, it may also mean that A.S. does not feel free enough at the present time to direct her creative energies toward achievement of her goals. This is supported by the loose succession, which suggests some weakening of control because of emotional conditions, as well as the low number of M responses which were previously discussed.

Hypotheses

1. There is difficulty in interpersonal relations because of lack of empathy.
2. There is little recourse to inner resources in stress situations.
3. A strong value system is absent.
4. A.S. has some difficulty in self-acceptance.
5. There is some awareness of impulses, but little insight, understanding, or acceptance of them.
6. A.S. has feelings of frustration because of her lack of self-acceptance and her failure to "act out."
7. A.S. has the ability to view the world in an impersonal, matter-of-fact way.
8. The affectional needs are well-developed and integrated, serving as a sensitive control function.

9. There may be some undue sensitivity to the needs of others and to hurt from others, suggesting some restraint in contacts.

10. A.S. has the ability to interact and respond positively in emotional situations but does not fully utilize this ability.

11. The reaction to emotional stimulations may be in a superficial behavioral manner.

12. A.S. has control over the impulsive expression of emotionality.

13. Although A.S. is most responsive to environment factors, suggesting a flight into reality adjustment, she shows marked introversive tendencies. This may be indicative of a state of transition, or of a direction of retreat, or it may be that the secondary organization is not realized and is a source of conflict.

14. A.S. is stimulated to productiveness by environmental impact, but her overt expression is inhibited.

15. A.S. has above-average to superior intellectual capacity, but the efficiency of functioning is average. This seems to be the result of inhibition and tension.

Sequence Analysis, Case of A.S.

As a rule, we become acquainted with the Rorschach information given by a subject by reading through the record even before we look at the quantitative summary. Naturally, any conclusions drawn from the sequence of responses have to be consistent with the other findings; the two procedures actually go hand in hand. Analyzing the sequence of responses, we relate this to other information available about the subject.

Card I

The one response that A.S. gives to Card I has the following characteristics: She immediately tries to organize the blot material into a whole response with a family shield. She goes beyond the very superficial approach; such a concept frequently covers up by specifying in detail the animal heads, the nose, and ears. But she remains conspicuously ambivalent about the central figure, most frequently seen as a female. She says "the thing in the middle is just something decorative to hold the whole thing together."

A glance at the summary sheet shows us that there is no undue stress on a W approach; therefore, the concept shield is not an excuse for being unable to cope with the situation otherwise. She shows a concern with authority—and attitude toward authority is often revealed in the concept of emblems or shields. The question arises as to why can she not see the center detail, often seen as a female figure that "holds the whole thing together." Her feminine role, which she conceives of as a rather submissive one, has apparently not led to any satisfactory solution.

Card II

Card II provides us with as neat a description of "color dynamics" as we may wish. For 45″ she is very troubled and turns the card, saying: "This will take me a little while." Then she expresses her regret that she cannot give a W response. Finally, holding the card upside down, she interprets first the center red, and then, turning the card around again, gives a vague interpretation of "unicellular animals" to the top red. Only in the inquiry, when the total test situation has markedly changed, is she able to use the black part, in a most revealing manner.

This is a clear-cut case of subjective color disturbance. But also she reveals the strength of the color attraction for her, since she selects just the three red spots for her responses in the performance proper. However, the color comes through only hesitatingly. Only in the analogy period, after having given other clear-cut color responses on the last three cards, does she finally admit that the red helped her in seeing a crab, and it is "one which doesn't bite." Since a crab is red only after it's cooked, she's quite right. The struggle goes even further in the second response. First she flees from the hot color to the cooler shading in specifying the unicellular animals. Only when confronted with the fact that she has called them "these two red things" in the performance proper does she admit that they may be stained." Then she turns spontaneously to the rest of the card, and combines in a somewhat doubtful anatomical response "a male pelvic bone and this his—you know what." She is unable to use the word "penis" without help. Even though such a combination of anatomical or dead animal objects with live parts of the same organism has once been noted as suggestive of paranoid thinking, she is too much aware of the inconsistency for us to worry about this pathological condition. However, it is not farfetched to relate this response to the sexual difficulties with the young professor mentioned in her autobiography. We should keep in mind that the combination of the "not-dangerous' crab (which is frequently seen as a female organ) and the penis, which is attached to a diagram of a male pelvis, may possibly be an indication that she plays some part in contributing to the difficulty in their relationship. But we know that even her friends describe her as argumentative with men, which seems in contrast to her otherwise feminine and submissive approach to life.

It is clear from A.S.'s response to the first colored card that initially she is not able to cope adequately with situations that are emotionally tinged, but also that she has the capacity to make an adequate recovery.

Card III

Card III continues to add a great deal to the picture as it unfolds. She starts with a usual popular response to the black area, with two strange variations. On the one hand, she refuses to commit herself as far as the sex of the two people is concerned, and uses a somewhat far-fetched excuse for doing so ("rough drawing"). On the other hand, she adds an original addition to the concept, namely, that the inner center red is a ball in motion. It seems that these two variations are interdependent. What moves between these two people makes it more difficult for her to say whether they are men or women.

The separation of the red spots from the black area gives people who are uncomfortable with the color the opportunity to avoid using it. Nevertheless, the fact that she sees two people "playing a game together" indicates that she is capable of warm, happy interpersonal relationships. She is responsive enough to the color to want to include the red areas, but is yet unable to use the color in her responses.

Card IV

This card is the first of the strongly shaded cards and has two associations that are almost equally frequent. One is the "winged animal" and the other, using the shading, is an aggressive male figure such as a giant or gorilla. Her reaction is a strangely ambivalent one, "an amphibious animal" that "has wings" and "crawls along the ground." In the inquiry, she reveals further that the creature is "asleep," in a "sleeping position." The inquiry did not quite make it clear that the "tough, scaly skin" was based on shading, but we may safely assume that this was so.

Associations to this card are often interpreted as attitudes of the individual toward male authority figures, particularly the father. The prehistoric character of this strange monster may be related to the fact that her father is 73 years old and that one of her difficulties is the lack of differentiation of the father image in her, resulting in a confusion with regard to her feminine role.

Card V

Card V is immediately interpreted as the popular concept of a bat flying. It is not surprising that this essentially intelligent and well controlled subject makes immediate use of the popular connotation to Card V. However, her insecurity about this concept is rather puzzling. The critical remark about the upper extension has some objective validity, but the remark concerning the lower extension, "I did not know it was split up the back either," seems to reveal a tendency on her part to be hypercritical of herself rather than putting the blame where it rightly belongs.

It may be interesting to observe that A.S. selects to use the concept "bat," which is something ugly, rather than "butterfly," which would represent a pleasanter, more optimistic approach.

Card VI

Card VI has two major characteristics: It is the most strongly shaded card, and the one card in which the blot material offers a striking contrast between top and bottom portions. She reacts to both these challenges by interpreting the top part and establishing an interesting connection with the bottom part. She also uses the shading aspect clearly for the bottom part and implicitly for the top.

The bee may reflect the image she has of herself as a hard worker (a fact noted by her supervisor). In addition, the "bee bringing up something edible for the rest of the clan" suggests that she feels an overwhelming sense of responsibility toward others.

This card frequently evokes both masculine and feminine sexual associations, either in direct or symbolic form. Apparently A.S. is not able to handle such material comfortably either overtly or in a more socialized manner, and so both sexual symbols are replaced by the oral symbolism of providing food.

Card VII

Card VII does not present any difficulties for A.S. since, after six seconds, she organizes the whole material into three concepts. The upper two-thirds are nicely specified as "two dogs standing on their heads." The shading is used for the curly hair. Then, with the card upside down, she uses the remaining third for the concept of butterfly. The only original addition to the butterfly is the fact that she sees it "on top of the flower. He's getting his pollen from the flower." Finally, she returns to the original location, and interprets the area quite carefully as a map.

Card VII often facilitates responses involving an adult female figure, which may reveal an attitude to the mother image. In addition, the bottom center detail is considered as symbolizing vaginal sexuality.

A.S., however, sees dogs standing upside down in the area used for the usual adult female figure, which may indicate an immature level of social development, possibly as a result of poor mother-child relationships. This in turn implies that there will be difficulty in adult heterosexual relationships (a fact clearly revealed in the autobiography).

The sensuous impact of the bottom center detail is sublimated in her response of the butterfly on top of the flower (the flower, given to the usual vaginal area, is a female symbol; at the same time A.S. refers to the butterfly as "he"). The carefulness with which the map is described also indicates uneasiness concerning sexuality. The map response reveals also that A.S. uses intellectuality as a defense.

The sequence of responses to this card clearly demonstrates the way she handles heterosexual relationships; first, there is an immature reaction, followed by a sublimation, and then an intellectualized withdrawal.

Card VIII

The appeal of the first all-colored card immediately evokes the remark, "That's very pretty!" This is followed by five responses in rapid sequence. She is obviously stimulated by the color and uses it with increasing intensity, but she also has difficulty with it.

The first response is the frequent response of polar bears, but she adds, "pink ones," and explains, in the inquiry, that it must be the "drawing of some kindergarten child." This represents a pathetic attempt to include the color that is automatically excluded by the concept of "polar bears." The second response refers to the top area, which she sees as a "horseshoe crab"—an aggressive symbol. The next response, "some under-sea growth, algae or something," is seen as "food for the crab, but the crab is going away from it, not toward it."

In sequence of these three responses, it may be seen that A.S. is stimulated by the color but does not know what to do wth it. Her first response shows a forced use of color, and the second, controlled aggression and the algae is vague and also suggests withdrawal in the action of the crab. Such a reaction indicates a responsiveness to environmental stimulation but an inability to react spontaneously and freely.

Her next response shows an ability to recover in the face of emotional impact, and she uses the whole card to see a painted vase with natural flowers, a passive but pleasant concept. This response implies that she gives in to emotional challenges in a submissive way that creates conflicts for her. The final response combines a positive use of form with color, thus indicating a capacity to face emotionally stimulating situations after continued exposure.

Card IX

The positive reaction to color is continued in Card IX, which creates a good deal of difficulty for many subjects. She turns the card upside down and definitely identifies "the pink thing with a green stem" as a carnation. After this, however, the confusion of variegated forms and mixed-up colors becomes too much for her; she can't see anything and repeats in the inquiry, "I really can't see anything."

In responding in this passive manner to a card that often evokes responses such as "witches," "clowns," and "explosions," A.S. again demonstrates her tendency to withdraw in the face of emotionally threatening situations.

Card X

On Card X she continues with positive reactions. She moves quite freely over the card, picking six of the usual details and adding one in the inquiry.

First she picks up the popular rabbit's face, but adds the green tears which she simply explains by calling it "modern art, or something." Then she sees the usual wishbone and gives it a definite specification, as belonging to a turkey. This is followed by the usual two top animals, described as "sniffing up a tree." Then comes two mountain goats where the animal action reaches the height of expressiveness, "moving very rapidly, gracefully, galloping off in opposite directions." She adds a part of the adjacent detail to give a good account of the head. Finally, she adds the usual octopi, and two islands, connected by a strip of land, and in the inquiry, the brown collies.

After the forced way of using color with the green tears of the rabbit, she avoids the color issue in the following five responses and only comes back to it in the additional response in the inquiry. This avoidance is facilitated by the use of obvious form-associations. In the inquiry to the last response, she states, "simply shape—the color is all off," but immediately makes her reconciliation with the color by seeing the collies where "the color is right, too." She concludes with an expression of regret that there was one more detail that she failed to include—like a child who has been trained to finish the plate of food put before it.

It should be noted that the one additional M in the entire record appears unexpectedly in this card, and that the human-like behavior is attributed to animals. The one main M response, which appeared in Card III, depicted a pleasant cooperative relationship. In contrast, the action on this card is aggressive and hostile, as indicated by the animal's dislike of each other and their yelling at each other. These actions suggest that A.S. may be basically hostile and aggressive but that she is unable to accept these feelings, and thus her energy is directed toward suppressing them. Her submissive, passive mode of behavior, noted throughout the record, is epitomized in the collies, which she sees as "sitting down at their master's feet."

Testing the Limits

When A.S. was directed to find human movement responses in the testing-the-limits period, she was easily able to give such responses to Cards VI, VII, and X. It should be noted that the action depicted is friendly and cooperative.

It seems likely that A.S.'s inability to give more than one M response during the performance proper is a reflection of her insecurity in human relationships, but that she has the potential to form warm, lasting relationships.

Summary

The statement A.S. makes in her autobiography that "relationship with my parents is very good, so long as I am not living with them" puts into focus the defense mechanism to which she resorts in order to maintain a relatively adequate adjustment. She has neither wanted to nor been quite able to sever completely her relationship with her parents and, by extension, with the authority under which she grew up. Yet she is unable to ally herself with this authority, since she is critical of it. Her solution has been to remove herself to a safe distance so that she is not too easily hurt, and at the same time is close enough to maintain the contacts that give her pleasure and that satisfy her submissive needs.

That this adjustment is not working quite well enough is indicated most strongly in the effect it has had on her intellectual functioning. Although there is indication that her intellectual capacity approaches the superior range, she has not made full use of this capacity. While she does operate on an efficient level, she presents the picture her colleagues have noted of "a hard, conscientious worker, though not particularly creative." Her method of dealing with the conflicts created by her ambivalent feelings (for example, toward her parents and other authority and the necessity for conformity) has been to inhibit the overt expression of her feelings and to busy herself, instead, with the obvious, routine matters to allow little time left to think. She has a great deal of difficulty in facing unpleasant truths, and since she does not have a strong value system on which she can rely, she resorts to a superficial, "socialized" manner of dealing with problems.

The same mechanism of detachment is again evident in her interpersonal relationships. She has a warm positive feeling about people and is aware of their needs. At the same time, her self-esteem is very low and she is unable to understand or accept her feelings of hostility or aggression, although she has some awareness of them. On the rare occasions when she permits herself to "act out," it is in a negative manner (for example, the argumentative quality that has been noted), which is contrary to her submissive tendency. Her reaction has therefore been one of controlling the spontaneous expression of her feelings, and this, in turn, has resulted in some restraint in her contacts with others. She presents a pleasant, friendly facade, but does not let people get too close to her for fear of being hurt by them. In addition, another purpose is served by not permitting herself free expression of her feelings: she is able to keep from awareness the objectionable nature of some of these feelings and therefore to avoid dealing with the conflict that arises if she becomes critical of anyone or anything.

The professional career and the total adjustment of A.S. fully justify calling her a normal subject. However, it is quite apparent that she is not using her capacities, both intellectual and emotional, to the fullest ,and so is denying herself a great deal of the pleasure of living. She has some awareness of this lack, and it therefore seems quite likely that if the stresses in her life are kept to a minimum she will be able to achieve the greater self-realization of which she is capable.

A BECK INTERPRETATION

G.A., MALE, AGE 39

Under need to gain wealth quickly, this man gambled recklessly and lost large sums. Psychiatrist's question: rule out schziophrenia?

Response Record
Figure I (35″)

1. DWF + A

'A bug . . . a flying bug (because of D 1); its wings are wilted away (should be filled out)—it's dead and its wings are wilted away. It's a dead bug, wings apart. That's all I got out of it. (Very slow.) I've must never seen anything like this . . . this way?' <V (Keeps shaking his head. Still Studies test card; does not give up.) "That's all I can see."

Figure II (13″)

2. DM + Hd
   5.5

'Red part on top, two faces looking at one another.' (Mean looking man and woman, anger, he is meaner, they look alike, brother and sister, or men, one of each.)

3. DdsCF + Hd, sex

(Hesitates) 'Would remind me of a woman's organs down here.' (Dds 24 and adjacent Dd: color and form.)

4. DsF + Rc

'Looks like a top of some kind.' (Ds 5)

5. DF + AP
3.0

<V∧ 'I see two dogs or two bears facing each other (playing). I didn't see it before, looks like they are doing something.' ('I can't figure it—coming from their nose,' i.e., D 1 and Dds in this section, D 4.) 'Can't see anything else, does color have anything to do with it?'

6. D C Bl

'Looks like it's covered with blood in places.' ("Unrelated" to other responses. He asks examiner what D 4 is.)

Figure III (37")

7. D M + H P
4.0

'Two people dancing here.' (Holding something in hand and I don't know, women, dog, women, odd faces, standing on high heels, dog faces; D 1.)

8. D M + Hdx

V∧<∧ 'I can't V∧ (deep sigh) V 'Two arms coming back (graceful hands towards middle and nothing there) in the back, 'I don't know, a finger pointing' (pointing at something and 'I just don't know what, to show something, I just don't know').

9. D F + Hd

'Two heads with a beard' (D 4), 'odd-shaped heads.'

10. Dd F − A

>∧ 'Two types of chickens or birds with feathers sticking . . . out of the chest on this man, a polly' (Dd 27 could be; a polly).

11. D F + A

'The red spots don't mean anything, I keep looking at these' (D 2); (tremendous struggle) 'a horse that has fallen down' (on his back, fell, tripped) 'with his nose in the air and the snoot on the side.'

12. D F + A

V 'This way a monkey looking at his tail' (D 2). ('The middle intrigues me, D 3, but I can't make it out. I looked and looked and couldn't think of a thing.')

Figure IV (18")

13. W FY + A P
2.0

'Someone had a bear's rug in front of the fireplace' (W; form, shading). Some kind of animal.'

14. Ds M + Bt, Ls
5.0

(Long delay). <V 'A feeling this is emerging from something but I can't figure out what' (D 1. 'A crevice, with an opening, ground around it,' D 2, and D 1 is coming from the bottom, 'What, I have no idea, an old tree, hollow.).

15. D F + A

Λ 'Snakes or something coming around, heads down' (D 4. Snake's head).

16. Dd M + Hd

'I seem to see two faces here (mean, eyes high, both very vivid), one a man (square), one a woman' (Dd 22, 'kindly, grey hair, a smile, my mother') >Λ Before, I couldn't see the face, now I just keep seeing it.' V 'I just don't see anything else.'

Figure V (90″)

17. D F + A
2.5

'Two bulls charging (W excluding D 2 and D 3), can't see heads, only shoulders and the driving legs.

18. Dd M H

VΛ 'A little old person there stopping, and doing something with his hands, working on a slab or table.' ('Fixing' Dd 23, 'or building, or cooking, very blurred, doing something, can't tell, can't tell if male or female.')

19. D M + Hd

'A man's head with patch over his eye and nose funny shaped' (D 6). ('Like one I saw before, something coming from his nose again, blood, he has been hurt, deformed, well beaten; maybe a black eye'.) <Λ 'Doing something' (shakes head)— 'this looks so funny, I can't figure what it is' (D 2). 'Someone standing on head and legs up—but legs are so funny.') (Patient is very tense, almost agitated.) V 'Can't. I don't see anything else.' (A morbid card, dark.)

Figure VI (40″)

20. D F + Ay

'An old totem pole' (denies); 'top head and things coming out' (decay, rotting at D 6).

21. D F + Hh
2.5

'Resembles a little light shining there, a candle, lit up this way' (center with D 12; 'burning a leaf', i.e., upper of D 2; 'is in candle, something will burn, a bed post now, can't).

22. W VF + Ls
2.5

> 'A water bank and reflection of grass and dirt (high grass, quiet, secluded), look-

ing from a boat' (entire; form and in distance; not too far, calm, peaceful).

23. Dd F + A

V 'I see two faces here but very odd shaped, hair down the back and beard, an animal face with nose here' ('I don't know, some kind of animal'; Dd 29). (Very, very slow, very resigned, throws up hands.) 'I don't see anything' (now, a man's penis, hair around there, couldn't make up my mind,' outer Dd to the side; 'I don't know, really don't know').

Figure VII (60")

24. DFT + A

(Deep sigh). >V> 'A Scottie dog or something here (D 2) look like he is kissing another dog, a furry dog, pretty furry, gosh!' (his fullness, face is so little, knew by fur).

25. Dd VF + Ls
1.0

(Looks very troubled). >∧ 'The sun is coming up in the morning, clouds, like looking through a mountain or (just the light of the sun—now a woman's lips,' Dd of D 6, 'very voluptuous, full').

26. D M + Hd P
2.5

>V (Deep sigh). ∧ 'Two women looking at each other (D 1) with hair flying or something ('don't like, they don't like each other, look mean, no identity, faces are so funny') or a feather?' (Studies D 6 closely.)

27. D F − Ob
1.0

'I can't make up my mind what this is here' (D 6). 'A needle (D 11) coming out of this but I can't imagine what this is' (head in hands and keeps shaking head). > (Can't give up card. D 6, not a syringe, I don't know). I can't make up my mind what that is' ('two chins meeting each other against the syringe, can't; neck and hair; D 1 are no features of a person but blurry features of a person').

Figure VIII (10")

28. D M + A P
3.0

'Two mice or two rats on end' (D 1).

29. Dd F + Hh
3.0

'Looks like a candle' (Dd 30, form 'that's been, not burning, but tallow came running down the candle').

30. Dd C.V Ls

V (Very long delay.) >∧> 'Part of a body

of water.' (Dd of D 5; color and depth.)

31. Dd F Tr
    3.0

< 'And a boat on the body of water' (**Dd** in D 5; form).

32. Dd M Hd

∧<∧ 'Two feet hanging, someone is hanging instead of walking' ('It's dead, a man!'), dangling there' (Dd in D 3; the ankles down. Deep sigh; shakes head).

33. Dd VF + Ar

<∧ 'A feeling these are buildings in this little area here and here.' (Dd 29; I'm on water and looking to shore, I'm looking from a blank space toward land; it's far.')

34. D C An

'A person's stomach cut open, veins and' (arteries D 2, color).

35. Dd F – A

'And front form, hanging, a real long animal' (Dd 22 only).

36. Dd M + Ab

'On a shield? I can't figure it out' ('rat will fall if he lets go, he looks like he will; both will fall. Shield is part of center of D 4; shows strength').

Figure IX (95″)

37. D F Ad

>∧<∧∨ 'A long dog's face' (D 2).

38. D F – Ad

'A horse's face here' (Dd 27).

39. Dds CF – Hh

'I see two lights shining at each other, a glare' (Dds 22; 'green cage over a bulb, but it is wrong color; also form').

40. Dd M + Hdx

< (Keeps shaking head) ∧< 'A person a person just going into space' ('reaching and can't find a solid place for his feet, grasping for something that won't hold him anyway, he'll fall').
coming down from a mountain and trying to hook his finger on something' (Dd 25 on to a ledge), 'getting ready to fall, like

41. Ds M – Hd

∧ 'I start seeing a face here, odd with eyes, more like a mask with hands sticking up' (upper Dd in center of D 10; 'a mask D 10, nothing behind; white eyes, dripping blood on chest, not dead, never alive, so weird; blood from nose, but can't understand.' Dds are hands. < 'No a crocodile, just head of it).

42. D F + Ad

>∧ 'A lobster's claws or something (D 7

form. This card was troubling, I couldn't find anything').

Figure X (40")

43. D M.CF – H

'A face, swimming, with a yellow body, a different face there.' (D 2, moving easily, color form. 'Child's face, red cheek, yellow body, I don't know; I see legs, whether it's drowning? That costume?').

44. D M – A
4.0

'Two angry birds but without beaks, angry bird as I look at a bird.' (D 8; 'mouths open, body of bird, no beak, not nice, angry at each other, I can't tell').

45. D M + A P
4.5

'A rabbit with ears up. The green, I don't know what that is (D 5), alert to children swimming towards him, pretty children, can't tell.'

46. D M + H
4.0

'These look like bodies here with heads up here that were birds before (D 9 with D 8), bodies holding on to something with their arms.'

47. D F + A

'Like they are holding ducks (D 6), in their hands and ducks' heads not coming together, I can't figure that out' ('something in middle [Dd 34] is salt shaker? Long dresses, tails, musketeers, heads, odd to me, I'm dreaming, it is very confusing to me').

48. D M.V + H

∨ 'A man now with his legs, gives impression he is floating in air, like from a parachute or something' (D 5; free form, hanging from arm level; 'will fall, funny place, a very precarious ledge through two mountains; I can't).

49. Ds F + A
5.0

'Fish going through the water' (D 12, with space, form).

50. D F – Ob

(Looks closely) 'Long trumpets with a thing, (form) at end. . . Can't figure it out' (D 3).

51. Ds CF – Hd
5.0

'Looks like a head should be there, a green wig, I never saw one but a face should be in these' (Dds below D 5; with D 4 as wig). 'A woman's face, pretty, young, very vivid, my wife's face.' (Gives up in resignation, sighs, keeps).

Time: 53' 12"

Response Summary

W	2	M	16 (2–)	H	5	F+		76%
DW	1	M.CF	1–	Hd	11 (x2)	A		37%
D	33 (s 5)	M.V	1	A	16	P		6%
Dd	15 (s 2)	C	2	Ad	3	s		7.14%
	51	C.V	1	An	1			
		CF	3 (2–)	Ar	1			
		FY	1	Ab	1			
		VF	3	Ay	1			
		FT	1	Bt	1			
		F+	16	Bl	1			
		F–	5	Hh	3			
Z f	21	F	1	Ls	3			
Z sum	69.0		51	Ob	2	Af r		0.89%
Ap. D Dd!!		EB	18:8.5	Rc	1	L		0.76%
Sep: Ir, with		EA	26.5	Tr	1	T/IR		43.8%
	trend cnfn.				51	T/R		62.6%

Interpretation

A dangerously denarcissized state of mind. The patient screens this by rigid conscious control. But thought pathology emerges and his fantasy regressions are from very deep sources. The man is especially vulnerable to emotional disturbances consequent on impacts on him as he transacts with his environment. A suicidal threat is present, the more ominous in the light of the man's verging on a psychotic disruption. While delusions would be among the symptoms, the structural picture is primarily reactive. Immediate hospitalization is critically indicated from these Rorschach test findings.

The painful mood state at present dominates GA's mental life, both conscious and unconscious. It is endlessly apparent in his expressions of inability to associate or to recognize what he does see ("Never" saw the like in fig. I; "Can't figure it" in II; "I don't know," "Can't tell;" and similar expressions at all ten test cards); in resignation and attitudes (the formula of "That's all" or "I can't . . . any more") with which he terminates his associations in fig. I, IV, VI, VIII, IX, and his slow, impeded behavior in figs. VI, VIII as recorded by the examiner. At the same time he maintains a rigid hold on his perceptions (the long stretches of F+, i.e., in the first nine responses; then after one F– in fig. III, a series of 15 F+). In fig. VIII where he associates with a total of nine responses, he deviates perceptually (F–) only once. It is not until fig. IX and X where color shock and fatigue are having their effects that he conspicuously departs from accuracy. Even for these two figures the F+ per cent is only moderately lowered, as in one not daring to err.

The emotional drag on G.A.'s intellectual processes is evident also in instances of severely retarded response time (figs. V, VII, IX). He is also much slower than most normal adults in figs. I, III, VI, VII, X). For other symptoms of inhibition examiner notes that the patient is slow between responses, hesitates, is struggling (as in fig. I, II, III, IV,, VI, VIII). These expressions of inability have been known clinically to identify persons who hold devalued self-percepts. In order to act as without ability a person first sees himself as without it. The dynamic behind the symptom is the fear to act. That is the illness. G.A. accents this attitude even more sharply in his thought content. This is recurrently dysphoric. His first response is such (other: see R's 14, 19, 20). Some overt behavior stems from painful feelings, as the "deep sigh" at R 8; ideas of guilt and insecurity in his fantasy. The "dead" theme occupies him both at conscious level and in his fantasy.

Again the intense pain reflected in this mood state, G.A.'s ego is exerting a strenuous effort at intellectual control. He shows this in, aside from his unbroken series of F+, the excessive attention to Dd in the Ap, compulsion that this is for precision; while his reiterated apologetics are another symptom of the fear of being in error. The net effect of the ego's exertion is to aggravate the stress. This calls for cumulatively more ego effort towards maintaining his integration threatened by the new tensions. The man's unremitting struggle periodically drains the ego of its strength and his defenses show cracks. Intellectual disruption develops. He goes into confusion with contaminatory trend (R 10); distorts form in a penis percept (in the inquiry, fig. VI); deviates far perceptually again at fig. VII, (R 27). The thought process and content in an M in the inquiry for this figure is a condensation| He loses intellectual orderliness (confused sequence) badly at fig. VIII, somewhat less so (irregular sequence) at figs. II, V, VI, VII. His first response, a DW, is alogical, vague reasoning.

While the stringent self-hold is his principal defense, he has recourse also to avoidances. So in fig. VI he is aware of the "penis" but names it only in the inquiry. In fig. II he is circumspect in associating regarding the female genital and he blocks off the connection between that percept and the "blood" thus reassuring himself against grasping the meaning: the responses are "unrelated." By his inability to synthesize these percepts G.A. demonstrates how one's defenses have a pathogenic effect on intellectual freedom and higher mental functioning.

He at first avoids female genitality again in fig. VII. Reacting to the vagina-form detail, he postpones to the inquiry of the association, "woman's lips," itself an obvious displacing. He is thus here doubling his defense tactics: delays and continues to suppress by the displacing. He has difficulty in verbalizing a pleasurable idea (R's 5, 16, and see also R 25); devalues women (R's 7, 26). He is in some flight from his fantasying as he shows in his belated M at figs. V and VII. His failure to produce some very common M is another flight symptom in this man who is capable of 18. Notable among these misses are the M + H P in figs. II and IX: the W M + H in fig. IV; and also although with smaller expectancy one of the M + H at fig. I. Symbolisms recur. Whether any topic has symbolic value to the person and what the meaning to him only he can validate in the therapeutic exploring. The present patient produced numerous associations which are leads to symbolisms (R 14, 17, 20, 21, 25, 27, 29, 31, 33, 36, 39). In my own experience symbolisms are used largely by neurotics rather than schizophrenics. I judge them before to be an adjustive rather than a pathogenic defense.

It is his fantasy which is G.A.'s major tranquilizer when the going gets rough. The three all-color figures, VIII, IX, X, trigger ten, nearly 60 per cent of his total of 18 such responses. Excitement has weakened the ego's usual bar against the unconscious. In fig. X where his feelings have mounted to the most concentrated degree and fatigue has set in, he has recourse to five, or nearly 28 per cent of his inner living. His reaction at fig. X is an autistic withdrawal into a dream life, judged from the individualized content in most of it. The fantasying is regressive in structure (F−), deviating form in R's 43, 44; and animal actors (A) in R's 44, 45. He invests strong feelings in nearly all his fantasy associations, as he shows in his language: mean looking; hurt, deformed, beaten; someone dangling; eyes dripping blood; and others. In a pleasurable vein is "a woman kindly" which he himself reported as "vivid." In R 36 he produces an abstraction of quality, "strength," a kind of response which characterizes only persons highly charged with feeling. Dereistic as the structure is and the themes so personalized, the question is an open matter at some points whether this patient is distinguishing his own inner world from reality.

R's 41, 43, 44 are G.A.'s more seriously regressive inner living distortions of reality, dream imagery. Less regressive but still such as found mainly in children and in disturbed adults, i.e., in persons chronologically or functionally immature, are the M responses in part humans; and those in Dd (see R's 16, 19, 32, 40). Not regressive are: R's 2, 8, 26; these human heads and arms are frequently enough so seen as M by all normal groups. On the other hand, deep regressions are in evidence in R 28, for which the activity is verbalized at R 36; and in R 45, even though the perception in these two is as accurate as can be. They are not only F+ but also P. The animals in these associations are taking roles in human dramas, something which only children, young ones, and the mentally disturbed, quite artlessly articulate. Two other fantasies are also of either day-dream or true dream productions in theme, although both are F+ and whole human percepts (R's 46 and 48). In the latter the insecurity thinking is vivid, intense, fuses a painful emotion-inferiority feeling (in the vista determinant). The patient himself identifies the dream process in R's 46-47; "I'm dreaming."

As for pleasure-pain axis, G.A.'s fantasy life is most frequently of one tone with his dominant mood state, painful. The themes are about insecurity, death, mean persons, bodily injures. He refers to a pleasurable topic, R 7, "dancing" and denies this affect as he equates "dog" and "women" and in the devaluing observation, "odd faces." The feeling is noticeably benign in R 16, and the topic in this is, not by chance, "my mother." A faint pleasurable flavor emanates also in the fairytale imagery of R 45. In two others of his fantasies G.A. is, so far as can be overtly judged (R's 8, 18), affectless.

The patient twice lays open to view his present precarious situation and the related clinical state of mind. In R's 40 and 48 he states his desperate hopelessness in the language of the unconscious: he'll fall; a man floating in space, with no support. That is where his gambling has left him. In his distress he also has recourse to restitutional ideation. Such is the abstraction "strength" which the "shield" is in R 36. A benign flavor obtains in this thinking too.

Considered as sheer quantity, G.A.'s could be a richly imaginative life, a socially constructive asset. His total of 18 M is far above the mean and near to the high end of the range of my normal adults (Beck et al., 1950). It compares well with M findings in persons carrying on creatively in their vocations. (See, e.g., the record of T.V.) Our patient's EA, 26.5, marked him out sharply as capable of very broad emotional experience. His energetic feelings indicated in the color associations are a mobilized force behind his imaginative potential. As he is now he only too clearly is turning to a day-dreaming which is a theater of play for his worries.

Two leads emerge regarding the personal dynamics in G.A.'s illness. One he communicates at "mother' 'imagery (fig. VII). His very retarded time for first response at once discloses his mounting agitation. He is reacting mainly to stimulation from within: of his four associations, three are emotionally determined. (His lambda index for fig. VII, 0.25, is much lower than even his deviating low 0.76 for his entire response pattern.) When attending to the objective reality (F determinant) he distorts it in a confabulatory idea at the vagina detail (R 27). His attitude regarding this organ is threatening enough to cloud his thinking, something he showed also in fig. II (above). In his emotional processes he is here manifesting longing for erotic contact (T); strongly sensed inferiority feeling (VF); and an internalized hostility (M). The theme in his inferiority feeling process supports the indication of erotic need: "woman's lips, voluptuous," at first suppressed. He side-steps the love wish in R 24 in the animal actors, a regression that this is to primitive eroticism. In associating to the maternal profiles he ventilates hostility, the women are "mean." Who are they? This is something he shuts out. They have no "identity." Whether an unbroken attachment to his mother and the anxiety generated thereby have inter-fered with his heterosexuality, producing some defensive hostility to women (see above regarding R 7) is the question here. His open utterance of affection towards "my mother . . . kindly, smiling," will be recalled (R 16).

Second is G.A.'s reaction at "father" imagery (fig. IV). He produces here one of his most dysphoric toned thoughts, the symbolism in R 14. Is this identification as of himself? Or at an even more deeply unconscious level is the "old hollow tree" his father? To the degree of his identifica-tion with his father, does he carry a self-image of himself as hollow? It confirmed this identification as the core of this man's denarcissized view of himself with all its fermenting torment. It is essence of his illness. When he discloses a phobic attitude in R 16 he discriminates between his two parents: only the mother is "kindly;" the "man" is "square." To perceive a mother image at this masculinity stimulus is very rare. But what, in this patient, is effecting this linkage is an unanswered question. The patient gratuitously informs us that his emotions are here strong ones: "both very vivid."

G.A.'s thoughts and the question of unprepossessing self-attitude evoked as strong masculinity imagery (fig. IV) acquires added significance in the light of his ideation at the "phallic" figure (VI). His first association here was on the "old-decay-rotting" theme, a syncretistic blend in R 20 around this very common "totem pole." He follows this with the symbolisms, "light shining . . . candle lit . . . will burn." But regarding what his unconscious is here ventilating the test findings can only ask. His next association ex-poses a suicidal idea: R 22. Landscape imagery that accents repose and tranquility I have found too often in patients clinically suspected of being suicidal. One can rationalize it as that yearning for the ultimate rest. The "surcease from sorrow" (Poe), "peace of the grave" (Millay). Our man's thoughts at this phallic figure are not benign ones.

A characterological trait that plagues G.A. reducing his self-worth in his own eyes is his feeling of inferiority. His five Vista (V) responses are distinctly above the mean of 1.84 in our normal adults (1950). In three the scoring is VF, the feeling process (V) is stronger than his objective judgment (F), chafes at him intensely (R 22, 25, 33). In the two others he also experiences emotions along another dimension and churning up the pain. The excitement in the pure color determinant (R 30) fuses with the self-depreciation into an overt clinical symptom which is a troubling irritability. In his blending M with V (R 48) the man accents the depth in his personality which this damaging trait has invaded. The feeling is very much essence of his self. It is a trait which must further darken his sombre view of his life and would foster any suicidal ideas already breeding.

The thought content to which G.A.'s inferiority feelings relate are: the sense of distance twice. He fixes on an unattainable objective, the rising sun, in R 25. He identifies his percept with a woman's voluptuous lips. Whether the "light of the sun" is his symbolism for this same objective, is one more question which his productions are opening up. The "buildings" (R 33) is a theme which Rorschach interprets (1923) as communicating a person's feeling of inner incompletion. While distance enters into G.A.'s imagery at R 48, the M factor is here the dominating one, with its theme of the "precarious." In this blend, his feeling of inadequacy is rubbing salt into the wound which he suffers in this nightmarish experience of helplessness. Much here remains to be unraveled concerning his emotional state. The blends (M with C, Y, or V; C with Y or V; V and Y), experiences along more than one emotional dimension that they indicate, still present among the least analyzed of Rorschach problems.

Whether in the "reflection" association (R 22) G.A. is communicating his compulsion to look into himself, to scrutinize what he has done with his life, is again one of those questions that a Rorschach protocol can only ask. Regarding the general significance of the "reflection" topic, we do not have satisfactorily established information. This man's mental state is here wrapped up in thoughts of "quiet, secluded." The suicidal flavor of such ideation has been noted. It is more ominous in relation with "water" (which can drown), something which this patient sees both in this association and in R 33. In one of his fantasies he toys with a drowning idea (R 43). Another visualizes a man hanging (R 32). Hence, the suicide hazard was emphasized in reporting to the referring psychiatrist. Hence also we concluded that hospitalization was critically indicated.

To pleasure toned stimuli (figs. VIII, IX, X) our man is very responsive. He rates an Af r at 0.89 markedly above the range, 0.40 to 0.60 of normal adults. Exciting situations mobilize and free his feelings. His reactions are sure to be impulsive (pure C) or highly labile (CF). At the same time he suffers anxiety shock at these points. His feelings carry him away in fig. VIII, evident in six emotion-toned, as compared with only three strictly form, responses. His attention is claimed by seven Dd in nine responses, as this test figure alone accounts for nearly half of his 16 Dd. G.A. is here under compulsion to observe the minute. But something is unnerving him. His hold on reality weakens: his F+ per cent is 50 in fig. VIII as compared with 76 for the whole test.

The shock effect reaches a high point in fig. IX. It is a free anxiety into which the patient is precipitated. Thus his very retarded time for first response; his reduced productivity as compared with what he does at figs. VIII and X; field of vision is restricted, as seen in the Ad, Hd, and x responses; overly attends to the Dd; P failure blunders from reality, as shown in the 50 per cent "extended F+" (Schafer, 1954); fantasy regressive both in structure and in theme. He at first suppresses an anxiety-toned theme which, however, later escapes him, "blood" (inquiry of R 41).

By his reaction at fig. X, G.A. sets his psychological fragility in high relief. Persons with less serious neuroses regain their self-control following their disturbance at IX. This patient abandons himself to regressive and autistic fantasying; his thinking turns syncretistic in R's 46-47; he distorts reality in R 50. However, he also manages some moderation of the disturbance. In speed for first response, while he is still very slow he is much faster than at IX. He has freed himself from the hold of Dd on him and he turns to the obvious (D). In testing reality (F+ per cent) he is again within neurotic limits. The psychological gryoscope, the ego, is striving, feeble though it is, to restore the personality's balance.

It is at the three all-color figures finally that G.A. most drastically withdraws into his introvert shell. He fashions here some of his most idosyncratic condensations. Under his excitement he has gone thus into a dream-like state from which he inadequately recovers. Ego forces are scattered. Exposed as he now is to the peril of impulsive acts, the suicide hazard is that much greater.

G.A. harbors an opposition trait of above average degree, (s, 14 per cent). He is now directing it mainly against the ideas fermenting in his unconscious (inferred from the covariance of much s in a person markedly introversive. (See p. 68). Necessarily he is compounding his anguish as he fights within his innermost self for the very ideas from whose conscious significance he has escaped by converting them into unconscious thought processes. As a consequence he weights himself down further under his oppressive mood, since the psychologic stress deriving from a person's attack upon himself is among the most insufferable of human experiences. The clinical logic here points to the punishing superego.

Empiric data in the test support this deduction. The oppressive effect on him of figures: IV, VI, VII has been described above. It will be noted also at fig. V. His initial response time (90″) is very near to his slowest.

He misses the P, statistically the most frequent evoked by the ten ink blots. He turns principally to fantasy living although this test figure is among those least releasing this process. The themes in his two fantasies concentrate on the disadvantaged, the injured. Anxiety is tormenting G.A. at these four heavily black figures. Such stress originates in central, i.e., superego, layers of the personality. While still more hypothetical than validated, this is a lead always to be pursued (Beck 1952). Any indication that a person is attacking himself necessarily heightens the suicide threat.

In the overall, G.A. dots this test record with sporadic signs of thinking disturbance. He uses an alogical thought process (the DW in R 1); with trends to syncretism in R 7 and in R 10. He places his human in an odd position in the inquiry of R 19. He visualizes a queer synthesis in R 21. His language confusion is severe in R 27. Orderliness is moderately upset (sequence irregular) in fig. II; more so in fig. VI. But the man's thinking remains formally intact as does his perception, until his excitement disrupts him. It will be noted that in the first six test figures he deviates perceptually (F−) only once. His F+ per cent for these is 91. From fig. VII on his affects overpower him. His F− count rises to 4 and F+ per cent deteriorates to 56; ("extended F+," 62 per cent). For his entire reaction pattern his grip on reality (76 per cent) is above the compromise level of neurosis (60 to 70 per cent); and his recognition of the convention (P) is in normal range.

G.A. possesses a high intellectual endowment. His Z score of 69.0 shows him well able to grasp complex relationships. Then he elaborates one of his ideas richly: (R's 14, 21, 22, 25 with 28, 36, 40-41, 45, 48.) Diction uncovers signs of exposure to education and of the ability to absorb it, as e.g. "wings wilted away," "graceful hands," "intrigues me," "a morbid card," and others. Yet the man's achievement is now badly reduced. For one with the ability to synthesize his percepts at the level of Z 69.0 his responding with only two W is pathologically low. He betrays here his pitifully weak intellectual drive, a lack of initiative. By channelizing his thinking as symptomatically and at times as pathologically as he does he is rendering his abilities ineffective. He fails to turn them to socially worthwhile goals. However, many of his associations are to be explored as symbolisms (see, e.g., on p. 275). As defenses more adjustive they are stronger ego operation and to this extent relieve the deleterious outlook. His one anatomy association in R 34 is very pathologic thinking. Released at fig. VIII it is also a measure of how disrupting his neurotic anxiety is. His one cheerful and potentially most healthy thought was his final one: "a woman's face pretty, . . . my wife's face." It is one sign that he can experience emotional warmth towards another, someone of closest life importance to him.

In overview, while the structure of G.A.'s illness is reactive, and the depressed affect must be judged as of neurotic order, the intensity with which he lives it, the extent to which it dominates his thinking, his vulnerability to emotional impacts, and the regressive nature of his fantasying, all converge in the conclusion: this man is on the verge of a psychosis, the symptoms of which will probably include delusions, with serious suicide hazard.

In terms of the processes and the manifestations of them, G.A. is seen as follows:

> *Intellectual functioning.*
> II-A, integrated; but also
> II-B, disrupted severly, under stress

> *Emotional state.*
> IV-B, depressive tone, of psychotic
> severeity; with IV-A,
> high volatility.

> *Fantasy activity.*
> III-B, regressive, deeply; V-A,
> autistic solutions. IV-D,
> traces of potential for
> constructive imagination.

> *Defenses.*
> I-A, constrictive; with recourse
> also to I-C, adjustive.
> (the symbolisms).

> *Social adaptation.*
> V-B, self-derogation, acute; traces
> of V-C, restitutional.

Treatment Implications. Hospitalization is immediately indicated. Initially the therapy is to support this man's dependency need until his present crisis subsides. A necessary early step will be to breed confidence and nourish his self-esteem, traits that are now so nearly nonexistent in him. Towards promoting the therapy G.A. himself provides important assets. Principally these are the fluidity of his emotional state, his Experience Actual (EA) and its depth, a trace of evidence for healthy marital relationships, and a high intelligence. All these can be mobilized as counterforce against the depression. A long-time supportive program is further indicated. The question of deeper treatment is to be considered later depending on his course.

A PIOTROWSKI INTERPRETATION

Delia: A Relatively Well-functioning Young Woman

and Her Bizarre Rorschach Record

The Patient and Her Problems. Delia, a single nineteen-year-old female art student applied for out-patient psychotherapy on her own initiative because she had become extremely sensitive to remarks of others about her, had developed crying spells (for which she could not always find a reason) and sporadically had felt "strange" since the age of sixteen. The oldest of three children, she had a sister who was four years younger and a brother, six years younger. She liked the brother and got along well with him but resented her sister whom she believed to be prettier than herself and the father's favorite. Delia described her father, an independent repairman, as "a bore who has frequent outbursts of rage and no consideration for the feelings of others" and her mother as "a bright but gutless woman who married beneath her." The parents belonged to different Christian denominations which did not cause friction, but the children were members of their mother's church. Delia had enjoyed elementary school where she had been "a star." Grades continued to be very good in high school although her attitude toward school changed. Her peers "bored" her and she made no friends. Having more than one teacher in high school made her uneasy. Menarche for which she had been prepared occurred at the age of eleven. She wished it had never occurred.

Later Delia complained also of inability to do the work she had previously been doing well and of decreased interest in art, her chosen career. She remarked: "I have no idea what I'd like to do." She wondered about her social relations and communication with others. "People can't take me except in small doses," and "I guess I can't trust anybody," she said puzzled. Men "chasing" her and trying to stroke her legs on a bus annoyed her. Delia suffered from physical illnesses: gynecologic difficulties (menstrual irregularities, resection of an ovary, cramps), recurrent eye infections, and a protracted virus infection.

The sporadic strange feeling occurred when she was resting or lying in bed before falling asleep. She felt flattened out and encased in something heavy which made breathing difficult. These states were horrifying and at the same time oddly pleasant and reassuring. They aroused neither thought nor fear of death. Delia experienced them also every time she had an orgasm.

Delia's intellectual capacity was very superior. If the IQ were based solely on the WAIS vocabulary, it would have been at least 150. The lowest verbal performance score was on the arithmetical problems, passed on an average level. The verbal WAIS quotient was 122 and the non-verbal one 140 with an excellent performance on the digit-symbol test and superior performances (with hardly any corrections) on colored block designs and object assembly.

The Rorschach Record and Procedure for its Interpretation. Delia co-operated readily and frankly. Her Rorschach record has been scored and interpreted in accordance with the rules in Perceptanalysis[5] and more recent findings, especially concerning long-term prognosis.[10]

As theories are improved in scope and validity, they become applicable to increasingly finer observations. This is true of all empirical sciences, including perceptanalysis. When, however, in the early stages of develop-ment, a theory is incomplete or unsound, single test components permit limited valid inferences. At this point, interrelating many test components is necessary if conclusions are to be comprehensive and predictions valid. Since action tendencies (appetitive drives) are more consistent than overt behavior (consummatory actions), the former can be inferred from fewer test components than the latter. The etiology of psychosocial behavior is much more complex than the detection of some potential action tendencies. Total personality including all action tendencies escapes us. The "principle of the interdependence of components" (5:390-413) must be followed in attempts at predicting overt psychosocial behavior, especially in "blind" analyses, because of the complex etiology of overt psychomotor behavior.

Rorschach suggested[14] that the interpretation of a test record begin with the most conspicuous or statistically least frequent test reactions and then gradually include the less conspicuous features. This procedure was suggested for its relative convenience and not as the only valid approach. If nothing is overlooked in a test record, it does not matter how the interpretation begins or ends.

Rorschach Record

No. of Resp.		Score		Response
				3″ I
(1)	Dr	Mc′	(h)	∧ An angel groping, from the rear (to-ward observer).
(2)	Dr	FM−	a	A bird flying.
(3)	W	Mc′−	(h)	A batman type of person, standing still; a person standing behind a lot of clouds.
(4)	W	mc′±	ntr	∨ Something tossed out of a volcano, an eruption.

| (5) | D | M | (h) | ∧ Two angels facing each other doing a Russian dance. |

(1) (Whole except bottom halves of sides.) Feeling for her way out in darkness. (2) (Same as 1.) It has giant wings taking off. (3) (Whole. Clouds were seen inseparate from batman.) Black clouds. He's standing on the top of a mountain. (?) It's a batman because it's black; looks evil, sinister. (4) (Whole. Dark shading.) Little thing flying around. It fans out, erupts. (5) (Same area as 1.) Holding hands, doing a knee-bend dance.

7″   II

(6)	Dr	M	(h)	∧ Two people in long gowns, and they're playing patty-cake.
(7)	DS	mC	obj.	Airplane.
(8)	D	F	sex	This is really female.
(9)	D	F	a	Bug or butterfly—
(10)	D	C	bl	Bleeding.
(11)	D	Mc'–	(h)	Little spirits doing a ritualistic dance. Coming out of a lamp. They're evil because they're black.
(12)	D	CF	ntr	And hot lava things.

(6) There are their heads (top reds), their gowns (grays without bottom red). Women. (7) (Inside white space and bottom red.) It is pointed, and the fire is coming out of the back of it as it flies. (8) (Bottom red.) Vagina, everything is there. (9, 10) (Bottom red.) Because it is red and the antennas are coming out of it. (11) (Grays.) They're vaguely human. No, not solid. Vague. Their form is changing constantly. It is not really a lamp. Just some object. (Bottom center gray.) (12) (Top reds.) Hot because red.

5″   III

(13)	W	Mc'	(h)	∧ Two African fertility gods.
(14)	D	Fc'	(h)	First they looked like females, but now they are males. Male fertility gods.
(15)	D	F–	at	Stomachs are attached to their wrists. I don't know why, but they are very strange.
(16)	DS	F–	(a)	∨ A fly's head with big eyes, with crayfish arms; and it is wearing a bow tie.
(17)	WS	F	a	A frog's body.
(18)	D	C	bl	It's a wounded body.

(13) (Usual figures.) They have egg-shaped heads; black. They have a bosom and high heeled shoes. It's so exaggerated. Their head, their posture, the body is bent; an impossible posture, they're pointing. (14) Males because of extention at the "knee." It looks phallic; very obvious. (15) (The stomachs are two halves of the bottom center gray.) Has that configuration. It's peculiar. (16) (Reversed posi-

tion. Eyes, top center gray. Arms, top sides of gray. Tie, center red.) The whole face. Flies have claws. A strange-type of animal. (Bow tie?) This is a cartoon (and that is why this fly has a bow tie). (17, 18) (Whole plus white space between is the body. The red areas are blood.) The frog has a wounded body. (?) Maybe still alive.

				17″ IV
(19)	Dr	M	h	∧ A person is wearing a mask. The feet are big. He's tremendously large.
(20)	W	Fc	(a)	∨ A king bird wearing a crown. That doesn't mean much at all.
(21)	Dr	M–	(pl)	∧ An evil tree, a live tree, a people-eating tree. It's going to attack people.

(19) (Whole except middle bottom part. The mask is top center.) He's big and fat, lying there with his legs spread out. (20) (Whole. The crown is the top center part; feet, bottom corners extensions.) He's a king bird because he is wearing a crown. Bird with feathers (feathers sugggested by texture). (21) (Whole except bottom center part.) It's almost a person-tree. It has a head and can move like a person. Could not be a nice tree because it has these evil-looking arms (arms, top corners extensions).

				18″ V
(22)	W	FMc	ad	∧ Horses coming out of a cloud from two directions, from each end. You see the heads and forelegs on each side.
(23)	W	Fc'–	a	A bat. His wings got caught in a dryer. He's all mangled. Was in a fight. He had beautiful wings before.
(24)	W	F–	a	∨ Upside down, it looks like a butterfly was caught in a fight.
(25)	d	F	sex	∧ This shape looks very female. Looks like the mount of passion.

(22) (Whole.) There is no particular form, just a puff of smoke (center part, the cloud). The horses are running out of the cloud. (23) (Whole.) It's damaged; something is missing. There should be more. It's a black bat. (Patient was unable to specify and locate missing parts.) (24) (Whole; antennas, top center.) It's not complete. Something is missing, parts of wings. The colored part is missing. (25) (Bottom center including some small adjoining areas but without the thinner lower parts of bottom center.) A woman's legs with the mount of Venus.

				1″ VI
(26)	D	Fc	sex	∧ A sexology diagram, the interior.
(27)	d	FM	a	A crown that some country has as its national symbol. A bird is at the top of the crown.
(28)	d	F	arch	A bird on top of a castle.

(29)	d	M–	h	Two people holding on to the mountain, and doing pushups against it, going back and forth.
(30)	dW	Fc–	bl	Somebody bled on the floor. Little flies are gathering around to nibble at the blood.
(31)	D	FM	a	Two little snakes or worms approaching each other. They're going to bite each other.
(32)	D	M	sex	One worm is extremely phallic looking.
(33)	D	M–	(h)	V Embryo forms. Ugly and deformed.

(26) (Large area. "Vaginal canal," top vertical middle lights spots.) This is the vaginal canal and the skin all around it. It's all bubbly. The skin has little disturbances on the surface; no smooth surface. Hips. (27) (Small top area of left third of large part.) The bird is perched on the crown (bird, upper left corner). The bird is taking a rest. (28) (The same area is reinterpreted as a castle with the bird on top of it.) (29) (Same area as 27 and 28. The birds, on both sides of the plate, are the upper part of the human bodies. Patient would not identify the sex, but got up and demonstrated their movements leaning against a wall at an angle but keeping body straight.) They are not too clear because it is in the distance. They're holding hands against the mountain. (30) (Whole. Flies, suggested by top part extensions and small protuberances all along the edges.) The little flies are on the top. The fact that these little creatures are there, this (the whole plate) has to be blood. Otherwise they wouldn't be there. It's messy and jagged. (31) Darkest parts of vertical middle, divided by light spots. They look like snakes slowly approaching each other. (32) (Top darkest part of vertical detail.) The only things I could think of as long are snakes, but this (top) looks like an erection, a phallus. (33) (Top two-thirds of external edges of large part.) They have funny heads. They're curved in an embryo position and are not standing straight.

				15″ VII
(34)	D	Fc	(hd)	Λ Fire flames. They have human characteristics to them. The trunk from the waist up.
(35)	W	M	hd	Egyptian belly dancers with headpiece as part of their costume. They have little snakes as their headpiece.
(36)	D	F	(hd)	The queen chess pieces in Alice in Wonderland.
(37)	W	F–	a	Four-legged butterfly on dissecting table. They cut out the middle of the poor thing. They took the antennas off, too.

(34) (Upper two-thirds.) It looks like fire because of these ends (top extensions).
(35) (Whole.) It is something exotic. They have snakes on their heads, these

pointed ends. Their bellies are practically touching. This (bottom detail) hides their legs. (36) (Top two-thirds.) (37) (Whole.) They removed the middle of it and its antennas. (The legs were the thin top extensions and the outer top extensions of the middle parts. The head was the entire bottom detail. Delia spoke of the four-legged butterfly as if it were a matter of course.)

				6″ VIII
(38)	D	FM	a	∧ Ehm! A colored one. Two bears coming straight up, vertically. Doesn't look like anything else.
(39)	D	mC	obj	Maybe an airplane. Some sort of jet with lots of flames and fire coming out of the back.
(40)	d	F—	hd	Little hands on the end of the wings (of the plane).
(41)	W	CF	pl	Fields of flowers. A very well-planned landscape.
(42)	WS	F—	hd	Like a face with a moustache. He has a pointed head and is wearing motorcycle glasses.

(38) (Side pinks.) (39) (Jet, gray and blue; flames, orange and bottom red.) It's pointed toward the front and moving fast. (40) (Bottom corners of top gray.) (Jet with hands?) It's not a real airplane. (This remark was made in response to a question, the patient realizing the unreality of a jet plane with human hands.) (41) (Whole.) It's all colored. (42) (Whole and inner spaces.) These are his eyes (blue). He has a large moustache (bottom red), and ears (side pinks). (Not a color response.)

				19″ IX
(43)	D	MC	(h)	∧ Two witches out in the woods. There is a fire burning. They are evoking the evil spirits.
(44)	S	FCw	ntr	There is a full moon out.
(45)	D	MC	h	> A man riding a horse. It is not really a horse; a dragon rather. Flames are coming out of it, from behind.

(43) (Witches, orange. Woods, green.) The fire is reflected on the witches (vertical middle detail is part of fire). It's a fire in the (green) woods. (44) (Top inner space.) It's a light pale moon. (45) (Turned to the right. Rider, top green. Horse, top orange and presumably extending to the red.) The fire is red. He leaves a trail of fire wherever he goes.

				4″ X
(46)	W	FMC	a	∧ Like looking through a microscope, all these worms and insects, floating around. An underwater scene with worms, sea horses and things like that.
(47)	D	M—	(h)	Two devils shaking hands. Their fore-

				heads are touching. The heads are together.
(48)	D	FM	a	Two wormy animals with bull dog heads. They are growling at each other, going to fight very soon.
(49)	DS	F–	(ahd)	∨ A face with two horns coming out of it.
(50)	W	mC	fr	A Fourth of July fireworks display.

(46) (Whole.) It's colorful, horribly diseased. The forms are vague. (47) (Top gray, reds and middle blues; the latter are the hands, the gray the foreheads.) (48) (Reds. Heads, top third down to top of middle blue, resembling humans.) They are sort of standing up. (49) (Top green, horns; eyes, middle blue; nostrils, orange triangle; chin, gray. Not a color response.) (50) (Whole.) Color and movement.

Tabulation

W	12	M	10 (3–)	a	13	No. Resp.	50
dW	1	Mc'	3	ad	1	R (VIII-X)	13
WS	2	MC	2	ahd	1	R (VIII-X) %	26
D	21	FM	5 (1–)	h	13	Time	34'
Dr	5	FMc	1	hd	5	T/R	.68'
DS	3	FMC	1	at	1		
d	5	mc'	1 (1–)	sex	4	IRT (I-X)	9.5"
S	1	mC	3	bl	3	IRT (col)	8.2"
		Fc'	2 (1–)	pl	2	IRT (nc)	10.8"
		F	14 (7–)	ntr	3		
F+%	55	FCw	1	fire	1		
a%	29	Fc	3 (1–)	obj	2	W : M = 15 : 15	
h%	37	CF	2	arch	1	W : ΣC = 15 : 11	
sex%	8	C	2			Σc: ΣC = 3.5: 11	

Diagnosis and Long-Term Prognosis. Delia's test record contains many peculiarities which indicate both schizophrenia and a poor long-term prognosis.[10] Among them are two contaminations, responses 3 and 21. A contamination is the unwitting overlapping and fusion of at least two different visual images projected onto a single blot area. The result is an unintelligible percept which the patient cannot disentangle, although he may sometimes deny having produced it (5:75). Percept is defined as a visual image located in a blot area. Thus rigorously defined, a contamination is pathognomonic of schizophrenia. The man masquerading as a batman and the clouds in resp. 3, the tree and the person in resp. 21, have—in empirical reality—different shapes; yet they cover, at least in part, the same blot areas. Delia could unravel the confusion neither on the level of imagination nor perception. She was not being playful or humorous, i.e., there was no deliberate attempt at creating an unrealistic effect (in which case her responses would not have been classifiable as contaminations). She was rather the helpless victim of her confusion. An "inconstant percept of variable dimness" (5:85) is another sign pathognomonic of schizophrenia. The characteristic feature of such a percept is to keep part of the percept clearly and firmly in mind while "perceiving" other parts of it vaguely and in a state of fluctuating size or shape. Resp. 11 is a good example.

Delia manifested in other responses, 15, 16, and 37, another type of defect: details were well and meaningfully perceived but the wholes of which they were parts were incongruous and unrealistic. Again, Delia was serious when producing these peculiar responses. The bottom center gray areas of pl. III do resemble "stomachs" but attaching them to the wrists of human-like figures, as if they were ladies' pocketbooks, is bizarre. The defective abstract reasoning is revealed by perseverating with the image of the "stomach" instead of abandoning it or changing it appropriately to fit the image of the bending fertility gods. The mental synthesis was faulty and gave rise to the peculiar idea of wearing the stomach on the wrist. Delia was genuinely puzzled by her percept but incapable of correcting or suppressing the "very strange" gods. Every part of resp. 16 is a good form, the fly's head, the crayfish arms and the bow tie, but combining them into "a strange type of animal" showed an impaired ability to maintain a separation between concepts logically incompatible but visually contiguous. She was mystified by these responses (15 and 16), as if coping with a real event and not a product of her own imagination. Delia did not attempt and could not (when urged to do so) unravel her peculiar percept. This was a manifestation of perplexity, Plx, found in test records of some patients whose reasoning has been affected by brain damage and some schizophrenics who fail to improve in a long follow-up period (3; 10:315).

Resp. 37, on the other hand, was acceptable to Delia although its form quality is very poor. It appears that self-criticism vanished along with a marked drop in conscious control over thought processes. The quality of form responses varies with the level of conscious control over thoughts.

The psychosis seems mild in degree for three main reasons. First, Delia was sometimes aware of the peculiarity of her responses indicating that she realized the irrelevancy of some of her reasoning. Quite frequently she referred to blot details to justify a response, revealing awareness of the significance of impersonal and empirical evidence. Finally, the rich fantasy life displayed by the number and variety of movement responses is inconsistent with a severe regression of intellectual and emotional functions.

Long-term prognosis, however, i.e., prediction for the period of three to six years after the Rorschach examination, is unfavorable. Delia's record contains five LTPTI signs; each sign is scored once regardless of the frequency of its appearance in the test record. Four of the signs Delia produced have a weight of +2 points each. Sign 2 is repetition or intellectual perseveration: "bird" occurred four times and two of the "bird" responses were of poor form quality. Sign 3, vagueness and tentativeness of perception or explanation, occurred in resp. 3, 11 and 21. Sign 5 breakdown of interpretive attitude, is manifest in resp. 15 and 40 when stomachs and human-like figures, hands and jet planes, were illogically combined in moments of concretization or loss of mental flexibility. Sign 6, inconclusive explanation devoid of any concern for accuracy, was given in resp. 37. Sign 12 the only LTPTI sign with a negative weight (of –2 points) requires at least five human movement responses regardless of form quality. The score then was 8–2 points, or +6 points. This high score strongly suggests lack of improvement three to six years after testing and points to the likelihood of further breakdown.

The twelve LTPTI signs were subjected to a factor analysis utilizing test records of 259 followed-up adult schizophrenics. Four factors were extracted. The solution was satisfactory psychometrically (1, 10). Factor B consists of signs 3 and 5 which Delia produced and can be described as "doubtful perception or interpretation" of stimuli. It is associated with sporadic difficulties in producing precise ideas and in applying ideas to empirical reality. Factor B is clearly indicated in Delia's test record. Factor C consists of four signs of which Delia had only two, signs 2 and 6, that were congruous, and one, sign 12, that was inconsistent with factor C. "Inappropriately applied energy," spontaneous but ineffectual expenditures of energy, are correlated with factor C. Vagueness of perception, thought and speech was clinically prominent and Delia was aware of it in an exaggerated degree. Inappropriate applications of energy were not striking.

Rorschach Record and Overt Behavior. What can be said about Delia's actual, everyday behavior and adjustment in view of the grave diagnosis and pessimistic long-range prognosis? The thought disorders are called primary because they are believed to be due to qualitative changes in the central nervous system and not merely to emotional stress. As long as a schizophrenic is aware of, and tries to correct, the deviant perception, reasoning, or behavior reflected in the thought disorders, he is an incipient psychotic; his malfunctioning is likely to occur mainly in stressful situations. This may cause observers to think that the symptoms are neurotic and can be explained by the environmental pressures. Delia was at times aware of the inadequacy of at least some of her percepts. She was capable then of exercising some caution when she realized that she was not in control of her thoughts or behavior. This fear of acting when she was at her intellectual worst can be assumed to decrease the instances of maladaptive overt psychosocial behavior. Even with this deliberate effort, however, Delia's thought disorders sporadically interrupt her attempts at prolonged and consistent reasoning, seriously weakening their efficiency.

Another sign of caution and control which reduce the chances of overtly manifesting inappropriate reactions is the direct relationship between prolonged initial reaction time and reduction of responses. The plates with the four distinctly longer IRT elicited an average of 3.25 responses compared to the remaining plates with an average of 6.00 responses. When most anxious, Delia restricts her behavior and thus decreases the likelihood of being conspicuously deviant. Moreover the longer delays were associated with plates VII and IX which reflect psychosexual problems, and with plates IV and V which are sensitive measures of self-esteem. Lack of self-confidence and/or psychosexual difficulties would lead to avoidance or reduction of social involvement and thus decrease the chances of undesirable overt behavior.

The high number of inanimate movements (resp. 4, 7, 39, 50) implies that the frequency of day-dreaming is so great as to appear obsessive and this constitutes another sign of restraint. The m indicate action-tendencies which the individual feels are desirable but which he can indulge only in fantasies and not in overt interhuman relations (5:206-16). The movement in Delia's m is freely assertive depicting forces easily overcoming the pull of gravity or other obstacles. Delia, however, experiences these impressive successes only in her fantasies.

No such successful power is apparent in her human movements (5:155-64). The first and most expansive movements with "same-sex figures," i.e., females appear in resp. 5 and 35. The action tendencies of same-sex figures have been found to be activated more readily than those projected onto opposite-sex or imaginary figures (9:513-4). Even these vigorous exhibitionistic movements are limited to one point in space, the Egyptian dancers moving only their bellies and the angels hopping up and down, doing kneebends, in a dance hardly becoming angels. The relatively most vigorous opposite-sex figure M is the rider of the dragon in resp. 45; while he travels through space, however, he is carried. Thus the assertiveness is greatly limited. The dragon also leaves a trail of fire behind it. Potentially destructive fire signifies negative emotion, i.e., repulsion, hate, or anger (5:224-9). If every M is a dynamic self-portrait of at least some aspect of the personality, Delia is, time and again, figuratively carried away by strong anger; she justifies this anger by rationalization but feels uncomfortable nevertheless. Discomfort and rationalization are inferred from Delia's use of opposite-sex or imaginary figures in the human action tendencies motivated by anger.

Delia's record indicates a capacity for playing numerous, diverse and unusual roles in interhuman relationships as her many M vary greatly in type. The pressure exerted on the motor system by the different M action-tendencies is never an average or vector of all the M, but each of these tendencies takes its turn in influencing the motor system when conditions are favorable for its appearance. These tendencies, however, remain incompatible with one another; this incompatibility weakens the strength and effectiveness of any particular manner of dealing with others. It encourages thought rather than clear and consistent action. The animal movements are less restrained and more expansive as a group than the human movements. From this it can be inferred that Delia had been more self-confident, independent and spontaneous in the early part of her life than in her adult years (5:196-201).

In resp. 32 a worm or snake looked to Delia "like an erection, a phallus." It is reasonable to score such a response as M because in every case where such a response had been given and the patient was treated, the therapy revealed that the individual, male or female, wanted to assert himself (at times) as a man. Women who give such responses have "penis envy." (Only a small minority of men or women produce an "erect penis" response.) Delia's deep dissatisfaction with being a woman is manifested in several other responses. The most striking is resp. 13. Not only was there hesitation about the sex of the "fertility gods," but also about their "exaggerated, impossible posture." This certainly is a blurring of the difference between the sexes. Moreover, those gods wear their stomachs on their wrists and are thus vulnerable rather than intact and strong. The preoccupation with fertility was associated with Delia's most conspicuous breakdown of reality testing, suggesting that impregnation as well as fertility cause grave conflicts. It is not surprising, therefore, that pl. IX, which is particularly sensitive to neurotic ambivalence concerning heterosexual intercourse (5:308-9) caused the longest initial delay. The phallus was compared to an aggressive, biting worm (resp. 32). The unusual "sexology diagram" in resp. 26, the "vaginal canal," with the surrounding skin being "all bubbly," with "little disturbances on the surface, not smooth," suggests a disease, as if Delia meant to say that it was sick to be feminine. The very large size of the "canal"—a much smaller and more appropriate one in pl. VII was overlooked—is closely associated with frigidity in women and impotence in men.

It is quite probable that sometimes there is no ambivalence and that then Delia has a distinct preference for her own sex. In resp. 35, the Egyptian dancers with "snakes (cf. resp. 32) as their headpiece" are practically touching each other with their bellies, but their legs are discreetly "hidden." As a result of such basic indecisiveness, confusion, and inconsistency regarding sexual drives it is likely that Delia's actual psychosocial life is much less disorganized than the Rorschach responses would make one expect. The seriously weakened capacity for the actuation of any action-tendency suggests a discrepancy between potential and overt behavior. While Delia's fantasy is richly diverse to the point of being incoordinated, her daily living is probably much more subdued.

Since the inability to give full and easy expression to potential action tendencies appears permanent, Delia probably feels somewhat frustrated at least much of the time. Depression is also indicated in a number of responses, e.g., 4, 23, 24, 30, 31, 45, referring to eruption, deformation, disease, injuries, bleeding, ("little flies gathering around to nibble at the blood"), seen in various stages of disintegration, indicating that Delia felt overextended and in immediate danger of failure. Therefore, she would be in a state of moderate chronic depression without psychomotor retardation. The absence of retardation is indicated by the brief initial reaction times and the spontaneous elaboration of her responses. The pace of interpretation was normal, being about 40 seconds per response. This depression functions as still another restricting and constraining influence.

In addition to the obsessiveness implied by the presence of four inanimate movements, there is direct evidence of obsessiveness. This is indicated by several instances of spontaneous criticism of her own productions, such as "that doesn't mean much at all" (resp. 20), "something is missing, there should be more" (resp. 23). In several responses, events are projected into the future instead of seen as on-going occurrences (resp. 15, 21, 24, 31, 40). This need to delay action is another form in which obsessiveness is manifested.

The human movement responses reflect important action tendencies which motivate overt psychosocial behavior. Experience has shown that each M functions sporadically as a more or less independent motive. When the nature of the M varies, the different types alternate as forces shaping the individual's interhuman relationships .Thus in Delia's resp. 19, the "person wearing a mask, lying there with big legs spread out," is not only a compliant but a very passive movement posture. The implication of this M is that at times Delia gives up responsibility for herself and passively waits for others to take care of her. By handling some vital situations in a very passive way she again acts to reduce the chances of inappropriate overt behavior. As the number of M increases, the tendency to feel pride and be hurt by lack of respect increases. This characteristic would be marked in Delia since she has 15 M. Other conditions being equal, a person who does not wish to have his pride hurt exercises caution in social relations (2; 5-144).

Delia is likely to be very suspicious of the motives of others. This is inferred not only from the large number of M in a schizophrenic test record but even from the content of some of the M. The angels in pl. I do not behave according to expectation (resp. 5); a tree is not supposed to move by itself and is not associated with evil intent yet Delia's tree eats people (resp. 21); "a puff of smoke, horses are running out of the cloud" (resp. 22), the horses are appearing suddenly. In other words, objects or creatures do not behave according to expectation which implicitly requires alertness. Since any M is also a dynamic self-portrait it can be assumed that Delia is anxious lest she actuate the action tendencies disclosed by these M (2; 5:121-186).

The sum of weighted positive color responses in Delia's record is four (resp. 7, 39, 41, 50) and the sum of negative color responses is seven (resp. 10, 12, 18, 43, 45, 46). Practically all of these responses, negative as well as positive, are earthy. In other words, Delia is capable of strong desires to associate with and dissociate from others in order to continue or discontinue the exchange of pleasures and pains.. Her negative emotions, however, are much more frequent than the positive ones. It can be expected that negative emotions leading to the avoidance of others, would affect her social relations far more frequently than would the positive. Here again we have an indication that overt acting out of her tendencies would reduce the chances of clashing with others.

One seeming contra-indication to the above is the absence of color shock. A color shock is an expected finding in the records of those who are well adjusted in their overt behavior as well as in their inner lives. In the records of obviously disturbed individuals, the presence of color shock is desirable as it is advantageous for these individuals to be hesitant and ambivalent about acting out in accordance with their emotional impulses which arefrequently disruptive in nature. Delia's overt behavior, however, may not always reflect her strong desire to avoid emotional involvement with others. The absence of color shock would indicate that this is not due to repression but rather in this case may be attributed to the inconsistencies and disorganization induced by the recurrent psychotic thought processes.

The test record contains reactions which are associated with facilitation of overt behavior. However, the forces which reduce the chances of easy and frank overt behavior are so strong that they obviate, to a very large extent, the danger of direct overt action which some of the components disclose. Among these action facilitating components is the large number of dark color or dark shading responses. Their weighted sum is seven, which is large, Delia has a tendency to increase motor behavior in situations of anxiety as a way to alleviate tension (5:262-71). The ratio of weighted light shading responses to color responses is 3.5:11.0. The implication of this ratio taken by itself would be that Delia has serious difficulties in adequately controlling undesirable motor impulses (5:281-2, 287). The possibility of impulsive acting out is diminished by her weakened overall ability to act in a purposive manner for any prolonged period of time and by her great fear of getting emotionally involved with others, as shown, above all, by her obsessiveness and the large number of negative color responses.

The number of whole responses reflecting readiness to plan for the future and achieve something noteworthy through personal effort, is normal for a person of her intellectual capacity. A closer look reveals, however, that this drive for personal achievement is weakened by a very low W+ per cent. This is only 33 per cent when computed by dividing all the good-form W by the total number of W's. Moreover, there was not one good-form constructive W (13:65-8). Thus her planning is likely to be of poor quality. This conclusion is reinforced by the low percentage of sharply perceived forms, the F+ per cent, which is only 63 per cent. Delia, therefore, would not be capable of persistent and prolonged constructive effort. She would be an under-achiever relative to her high intellectual capacity. Her potential would remain conspicuously unfulfilled.

Delia does not always use common concepts in the usual way. She does not always mean what others mean even when employing the same words. She qualifies her meaning, and these personal qualifications are easily overlooked. This is evidenced, for example, in locating responses in areas different from those which healthy subjects use when giving the same verbal response. For example, when pl. I elicits the association of a winged figure, and the figure itself is placed in the vertical middle, the wings are nearly always the whole symmetrical sides. Delia, however, eliminated the lower halves of the sides. One might argue that such a placing on the blot improved the percept of a winged angel, but then Delia projected a bird onto the same area which is a poor performance. Her third response finally succeeded in covering the whole blot.

In conclusion then, the inner self is much more in flux than the outer self. The internal personality (the afferent or perceiving personality, the one that embodies readiness for particular actions) varies much more from time to time than the outer, overtly acting personality. The rate of recovery from her intellectual lapses is quite low in view of the fact that

the contradictions are so marked. There are very severe internal inconsistencies. On the one hand she prefers to alleviate anxiety by ovrt motor
behavior, but she also has a tendency, though a much weaker one, of
doing the opposite and alleviating anxiety through inhibition of overt motor
behavior. She feels quite passive and compliant and would like to be taken
care of by others, surrendering self-confidence and responsibility in order
to have somebody else take over for her. At other times she is rather assertive though in a somewhat unrealistic manner. Her affects, desires to exchange pleasures or pains with others, are strong (5:228-9) but most of
the time they are negative; that is, she avoids powerful emotional experiences most of the time, while the rest of the time she seeks out such
experiences with equal intensity.

The tendency to under-reaction seems to prevail with greater frequency
and is much more powerful than is the tendency to over-reaction. Much
of her energy is expended in the search for security, rather than in the
pursuit of more constructive goals. She is strikingly on the defensive rather
than on the offensive. Her activity may be characterized as aimed at
avoiding failure rather than achieving success.

Resistance to Psychosis. There is one final issue that we ought to face,
an inquiry into her resources for resistance to the illness. How much passive resistance is there? We know that there is relatively little. Her most
active asset is the capacity for noticing that she is reasoning delusionally at
times and making an attempt at recovering her grasp on reality. The test
record contains several indicators of constitutional strength, which permit
the inference that she is capable of a good deal of resistance to the consequence of her psychosis on this level. One such indicator is the relatively
large number of white space responses, six. The correlation between white
space responses and resistance to psychosis as well as to fatigue in general
has been established on a purely empirical basis and was an unexpected
finding. It discriminates even between more successful and the less successful top industrial management personnel (9:515; 13:85). Schizophrenics
who resist the psychosis also have on the average a large number of S
than those who succumb to it, other conditions being more or less equal.
Another sign of constitutional strength is obsessiveness, which is also correlated with the ability to resist the onslaughts of schizophrenia. Patients
who deteriorate the least, for example, chronic paranoid schizophrenics,
are far more obsessive than hebephrenics or catatonics who deteriorate
much more rapidly and also fail to recover.

There is a positive though not high correlation between producing frank
genital responses and improvement. Delia produced four sex responses each
distinctly different from the others. She also has a very high percentage of

responses with human content. Both the frank sexual responses and the high percentage of human responses reveal an interest in people. Thus even if the capacity for purposeful, consistent, and prolonged action is weak, interest in the environment, the afferent personality, is fairly well developed.

Finally, among the assets which indicate resources for attenuating the effects of the psychosis is the great variety of content. The patient is imaginative; she has very many original responses and thus is intellectually quite flexible. The chances of her learning new ways of handling herself and others, ways of learning to live with her psychosis, are facilitated. It is true that some of the imagination and originality are due simply to lowered standards of reality. A number of inadequately structured original responses, which do not fit their respective blot areas well, are produced as a result of primary thought disorders and weakened capacity for prolonged voluntary attention. Nevertheless, the imagination is striking and keeps Delia sensitive to her environment. She perceives a great many events meaningfully which escape the notice of others.

Future Development. So great a discrepancy between the afferent and efferent personalities is not likely to be stable because of the amount of tension which accompanies it. Will the psychosis become more blatantly manifest or will the personality retreat to a lower level of adjustment? What is Delia's future?

According to the LTPTI the patient is not likely to be improved six years following the initial testing. On the other hand, Delia seems to possess assets sufficient to resist the destructive effects of the psychosis for the next three to six years. If our reasoning is correct so far, we cannot expect changes which require a significant improvement in the quality of thinking or an increase in constructive achievement. The inner balance can then be restored only by changes in more peripheral personality traits, those which are related to the patient's reaction to her psychosis and its effects. Improvement in the subjective attitude toward the psychosis, which is so vital in incipient psychotics, could be obtained by a reduction of futile striving and diminution of sensitivity. The best way to adjust to an unimprovable psychotic condition is to constrict the afferent personality. This Delia can do by becoming less sensitive to the environment, less ambitious and active, limiting herself to activities in which she is not likely to fail. Such an impoverishment of personality would create a chronic depression but it would also avoid disappointments and reduce inner turmoil. The overall personality gain would lie in the disappearance of most of the reasons for fearing social interactions and in greatly diminished inner tensions. By becoming less competitive and free of the strain associated with failure, Delia will have fewer problems though a duller existence.

There are two factors which may facilitate this transition to functioning on a lower but less frustrating level. One of them is her fear of the potential destructive and dangerous forces in the environment. While movement responses appear to be dynamic self-portraits reflecting genuine action tendencies, it is believed that form responses among other things reveal the subject's fear of threat from the environment. Delia visualized considerable destruction in some of her form responses (resp. 23, 24, 30). A constriction of her afferent personality, by reducing contact with the environment, would eliminate most of these fears.

The second factor is related to Delia's great pride. Any person with many human movements is proud. Since Delia is on the defensive and must experience many humiliating frustrations, including failure in competition, she must feel angry, envious, and revengeful. Her most direct destructive aggressiveness toward fellow humans is expressed in resp. 21. Trees do not have a nervous system; they are literally heartless. Projecting a heartless aggressiveness onto a tree (which, however, behaves like a human making the response an M) signifies that Delia deeply represses her strong destructive aggressiveness. Nevertheless, the aggressiveness is there, at least potentially. The enervating effort of maintaining the repression would be largely superfluous if Delia constricted her responsiveness to the environment and her readiness to react to environmental stimulation. Delia can save her pride from hurt by criticism or ridicule by diminishing the frequency and intensity of social contacts. She has already produced a most passive human movement in resp. 19; the figure is not only other-sex (male), but he wears a mask. Perhaps one day Delia will find an excuse to remove the mask and will be able to "lie down" without guilt or anxiety; she would then become passive in interhuman relationships without guilt or anxiety.

Saving her pride, avoiding chances of being injured or destroyed, and becoming more frank with herself, may provide the motivation to change gradually into an underactive but fairly stabilized so-called alpha schizophrenic.[4,7,8,11,12]

Summary. This is a systematic analysis of the Rorschach record of a very intelligent, young schizophrenic woman. The psychosis had already made serious inroads into the intellectual functioning and capacity for achievement at the time of testing. In spite of this, the patient's overt behavior was not markedly deviant. This has been an attempt to reconcile the discrepancy between the obviously psychotic thought processes and imagery, on the one hand, and the strikingly less impaired social functioning, on the other, in terms of principles derived from the perceptanalytic approach to the Rorschach and other sources. An analysis of what enabled the patient to function relatively well despite her dereism, complexities, and very inferior conscious self-control has been our main concern after establishing the diagnosis and prognosis. It is clear that many more conclusions could be drawn from a Rorschach record which contains so much information. The analysis could have been carried further and other avenues of approach explored.[6,7,8,9,13] The richness of the record is a function of the changes associated with the psychosis and the patient's fear of their implications as well as of her very superior intelligence and her artistic talent. But perhaps it is better to stop wanting to say more than to risk losing sight of the forest for the proliferation of trees.

REFERENCES

1. Efron, H.Y. and Piotrowski, Z.A. A factor analytic study of the Rorschach prognostic index. J. Proj. Techn., 30:179-183; 1966.

2. Parker, R.S. and Piotrowski, Z.A. The significance of varieties of actors of Rorschach human movement responses. J. Proj. Techn., 32:33-44; 1968.

3. Piotrowski, Z.A. The Rorschach inkblot method in organic disturbances of the central nervous system. J. Nerv. Ment. Dis., 86:525-537; 1937.

4. Piotrowski, Z.A. A defense attitude associated with improvement in schizophrenia and measurable with a modified Rorschach test. J. Nerv. Ment. Dis., 122:36-41; 1955.

5. Piotrowski, Z.A. Perceptanalysis. 1st print. N.Y. Macmillan. 1957. 2nd print. Philadelphia, Ex Libris. 1965.

6. Piotrowski, Z.A. Rorschach diagnostic evaluation (blind analyses). In The Genain Quadruplets. Rosenthal, D. et al., eds. N.Y. Basic Books. Pp. 269-306; 1963.

7. Piotrowski, Z.A. The Rorschach inkblot method. In Handbook of Clinical Psychology. Wolman, B.B., ed. N.Y. McGraw-Hill. Pp. 522-561; 1965.

8. Piotrowski, Z.A. Theory of psychological tests and psychopathology. In Approaches to Psychopathology. Page, J.D., ed. N.Y. Columbia U. Press. Pp. 165-194; 1966.

9. Piotrowski, Z.A. Psychological testing of intelligence and personality. In Comprehensive Textbook of Psychiatry. Freedman, A.M. and Kaplan, H.I., eds. Baltimore. Williams & Wilkins. Pp. 509-530; 1967.

10. Piotrowski, Z.A. and Efron, H.Y. Evaluation of outcome in schizophrenia: The long-term prognostic test index. In Psychopathology of Schizophrenia. Hoch, P. and Zubin, J., eds. N.Y. Grune & Stratton. Pp. 312-334; 1966.

11. Piotrowski, Z.A. and Levine, D. A case illustrating the concept of the alpha schizophrenic. J. Proj. Techn., 23:223-236; 1959.

12. Piotrowski, Z.A. and Lewis, N.D.C. An experimental diagnostic aid for some forms of schizophrenia. Am. J. Psychiat., 107:360-366; 1950.

13. Piotrowski, Z.A. and Rock, M. The Perceptanalytic Executive Scale: A Tool for the Selection of Top Managers. N.Y. Grune & Stratton. 1963.

14. Rorschach, H. Psychodiagnostics: A Diagnostic Test Based on Perception. 1st ed. 1921. Translated. Bern. H. Huber. 1942.

A SCHAFER INTERPRETATION

The first patient is a 41-year-old, married, childless woman with three years of high school education and an IQ of 110. She was born into an old, aristocratic Southern family and long played the role of the Southern belle. The clinical diagnosis was "conversion hysteria in a hysterical and narcisstic character." Among other symptoms, she had developed localized abdominal pain which seemed to involve hysterial identification with her long-ailing, semi-invalided husband—a man many years her senior and several times close to death not long before the patient's symptoms appeared.

Card I   Reaction Time: 3".   Total Time: 25".
1. (W F ∓ Plant, Dec) That looks like an orchid. [What made it look like an orchid? It could be. How was it like one? I think the shape of it. Anything else? No.]
(a) As the opening response, this unusual image forcefully suggests emphasis on narcissistic-decorative values. (b) The orchid image also seems to include noteworthy passive-receptive connotations: to a woman an orchid is something she gets as a tribute to her attractiveness. (c) Note the utterly unreflective initial response to inquiry.
2. (DF ± Ad) and it looks like elephants, too, with long ears (upper side D).
3. (D F + Cg) And I see a woman's dress (middle D).
The emphasis is on the dress (the outside) and not the equally or more often seen woman (the inside or substance). Thus, the opening narcissistic-decorative theme (I-1) seems to be restated.
That's all.

Card II   Reaction Time: 6".   Total Time: 35".
1. (D F + A P) It looks like a bear to me.
2. (D F (C) + (Hd)) Looks like two little dwarfs or something on top of the bear's heads (upper red). [Dwarfs? They had little caps on their heads and they remind me of the seven dwarfs in Snow White. What made them look like caps? Just the head.]
(a) Dwarfs, like gnomes, leprechauns, midgets, Pinocchios, male puppets or clowns, commonly suggest disparagement or mockery of men. (b) Introducing the idea of Snow White and the seven dwarfs suggests, in addition, the fantasy or hope of being the lovely, innocent, virginal (sexually repressed) little girl who is waited on hand and foot by gallant, sexless and somewhat foolish, depreciated beaux. In these respects, the psychology of Snow White and that of the Southern belle are not far apart.

(c) In this record, as is common in hysterical settings, childhood fantasy and story are major sources of nonbanal Rorschach imagery.

That's about all I see.

Card III   Reaction Time: 10″.   *Total Time*: 35″.

1. (D Ms + H) It looks like two people taking exercise—the little red spot (upper red). [Exercise? They're on their back with their feet in the air.]

(a) This is the only M in this quite repressed record and it is a moderately uncommon M. Its occurrence is all the more striking because the most common M—which is on the same card—is not seen. The image and its theme are likely therefore to have originated from an especially important value or source of anxiety. Also, the image shows us she has the ability to see the popular figures here. The failure of these figures to appear suggests the operation of repression—perhaps in response to the breast-phallus, masculine-feminine problem of integration often posed by this popular M. (b) The image itself suggests concern with physical condition, which in turn could refer to narcissistic interest in appearance (see I-1, I-3, II-2), or to preoccupation with physical symptoms, or both.

2. (W F ∓ A) I don't know what these black spots remind me of; maybe of beetles or something (all black). [Beetle? It looks like an enlarged picture of a fly or something. How? Just the feet (P leg) and the head (lower middle).]

That's all.

Card IV   Reaction Time: 35″.   *Total Time*: 1′.

It doesn't mean a thing to me.

1. (D F + Cg) This . . . (shakes head) . . . looks like a pair of big feet (lower side D). [Any particular kind of feet? Sort of a boot. Can you say any more about it? It just looks heavy to me. It looked like a boot would look if it was drawn by me, for instance, who cannot draw a line.]

That's all I can see. (Anything else?) No. I'm afraid my imagination is not very good.

Emphasis on the bigness of these feet, while not rare, is noteworthy. It seems to express feelings of smallness and inadequacy. In the coming about of this "big feet" response, it is likely that first the entire blot is seen as or sensed to be a large, threatening figure, then the anxiety stimulated by this forming image leads to its partial repression or to disruption of its crystallization, and finally the relatively innocuous "big feet" response forms and is accepted as safe. Three aspects of her response to this card lend support to this inference: (1) the delayed reaction time of 35″ (previous reaction times were only 3″, 6″, and 10″) suggests an initial anxious, repressive response to the blot; (2) so do her repressively-toned opening comment and her hesitation in verbalizing the response; (3) her spontaneous self-disparagement after the response and her self-disparagement in inquiry appear to parallel the implication of feelings of smallness and inadequacy in the "big feet" image itself, and could well have issued from the same source.

Card V   Reaction Time: 1″   Total Time: 30″.
1. (W F + A P) That looks like a bat to me. That's all. (Make sure.) No, that's all that means to me. . . . Nothing else.

Card VI   Reaction Time: 20″.   Total Time: 50″.
1. (W F + Ad P) It could be a bearskin or some animal skin—I don't know what. It could be anything. It looks like some taxidermist has been at work here. [What made it look like a skin? Have you ever seen— you have, of course—a skin stretched out? You see the feet and the tail. Anything else make it look like that? No. Just the shape of it.] (Anything else?) No, that's all. All animals!
Possibly more self-derogation, or else uneasiness about the possible unconscious, instinctual significance of her "animal" fantasies.

Card VII   Reaction Time: 25″.   Total Time: 55″.
1. (D F + Hd P) It just looks like two figures of two women (upper 1/3, two heads facing each other, with some kind of exaggerated hairdo (rejects card). (Keep on.) . . . Nothing.

Card VIII   Reaction Time: 10″.   Total Time: 35″.
1. (D F + A P) More animals! It looks like a rodent of some kind to me; a rat. (Anything else?) No. . . .
2. (D CF Rock) A rock at the bottom (lower pink and orange). [Rock? Just the color and the way it's shaped. Coral or. . . .]

Card IX   Reaction Time: 15″.   Total Time: 1′ 20″.
1-2. (Dd F ± Ad; Dd F ± Plant) I wouldn't know what that was, unless it's some kind of beetle on top there (upper middle orange projections). [What made it look like a beetle? The antennae; maybe the head. Could I see it? (Card shown.) No, not a beetle. It could be a stick, a branch of a tree, a dead branch.]
(a) The appearance of the dead branch image only during inquiry, as

well as the long pause between No. 1 and No. 3, suggests that this image may have been repressed to begin with. (b) This dead branch image appears to express the theme of the male figure's death or impotence through age. In turn, this inference suggests intense ambivalence, anxiety and repressive efforts in the area of fantasy and feeling about her husband's age and illness.

I couldn't tell you. (Nothing else?) No. (Take your time.). . .

3. (D F ± Cg) It looks like a . . . it could be an armor too. You know, knights in armor: the helmet and steel (lower center is helmet; lower red areas are steel shoulder plates.

(a) This response, like Snow White and the seven dwarfs in II-2, sounds the theme of gallantry, ladies fair and damsels in distress. This is hysteric imagery, Southern-belle style. (b) It is also conceivable that this image was partly determined by the patient's own need to ward off hostile intrusion.

Card X   Reaction Time: 15″.   *Total Time:* 1′.

1. (D F + A) I see a dog (middle yellow).

2. (D FC + A) And some caterpillars (lower green). [What made it look like a caterpillar? It was long and green and I just despise them.] Her volunteering "I just despise them" appears to have two major implications: (1) it is a naive, egocentric response to inquiry in that she gives a feeling as a determinant of the response instead of a perceptual aspect of the blot. It is not unusual for repressive, hysterical women to respond in this egocentric manner during the test; (2) the verbalization may have phobic implications, and, because phobias typically develop where strong repressive emphases prevail, it suggests noteworthy repressiveness. That is not to say that all people with bug-phobias are primarliy repressive in their defensive strategy. The phobic and repressive inferences derive their chief support from this patient's naive, egocentric and spontaneous style of verbalizing this fear.

3. (D FC + Plant) And maybe a flower bud (side yellow with gray base). [Flower bud? Just the shape: a half of it, not a full. . . . Anything else? The coloring: the yellow and the . . . I think it was green. I'm not sure; I can't remember.]

The theme here is one of birth and youth, a theme that may in one respect express concern over her childlessness and in another respect nostalgia for her youth and worry over losing her youthful charms.

4. (D F + A) At the top it looks like some more bugs, beetles or something (upper gray).

That's all.

All through the test the patient has been in great haste to give back the cards. Her average total-time-per-card is only 46″, despite relatively strong pressure from the testor that she take her time. Like delayed reaction times and card rejections, short total times frequently betray a repressive (and avoidant or ego-restrictive) defensive emphasis. The repressive person flees from this situation because he is deeply afraid of free fantasy, that is, of relaxing repressive barriers in the interest of imaginative, creative, self-expressive responses. This patient leaves the game while she's ahead, so to speak.

Summary of Scores

R: 19   EB: 1-2

Average Total Time: 46″

W	4	F+	9	A	7	W%	21
D	14	F±	3	Ad	3	D%	74
Dd	1	F∓	2	H	1		
		Ms	1	Hd	1	F%	74-95
		FC	2	(Hd)	1	F+%	86-89
		CF	1	Plant	2		
		F(C)	1	Cg	3		
				Dec	0+1	A%	53
				Rock	1	H%	11-16
						P	5
						P%	26

In summary, thematic analysis suggests that this is a naive, egocentric, repressive, narcissistic woman with significant feelings of smallness and inadequacy. She appears to try to view herself as a fair, innocent, virginal damsel in distress who needs somewhat depreciated and sexless but attentive beaux to admire her and minister to her, and who also needs a hero to save her. Also suggested is noteworthy anxiety over physical status, aging, infirmity and death, particularly that of the male figure but possibly her own as well. A phobic trend may also be present.

The summary of scores strongly supports the inference of heavy reliance of repressive defense: R is relatively low; there is only 1 M and that is a small one (Ms); the variety of content is limited and the responses generally banal (A%, P% high); she spends short total-times-per-card despite the tester's pressure; and the low W and Dr are consistent with this repressive picture. The relative absence of emotional lability and anxiety in her manner of taking the test is paralleled in the scores by the absence of shading rsponses, the relatively low sum C, the prevalence of FC over CF, the adequate F% and the moderately high F+%. We may infer therefore that this patient's repressive and narcissistic defenses and her symptoms are working fairly well to seal off anxiety; however, her eagerness to get rid of the cards and the breakthrough of anxiety-arousing images (or its clear imminence) suggest that her defenses are by no means invulnerable.

The role of the patient's intellectual level in this test picture is, of course, relevant. Her level—IQ of 110—is not high enough to allow for a rich record. But this consideration only leads us into the problem of the genetic interrelationship between endowment and choice of defenses. As a rule, repression seems to be favored for defensive purposes by those who are intellectually mediocre or relatively limited, just as the obsessive-compulsive defenses seem to be the defenses of choice among those who are intellectually precocious. We do not seem to be dealing with an either-or proposition. More or less limited endowment seems to favor turning away from mastery of reality and conflict through intellect and tends to foster repressive solutions to problems; in turn, these repressive solutions may lead to neglect and even devaluation of such intellectual assets or potentialities as are present. In the end the IQ is the resultant of interaction of, on the one hand, the limits set by endowment, and, on the other hand, the defensive and adaptive solutions which produce significant variations within these limits. Early environment also seems to play a major part in this interaction.

The question of the evidence for neurosis must also be considered. A repressive emphasis is clear in this record, but experience with relatively well-functioning women of average intelligence indicates no distinctive features in this record that prove that this woman now has a moderately disabling hysterical symptom requiring psychiatric treatment. Narcissistic character features are also plain but there is no evidence that these extend outside the normal range. In fact, some warmth and adaptiveness is implied by her FC-CF distribution and by the content of her color responses. Of course, if we define "neurosis" very broadly, we could say that a neurotic pattern is evident, but this definition probably would bring most everyone into the domain of neurosis. Moreover, it still would not differentiate the relatively well-functioning, asymptomatic, non-patient "neurotic" from the poorly functioning patient with symptoms. It can only be concluded therefore that this Rorschach record shows neurotic hysterical-repressive trends.

A HERTZ INTERPRETATION*

ELLEN: A GIRL, TEN YEARS OF AGE

Stated Reasons for Referral

Mother: Ellen has been expelled from two boarding schools and now has been asked to leave the day school she is presently attending. She has failed repeatedly. She is a reading problem. She has engaged in all sorts of misbehavior and minor delinquencies. The mother listed disobedience, belligerence, destructiveness, lying, stealing, and "sexual precocity." The mother is requesting examination to determine the nature of the child's disorder" and to get guidance as to what kind of school or "institution" would be appropriate for the child.

Ellen: "They want to know what to do with me. I guess I'm pretty bad."

Behavior in Test Situation

At first Ellen was very friendly to the examiner and seemed to be co-operative. As the test proceeded, however, she showed more and more irritability and impatience and became increasingly petulant, demanding and negativistic. When the eighth card was presented, she was openly hostile.

Throughout the test she seemed to fluctuate between childish dependency and demandingness and then independence and rebellion. She continually demanded help, comfort and reassurance. She courted approval and praise. Sometimes she adopted a helpless attitude and indulged in considerable

---

* Our procedure is first to analyze the total Rorschach situation blindly, i.e. without knowledge of the case history or of the interview material. We start with observations on Behavior in the test situation. We then consider the *Sequence Analysis* and proceed to an analysis of the psychogram. We then summarize the results of the "blind" analysis based on formal patterns, content, and behavior. Our second step is to write a summary of the Rorschach results integrated with other test data, case history and interview material, with recommendations as to intervention. This final summary is the report.

For a description of the scoring symbols utilized with definitions, scoring formulae and qualitative notations, reference should be made to Hertz, M. R.: *Rorschach Scoring Symbols* (mimeo), Department of Psychology, Case-Western Reserve University, 1966.

For a description of the location symbols used and for the scoring of form quality, original and popular responses, references should be made to Hertz, M. R.: *Frequency Tables for Scoring Rorschach Responses,* The Press of Case-Western Reserve University, Cleveland, Ohio, 1967 edition.

		W	FM+	A	P
I. (3") that looks like a butterfly//	Because those are like feelers and wings and his feet are here (3)// He looks as if he is flying and you know what, it's scared or something and it is flying away//	W 0.5			emot!
there's a person on each side sort of...but I think it's more like a butterfly//	I see the head(12) and even the nose of this person, and here the coat and arm(2) and oh yes, the leg(29)// It is as if someone is fancy dressed// One is facing outward here and the other is facing the other way// Yes, this is the arm(2) out and the coat is back here(4,5)// You know like in folds(4,5)//	D ----	M- Fc - Rep of R ---	H App	O-
this little creature in here is like a flying animal (31)//	Well I saw the animal and it has big eyes(9) and his feelers are out(1) and he is going up and out like this//	D	FM+	A	
and I guess these look like people don't you think so? Well don't they?..................... ....I see them plainly, these persons going this way and that//	I don't believe this is just an inkblot and I don't think ink was just dropped// It is like someone painted it, don't you think so//	---- ---- ----	Rep of R --- Questions --- Suspicious ---		
Here's like a stand..... or a tail of something//(3)	Yes it is a stand, like for a Christmas tree// You know how they have a stand at the bottom to hold them up//	Dr	F+	Hh	O+ wt-bal
	Well it is a plain tail of an animal, like an alligator's tail// It looks just like it//	Drf	F+	Ad	
That looks like a head (12) and arm (2) and foot (29) and there's the tail of each man's coat(4,5)//		----	Detailing ---		
These little dots look like dots of black...I mean of coal... just like pieces of coal//	That's all it could be, pieces of coal// Coal is black...and these pieces are all around//	Dr	Ch"F+	Coal	O+
I guess that's all there is here//					

Oh wait,there's a pumpkin there (V upper 2/3), don't it look like that? Right here you see eyes and nose and mouth//	Well it is cut out, with eyes (6), nose (8) and mouth (7,7)// It is cut out that way// I didn't count this(lower third)	Dr(s)	F+	Bo-obj	
Here I also see legs(V 12), and two arms (2),like a person with legs out like this(shows)// (W)	Well it just looks like it// Thats is all I can say// (looks off, disregards another question)	W ——— 0.5	Me-	H	O-
Hey wait, wait a minute, that's sort of like a stage coach in olden days. ...you know two men to sit there and some in back..	Well you hold it this way (V), and this part (lower 2/3) is the coach with windows (6,7)... and men are sitting in it// (Where?)well they are there anyway............... this could be the man's horse (2) if you want to put it in (laughs)// (where are the men in the back?)// Here don't you see them, here's the head (34)//	Dr(s) + Dr g 0.5 ((D	F- F- ----- F- Humor?	Str H ----- A	O- O- O- O-))
(150")					
II. Oh,oh, another one...I really don't know if I can answer this//					
(20")well you can say, here is a heart (V2))// and then	Well that's a person's heart, like in a valentine// You know how they are cut out//	S	F+	Art	O+
here is a light (4)//	It could be a fire, it's red// It shoots up//	D	CFm+	Fire	
(3) stockings are here//	Don't they have the shape? Don't they look just like socks?	D	F+	App	
Oh, here are two men (S) raising some candles (12) like this//	Here is the heads (3) and their coats and their feet are like this (shows) and this is the way they hold the two candles//	W ——— 1.0	Me+ Fc+	H Hh	P
could be a bridge in the background (36)//	These tiny lines, so tiny it's the only thing it could be// It is far off I guess//	Dr! ——— 1.5	F(C)+	Str	O+

Page 4

Case: 20-13-9

two feet here (6,7)//	These are the men's feet//	----	Detailing	----	
Hey, I changed it, that looks like mean faces//(3)	Because they are witches//				emot!
that's all I can think of here//	They're witches because they are so wicked and powerful, and their tongues are sticking out//				power!
V I don't see anything more (holds card, looks intently)					(agg)
V you know, these are two men upside down and there's fire up here in the middle//	Well I told you before, these are the men (same as above, but upside down), the same ones but now they are this way// Fire is the red that I said before//	---Rep of R u.d.--- + g 0.5------------0- comb			
V looks like a mountain here (top of 5) and big flames are coming off the mountain// (4)	This is the mountain (5+5)// Don't that look like a mountain? And the fire is on top, the way it is formed, sort of shooting out//	+ D 1.0 comb	F(C)+	Mt	
that's all I can think of// (110)					
III. Now that's a hard one...I don't know if I can do this		-- complains re difficulty-- -- self-depreciation--			
10"Well here is a butterfly (5)//	The wings are formed like this and inside is the body// that's all// It is just a butterfly//	D	F+	A	P
And here is red iron hanging down, red hot I mean// (V 4)	Well red iron hangs that way you know like things hang from a tree like...the iron is cooking, and then it gets hot and bulges// No I do not mean it is hanging from a tree, it is just hanging from something..it is just red hot iron bulging, and dripping//	D	CF+ cFm+	Iron	O+
that...these men..they look like skeletons, and sort of like......	Well these are skeltons just sitting..or on a rock or near a rock(1)// they are not fat and have no clothes on them// Then look at this space, they have to	W(s) 1.0 ((g 0.5------------0-))	Me-f+	Anat-obj Rock	P

	be skeletons, what else could they be// Just as if they are on a rock, waiting for the iron to be done, and while they are waiting they are trying to catch the butterfly//				
	They are skeletons, because they are as I told you, they are so skinny, and there is an open hole here//				
a face, sort of, here (1+1) and then I suppose it could be........	Well you see the spaces for the eyes (35) and nose, (20) and the mouth could be down here(33)//	D(s)	F-	Hd	
the yarn you buy (5)//	It is bunched out and squeezed in here in the middle as you see yarn // It is nice and soft//	D	Fc+	Yarn	O+
V (4) cranes//	cranes have legs, as if standing in something, you know how they stand in ponds, with one leg up//	D	FM+	A	
V this way, a man's arms (2), and eyes and forehead (1+1) and a crack in the nose//............ and you could say his feet are here (6,6) (84")	Well you can see him raising his hands, no arms like this (gestures) and he is very happy//	W(s) 1.0	Me+ ↓ F-	H	split! emot!
IV. Oh, I just don't know what I am going to do with this......			----Self depreciation---		
(10") V feelers and eyes and there's prickles on him//	Well it is all this (2), but I don't know what it is or he is I don't have the slightest idea....All I see, something with feelers, eyes, lots of prickles//	D	cF-	A?	O-
like a fairy-sea animal, too, you know, half lady and half fish (V3)	Well, these (9) are like people down to here(shows) and then the tails (4) swoop up//	D 1.5	F+	HA	O+

Date.....................

Examiner: Hertz

man with arms and big feet sitting on a prickly bush//	Well you see the prickles here (6), and this is the man's head (5+5) and his arms (4) are flung out and here are his huge feet (1)// He's on this bush (2). It is all, you know, bushy and prickly//	W 1.0	Mf-è+ Fc+	H Bo	P size
(55") That's it//					
V.					
(3")That's all together...here are the wings and feelers and legs, and that's all I can say because it is a flying animal//	It's flying because it's scared, but you really can't scare a bat// Well someone scared him, but you really can't scare a bat// Well as I said, it's a big black bat, scared//	W 0.5	FM+ FCh+	A	P emot!
a crooked prickler bush this (W)//	Well it's bushy all over and it's got pricklers on each side//	W 0.5	cF-	Bo perseveration "prickles"	0-
This way (V) the same bat, but his arms are downward now// Of course, I mean bat's wings//	Yes, it is the same bat, and his wings are down now// Well I meant wings//	----	Rep of R,u.d.-----		
Here//	Wait, well if you don't count the feelers (5,2) and take these ends off (6+7) like a banana, sort of crooked banana, on its back//	((Dr!	F-	Ed	0-)) Proj!
(45")					
VI.					
(5") Whew, this is a turtle//	The whole thing// because it is big and round//this could be the shell (S+S), and here the head (1)//	W 1.0	Fc+	A	
a starfish//	Well, it has these things out, 1,2,3,4,5,6...Just like a starfish// It looks like it//	W 0.5	F-	A counting	proj!
a humming bird up here// (1)	It just looks like it//these are wings (18) and in the center, the body//	D	F+	A	
The same upside down//		---- u.d.		----	

Page 7

Case: 20-13-9

Date............................

Examiner: Hertz

V and here is a high mountain (5) and there are two guards in here (24) standing up there with knives (8)//	Well it is far away, this mountain, see how it goes up and these are the heads (32) that's what you can see, and these the knives// they are guarding something//	D + Dr	F(C)+ F+	Mt Hd Weap	
		g 1.5 comb	-------	-------	-O+
A country sort of all around in here (area around center)//	Well country is sort of formed like that...on Television you see American...well like map of where it is// it's shaded like that on maps to show it//	Drv	ChFv+	Map	
(60")					
VII. What in the name is this? Really!					
(12") sea or land//	Well this is the sea(10) and there is land all around,like on a map//	S(W) 0.5	Fv+	Map	
A flashlight (V 12)...... ....or...............	It is the form of it and it lights up here (6)// this here makes me think you know how the light goes out// I mean the fuzzy shading like//	D 1.5	FCh+	Hh	O+
it could be a bomb (12)//	I said a bomb because they are made that way and that's how they look when they are lying down// Just like inlets in here and here (indentations inner side of D 2 and D 3)//	D	F+	weap	O+
V A fat lady, head is somewhere here (3+3) and here arms are out(4) and here are her legs (8)// She is like this (shows)//	Well just like a big fat lady, with her body here(10) and you can see her sort of standing up// Well I suppose there's a nose in the center and the eyes would have to be here and here (inside D 3)//	W(S) 0.5	Me-	H	O- H derog.
(55")					

VIII. What more? How many more must I have?					
(9") well that's like a map sort of like rivers around and land and more land??	Well here are the rivers (all spaces) and it just looks like you see, a map// could be of anything// This is one country and this is another country// like on a map, these colored maps//	W(s) 0.5	C/F+	Map	
Wolfs crawling (1)//	Well it just looks like that// Just here (1)//	D	FM+	A	P
I can't get much more out of here// (holds card)					
V animal flying here (5+5)// The arms, I mean wings are out//	It could be any kind of flying animal//	Dr	FM+	A	
That's all// (emphatically) (50")					
IX. Say I want to get rid of these ....I have been here hours and hours...what do you think!					
12") These are the same thing, all over again...land and sea... and in here (30) little green patches (20) in the middle of the ocean//	That's all it could be...looks like that, that's all// It's like map in a book like I said before//	W(s) 0.5 + Dr(s) 1.5	C/Fv+ F+	Map Island	 O+
this is not much like animals... no..no..there are no animals in here//	Well all this could be ocean, and here little green patches all alone out here//				
(45")					
X. Oh...now... (5") big round things that have lots of legs...you know what I mean//		D	F+	A	P
a fish here (9)	Well it has the shape of a fish, that's all//	D	F-	A	

Page 9

Case: 20-13-9

Date.........................

Examiner: Hertz

and a snake (3)	The snake has that form, and there are snakes that color//	D	FC+	A	P
lions (7)//	See the form here, they are lions//	D	F+	A	
sea monsters (4)//	You see pictures of sea monsters like that//	D	F+	(A)	
little red land (1)	This all could be land, and it is that color on a map//	Dv	C/F+	Map	
(50")	Could be a walnuts hanging down from a tree or something (14)// No I mean just hanging down//	((Dr	F+	Bo	O+))

Probing:
  (Color) Yes I said maps because maps are colored that way
           to show different lands or countries. No, I said yarn
           here, because that is the shape it comes in// yarn
           can be in any color//

  (Human movement) These are skeletons here, not people
           because they are bony and separate here, see the
           hole. They could not be people// Yes they are
           sitting down or bending, no crouching...

  (Populars) This here? It's the yarn.

       IV. I told you what this was. That's all it is//

      VII. I told you about the land, didn't I?

self-criticism and self-derogation, expressing feelings of futility as to the success in her handling the test. She anticipated failure even before she attacked a blot. She tried again and again to give up. Occasionally she flared up, belligerently refusing to apply herself. With persuasion, she continued but gave only minimal response.

Ellen seemed uneasy because of the relative freedom which the Rorschach situation provided. She needed, wanted and demanded more specific directions. She seemed unwilling to make her own decisions as to meanings. She seemed to define each Rorschach task as an authoritarian one, visualizing certain demands and expectations which were never imposed, but which she herself superimposed. She felt for example under pressure to give responses which were "expected." She felt she should find "animals" in one card. She needed the agreement of the examiner as to what she was seeing. As a result she seemed to be under considerable pressure to meet imagined rules and demands in the test.

Despite the fact Ellen wanted help and reassurance from the examiner, she seemed to fight these dependent tendencies an dassumed an air of bravado and became negativistic, hostile and rebellious. She tried to provoke the examiner by openly expressing her distaste of the test and her resentment toward the examiner because there were "so many blots."

Ellen seemed to distrust the examiner. She was suspicious of the test. She did not believe that the blots were just ordinary inkblots. She seemed to be threatened by the examiner, the test, and the whole testing situation. She therefore became more and more cautious and inhibited as the test proceeded and restricted her productivity. She appeared to have one goal in mind: to finish and to escape. Ellen was highly distractible. She frequently looked around the room, making comments on the books and papers on the desk. She was easily fatigued. She seemed to have difficulty in persevering to the end of the test.

Thus Ellen appeared to be a contradiction, at times compliant, childishly submissive, demanding help, reassurance and praise, at other times uncooperative, negativistic, independent, and rebellious.

Sequence Analysis

Card I

Our first impression is that Ellen is highly productive since she gives seven responses to the first card. Her mental procedure in attacking the blot appears on the whole to be adequate. She sizes up the whole situation in a short time, then analyzes the blot into parts, reacting to usual areas, and finally differentiates the blot into smaller areas. This is the usual procedure which most people take. Ellen is, however, prone to focus more on rare and unusual details. Emphasis on rare details sometimes reflect a a need for accuracy and correctness. With Ellen it may also indicate that she is awed by the complexity or the novelty of the situation. She may therefore prefer to handle the smaller areas, because she fears she cannot succeed with the larger blot. Again, the overemphasis on rare details may reflect a kind of fragmented attention, a swing of the attention from one area to another. Finally, her procedure suggests a kind of escape reaction from areas which stimulate anxiety within her. She may turn to the smaller areas because she is unwilling or unable to face certain imagery which the larger areas stimulate.

We note that Ellen goes from the top area (D 31) to the bottom (Dr 3) and then to the tiny spots off the side figure (Dr 20) omitting the center figure which frequently is seen as a female figure (D 17). The female figure which may represent for her the mother figure may threaten her so that she tries to ignore it (denial). This appears to be corroborated by the fact that she gives a fragmentary detail (Drf 3). Further, twice she arbitrarily delimits the whole, responding to two-thirds of the figure. We believe therefore that Ellen's procedure reflects at least in part an attempt to avoid certain areas which stimulate imagery she cannot tolerate. It may be the center "female" figure (D 17), or the side figures which frequently elicit human responses, or the center pincer-like projections which frequently arouse imagery of hostility, attack, violence and even destructiveness. With the fragmentary detail she handles only a part of an area which no doubt arouses disturbing imagery, thus decreasing the impact of the threat and preventing the whole image from jelling into something which is disconcerting to her.

Ellen's reality testing is uneven. While she is capable of seeing her world clearly (F+), too often her grasp of reality is poor (F–). Her thinking tends to be illogical and even distorted (O–). Analysis of the content of her response suggests that it is not lack of ability which is causing the misperceptions and the distortions, but personal problems.

At the beginning, Ellen is able to see the things which most people see (P). She gives the "butterfly." The response is a conventional one but it is saturated with details of perception and comments that individualize it. The "butterfly is scared" and it is "flying away from something." These elaborations are made with such feeling and intensity that we hypothesize that Ellen is projecting her own feelings of fear and her own preoccupation with escape and flight. We have noted her escape tendency in her reactions to rare areas. Our question is, of what or of whom is she scared. Why does she feel the need to flee? We get some answers from the responses which follow.

Ellen sees "persons on each side" but they are not the usual forms which are sometimes given (the usual F+ H). The human figures she sees are facing away from each other, with arms extended (D 2) and profiles along the outer edge of the top area (Dr 12). Usually when human forms are projected into the side areas, they are most easily seen as turning inward. This is fantasy in which the form percept is inaccurate (M−). It is a distortion in fantasy. Ellen seems to be revealing something very personal in this response. There is the possibility that the figures which sometimes present parental figures for children are going in opposite directions. We wonder whether they disturb Ellen because her parents are separated or divorced or because there is some dissension in the home.

We note that the human figues take a passive attitude at first—they are just facing outward. It is only in the inquiry that she suggests some extensor movement ("arms are out"). She may be projecting her feelings of tension and conflict because of some impending and disturbing activity on the part of the parental figures.

We hypothesize then conflicts in reference to parental figures, conflicts which are severe enough to root up material from the deeper unconscious. We also hypothesize that Ellen may take recourse to daydreams and use her imagination autistically, fleeing into an inner world and living in unreality.

It is of interest that Ellen dresses up the figures. This may just be a childish elaboration. Children like to get dressed up. Again, it may be a covering concept. Ellen may feel the need to hide the figures because she cannot face them directly. She may be "prettying them up," really seeing them as dark and evil (reaction formation). She may feel guilty because of her feelings toward them and try to make up by using happy or benign figures (denial).

In seeing clothing and "the folds," Ellen reacts to the texture (Fc). This suggests sensitivity to the environment, especially to social contact and social interaction. Further, texture responses frequently reflect a need and a longing for affectionate contact, a kind of affect hunger. Implied are feeling of deprivation of contact, dependency longings and feeling of rejection. Since texture is used in conjunction with the human figures, which appear to disturb Ellen, we feel that affect hunger is definitely in the picture.

We have further evidence that the figures disturb Ellen. She returns again and again to them, lingering descriptively on body parts (stimulus perseveration) and describing them in detail (detailing) sometimes with minor variations. Detailing is not unusual in the records of children six or seven years of age or under. Here then it suggests anxiety. Ellen tries to handle her anxiety by breaking the percept into parts and dwelling on them separately. It is a kind of anxious restriction in functioning to that which is definite and certain. Indeed constant repetition and additions of this nature suggest the defense of undoing. Not only does Ellen try to contradict the imagery with its associated feelings which she originally experienced but she tries to do something about it, to set right the original imagery which was intolerable to her. By repetition and elaboration she discounts the implications of her original experience. If you talk long enough about something, it may lose its original meaning.

The next response "flying animal" is acceptable in form quality (F+). The emphasis on the "big eyes" however may point to suspicious attitudes. This is substantiated in the inquiry where she frankly shows her suspiciousness. She does not believe that these are just inkblots. They must have some hidden meaning and purpose.

We note that Ellen asks the examiner for reassurance. In fact she does this throughout the card and throughout the test. Indeed she demands help rather aggressively. She appears insecure and uncertain of herself. She is unwilling to make decisions on her own. This reflects dependency.

We next get alternatives to the bottom detail (Dr 3) both of which are realistically perceived (F+). Ellen sees a "stand for a Christmas tree" and an "alligator's tail." The stand appears to be a support concept. It may well be that Ellen is concerned with support, either physical or psychological. Since her physical needs seem amply met and since we have already noted evidence of dependency, we again hypothesize feelings of insecurity, concern and fears that she has not firm ground upon which to stand. She may feel she cannot stand on her own feet. She appears to have a deep need for psychological sustenance, comfort, encouragement, approval, and acceptance.

As we have indicated, the "alligator's tail" (the fragmentary detail) is not usual by itself. The whole alligator is sometimes seen in the center detail (D 17). Why does she limit her image? Fragmentary details sometimes are due to limited ability. They also suggest some inhibitory factors at work. Sometimes strong anxiety prevents an individual from seeing the whole object. Ellen may be fragmenting her perception because she cannot deal with the disturbing image as a whole. It has been observed by some clinicians (Phillips and Smith) that the alligator image is often given by hostile, aggressive and strongly negativistic individuals who try to attain their ends, often destructively, by whatever means available, with little self-reproach for their wrong-doing. This hypothesis may apply here. Ellen may be avoiding the image and the destructive impulses associated with it by denying the whole (defense of denial) and by restricting herself to a part (isolation)'.

Alternatives in perceptual choice frequently reflect indecision. We often have this kind of response in pictures of dependence. In giving alternatives, Ellen may be trying to defend against the admission of her need for support. Or she may have been trying to censor the alligator image by giving a more acceptable Christmas tree image. Repression partially fails, however, and she reveals part of the disturbing image.

Another hypothesis should be considered, despite the fact Ellen is only ten years old. It may be that the area (Dr 3) which sometimes elicits a symbolic image, disturbs her because of the sexual implications. If this hypothesis holds, Ellen uses several defensive techniques to handle the anxiety which is aroused. She renders the image lifeless and hence less threatening ("stand") in which event we have objectification and displacement. She resorts to a childhood image ("Christmas tree") which may be a form of regression. Again she uses symbolism ("tail" for the phallic object).

Ellen next escapes to the rare area (Dr 20) seeing "pieces of coal," stimulated especially by the black color. Reacting to black color points to underlying fear, anxiety and depressed feelings. Some clinicians suggest that it also reflects withdrawal from outside stimulation because of traumatic experiences in one's life. Klopfer calls this the "burnt child reaction." Piotrowski goes further and suggests that black color responses also reflect a need to protest only and actively when faced with anxiety situations. We hypothesize then that Ellen is filled with doubts and uncertainty, that she has forebodings of threat and danger and that she feels the need to act and handle the situation which provokes so much anxiety. She may act out in similar situations which threaten her.

Ellen now tries to give up the card saying "I guess that's all there is here." This terminal statement again reflects her lack of certainty and indecision. She only guesses that she can't do better. Yet Ellen holds the card and persists. Perhaps something in the blot is holding her, compelling her to attend. Or she may be defining the task as an authoritarian one. She may feel that she is supposed to give more responses. In this event, she is projecting her own super-ego-based pressures onto the situation.

After a pause, Ellen sees the "pumpkin face," holding the card inverted, reacting to the upper two-thirds of the blot, and cutting off the bottom area. While we frequently get a face of some kind for the whole blot, we rarely have subjects restrict themselves to the upper part. We have already indicated that certain imagery is disconcerting to her and hence she denies it. In addition her dependency is again revealed. With this comparatively easy response, she again asks for reassurance. She seems to be in desperate need for direction, authority, and acceptance.

A highly different response follows. Holding the card inverted, Ellen sees "a person . . . with legs (D 12) . . . and arms out (D 2)." This again is human movement where form quality is very poor (M–), which, as we have indicated, is commonly associated with regressive and/or autistic thinking. What this figure means to her and what is the substance of the fantasy we cannot say at this time. Suffice to say here it points to faulty perception of the human form.

The final response is a childish one, which, however, is highly forced. Again she limits herself to the upper two-thirds of the blot. With the card inverted she sees "stage coach . . . in older days." This may be a confabulatory percept, since, in the inquiry she indicates "windows" for the spaces. Again, the percept may have been induced by the previous response of "pumpkin" and she may have associated freely. In the original response, she indicates "two men used to sit there and some in the back." She explains this in the inquiry by showing the "heads" of two men (Dr 34)'. Again this points to confabulation, a highly primitive mode of thinking. It is what Piaget calls transductive thinking.

In the inquiry, she elaborates even more, giving far-fetched additions, and combining separate percepts into impossible combinations (g-O- combination). Whatever was her initial percept, she extended it inappropriately. The image suggested by one or two areas initiated a series of elaborations, almost in the manner of free association. Such combinations suggest irrealistic and autistic ideas. Such combinations and confabulations are common in very young children. In Ellen, they suggest regressive modes of thinking. They imply the probable presence of irrealistic autistic thinking. Yet Ellen seems to be aware of what she is doing. She sees things in relationship which aren't there ("men sitting in the coach," "the man's horse")' but she laughs in a pleased way as if she is getting pleasure in misperceiving and distorting. This implies a kind of malicious aggressiveness and stubborn persistence in putting things together which do not belong together. In real life, she may make up stories and enjoy the deceptions.

Card II

There is a long delay before the first response to this card. It is the longest initial reaction time in the whole record. Strain and tension are immediately inferred. The question is why?

First, she appears filled with fears of failure. She has little confidence in her ability to handle the task. Indeed we note such expressions of inability and self-disparagement throughout the record. Second, the impact of the color may disturb her. Color arouses affect; red color, hostility and violence. It may be she feels she cannot cope with her hostile impulses. Third, it may be the massive darkness of the side areas which arouse anxiety. Fourth, it may be the side figures which frequently are seen as human forms and for children often represent parental figures. We have already noted this disturbance in her reactions to the preceding blot.

We feel that all these factors contribute to her disturbance. We have color shock, possibly shading shock, and human-form shock. We say this because her general mental procedure in attacking the situation is highly erratic. She reacts first to a large space, then goes directly to the red areas, top and bottom, and only later reacts to the whole (reversed succession). She then continues to react to a very rare and minute area and finally to a usual detail. In addition she reacts to color with explosive content. The popular human form is delayed but when given, is repeated and elaborately detailed. The popular animals for D 5 are not given. Ellen's whole behavior reflects the strain and tension she is experiencing.

Ellen's first response is highly significant since it is a reaction to the space (S 2). This is most unusual for the first response, since it is a complete reversal of figure and ground. It is a childish response, "a heart" like in "a valentine." This appears to be a defensive operation, an escape reaction, enabling her to withdraw from the sources of disturbance (the red color representing violent emotions) or the silhouettes (representing parental figures). The complete reversal points to strong oppositionalism in her make-up which may take the form of resistiveness, stubbornness, or hostile negativism. Again it may also point to a need for mastery either of the situation or of her underlying hostility.

The content of the response is childish but not unusual for a child of Ellen's age. It may however be a regressive operation, a negation of the threatening implications of the other aspects of the card.

After the space, Ellen turns to the color areas, which no doubt she had tried to avoid. She sees "light" for D 4, but it is really "fire shooting up." Fire is an aggressive destructive erupting image suggesting explosive emotions. It is associated with anxiety and foreboding (Ch). Some clinicians suggest that explosive fire of this nature (negative color) reflects strong fear of close contact with others, which may develop into hate when an individual feels cornered and is unable to sever emotional ties with others (Piotrowski). This hypothesis appears to be verified by another pattern, the inanimate movement (m) which frequently appears in the records of individuals who experience certain impulses which they dare not gratify and which are repressed, resulting in tension and frustrations.

Finally the usual human figures are seen (P delay) in movement. Structurally the response is a good one (M+). She is able to analyze the blot into its relevant parts, project forms into them which are accurate (F+), see relationships and build up an accurate combination (Wg), utilizing her imaginative resources (M+). Her human figures, however, are not "clowns dancing" as we often get, especially with children. They are not figures in hostile interaction as we sometimes get. They are men in an inocuous sort of activity, just "holding candles." This is a kind of a "static M" which is often a disguise for some other desired but unacceptable activity. Our subject may be denying the hostile interaction between the figures perhaps repressing or inhibiting her own hostile impulses. The content "candles" is a household object and a feminine interest. The men really are females in her imagery. This is verified later.

Again, even though our subject is not yet ten, we keep in mind that this area sometimes has special phallic significance for adults. They often objectify this area, thus dehumanizing it and making it safe and acceptable. A "phallic" area was objectified in similar fashion in Card I.

Characteristically our subject runs away from areas which evidently have conjured up disturbing imagery and escapes to two very rare details, too little lines (Dr: 36) which she sees as "a bridge in the distance." Why a bridge? A bridge is often an escape symbol. Clinicians have noted that "bridges" are sometimes given by insecure people who search for security and who feel that they have no one on whom they can depend. In children, "bridges" often reflect disturbed relationships with nurturing or parental figures so that they want to escape. We have already noted such a problem. She has shown her insecurity and the need to escape before. But the bridge is tiny and far away. It is beyond her reach. It does not offer her much means of escape. Thus she may be expressing the futility of her position. There is no way out.

It is obvious that the human figures "hold" Ellen. She is so riveted to the disturbing figures that for a time, all other content is blotted out. She returns again and again to them (stimulus perseveration) and describes them minutely (detailing). Again the intensity with which she responds reflects her personal involvement. The "men with candles" become figures with "mean faces" and then they become phobic female figures, "witches," who are menacing and frightening. The witch symbol generally expresses a conception of the mother as hostile, evil and all powerful. This may then be what Ellen is defending against, first by attempted repression, then by delaying tactics, and then by reaction formations (making them innocuous figures at first). The childish elaboration, "the witches are sticking their tongues out," suggests to us that Ellen identifies with the witch mother and is really projecting her conception of herself as mean and evil. Possibly it is because of the hostile and aggressive impulses she experiences in conjunction with the figures. Whether or not she ascribes such sadistic attitudes to herself or to others, we know that she is intensely preoccupied with them.

Ellen tries to give up at this point. "That is all I can think of . . . I don't see anything more." This again suggests her pessimistic attitude that she cannot cope with the situation. But Ellen still retains the card. The figures continue to hold her. Wtih the card inverted, she sees "men upside down with fire shooting from between them." There can be no doubt that violence is associated with the figures.

It is a question why she sees the men upside down. With certain schizophrenic patients, forms are seen upside down, sometimes without turning the cards. This is Rapaport's "autistic logic." The patients accept the upside down position as the real one and draw far-fetched conclusions that they must represent something real that way. Ellen has turned the card, however. She is fully aware they are the same men she has given before only they are upside down. We feel therefore that rather than reflect any serious pathology, her handling of the figures represents her hostile and violent wish to manipulate parental figures as she will. She may be projecting a sadistic wish to stand the figures on their heads.

Finally Ellen sees a "mountain" but "flames are coming off the mountain." We note again indications of explosiveness, this time associated with feelings of inadequacy (Vista) no doubt in reference to her ability to handle her hostile impulses. She tries to put distance between herself and her seething emotions.

Throughout her performance in this situation, Ellen asks for confirmation of what she gives. She is in constant need for reassurance. She fears she may be wrong. She fears retaliation from the examiner and perhaps from herself. Her aggressive demandingness again reflects her deep dependency.

Ellen fails to see the popular animal for D 5 (P failure). She seems so preoccupied with her own problems that she does not react as others in her group frequently do. We would not expect her to behave in a conventional manner in situations where she is deeply disturbed.

Card III

Again Ellen protests that the blot is difficult even before she tries to handle it. She is really weighed down by lack of self confidence and feelings of failure.

When she attacks the card, sequence is reversed. She first elects usual details and only later responds to the whole. She then turns again to usual details and finally ends with a cut-off whole. Despite the irregularity, she appears in control of the situation. Her reality testing is more than adequate (F+), her emotional responsiveness though violent is controlled (CF+), her imaginal ability is utilized appropriately (M+).

It is significant, however, that her first response is to a colored area, where she sees the popular "butterfly." She reacts only to the form. Generally color is involved in this response. She seems to shy away from the color insisting that the shape determines the response. This is verified in the probing. This may be a form of denial. She resists the emotional impact of the area; she is reluctant to become emotionally involved. She handles the situation, impersonally. This is a sign of ego strength.

Her control is short-lived, however, because she immediately reacts to the strong red area at the side with a highly personal image. She sees "red iron handing down . . . red hot . . . bulging." Here she reveals seething emotions (CF), deep need for affectional relationships (cF), a need or wish to express hostile impulse but a fear to express it because it is unacceptable and will meet punishment and retaliation from the outside world (m). The formal patterns and the content suggest to us considerable tension, iner turmoil and disharmony in conjunction with hot and dangerously explosive emotions.

The usual human figures in movement finally appear (P delay). Even though this response is frequent, her special imagery and elaborations point again to her preoccupations and problems. The figures are "skeletons" but she treats them as living human beings. She tries displacement. She still cannot face living people. In addition, her use of skeletons seems to have belittling implications. She may need to derogate the human figures she actually sees. Again, she may be highly sensitive to spaces as gaps. She refers to the spaces several times. This may point to special sensitivity to lack of solidity in a figure or an object. She may be projecting lack of solidity and stability in her own being or even in her own life. We sometimes get emphasis on spaces as gaps in the records of children whose parents are separated.

In the inquiry, Ellen weaves a story with her percepts as she did in Card I. She elaborates by combining areas separately interpreted, in inappropriate fashion. "The skeletons are just sitting . . . on a rock . . . waiting for the iron to be done and while they are waiting they are trying to catch the butterfly." This is a confabulatory-combinatory response where arbitrary and irrealistic relationships are established between relatively autonomous parts of the whole. This suggests thought disorders often met in psychotics. Again it points to the transductive reasoning of Piaget: because things are seen together, they belong together. Again, however, Ellen is aware of what she is doing and even seems to enjoy the impression she is making on the examiner. She did this also in Card I. While the serious implications of this response cannot be entirely eliminated, their weight is lessened. Rather than suggest serious pathology, we would hypothesize that Ellen is prone to resort deliberately to irrealistic and highly imaginative thinking when confronted by a situaton which she finds difficult to handle and which arouses deep anxiety within her. This reminds us of "regression in the service of the ego." She permits herself imaginative liberties but she is in control of her thinking. We might consider this successful defense, if we did not think that this tendency may manifest itself in real life in similar imaginative flights which might take the form of weaving tales and fabrication.

We note that the skeletons just sit (flexor stance), wait (neutral or static stance), and try to catch (extensor stance). This suggests to us considerable ambivalence as to hat kind of activity she is projecting. Passivity is reflected by the flexor stance, assertiveness by the extensor, and inhibition of some desired activity by the static M. This may reflect her own ambivalent orientation and her conflict over passivity and activity, submissiveness and self-assertion. The extensor M, "trying to catch" something, has sadistic implications.

The "full-face" response which follows to the lower middle area (D 1+1) is poor form and arbitrarily organized (F−). Most faces seen in the Rorschach with few exceptions are seen in profile. This one is infrequently given. The "eye" (s 35) and the "nose" (s 20) are located. "A mouth could be down here (s 33) but it isn't there." She herself is aware of the vagueness of the image by her remark "sort of." In adults, unusual full-face responses are associated with paranoid thinking and psychosis. In this 10 year old child, we prefer to think of suspicious attitudes. Further the fact that she projects a mouth which isn't there again suggests that oral (dependency, demand) conflicts are especially acute.

Ellen is in good control of the situation. Her response to the red center (D 5) as "yarn" is highly different and acceptable (O+). It suggests a feminine interest. Sensitivity is controlled (Fc). Ego strength is again indicated in the fact that she again shies away from the color and gives a straight form answer. She is able to repress emotional expression. She can prevent herself from becoming emotionally involved in an emotional situation. Control is likewise in evidence in her next response which is well perceived and original, "crane" as they "stand in ponds with one leg up."

For her last response, Ellen inverts the card and sees "a man's arms (D 2) and eyes and forehead (D 1+1) and a crack in the nose." The man is raising his hands. It is not unusual to get a human figure with arms upraised either directing, threatening, or in supplication. The extensor movement here points again to aggressive striving and self-assertiveness, or Ellen may be projecting fear that someone is threatening or directing her. She may be identifying with the individual and be the threatening one. Again she may be expressing her own need to control and master the environment or her own impulses, a need which we have already noted. Finally, she may be the figure who is begging for help and sustenance, which we also have noted before.

The crack in the head is interesting. Split concepts have destructive connotations. They suggest hostility and violence or fear of attack. Again Ellen may be projecting her own sadistic need to attack the figure and crack the head. Her style of wording itself represents this underlying sadistic orientation. Again she may be projecting her fear and apprehension lest she be attacked. The fact that she makes the figure "happy" in the inquiry appears to be an undoing operation to reduce the threat either of some one else or of her own impulses. Finally, the additional elaboration of "feet" for the bottom areas (D 6) again shows her tendency to make things work out. They are poor form (F–). She arbitrarily manipulates the figure and puts things together to justify her ideas.

Card IV

Again Ellen expresses feelings of failure. Before she starts she knows she cannot succeed. She does attend to the blot, however, but her productivity is markedly reduced. She is obviously tense and disturbed (Shock). The succession is reversed. The first response is vague and indefinite. She delays seeing the usual human figure sitting. She fails to give the popular "animal skin." This all suggests disturbance, either because of the dark shading, the massive figure which is frequently seen as an overwhelming authoritative figure, and/or the areas which often elicit sex symbolic imagery.

Ellen's first response is a vague impressionistic one. She is attracted to the center projection, especially to the sharp projections and the "eyes." She sees only "feelers . . . prickles . . . and eyes." She cannot combine them into a definite form. The blot simply arouses a vague scary image and painful feelings. Ellen may be projecting her sadistic desire to inflict pain or her fear that pain will be inflicted on her. She desperately tries to repress the threatening image. The question is whether she has sex thoughts in relation to male sexuality because they are projected onto the area which frequently elicits ideas of masculinity. Is male sexuality viewed as threatening, harmful and injurious? Again we hesitate to make this hypothesis because of Ellen's age. It has recurred so often, however, that we must consider the possibility that we have a sexually precocious child who is frightened and intimidated by male sexuality and who appears to be extremely anxious over possible sexual attack.

After this first impressionistic response, Ellen takes refuge in a childish image, a "sea animal" which is "half lady and half fish." This imaginary object is well perceived (F+) and highly different (O+). The dark figure (D 9) is frequently seen as a female figure. She combines it with another detail (D 4) which are "tails . . . which swoop up." Ellen has avoided the female figure before. This may well be a displacement, a kind of undoing or a device by which she screens a threatening female figure, makes it imaginary, and thus puts distance between herself and the female. In this way she makes the female acceptable, pleasant, and harmless. Further she handles the projection, which is frequently given a sex symbolic response, in a childish regressive manner, reducing its threat. Her defensive operations are successful.

Finally she sees the human form sitting on a bush, a response which is not infrequent, but which she has delayed (P delay). "The man . . . has arms out . . . big huge feet . . . sitting on a prickly bush." The "prickly bush" is highly different (O) and at once betrays personal involvement. Putting the figure on the prickly bush has cruel implications. It points to a sadistic need to hurt the figure. Even her verbalization is sadistic, "arms are flung out." Generally the arms are down, drooping.

The crucial question is, whom does she want to hurt? Who is the focus of such destructive desires? Who is the individual who is being tortured? Generally the image is an authoritative figure who is big, powerful and threatening. It would appear that she is fearful of this powerful figure. Her emphasis on size and her redundancy ("big huge feet") suggest strong feelings of being small, weak and vulnerable in the face of this threatening figure. Sometimes it is a powerful punitive father figure. In Ellen's life, it may well be a dominant, threatening, overpowering mother. We have noted before the hostility which Ellen harbors against someone and her deep need to punish and inflict pain.

Her sadism may be directed toward herself, too. She may be identifying with the figure and experiencing a need to punish self. We note that the stance of the movement is both flexor (sitting) and extensor (arms flung out). Ellen may be in conflict as to what should be her role in life. Should she act out aggressively and independently or should she be submissive and resigned? Thus she may be expressing ambivalent, perplexed and conflicting attitudes.

We should note that Ellen is responsive to the texture, both to the softness (bushiness) and to the hardness (prickly). We have already noted evidence of her cautious sensitivity to others and of her affect hunger (texture). There is strong need in Ellen to feel near and close to others, to belong and to be in contact with others. The texture however is also hard and brittle. It has been hypothesized that such use of texture implies anticipation that affectional needs will not be satisfied (Klopfer). Other clinicians observe that reactions to texture as hard, rough, and brittle are found in the records of individuals, often sociopaths who conform on a superficial level and who appear to be compliant, submissive, and subservient. Such conformity however is only a facade which covers their deep hostility toward those who fail to satisfy their dependent needs (Phillips and Smith). This hypothesis may well apply here.

Ellen fails to see the popular "animal skin." She no doubt is so preoccupied with her impulses, feelings, and thoughts that she just does not see what others generally do.

Card V

Ellen readily gives the popular "flying animal." Here she shows she is in tune with the thinking of her fellows (P). Again, however, she elaborates in a highly personal manner. The bat is "scared . . . but you can't scare a bat . . . but it is scared." Even this simple situation is permeated with intense personal material. Her fears and dysphoric thoughts and moods are projected onto the popular bat. She tries to take back and undo what she says, unwilling to admit her feelings of being scared. She is unable to suppress them.

She next perseverates with a sadistic percept, "a crooked prickler bush." Any repetition of motif especially when it is so different (O) projects considerable personal involvement. She shows again she is highly sensitive to projections which hurt and sting. There can be little doubt that sadistic attitudes, motives and conflicts are central to her adjustment and that she is likely to be aware of and concerned about them.

Again she repeats, seeing the bat upside down. This may be a desire to give another response to satisfy the examiner. Again it may be that she feels the need to manipulate objects turning them and twisting them at will.

An additional response in the inquiry, "a crooked banana," merits exploration. First she takes off projections, stripping her image of its sadistic implications. Food is an obvious symbol for dependency needs. It is an oral receptive image reflecting again the dependent orientation we have already noted. Her need for nurture and gratification of needs is so intense, that she misperceives, distorts, and manipulates reality to suit her needs (Dr! F− O−). It should be indicated, however, that she is vaguely aware of the inadequacy of her percept. She rationalizes by making it "crooked."

Card VI

Ellen is more productive in this situation. Her mental procedure is more orderly. For the most part she displays adequate intellectual control (F+).

The first two responses are similar to those given by young children, "a turtle" and "a starfish." In the former, texture is involved in her reaction, "a shell." Again she appears to be sensitive to the hardness and the brittleness of the shell. Again we think of the compliant behavior which is a facade for latent hostility toward authoritative figures. In addition, it has been hypothesized (Phillips and Smith) that content like "turtle, crab or bug" symbolizes the rejecting, punitive and destructive mother figure. Such content is given by highly dependent individuals who view the mother as rejecting and punitive. Again then we repeat our hypothesis that Ellen has deep rooted dependency needs, that she fears rejection, anticipates rejection, and is hostile because of the denial of gratification of her needs.

The response "starfish" is considered poor in quality (F−) for a girl of Ellen's age. Again it is the projections which interest her. In childish manner, Ellen counts the projections. Counting often reflects an attempt to overcome anxiety. It is sometimes a tactic in handling something which is disturbing or confusing. We again suspect apprehension in relation to ideas of male sexuality.

Ellen next reacts to the projection of (D 1). She makes it a "humming bird." We get a flying object frequently for this area. Why it is a "humming bird" merits exploration. If Ellen is seeing a bird that is attractive and happy, she may be denying an image which fills her with fear and foreboding. It may be the phallus. Again, if Ellen perceives a brightly colored bird and hence projects color into the gray-black area, our feeling is that she is trying to hide a depressed mood and that she is trying to display happiness while she actually experiences deeply felt sadness, a form of denial. The fact that she clings to it and repeats it upside down corroborates our suspicion that some personal conflictual material has been aroused. With preadolescent children, this area sometimes arouses the stirrings of heterosexual needs which are likely to cause anxiety. This may be the case with Ellen. We feel, however, that there is more in the picture than normal sex interest of the preadolescent. We have noted too often Ellen's sexual concerns.

This last is corroborated in the next response. With the card inverted Ellen sees ". . . a mountain and two guards (Dr 32) up there with knives (Dr 8)." Here she turns to vary rare areas which lead to the invaginated area in the center which frequently symbolizes feminine or vaginal sensitivity. She really sees only the heads of the guards and the projections as knives. She proceeds however to combine and fabulize and see the whole human forms in movement. This is really not human movement in the Rorschach sense. It is a made up "confabulatory M," movement being superimposed rather than actually experienced. The content may well be symbolic of a sexual theme: the vaginal area must be protected aggressively. The use of shading as vista suggests feelings of inadequacy in reference to this feminine area. Does Ellen feel the need to protect her virginity? Will she do it aggressively and sadistically (knives)? Or does she need someone else to do the protecting? We think by this time Ellen is not sexually naive. The formal score patterns and the content again point to deep concern in relation to sexual activity. They also suggest potential for overt and sadistic acting out. It should be mentioned that we have observed this type of response in adolescent delinquents.

In the final response, Ellen sticks to the center invaginated area. She gives a vague but safe "country" which at first is an aerial scene such as you see on television, but which is changed in the inquiry to a "map." The first vista response points to feelings of inadequacy, again, we think, in reference to her sex role. The change to a safe "map" may be a childish reaction. Children give many maps because they view the test as a school task. Again, maps are frequently evasive responses which reflect frustrated dependency, associated with attitudes of resentment and unhappiness. This hypothesis is relevant here since we have noted several times her strong dependency needs and her frustrations in this area. The very fact that she wavers between the vista scene and the flat map emphasizes we think her feelings of personal inadequacy, helplessness and hopelessness.

Again we must note P failure. Ellen fails to give the usual and popular "animal skin."

Card VII

Ellen's behavior is now beginning to show open hostility. The controlled facade which she has manifested up to now is disappearing. She can no longer cover up. It is significant too that the break comes in the card which contains an area which frequently is seen as a mother figure and which sometimes arouses anxiety in reference to this figure. Indeed considerable strain and anxiety (shock) are in evidence in her disturbed behavior, her initial reaction to the space, her focus on the center axial area, her poor human movement response (M−), the P failure and the content of her responses.

Ellen's first response is an evasive water landscape or a map. She sees "sea" and adds "land all around." It is significant that she avoids the conspicuous mother figure common here. She guards against the mother imagery which the card triggers and becomes vague, general, and superficial. She escapes to the space and vagueness, in characteristic fashion.

Ellen is next drawn to the center bottom area (D 12) giving alternative objects, "a flashlight" and "a bomb." Both are elongated objects often symbolic of the phallus. It is of interest that this area receives many different kinds of symbolic variations. It is sometimes frankly seen as the "anus" and sometimes as the "vagina." Rarely does it elicit a masculine sex object. This suggests again that Ellen is concerned, confused and in conflict over male sexuality. It is of interest too that both objects are explosive, the "flashlight" having a disguised explosive top (the light shoots out), and the "bomb" being an aggressive explosive weapon. Ellen's reaction to the diffuse shading (Ch) and the projection of inanimate movement (m) reflect mounting tension. In conjunction with the content these patterns seem to point to the urgency of sex drives which are crowding for expression. We might almost anticipate the discharge of accumulated tensions. There is the possibility that Ellen may act out and indulge in some form of sexual activity.

Ellen's last response "a fat lady . . . with legs out" is a highly personal autistic movement response (M− O−). She departs radically from the reality of the blot. She arbitrarily organizes the whole including the space. She imposes eyes on the figure which are not there. She concocts a nose. She projects a solid into the space making it the body. She inserts a mouth, which is missing. She sees a living figure unrealistically with arms and legs out (Me−). Again we see that Ellen resorts to highly autistic and regressive thinking (M−). She ascribes assertive and aggressive attitudes to the lady (Me). She expresses contemptuous attitudes toward the female figure (fat lady). She shows her intense feelings of oral deprivation (missing mouth). She stubbornly adheres to her ideas especially about the female figure (S or reversal reflecting intense oppositionalism). Finally she high-handedly manipulates the figure and makes it work for her to satisfy her ideas and her needs (manipulation, insertion of items).

In the inquiry, Ellen gives an additional response which may seem innocuous but which we think has considerable significance. For the indentations along the side of D 2 and D 3 Ellen sees "inlets." Inlets have harbor-like protecting qualities. Ellen seems to be expressing again her need for security and protection. We have noted her longing to be protected before. Further, by going outside the figure, she does not have to handle what is inside. She is again escaping and retreating from the requirements of the situation.

Card VIII

This card is supposed to be attractive and pleasant with its soft colors and harmonious design. Generally it readily evokes pleasant content and positive feelings. Yet Ellen does not react to the pleasurable stimuli. Instead she inhibits productivity and represses emotional expression. She avoids the emotional stimuli by giving three innocuous responses, first an evasive map with color used artificially, then the popular animal, and after trying to give up, a vague "flying animal" for Dr 5+5. Thus she restricts herself to the general and to the vague. She is unable or unwilling to become emotionally involved. She does put on an outward show of affect (C/F) but it is merely a facade. She represses her genuine feelings and emotions. She is probably prone to deal with social relationships in real life in a similar forced and artificial manner.

Card IX

Subject now is openly hostile. She blames the examiner for making her persist. She resents having to knuckle down to a task. She has not developed habits of perserverance, nor does she experience any joy in accomplishment. Again the powerful impact of the colors cuts down her productivity, this time to a single response, the easy and evasive "map." Again she shows that she is not capable of a genuine emotional response related to the reality demands of the situation (C/F vague). She avoids emotion-provoking situations. She puts on a superficial social-veneer type of control. It is significant however that she does not disintegrate.

Despite her attempt to repress her feelings and to evade the imagery which no doubt has emerged, she does give a highly personalized meaning to a small area of the map: ". . . this little green patch in the middle of the ocean." She explains in the inquiry "all this could be ocean (S 30) and here little green patches all alone out here." Because we feel this is a highly personal projection, we have given it a separate score. No doubt Ellen is projecting her own feelings of being alone, isolated, deprived and rejected. Such imagery is frequent in depressed persons.

Card X

Ellen is more productive and more realistic in this last card. She gives a series of six responses. Her first response to D 6 is really a popular, although she fumbles a bit for a name. It is a "big round things that have lots of legs, you know what I mean." This is followed by a "fish" for D 9, which is poor form quality (F−). This may be a childish answer. Yet it may have some symbolic significance. Some clinicians believe that the inappropriate selection of fish for an area may suggest giving up strivings for independence because of an overwhelming and possessive mother figure. This is associated with a profound passivity and inertia and with a clinging dependency (Phillips and Smith). We have noted these attitudes in Ellen.

Again her apprehensiveness and fearfulness in the face of a threatening environment and her general feelings of weakness and inadequacy may be reflected in her reaction "sea monsters" to D 4.

Ellen gives the popular "green snakes," her only FC. This suggests that there is some slight capacity in her for emotional rapport with her world. The final response, "red land . . . it is that color on a map," is again a forced color response (C/F vague). Genuine emotional reactivity is seriously repressed. Indeed her general reaction to this card underscores her inability or unwillingness to be emotionally responsive to the demands of the situation. An additional response to the center area (Dr 12), "walnuts . . . hanging from a tree," is a food response, again showing her dependency needs.

Ellen's failure to give genuine color responses to the color cards corroborates the hypotheses we have repeated throughout the sequence analysis. There is a strong need in Ellen to repress emotional responsiveness because of threats from without in her environment and because of threats within her from her impulses. She is constantly threatened with pain, punishment and rejections from her world. She is threatened by her own unacceptable, forbidden, and destructive impulses which may erupt without self-control. She rigidly inhibits self-expression in situations to which most people are emotionally responsive. In general, her emotional responsiveness is both inappropriate and inadequate.

Probing

In probing for color, Ellen explained that maps are colored to show different lands or countries. The area she selected in Card III reminded her of "yarn" because that is the shape in which it comes. She could not give any additional color responses.

In probing for human movement, we satisfied ourselves that she really experienced the "skeletons" as living human beings. She explained again that she saw skeletons because they are "bony and separate here with a hole." While she said they could not be people, she did insist they were "sitting down or bending, no crouching. . . ." She gave no further human movement responses.

Ellen could not see the popular responses which she did not give, even when they were suggested to her.

Analysis of Psychogram

Intellectual Aspects of Functioning. The formal Rorschach patterns point to a child who is at least of average intelligence (2 good W, 19.5 Sum g wt., 7 M of which four are good, 31 per cent A+Ad, 22 per cent O+,

---

Summary Sheet on facing page designed for use with Frequency Tables for scoring responses to *The Rorschach Ink-blot Test* by Marguerite R. Hertz, Ph.D., published by The Press of Western Reserve University, Cleveland, Ohio.

Name	20-13-9						No.	
Birthdate		C.A. 10						Delay
Address			Tot RT(Sh)(1) 33 Av 6.6					π
School	Grade		Tot RT(C) (1) 56 Av 11.2					possibly VII
Occupation			Tot RT (1) 89 Av 8.9 ±AD3.9					
			Tot T 704 Av(B)70 Av(R)'14					quick - possibly V

TOTAL R 49   FAILURES X

I. MENTAL APPROACH					II. DETERMINANTS					III. CONTENT		
R-Rx	Factor	R+ 39	Total +,-,x	Total 49	%	R-18 Rx	Factor	39: R+	Total +,-,x	Total 49	%	
							Differentiated Scoring					
3	WO					3	MO					A 14 (A) /
1	W	2	9(1)+ .3		27		M	1	4+	7	14	Ad / (Ad)
	Wv	2(1)	4 -				MP	3	3 -			Σ(A+Ad) (15) 31
	WP	5					M trend					H 7 (H)
							FM	6		6		Hd 2 (Hd)
2	DO	5					mF	(2)		(2)		Σ(H+Hd) 9 18
2	D	9	19+	23	47		Ch					Anat-H
	DP	4	4-				ChF	1		1		Anat-A
	Dv	1					F Ch	1		1		Anat-obj /
2	DrO	+										Blood
	Dr	3	8+	10	20	5	Fcrude	15		20	41	ΣAnat (1) 02
	Drv	1	2-									Sex
	Dv						F(C)	3		3		Ad-obj
	Drf	1	1+	'1	02		(C)F					Hd-obj
							(C)					
(1)	SO	1		2(8)		(1)	Fc	2(1)		2(3)		Bo 1(1)
	S	1(1)	2(6)+		6+...	2	cF	(1)		2(1)		Cl ccal /
	sO		(3)-		22		c					Ed /
.2(1)	s	(5)					F Ch"	(1)		(1)		Fire
							ChF	1		1		Geol
	ΣW		13	27			Ch'					Mt. YUCK 2(1)
	ΣD		25	51			FC	1		1		Sc
	ΣDr		11	22			CF c/F	2+3		5		Vol
							C crude					Wr

IV. ORIGINAL - POPULAR

							C resp.	(6)		6	1.2	iycn
7	O	10	22½	20	41		ΣC wt			5.5		ΣNat (6)(2)
2	gOcmt	1										
	P			9								App /(1)
	Pfail I, IV, V, VII											Arch
												Art /
	Rv		5									Emb
												Hh 2(1)

PERSONALITY PATTERNS

				Map 6 12
				Mech
W 13	(W)	(2)	Me 4 Mf-2 2 My static 1	Orn YARN /
Dr+Do+S+s		26%	M:FM	7:6	Orn Sci
Mental App W (0) Dr				St
Succ.: Reg. 3 Irreg. +			Color Deviations	—	Str
M+ 4 M Hd			low Color VIII - X		Weap 2
Dr M M- 3 (M)		(4)	[FC-(CF+C)] wt .5-5.0	-4.5	B..cbi /
M trend M! 3					ΣObj (15)(3)
W:M 13:7	(W):(M)		Σ[F(C)+(c)] wt	4.0	Abstractions
				1.5	
F+: Σ F prim 32/40		80%	ΣSh wt	7.0	ΣOB (2)(5) 43+
R+: Σ R 31/49		86%			References
F+ F- Variability			Fc+F(C)+FCh	6	mythology
gO+ + P 2 gv3			F:Fc+F(C)+FCh	20:6	Christmas
+ 5 - 5 Σg 19:5					
gcomb +1.;cr - 3			[FCh-(ChF+Ch)] wt	-0.5	
g+ g- Variability org.acts —		23	[FSh-(ShF + Sh)] wt	-1.0	
H 7 H-Hd 7-2 = 5			M+ Σ C wt	12.5	Qualitive Patterns
			M: Σ C wt	7:5:5	agg! split!
A+Ad+Anat+Sex	ΣOB	33%	Erlebnistypus Introversive		counting u.d.
Var 18		+3%			detailing vt-bal
O Bizarre		—	VIII - X 10 R	10	emot!
Contamination		—	X : VIII - X	6:10	H derog
Confabulation		✓			Perseveration
Fabulation		✓	F crude:M:C 41%:14%:12%		Power!
Shock		✓	%oF+ 2M:C 80% :14% :12%		proj.!
Recoverability		✓			repetition of R
Tempo	Irregular		7.0 ΣSh wt > 5.5 ΣC wt		size

adequate spread of content as seen in Var 18, per cent OB 43). Form quality falls within the range of normality (80 per cent F Prim $+$). A few of the Rorschach patterns exceed the norms for her age group (good M, high g, high per cent O) suggesting a higher intellectual level of functioning.

Her functioning is however uneven and erratic. She appears highly productive (49 R) exceeding the norms published by other authorities for a ten-year-old group. Her productivity, however, is not consistently constructive. Many of her responses are extravagant interpretations of tiny details. Rather than rich productivity, the total R reflects restlessness, distractibility, escape reactions, and possibly the presence of ideational symptoms.

In addition, the tempo of the responses is uneven. She gives many responses at first, then gradually slows up and peters out, only to revive somewhat in the last card. Productivity and activity are not sustained. She fatiques readily. Her attention laxes. She becomes more and more resistant and inhibited as the test proeeds.

There are several reasons for the unevenness of her performance. First, she is extremely anxious in the test situation. She is completely lacking in self-confidence. She is unwilling even to face the problems because she is sure of failure. In addition, she resists being compelled to persevere. Even more important, certain aspects of the blots are threatening and disturbing her. They cause her to become guarded and evasive.

This unevenness is seen in Ellen's mental procedure (W (D) Dr). She shows some capacity to take an overall view of the blots, but it is limited. Further, she is so intent on concentrating on small irrelevant details that she is prone to overlook the obvious parts of the blot. Her mental procedure then tends to be unbalanced and inefficient.

Of the 7 W's which Ellen gives, only two require much effort. Most of her W's involve vague content and four are popular. These then are easy and lethargic W's. She seems to follow the path of least effort. It is not however a matter of lack of ability since her g score is high in the superior range. She has good capacity to analyze a situation, to see relationships between and among its parts and to come out with an organized response. Thus while she has analytic and synthetic ability, she does not achieve constructively commensurate with that ability. She lacks initiative and drive for more constructive achievement (few good W with high g).

On three occasions, Ellen's whole responses are poorly combined pointing to unrealistic and illogical relationships. Confabulatory and fabulized-combinatory whole responses are common in young children. They are rare, however, in ten year old children. We note this tendency also in other responses where organization takes place in smaller units (g– 0– combinations in conjunction with usual and rare details). Like a very young child, Ellen makes false deductions and jumps to erroneous conclusions on the basis of inadequate evidence (Confabulatory responses) or she relates parts of situations in unrealistic and illogical fashion. Again she childishly forces reality in line with her needs and her thinking (Manipulation).

The marked emphasis on the rare and the minute does not mean that Ellen is interested in fine detail. Rather she is driven to small areas because she is afraid to become involved in the larger aspects of the problems presented.

Ellen tends to be unsystematic and illogical in her mode of response to the cards (Succession). Irregular succession is noted in Cards II, III, IV, and VII; regular in Cards I, VI, and VIII. No succession can be evaluated in Card V where she gives two W's, Card IX where there is only one response, and Card X where response is only to the usual details. It appears that Ellen cannot handle in systematic, orderly, and efficient manner situations which are anxiety-laden and which disturb her.

Ellen's thinking for the most part is clear, realistic, and controlled (80 per cent F+ (Ror) Primary). Her score compares favorably with our norms for her age (76-90 per cent). Of the 39 F Primary which she gives, 32 are form fitting; of these 9 are P, 11 are 0+, and 5 are vague. She shows adequate capacity then for conscious, directed and prolonged control over thought processes. At times, however a weak kind of control is exercised by sticking to the easy or resorting to safe vague generalizations.

More than adequate intellectual ability and control are seen in the M score which is beyond capacity (7 M). The mean for her age group is 1.03 S D 1.54. Of the M which she produces, 4 are sound structure (M+). Ellen then has good imaginative ability. She can indulge in fantasy and wish-fulfilling activities within the context of good ties to reality.

At times however, Ellen gives free reign to her imagination and indulges in extreme fantasy losing herself in her fantasy world (M−). Sometimes she distorts forms and misinterprets relationships, giving meanings without objective support. Thus she sees "persons . . . facing outward" (Card I), "fat . . . lady . . . with arms out" Card VII. On occasion then her thinking tends to be regressive and autistic. She may resort to dream living, possibly daydreaming.

Indeed, Ellen's thinking tends generally to be highly different (20 0). A few of her originals point to genuine creative ability (11 0+ or 22 per cent of total R). She can see things in a different light, still adhering to reality. Most of her originals, however are highly personalized, reflecting special problems and preoccupations and personal fears and conflicts. The "Christmas tree stand" (Card I), the "tiny bridge" (Card II), the "mermaid" and the "man on the prickly bush" (Card IV), the "guards, with knives" (Card VI) and the "flashlight" and "bomb" (Card VII), all appear to be symbolic of basic conflicts and problems.

On occasion there are breaks with reality and wide deviation in her thought content (10 R− of which 9 are 0−). Personal interests and conflicts cause her to misperceive and even distort reality. This is seen in "persons facing away," "stagecoach," and "person with arms and legs out" (Card I), "prickles on something" (Card IV), "prickly bush" and the additional "crooked banana" (Card V) and "the fat lady" (Card VII). responses are all the more personally significant because they represent departure from reality and loss of intellectual control.

Despite these occasional lapses, however, there is no evidence that there is a pervasive weakening of ties with reality (adequate per cent F+ (Ror)). When she is not upset by anxiety-laden imagery, her thinking is adequately realistic. Further she is often aware of the lack of fit of her percepts, but she stubbornly even aggressively persists. She seems to relish making up stories. She enjoys indulging herself in fantasying, laughing at what she says.

Her stubbornness and persistence are seen also in her reactions to spaces which point to considerable oppositionalism in her makeup. She gives reactions to two usual spaces and to nine additional spaces. Twice she projects solids into spaces a procedure which is associated with strong will, determination, independent thinking and stubbornness. Ellen will stick then to her personal ideas whether or not they are appropriate to the situation.

The fact that Ellen is in good touch with reality is also seen in her score of 9 popular responses, which is well above the average for her group and which shows that she is more than adequately adaptive to the thinking of her group. She is well able to share in the thinking of those about her. Indeed, the weighting of the P suggests that Ellen forces conformity. It appears to be a defensive maneuver to put on a social front. We note this also in her use of color (C/F) which reflects a forced and artificial emotional responsiveness to her environment.

It is significant however that despite her ability to see things that most people do, she fails to give popular forms in Card II, where she experiences considerable emotional upset and in Cards IV, VI, and VII, where anxiety-laden imagery appears to overwhelm her (Sequence analysis). When emotionally disturbed then, she does not show the good ability which she possesses for adapting to the thinking of her group. She is too preoccupied with her own interests and problems.

Finally, Ellen's mental horizon is seriously limited. It is true that considerable width in range of interests is suggested by the 31 per cent A+Ad and the 43 per cent OB. We know however that the range includes six innocuous maps and nine popular forms. In reality, then, Ellen's interests are not broad. They are restricted to that which is of immediate concern to her. This is verified by the high per cent 0 which shows that her interests are really idiosyncratic and symptomatic.

In general, then, while Ellen has adequate intellectual ability to function within the range of her age group, emotional problems appear to be reducing the level of her efficiency. She does not use her abilities for constructive achievement. While the ratio 13 W : 7 M appears to suggest adequate constructive efforts, there are only 2 good W as compared to 4 good M and we have noted that much of her energies are engaged in highly personalized, regressive, or autistic thinking. There is no real drive to intellectual achievement. She has lowered her aspiration level because of fear of competition, fear of failure, and habit of giving up (Behavior).

Affective Aspects of Personality Functioning. We have already noted that Ellen is moved by strong feelings which are introverted into highly personal fantasy living (M). Her orientation toward herself and toward her world is highly ambivalent (M stance). Part of her nature is asserting itself and fighting (M extensor) and part is submitting passively and submissively to her fate (M flexor). Thus we have extensor M in "men . . . bringing candles together" (Card II) and in "man . . . raising his hands" and "skeletons . . . straining to catch the butterfly" (Card III). Flexor M is indicated in "skeletons . . . sitting" (Card III), and the "man . . . sitting on the prickly bush" in (Card IV).

Again, M reflecting static pose is seen in "people . . . facing out" (Card I), "skeletons . . . waiting" (Card III). She appears to be in a state of tension, because hostile, sadistic, and dependent impulses (content) unacceptable to herself and to her world, must be inhibited. Indeed conflict between passivity and activity, compliance and self-assertion, and dependence or independence is even more in evidence in the M responses where there are combinations of static, flexor and extensor postures. For example the people (Card I) are facing outward but later she sees them going in opposite directions; the skeletons (Card III) are sitting, waiting and trying to catch the butterfly; the person (Card IV) is sitting in a bush but the arms are out; the fat lady (Card VII) is sitting but her arms are out also. Impulses seem to be frustrating each other. She is in a state of tension and indecision, unable to act forcibly and consistently in handling her problems.

Strong feelings are likewise suggested in her emotional responsiveness to the environment (12 per cent C responses and 5.5 Sum C wt.). These total scores suggest that Ellen has adequate affective energy for response to her environment. Of the color responses, 2 are genuine CF but 3 are artificial C/F and only one is FC. Thus while the total scores appear high, only three are genuine color responses. Of these 2 appear in Cards II and III and genuine color reactions are repressed in Cards VIII and IX and for the most part in Card X.

Ellen's emotional responsiveness then is really inadequate and inappropriate. It is for the most part curtailed and repressed. This is verified in the low number of responses to Cards VIII, IX, and X (20 per cent) which reflects her low capacity for healthy emotional reactivity to her environment. Further the low FC shows that she is not in emotional rapport with her environment. She has little capacity for harmonious relationships with people. She is preoccupied with people (H) but it is because of her conflicts concerning them, her dependence upon and antagonism toward them. There is little understanding or feel for people and little reaching out for warmth and contact. If anthing Ellen withdraws from them emotionally, and desperately represses emotional reaction to them. She seems unable or unwilling to permit herself any pleasureable experiences in relation to her environment. A few cheerful ideas are suggested such as the Christmas tree (Card I), the valentine (Card II), the costume of the people (Card I), and possibly the humming bird (Card VI), but for the most part pleasurable experience is stifled.

Ellen does try to make some feeling contact with her environment. She responds however in a highly superficial and artificial manner (C/F). She puts on a facade but her emotional reactions are not deep or genuine.

There is evidence of occasional release of emotions (CF). When Ellen does express herself emotionally, she is prone to be highly immature and explosive (Color with blood and fire). She is irritable, childishly demanding, self-centered, concerned about herself and her own interests (CF). She is apt to react in explosive fashion.

For the most part, Ellen holds herself back because she is in a chronic state of tension and anxiety. We have noted this anxiety in her behavior in the test situation with her fear of failure, her resignation, her proneness to give up, her childish demandingness for assurance from the examiner, her distrust and suspiciousness, and even her antagonism. In addition, as we noted in the seqeunce analysis, dominant themes provide leads as to personal fears, conflicts and anxieties. Thus we noted rejection, conflict with activity and fight, and confusion and fears in relation to sexuality.

Anxiety is also in evidence structurally in her reaction to the color cards (color shock) in her erratic reality testing, her regressive and autistic activity, the repetition of responses, the unsystematic intellectual procedure, the escape to the minute and the irrelevant, the detailing, the breakdown of defenses, and, in Cards VIII although X, the reduction in productivity.

Anxiety is likewise reflected in Ellen's reactions to the shading cards. She gives 10 shading responses and shading is involved additionally in five more responses. Shading seems to elicit feelings of fear and foreboding. We note shading shock in the P delay, the resort to mythology, and the defensive instability in Card IV, the proneness to the overreaction and overcontrol, the stimulus perseveration in reference to the phallus-like details and the evasive map to the invaginated area in Card VI, the P failure and the avoidance of the women, the reversed succession, the evasive map response, and the regressive and autistic M in Card VII. Such shock reflects deep anxiety and disturbance in the psychosexual area.

The reaction to the general shading diffusion in Cards II, VI and VII reflect a vague, unchannelled anxiety. She seems to adopt passive submis- sive resigned attitudes in the face of threat. Indeed in these cards, her passivity and resignation appear to be a kind of defensive operation against the discharge of intense emotional energy (Card II, explosive color with shading). The recourse to passivity and inactivity counteracts the strong impulses.

Feelings of inferiority and inadequacy are also shown structurally by the reaction to vista. Ellen feels grossly inadequate to meet certain situa- tions. She feels that things are beyond her reach (Vista with bridge). Further she longs for affectional contact (Fc). At times these feelings are overwhelming (cF). We think that this affect hunger stems from depriva- tion in early mother-child relationships. Such deprivation no doubt has led to the emotional withdrawal which we noted.

Ellen's anxiety is so deep at times her moods are dysphoric and de- pressed (black color response and content). Reactions to dark shading suggest that Ellen has had traumatic experiences in her life which have been so devastating, that anxiety is deeply imbedded in her character structure. Klopfer calls this "the burnt child reaction." These reactions also suggest that Ellen feels a deep need to protest openly and actively when faced with anxiety laden situations. She must do something about the threats and dangers which she fears.

Personality Gestalt

In general, Ellen appears to have emotional resources at her disposal to make an adequate adjustment to the challenges of her environment. Look- ing at the psychogram it would seem that she has more than enough affective energy which could be introverted into fantasy and utilized in outward release (Experience Potential 12.5). This is misleading, however. As we have indicated, she is too prone to constrict emotional expression and to avoid pleasurable experience. At best, she forces or simulates the feelings and emotions which she cannot experience spontaneously. At the present time then she is much more introversive (*Erlebnistypus*), stimulated more by inner thoughts and feelings and much more prone to indulge in fantasy experiences than to deal actively and aggressively with her world.

Ellen's introversiveness however is far from healthy. Her fantasying is used as a defense against her deep anxiety. Too much is diverted to autistic purpose and has little relationship to the solution of her real life problems.

Further the strong oppositionalism in Ellen's makeup (S+s) which we have already noted in the intellectual sphere, takes its toll emotionally. Because of her introversive orientation, opposition is directed against her innermost self, i.e., against her unacceptable and undesirable wishes, impulses and attitudes which are not consistent with current standards. She fights her dependency needs, her self doubts and self distrust because they reduce her self-esteem. She fights her smoldering hostility bcause of fear of reprisals and punishment and possibly because of feelings of guilt. We know too that opposition is likewise directed against her environment. This is seen in her impulsive and explosive themes of violence and hostile sadism, in her explosive color scores and in her use of spaces.

Ellen's adjustment then is in precarious balance. We would expect her to be emotionally inhibited, withdrawn, retreating within herself as a refuge from emotional and social difficulties. On occasion, we would anticipate unstable and unrestrained childish explosiveness.

Fortunately there is adequate control in the picture (per cent F+(Ror)). The ego is capable of holding emotions under control. She is in adaquate contact with reality (F+,P). She shows good capacity for inner control (M+) even though she has not developed her imaginal capacity to the point she can use it constructively. Control is likewise attained through various defensive operations which for the moment may serve her in good stead although they are far from healthy.

Thus strong repressive emphasis appears throughout the test in the formal patterns, the content and her test behavior.

She also relies heavily on denial and on reaction formation. Thus she uses pollyannish imagery and "pretties up" the threatening human figures (Card I); she makes the man with a crack in his head, happy (Card II); she makes the disturbing image innocuous at first (Card III). Further, she is prone to restrict her attention to small details in certain situations, denying the more threatening aspects. Or she tends to retreat from disturbing parts of situations avoiding anxiety arousing or depressing images. Thus she retreats from color in cards VIII and IX and from the mother figure in Card VII. Her ingratiating behavior is a denial of her intense underlying hostility and rage. Even her negativism and hostility may reflect denial of dependency feelings and lack of self-confidence.

Again Ellen defends by undoing, giving alternatives or repeating her responses again and again, sometimes with minor variations, sometimes detailing excessively as if elaboration relieves her of the apprehension the images have aroused. Again she minimizes the size of her images to render them less threatening.

Ellen also uses regression, reverting to a world of mythology and fairy tales. Regression is also seen in her passive, childlike helpless demanding behavior.

Another major defense is her withdrawal and self-insulation. She withdraws from the emotional impact of the environment thus detaching herself from genuine emotional involvement. She withdraws into fantasy, at times austistic fantasying.

Projection is likewise used. Ellen's behavior shows that she projects her feelings of distrust, hostility and sadism on to the examiner, the testing situation and the blots themselves. She projects also her own superego pressures and expectations, viewing the whole testing situation as an authoritarian one. Such projections suggest that paranoid features are in the picture.

Most of Ellen's defenses are pathogenc. They tend to bottle up her emotions and repress their expression. They are weak and ineffective in the sense they are not protecting Ellen from pain and anxiety. They are taking their toll in curtailing her mental and emotional freedom.

Ellen's debilitating anxieties, her deep and painful moods, her feelings of rejection, her fears of further rejection, her shallow interpersonal relationships, her mistrust and suspicions of people, her lack of understanding of people and her inability to relate to them, her need to fight back aggressively and sadistically, and her maladaptive defensive maneuvers have of course affected her social adjustment. She has, however, capacity to make contact with her fellows (H) and to conform (P). She is able to think as her fellows do. She is responsive to common conventional ideas.

Her contact with people is more a preoccupation with what they do and think in reference to her. She is not in emotional contact with them (low FC). She is not able to express genuine feelings and emotions in her relations with them (C/F). When she conforms she does so superficially with surly compliance (hard texture). As a matter of fact, she overconforms (excess of P) putting on a social front, which really is a facade which covers up latent hostility.

It is significant that when Ellen is threatened by a situation, she does not conform even in this superficial way. She does not recognize what is appropriate response in a situation (P failure). Then her reactions are socially immature and inadequate.

Differential Diagnosis. The Rorschach reveals an anxiety-neurotic child. The picture is one where Ellen shows dependency, passive anxious withdrawal and resignation, to which she reacts with aggression and hostility.

These in turn arouse anxiety and guilt against which she must defend, so she shows counter regressive impulses and maneuvers and again withdraws into passivity with attendant dependency feelings. Again these awaken in her inferiority feelings and, in order to bolster her self esteem, strong opposition and hostility are again released. We have then a neurotic condition, a kind of chain reaction, referred to in the literature as the passivity-resistance closed circuit (Beck).

We would then anticipate ambivalent behavior. On the one hand Ellen will show behavior which is childishly demanding, petulant, resistant and negativistic, and superficially compliant. On the other hand aggressive impulses may be acted out, in the form of self willed, destructive and perhaps delinquent behavior. Or aggressive impulse may be warded off by defensive operations such as reaction formation, denial, isolation and projection.

We have noted that Ellen has more than adequate voluntary self control (per cent F+Ror), ability to deal with reality on an imaginal level (M), ability to respond to common conventional ideas (P), and emotional control in the form of delay, guardedness, neurotic constriction. Further various kinds of defensive operations are utilized to deal with untenable impulses and anxieties. We feel therefore that she has the ability to control hostile and destructive impulses and acting out behavior.

Such control may not hold, however. If tensions build up and if pressures become too great, she will act out and become overly aggressive and possibly delinquent.

Case History, Interview Data

Ellen is a very pretty, only child She was adopted at birth (not through any official agency) by a woman who had been divorced and who had remarried. The foster mother had difficulty in her second marriage and tried to save that marriage by taking a child. When Ellen was three years old, however, the parents were divorced and the father disappeared completely from the child's life.

Ellen's foster mother is a very successful business woman, the owner of several foundaries. She is bright, alert, intelligent, and charming. She maintains an elaborate home with a staff of servants. She has little time for the home however. She is completely tied up with her business and has little time for the warm contact and intimacies which a child needs. Training is left to the household servants and to private schools. The mother professes deep love and devotion for the child. She indulges her every whim and overwhelms her with material goods and possessions. It is obvious however that she is too engulfed in her work to be able to establish good, healthy rapport with her child.

The mother expresses highly conventional ideas about child rearing and discipline. She believes in "good manners, respect for authority and good behavior." From what she says, her discipline appears to be authoritarian, inconsistent, and sometimes even harsh.

The help in the home is for the most part indulgent, undemanding and permissive. When Ellen misbehaves, more often than not, they pretend unawareness to avoid conflict with the child. Ellen therefore "gets away" with many things and she knows it. On occasion, they report Ellen's misconduct to the mother. Since she is away so much, there generally is a long time lag between the administration of punishment and the occurrence of the misbehavior.

The mother says she is a great "believer in education" which was denied her. She has aspirations for the child for high levels of academic and vocational success and for social recognition. Vocational success means to her following in her "footsteps."

According to the mother, Ellen's behavior is highly unpredictable. Sometimes she is "as good as gold." She will do as she is told. She sometimes remains at the table for hours while the mother discusses business with one of her associates. When Ellen accompanies her mother on a business visit, she is told to wait in a certain office. She will sit for hours without complaint until she is released. At other times, however, she is irritable, belligerent, and has temper tantrums. She lies and steals at home and at school. She also displays "sex behavior." At one time, she tried to get into bed with the butler. At another time, she accused a trusted servant of sexual advances, which, upon investigation, was a retaliatory measure because he refused to permit her to go out after dark.

The mother and the school are confused by the contradictory behavior. The mother is especially disappointed because of the child's failures in school. She feels the time has come when neither she nor the school can handle the child. The mother said she finally was convinced that Ellen is "subnormal in intelligence" and that there is some "mental disorder." After all, she says, "Ellen is an adopted child and who knows what her heredity is?" The mother requests examination to determine the nature of Ellen's "mental disorder" and to get guidance as to what kind of school or "institution" she should be sent to.

Ellen's attitude toward the mother is ambivalent. She loves her mother but she wishes she could be more like other mothers and be at home. She feels that she scolds and punishes her too much and is unfair. She wishes that her mother was not so "nervous." She says that when business is good, the whole house is "relaxed." When there is trouble everybody is tense. Apparently the home is dominated by the mother and her moods.

Ellen resents being left with servants. She does not want to be "bossed around," but she feels she can "handle" them. Evidently Ellen has learned ways to intimate and deceive them. There isn't anyone in the home whom Ellen really likes.

In Ellen's short life, she has attended many boarding schools, day schools and summer camps, all frequented by children of the upper social class. She has failed repeatedly in her work. Her relationships with her classmates have always been poor. She says, the girls are "mean." She is never included in their activities. She is always left out of everything. The girls "make up secrets about her" behind her back. Her teachers "pick" on her. They listen to "mother and not to me." "I guess it is because mother gives them so many presents."

In her present school, Ellen is failing. She has been asked to leave. The school lists as reasons, "poor achievement, reading disability, negativism, belligerence, lying, stealing, disobedience, destructiveness."

Other Test Data

Ellen was given the Wechsler Intelligence Scale for Children, achievement tests, the House, Tree and Person Test, the Goodenough Human Figure Drawing, the CAT and the Despert Fables, all administered by another psychologist. She was also sent to our Reading Improvement Center and given reading tests and the California Test of Personality.

Results of testing give a verbal I.Q. of 97, a performance I.Q. of 100 and a total scale I.Q. of 99, placing her in the middle of the average range of intelligence. Her drawing of the human figure, scored according to Goodenough's criteria and norms, confirms this placement.

The psychological reports indicate that the overall estimate in intelligence is in noticeable contrast with the clinical impression. Analysis of the subtests reveals inconsistencies in successes and failures. Emotional factors appear to be responsible for failure to function according to Ellen's capabilities in many areas, perhaps in all. The reports list anxiety and insecurity in the testing situations with strong needs for contact, acceptance, and direction.

The personality tests give evidence of hostile and aggressive feelings toward parents, especially the mother who is viewed as a threatening punishing figure rather than a nurturant affectionate one. They also reveal feelings of unworthiness, inadequacy, loneliness, alienation from people, fears and threats from the environment.

Summary

The results of the Rorschach analysis must be evaluated in the light of the case history, the interview material and other test data. They must be interpreted in conjunction with the influences within the home, in the school, and in the larger society of which Ellen is a part.

Ellen has been brought up in an environment of riches, where great emphasis has been placed on the physical aspects of her care rather than on the emotional. No one has been occupied in meeting Ellen's emotional and social needs or interests. It has been an environment where there has been little warmth and affection, little sympathetic understanding, and little communication between Ellen and her adult world.

Ellen's learning environment at home has been seriously impoverished. There have been no joint family projects, no joint activities and no fun. No one has read to or with Ellen; no one has taken her to museums, concerts, circuses or carnivals; no one has arranged social activities with children of her age. In the home, no one has encouraged initiative or spontaneity and no one has stimulated her intellectual curiosity in any direction.

Ellen then has little opportunity for intellectual or social exploration. She has developed no outside interests, hobbies, or group activities. She has participated in few group activities. She has had few stimulating and happy experiences.

There can be little doubt then that there has been and is now rejection in the picture. Ellen was rejected by her natural parents and by a foster father who abruptly disappeared from her life. She has been severely deprived and rejected by a mother who has never been responsible for Ellen's emotional succorance. Rejection by the mother is all the more severe because, while she professes deep devotion and pride in the child, she has really never valued the child as a person, but rather for her own self enhancement and for the gratification of her own frustrated marital and parental needs. As a result, there is little commonality of feeling, mutual understanding, or ease of communication between the mother and Ellen.

As a result, Ellen has not developed intrinsic feelings of security and adequacy or worth. Since support, assurance, and guidance have not been available, Ellen feels deprived, alone in the world. This has lead to a perceptual search to find security and acceptance. There is no one to which she can turn, however. She therefore feels alone, abandoned, helpless and hopeless.

Because of the recurrent exposure to depreviation and rejection, Ellen has acquired strong feelings about herself. Prolonged rejection has resulted in complete self-devaluation and has led to serious impairment of her self-esteem. She has accepted the negative evaluation that others have placed on her. She now perceives herself as unworthy, unlovable, inadequate, and a failure. She feels all the more apprehensive and fearful in the face of a threatening environment because of these feelings of weakness, inadequacy, and low worth.

Ellen wants desperately to enter into affectionate relations with her mother and with others but she is in a continual emotional state of fear because she anticipates rejection. She regards herself as unworthy of love and hence withdraws from involvement with people to avoid further traumatic rebuff. She is however in desperate need for acceptance, support, protection and direction more so than another child of her age. She is childishly demanding, then, fearful, apprehensive ,petulant and negativistic. She has not yet grown up commensurate with others of her age.

Ellen's self depreciation and dependency are accompanied by resentment, rage, and bitterness. She reacts to her plight with narcissistic protest. She resents depreciation from others. She resents the need to surrender to the authority and control of others. Hostile and aggressive feelings are directed toward her mother who rejects her and who threatens her self-esteem. Indeed, she views the mother as all powerful, evil, rejecting and punishing. These attitudes have spread to others in her environment, especially those who exercise authority. She has developed a deep seated need to fight back and to retaliate. Sadistically she wants to inflict pain and to take revenge.

There is a strong oppositional trait in Ellen. Strong feelings are mobilized behind this trait. She wants to assert herself stubbornly and persistently and to resist being overwhelmed by outside pressures. Ellen has ego strength. She fights. She refuses to knuckle under the domination of others. She is hostile and rebellious, then.

Oppositionalism is likewise directed against herself. Her feelings of inadequacy and dependency cause anxiety. She fights then her dependency needs, her self doubts, her self distrust and her desires to surrender to those who apply pressures.

Ellen's hostility and rebellion and her other socially unacceptable impulses generate anxiety within her. They threaten her with loss of acceptance from persons on whom she is dependent and who may retaliate with punishment. After all, she dare not aggress against those on whom she relies for support and affection. Her hostility then arouses feelings of guilt and remorse which result in further negative self-evaluation and which induce more anxiety. Dependency needs and feelings of inferiority are reactivated. She resorts again to passivity, submission, and resignation. She gives up her strivings for independence and resorts again to clinging dependency, becoming passive, submissive and resigned. She even takes recourse in inactivity, in doing nothing. This is her defensive operation to counteract strong impulses. This however results in further devaluation. Again opposition is induced in reaction to these dependency and submissive feelings, so that aggression is again released. It is a neurotic process which continues in circular fashion, a kind of chain reaction we call the aggression-passivity closed circuit.

Ellen's anxieties are increased by rejection and failure in school as well as at home. She is so emotionally starved that she tries to transfer her quest for love and status from home to school. She is not however able to establish an emotionally dependent relationship with her teachers. Because of her deep seated feelings of inadequacy and her anticipation of failure, she tends to give up. She does not try to live up to the requirements of the school or to compete with her fellows. She ignores homework and has low academic aspirations. She fails to achieve. Her habit of fighting back and of being resistant and belligerent antagonizes teachers and peers alike. She experiences further rejection then. She senses disparagement, ridicule and ostracism from her school mates. As a result, her feelings of inferiority and her low sense of worth have become exacerbated. So she fights back and becomes even more resistant and belligerent. Like the home, then, the school is also a source of conflict, failure, and ego deflation.

Another source of conflict which is creating considerable anxiety is in the area of sex. Ellen appears to be more preoccupied with sex than most children of her age. The case history contains no evidence of any actual traumatic sexual experience which Ellen may have had. We keep in mind, however, that Ellen has been exposed to differential experiences which children have in private schools where "sexual experiences" such as peeking, "show games," and sexual exploration are not unknown. There is always the possibility then that some form of sexual activity has been experienced.

There is no doubt that Ellen's attention has been focused on sex. She is more aware of and concerned with heterosexual activity than most children of her age. For some reason she feels threatened by male sexuality. She has sexual fantasies and vague forebodings of sexual attack. For Ellen, sex is a source of fear, conflict, confusion and anxiety.

There are many factors then which are endangering Ellen's self-esteem and inducing anxiety. Chronic rejection resulting in self-depreciation, further ego devaluation because of unacceptable impulses, guilt feelings, self-reproach and rebellion against the outside world, all threaten her.

Anxiety is all the more severe because Ellen is prone to view every situation as an authoritarian one. While many of the threats in her life are realistic and genuine, Ellen tends to ascribe rules, demands and pressures to situations which are unrealistic, inventing them, and then feeling constantly under pressure to meet them. Then, in characteristic fashion, she anticipates failure and with it rejection and punishment. These pressures are her own superego-based demands and self criticism.

Thus Ellen is prone to perceive threats and rejection in situations where none exists. Indeed the most trivial threat or obstacle is magnified. This makes her hypersensitive to rebuff from her environment. It causes her to overreact with fear and rage behavior to situations which in her judgment pose threat to her sense of adequacy. Her behavior is often disproportionate to the objective degree of the threat. Her anxiety then is all the more pathological because threats to herself and to her self-esteem are apt to be exaggerated because of the long standing impairment of her self-esteem.

Ellen then is in a chronic state of tension and anxiety. She is constantly coping with real and fantasied authority and threats. At times her anxiety is so deep that her moods are dysphoric and depressed. In addition, because of her aggressive-passive orientation, she is in a bind. She is in severe conflict. Part of her nature wants to assert itself and part must submit passively to her fate. She wants to be assertive but it is expedient to be compliant and submissive. She needs to be dependent but she also wants autonomy and independence. She wants to rebel against authority yet she is highly dependent upon it. She needs to fight back sadistically yet she fears the consequences of such behavior and she is threatened by feelings of guilt and remorse. She wants to make contact with people yet she must dissociate herself from them lest she be hurt again. Thus she is alternately submissive, compliant, passive, apathetically accepting authority and control and then noncompliant, active, assertive, resistive, rebellious and explosive. She is in a continual state of tension because activities and impulses which are mutually exclusive demand expression.

Ellen tries to handle her conflicts and anxieties by a variety of defensive operations which manifest themselves in ambivalent and often contradictory behaviors. Thus she tries to repress her thoughts and fantasies and block discharge of threatening feelings and impulses. She represses hostile and dependent impulses and sexual imagery. Situations which are exciting and pleasure-toned therefore cause her to repress feelings and block ideation. She is unable or unwilling to permit herself any pleasureable experiences. As a result she has little feeling contact with her environment. At best she forces or simulates the feelings and emotions she cannot experience spontaneously. She puts on a facade of emotional rapport. Because of her severe repression of feelings and emotions, she lacks zest, spontaneity and joy in living.

Ellen relies heavily on denial and reaction formation. She adopts superficial, compliant and ingratiating behavior which denies her underlying anger, negativism, suspiciousness and hostility or she becomes irritable and belligerent, denying underlying needs for dependency, help and direction. She puts on a show of serenity even happiness in her overt behavior but she really experiences deeply felt sadness. When confronted by a situation which to her is threatening, she handles only a part of it denying the threatening implications of those aspects which are disconcerting to her. She manipulates people and objects in her environment trying to strip them of their sadistic or sexual implications, in this way denying them. She pretties up people or makes substitutions to prevent seeing that which is evil and threatening. She closes her eyes to the painful and the unpleasant.

At times she becomes childish and regresses to infantile modes of thinking and behavior. Thus she shows childish behavior constantly demanding help, direction, assurance, and confirmation of what she is doing. She resorts to childish imagery and to the world of make-believe. Indeed her thinking at times is childishly irrealistic, fantasies and autisism replacing objective reality.

Ellen often seems aware of what she is doing when she regresses in this way. It is "regression in the service of the ego." She permits herself imaginative liberties but she is in control of her thinking, well oriented to reality. We might consider this a successful defense if we did not think that this tendency may be manifested behaviorally in imaginative flights which take the form of weaving tales and fabrication.

Again Ellen defends by undoing, repeating her ideas again and again, with detailed elaborations in order to reduce the fear which the thoughts arouse. She often minimizes and negates the threatening implications of the impulses and the ideas which hover near awareness.

Another major defense is Ellen's withdrawal and self-insulation. Ellen is narcissistically preoccupied with self. She avoids, evades and runs away from people and situations. She is dependent upon them but threatened by them. She is harrasssed by a constant and haunting fear of more and more rejection. She dare not make intimate contact with them lest they inflict more pain and rejection. She cannot then let herself be exposed to further frustration, failure and loss of self-esteem. Therefore she withdraws and cuts herself off from social intercourse, in the desperate attempt to escape her stressful life experiences and to retreat from the pressures and requirements of her life. She withdraws within herself then and harbors her conflicted feelings without immediate expression. Thus on occasion her behavior is passive, submissive and resigned. Or she appears apathetic and indifferent. Or she is inactive—she does nothing.

More often Ellen withdraws into fantasy life, using her imaginal ability to spin fantasies. Her fantasy world however deals with her sadistic, hostile, erotic, and dependency needs. Behaviorally this may show as daydreaming. Her fantasying is not healthy, however. The phobic, repulsive and paranoid images and thoughts of hostility and aggression in her fantasy world in turn stir up more painful anxiety. For Ellen, fantasy is not used constructively but as a mechanism of escape from life's difficulties.

While Ellen's fantasy life seems to afford her support and refuge and no doubt prevents her from excessive explosiveness, it is at the expense of her relations with the outside world. She has become overly introversive, concerned with self, immersed in her own problems. She is more prone to act in accordance with her own ideas and attitudes than in having close relations with others and submitting to their wishes.

Again, in unhealthy fashion, Ellen uses projection as a defense. She projects her own evil and hostile tendencies, her sadism, and her distrust and suspiciousness onto others. We have noted that she even projects her own superego-imposed demands and pressures onto her environment.

Finally Ellen utilizes aggression as a defense. She strikes out in anger and in fear and fights. She shows a deep need to protest actively when faced with anxiety laden situations. She must do something about the threats and dangers she fears. Her aggressiveness may take the form of negativism and rebelliousness. She may act out hastily, imprudently and without regard to consequences. Then her hostility may become explosive and destructive. Ellen's aggressiveness is a symptomatic aggressiveness because of her intense feelings of inferiority, rage and hatred, and because of her neurotic conflicts.

Most of Ellen's defenses are maladaptive. They tend to bottle up her emotions and alienate her from people and from her world. Or they cause her to explode in uncontrolled fashion. They are ineffective in the sense they do not protect her from pain and anxiety. They curtail her social adjustment and reduce the level and quality of her intellectual functioning.

What about Ellen's intellectual capacities? Is her intelligence subnormal as her mother believes?

The intelligence tests place Ellen in the middle of the average range in intelligence. Qualitative analysis of her tests however indicate that she has capacities above her present level of functioning. The Rorschach corroborates this. It indicates that Ellen has potential ability at least a high average level.

For the most part Ellen's thinking is clear, realistic and logical. She shows adequate critical and analytic ability. She has ability to discriminate, to generalize and to comprehend relationships. She has above average imaginal capacity and shows that she can utilize it. Some of her ideas are richly original. She can see things in a different light, still adhering to reality. She gives ample evidence of a capacity for independent thinking. At the same time, she is more than adequately adapted to the thinking of her group.

Ellen is not however operating at a level commensurate with her intellectual capacity. She is functioning under a burden of insecurity, anxiety, feelings of failure, resentment and rage, all of which interfere with her functioning, inhibit her productivity and block her judgment.

Further Ellen has not developed habits of perseverance. She is restless and easily distracted. In addition, her lack of confidence and anticipation of failure cause her to give up. She has lowered her level of aspiration and stifled initiative and drive for constructive achievement. Further, she has developed habits of guardedness and evasion, which reduced her productivity.

When Ellen feels threatened, and we have indicated that even the most innocuous details in a situation may cause threat, Ellen's whole mental procedure in approaching situations becomes unbalanced and her thinking unrealistic, illogical, and unsystematic. She often is prone to lose sight of the relevant and main objectives in a situation, to overlook the simple and the obvious, and to be overresponsive to irrelevant stimulation. As a result her ability to distinguish between the important and the unimportant is unevenly developed and falls below the normal range. She seems to turn to very small aspects of a situation as a means of escape from those aspects which threaten her. Or she clings to small things which seem to provide her with feelings of safety and security. Generally then we would anticipate that she will be illogical and inefficient in her mode of attacking problems. We would not expect her to deal realistically with day to day problems or to be practical in her approach to them.

Ellen has another handicap. Too often there are serious breaks with reality and wide deviation in her thought content. Personal interests, problems, and preoccupations cause her to distort reality, misinterpret relationships and give meanings without objective support. Like a very young child she often confabulates indulging in a kind of childish primitive or magical thinking which Piaget calls transductive thinking. Or she tries to manipulate a situation and change it to suit her own needs and ideas. We would expect then that Ellen often misinterprets events in her life situation and jumps to erroneous conclusions on inadequate evidence. We would expect her to force her reality in line with her own thinking and needs. She does not seem to be able to approach life situations from a more objective and detached point of view.

As we have indicated, Ellen's reality testing also suffers from the way she uses her imaginal ability. She sometimes give free reign to her imagination and indulges in extreme fantasy losing herself in her fantasy world. As a result on occasion her thinking tends to become regressive and autistic. This is all the more exaggerated by the fact that much of her thinking stems from personal needs and conflicts.

At the present time Ellen's interests are severely circumscribed. Indeed they are for the most part idiosyncratic and symptomatic.

There can be little doubt that Ellen's native endowment is not being fully employed. Emotional forces are restraining her functioning and bearing down on her efficiency. She does not use her abilities for constructive achievement. She has not yet found adequate outlet or focus for her potential abilities. Despite the many deviations in her intellectual functioning, however, there is no evidence of a general or serious weakening of ties with reality or of pathology. When not diverted by emotional problems Ellen's thinking is adequately realistic and controlled.

Ellen's behavior should be rational and controlled. She has the intelligence to understand people and their problems. She is responsive to common conventional ideas. She is aware of everyday things. She can recognize what is appropriate response to a situation and what is not. She is well able intellectually to assume socially acceptable patterns of behavior. She does not however have the emotional feel for her fellows or the necessary motivation to conform in a healthy constructive manner. When she conforms she does so artifically. It is a conformity on the surface, a kind of facade to cover up latent hostility. It is a veneer to hide the smoldering rebellion within her.

When Ellen feels threatened by a situation, however, she does not conform even in this superficial manner. She doesn't think as others do. She does not recognize what is appropriate response to a situation. She disregards social standards. Her behavior then becomes socially immature, inadequate and unpredictable. We would anticipate then that on occasion she will act hastily, imprudently and without regard to consequences.

Differential Diagnosis. In general, Ellen is a badly troubled child. She is suffering from a neurosis, a severe anxiety state which keeps her in a perpetual state of upheaval. There can be little doubt that traumatic experiences have been so great that they have caused serious damage by reducing the level of her intellectual functioning and the efficient use of abilities that she has. It has restricted her interests to what is of immediate concern to her. It has lowered her level of achievement. It has reduced her drive. What drive there is is hollow. If anything it is a drive to non-achievement. Damage has not only lowered her level of achievement but it has seriously affected how she lives emotionally and how she responds to her environment.

Ellen's debilitating anxieties, her deep and painful moods, her smoldering antagonisms, her faulty perception of people and of social realities, have seriously impaired her social relationships. Her lack of rapport with people, her mistrust and suspiciousness, her inability to establish and maintain warm relationships with people, all have alienated her from her people and have deprived her of adequate social outlets.

As a result, Ellen's social adjustment is seriously retarded and impaired. She has not yet developed the cognitive and social competence which normally takes place during the preadolescent years.

Understanding Ellen's Behavior Problems. In the light of our analysis, we can understand Ellen's problems in terms of her chronic emotional condition, her neurotic difficulties and her generally immature social development.

No doubt the schools to which Ellen was sent represent the highest of the social strata and cater to more children who probably are of upper level intelligence and who have had many opportunities for outside stimulation and activities. Ellen has not had the advantage of an enriched background. Hence, despite the fact that she is well able to function at a higher level than she is doing at the present time, she is handicapped. In addition, according to the report on the achievement tests, Ellen is chronologically relatively young for the school grade placement in her present school. Hence she has been in stiff competition with her school mates.

Ellen's failure to achieve may also be attributed to the unrealistic expectations of the mother and possibly the school where she is expected to function in a manner superior to that of which she is capable. She has apparently been under great pressure then to perform at a level incommensurate with her ability with resultant feelings of frustrations, inadequacy and insecurity.

Then, because of Ellen's emotional difficulties, we have noted deficiencies in certain cognitive areas: her inability to attack complex situations, her proneness to overlook essentials in a situation, her tendency to escape into autistic fantasy, her highly egocentric and subjectivistic approach to problems, and more. These are bound to affect her intellectual functioning and her social judgment, and have no small affect on her school achievement. Thus achievement will be erratic and below her optimum level.

Ellen's reading difficulties will be emotional. Her performance is said to be about one year behind others in her school grade. According to the reading tests reported, her silent reading tests scores show she is able to accomplish at the level of her grade on the basis of national norms. They show however in her oral reading she is about one grade behind the norms for children of her grade. This we think is the result of her emotional conflicts.

In general, school experiences have not been happy or satisfying for Ellen. They have been a source of ego deflation, of failure and of conflict. We know that chronic school failure with its associated emotional trauma and social rejection causes profound ego deflation. It can be understood then that chronic failure in schools has intensified Ellen's anxieties. We can understand too why Ellen has lowered her sights, stopped competing with her peers, and has given up. The child who anticipates that she will fail at schoolwork does not attempt it.

Thus Ellen's inattention, apparent indifference in school and her failure to participate in the activities appear to be forms of withdrawal because of repeated failure and rejection. As a result of her experiences, she is frustrated, suspicious, jealous and hostile. So she fights back. Her negativism and disobedience and other aggressive activities appear to be her way of coping with threatening situations, her means of reducing feelings of anger and rage and her way of retaliation for criticism, punishment and status deprivation. They may also be her mode of gaining the status which has been denied her.

Ellen's persistent stealing may reflect her immaturity. Like a child, she takes what she wants. She probably learned habits of taking what she wants at home, where the atmosphere is so permissive when the mother is away. She also probably developed sly habits of getting away with things in the process of learning to "handle" the servants.

Again stealing may emanate from Ellen's need for affection which has been withheld by others. The very fact that she is surfeited with material possessions given to her by others may aggravate the emotional void in her life. On her own, she acquires possessions, as a substitute. Accumulation of things on her own affords her some consolation. Of course Ellen may steal in anger, resenting the attitudes of her mother, her teachers, and her peers who ignore and scorn her. Again, she may steal in order to embarrass the mother and hence to punish her. Finally, Ellen may steal to get attention and to shock others into action because of their indifference and disinterest.

Ellen's "sex behavior" appears to be precocious. We have indicated that it may be the result of experiences which she may have had at various private schools. These may have accelerated the normal heterosexual stirrings which are characteristic of the adolescent period.

Again because of Ellen's history of emotional deprivation and because of her extreme need for contact and affection much of what has been called "sex behavior" may well be the desire of the young child for bodily contact of a nonerotic nature and for affectional closeness with a parent or a parent substitute. It may well be a childish reaching out for the warmth and affection of which she was deprived.

Finally, because of Ellen's rebellious and sadistic feelings toward people, she no doubt uses her "sex behavior" as a weapon for personal retaliation, to shock adult sensibilities, and to express defiance of adult authority.

In general, Ellen's misbehavior and delinquencies can be explained in terms of her emotional problems. We are inclined to believe that her misbehavior may well be indications of a healthy process rather than a pathological one. She is fighting back at a hostile world in an attempt to maintain her integrity.

Treatability

Assets. Can Ellen be helped. She has many assets which could be utilized to advantage. She has the capacity to achieve commensurate with her age group. She has potential for more constructive use of her intellectual resources and more meaningful and warm interpersonal relationships.

1. Ellen has good native intelligence and is in good contact with reality. She has the capacity for critical realistic and logical thinking. She has adequate ability to formulate abstractions and to reason.

2. Ellen has good imaginal capacity which could be used in more creative and constructive ways. While it is true she engages in much autistic wishful thinking, there is no evidence of run-away autistic living.

3. Ellen's thinking is adequately flexible and original. While her originality points to idiosyncratic and symptomatic thinking, it reflects potential which is not fully being put to use. With appropriate stimulation and direction, Ellen's horizon could be made to expand. She might be interested in things outside herself and become more detached and objective in her interests.

4. Ellen has emotional reserves which can be activated. Despite her overcautiousness in forming emotional ties, she shows signs of potential capacity for warm relationships. There is some small indication of a reaching out to form relationships with others.

5. Ellen has considerable ego strength. Her ego is sufficiently intact to hold aggressive urges under control. She has a strong capacity for oppositionalism. Strong feelings are mobilized behind this trait. She has a desperate need to assert autonomy and to gain self mastery. She shows fight and determination. She fights her dependency needs, her passivity, hostility and sadism. She fights her environment, resisting being overwhelmed by outside pressures. She does not yield her independence. Indeed, in the light of her traumatic experiences she has achieved rather remarkable feelings of independence even though it has been at great cost—severe neurotic anxieties and distorted relations with people.

If Ellen's need for love, affection and acceptance were adequately met, her need for self mastery, autonomy and for an independent role might be turned to constructive use. Her strong oppositional trait might be directed to a frontal attack on her problems. It might be converted into healthy vigor, energetic initiative and enterprise.

6. Ellen's thinking is more than adequately adaptive to that of her group. She can perceive what is expected and understand restrictions and social amenities. Further she is concerned with surface deportment. With proper motivation, she should be able to anticipate the consequences of her behavior and appreciate the advantages of conforming to social norms.

7. Ellen gives ample evidence of ability to control her behavior. She has the intelligence to react to life's problems realistically. She is capable of control through a kind of cautious holding back. She attains control through various defense mechanisms, which, while they are not healthy, they still

prevent more serious breakdown. In addition, despite corroding anxieties, Ellen's defenses are holding to some extent, and up to a point serve her needs. Her recourse to fantasy, for example, enables her to articulate personal feelings and problems without being threatened from without. It helps her to get vicarious gratification of frustrated hostile, dependent and erotic needs, and to restrain potentially disruptive impulses and feelings from expression. Thus fantasy absorbs some of her anxieties, even though they take their toll in constricting her personality and preventing more wholesome contact with her world.

The very fact that Ellen utilizes so many defensive operations shows that her personality is in a mobile state. She is vaguely aware of her problems. She is struggling with them. She is anxious about them. She is trying to cope with them. Her defenses then could be turned to good use.

8. Finally there is nothing in the record to suggest a generalized break with reality or a psychotic process at work.

Liabilities. Unfortunately there are more liabilities than assets in the picture at the present time.

1. Ellen lacks self-confidence and what is more important, she lacks self-respect. She feels inferior and helpless and is resigned to her fate. Her self esteem has been impaired for so long that it is deeply imbedded in her character structure and has led to a neurotic kind of anxiety where environmental vicissitudes and her own failings are exaggerated out of proportion to their true degree of threat. It causes her to overreact, with fear and rage or with withdrawal. It will require considerable effort to help Ellen appraise her environment and herself more realistically, to enhance her self-esteem and to develop self-confidence. In addition, Ellen's withdrawal and resignation may increase therapeutic difficulties. She may characteristically withdraw and be unable to develop the initiative and self assertion needed to attack problems.

2. Ellen's habitual mental procedure in approaching life situations tends to be too unbalanced. Thus her superficiality in sizing up situations, her overresponsiveness to irrelevant stimulation, and her inability to differentiate between the important and the unimportant may prevent her from seeing life problems in perspective and in analyzing them and focusing on that which is important.

3. Again, Ellen is so preoccupied with her personal problems that her thinking is highly subjectivistic. It will be difficult for her to take a more detached and objective view of herself and her world.

4. Further, Ellen is prone to misperceive and distort reality, and fashion it to suit her needs and ideas. She is apt then to misperceive and distort the efforts of people around her who try to help her.

5. Again, Ellen distrusts people. She is threatened by them. She with-

draws from them. This will make it difficult to reach her.

6. Again, Ellen has not developed any emotional rapport with people. She is unable to give of herself and to establish emotional relations on a fair give-and-take basis. As yet she cannot subordinate her desires and feelings to those of others. It may be difficult to make her aware of the needs, feelings, and interests of others and help her develop feelings of moral obligation and social responsibility commensurate with her age.

7. Another potential handicap is Ellen's introversive withdrawal and her inadequacy for free emotional response. Her emotional energy is not sufficiently liberated to help her respond to the emotional challenges of her environment. She may not then be able to develop the emotional freedom and fluidity requisite for accessibility to therapy.

8. Finally, Ellen's defenses are for the most part maladaptive. Repression is too stringent and constriction of emotional reactivity too tight. Withdrawal, especially her withdrawal into fantasy living is diverted to autistic purpose and has little relationship to the solution of her real live problems. It prevents her from dealing actively and aggressively with these problems. Her defenses on the whole do not serve adaptive problems solving functions. Instead they seem to magnify the sources of apprehensiveness and suggest unsuccessful solutions. Even worse, they sustain her immaturity and exaggerate her difficulties in making an adequate social adjustment.

Prognosis

There is little doubt that Ellen is suffering neurotic difficulties which may become more severe as times goes on. She is a deeply troubled child, full of fears and anxieties, and anger and rage which are impairing her intellectual functioning, reducing her efficiency and retarding her social adjustment. At the present time, explosive hostility is seething below the surface. Impulses are crowding for expression and tensions are building up. They may erupt at any time. While Ellen still shows capacity for some self control, it may not hold. Further exposure to rejection and deprivation and certainly any increase in environmental stress may bring her to the limits of her control and may threaten the integrity of her personality.

Ellen's condition is all the more serious because she is approaching adolescence where there are pressures inherent in the very nature of the developmental transition and where she will be exposed to the possibility of further frustration, failure and loss of self esteem. With the added stress of adolescence before her, the outlook is grim if Ellen is not helped.

Recommendations

Psychotherapy is definitely indicated for Ellen and intensive counselling if not psychotherapy for the mother. In addition, treatment should be instituted for both the mother and the child as a unit. Finally, radical modification must be made in the child's environment so that it is tuned more to the needs of the child.

We realize that for Ellen, complete insight into her problems may not be attained. She must however be helped to understand how and why her mother, teachers and peers behave as they do so that she may become more accepting of the pressures. She must also be helped to expand emotionally and make contact with her world. She must be helped to gain self-confidence and self-respect and rid herself of her feelings of "badness" and lack of worth. Finally, it is important that Ellen learn to know and appreciate her assets.

The school and the mother must cooperate and cultivate Ellen's assets. What skills she has should be put to use. Further, special tutoring should be instituted at once to help Ellen build greater proficiency in the skills which are below her general level. She needs special tutoring, especially in oral reading to help her gain confidence so that she will attempt new material without feelings of failure.

Ellen needs to taste success in some areas. Mother and school should provide opportunities for achievement and should set more realizable goals for success. They should provide a milieu which avoids the damaging personal experience of rejection and failure. Above all, they should avoid stigmatizing the child as a failure.

The home environment should provide stimulation. Obviously, it is important that the mother spend more time with Ellen. She should help the child develop outside interests and hobbies and participate in them with the child.

Above all, Ellen needs opportunities at home, at school and in the neighborhood for making warm contacts with others. She should be placed in contact with adults who will show her affectional acceptance and understanding and who will activate her potential for warm relations. She should be encouraged to spend time with accepting and fun loving friends who will help her release her bottled up emotions and enable her to have pleasureable experiences. Possibly Ellen could be encouraged to join groups such as the Girl Scouts where emphasis is placed on good times and fun and also on the development of social skills. Ellen is in desperate need to have successful and satisfying experiences.

Counselling is imperative for the mother. Whether or not Ellen will benefit from therapy will depend on the extent to which the mother is able to understand her own difficulties and those of her child and the degree to which she will be able to change her attitude and behavior toward the child.

AUTHOR INDEX

Abrahamsen, D., 153
Ainsworth, M., 89, 227, 245

Baker, E., 173
Bash, K., 4, 13
Baumgarten-Traumer, F., 2, 13
Bechtold, H., 248, 256
Beck, A., 120, 227, 244
Beck, S., 13, 15-18, 21, 28, 29, 37, 39, 50, 91, 93, 96-97, 101-102, 107-108, 113, 117-120, 227, 244
Belinsky, B., 153
Berg, D., 153
Binder, H., 17-18, 28, 199, 220
Binet, A., 1
Bleuler, E., 6
Booth, G., 18, 87
Boyer, L., 89
Bricklin, B., 154
Brown, J., 199
Buchard, E., 30, 51, 88

Candee, B., 153
Cronbach, L., 149, 172, 250, 256

Davidson, H., 30, 51, 57, 70, 87-89, 227, 245
Dubin, S., 199

Efron, H., 314
Elbert, E., 173
Ellis, A., 173
Emery, M., 89
Eron, L., 1, 5, 14

Faterson, H., 87
Frank, L., 6, 13, 23, 28

Gill, M., 13, 51, 175, 176, 199, 200, 227, 245
Goldfarb, W., 88
Guirdham, A., 18, 28

Hackbusch, F., 88
Harriman, P., 37-40, 50
Harris, J., 249, 256
Henri, S., 1
Hens, S., 3, 5, 13
Hertz, M., 18-19, 23, 25, 26, 28, 34, 41-42, 50-51, 172, 174, 227, 244-245, 321
Hirning, L., 89
Holt, R., 89, 175, 227, 245
Holtzberg, S., 153
Holzman, E., 30, 88

Jung, C., 6

Kelley, D., 25, 28, 30-32, 35, 51, 61, 73, 88, 152
Kenyon, V., 199
Kerner, J., 1, 13
Klopfer, B., 16-17, 21-22, 25, 28-31, 35, 46, 51, 57-58, 60-61, 70-73, 80-81, 84-85, 87, 89, 227, 245
Klopfer, W., 89, 227, 245
Knight, R., 176, 199
Koch, S., 250, 256
Kovitz, B., 200
Krugman, M., 1, 31-33, 51, 88

Lenkoski, L., 199
Levin, M., 126, 152
Levine, D., 154, 314
Levitt, E., 120, 227, 244
Levy, D., 7, 120
Lewis, N., 153, 314
Loehrke, L., 174
Loosli-Usteri, M., 12, 13
Lozoff, M., 176, 199

Margulies, H., 88, 89
Miale, F., 24, 28, 30, 50, 88, 199
Molish, H., 117, 119, 120, 227, 244
Morgenthaler, W., 1, 4
Murphy, L., 88

Nunally, J., 119

Oberholzer, E., 1, 3, 4, 6, 13, 89

Paolino, A., 174
Parker, R., 314
Pilot, M., 199
Piotrowski, Z., 17-18, 25-26, 28, 47-48, 51, 121-125, 137-139, 148, 152-154, 227, 245, 314

Rabin, A., 40, 51, 119, 120
Rapaport, D., 13, 24, 27, 28, 47-49, 51, 155, 175-177, 179, 181, 199, 200, 227, 245, 248
Rickers, M., 89
Robb, R., 200
Rock, M., 154, 314
Roemer, G., 1, 3, 6, 13
Rorschach, H., 2, 4, 5, 13, 89, 142, 220, 227, 245, 314
Rorschach, O., 2, 14
Rubenstein, B., 172
Rybakow, T., 2

Sample, B., 89
Schachtel, E., 18

Schafer, R., 13, 14, 28, 49, 51, 175, 176, 178, 179, 181, 198, 199, 200, 227, 245, 248
Schumer, F., 1, 5, 14
Selinski, H., 89
Sender, S., 16, 28, 51, 58, 60, 89
Shakow, D., 88
Sinclair, J., 119
Spiro, H., 199
Stein-Lewinson, T., 87
Symonds, P., 173

Tallman, G., 88
Thetford, W., 119, 120
Tillman, C., 199
Troup, E., 89
Tulchin, S., 1, 14

Von Arnold, B., 153

Wells, F., 29
Whipple, G., 2, 14
Wolfson, R., 30, 88, 172
Wood, A., 89
Wyatt, F., 250, 256

Zubin, J., 1, 5, 14

SUBJECT INDEX

Achromatic color, 66, 70, 82-83, 96, 99, 105-106, 133, 135, 186, 222, 225
Administration
  Beck System, 92-94
  Free association, 201-205
  Hertz System, 23, 158-160
  Inquiry, 54-58, 93, 94, 125-126, 159-167, 179-180, 203, 205
  Instructions, 202, 204
  Intersystem comparison, 201-205
  Klopfer System 54-58
  Piotrowski System, 124-126
  Rapaport-Schafer System, 178-181
  Rorschach, 54-55
  Testing the Limits, 55-57
Affect, 79-81, 101-105, 134, 145-146, 192-194, 229, 238-239
  See also Shading and color
Analogy period, 58
Anxiety, 81-83, 105-106, 146-147, 239-241
  See also Shading responses
Appendix, 257-374
  A Beck Interpretation, 282-296
  A Hertz Interpretation, 321-374
  A Klopfer Interpretation, 258-282
  A Piotrowski Interpretation, 297-314
  A Schafer Interpretation, 315-320

Beck System, 90-120
  Administration, 92-94
    Inquiry, 93-94
  Behaviorism, 9, 15-16, 18, 38-39
  Early development, 37-41, 90-92
  Interpretation, 97, 101-118
    Animal content, 103
    Case of G. A., 282-296
    Color, 101, 105
    Color shock, 106
    Erlebnistypus, 107-108, 112, 115-117
    F plus %, 104, 111
    Grey-black shock, 106

Mode of approach, 103
Movement, 101, 104-105, 111-112
Organizational activity, 101, 103, 111
Popular responses, 104
Ratios and percentages, 107-108, 288
Shading, 105-106
Whole responses, 103, 111
Blend responses. *See* Multiple determinants
Blind analysis, 22, 26, 34, 36, 71, 87, 113-115, 171, 228-231
Blotto, 1

Chiaroscuro responses, 65, 70, 79-81, 99-100, 135, 146-147, 186-187, 194, 220-225, 239-242
  Intersystem comparison, 220-221, 222-225, 239-242
  See also Shading; Scoring symbols (C), C', c, c', Cg, Ch', Ch", Cw, K, k, T, V, Y
Color responses, 64-65, 79-81, 98-99, 185-186, 192-194, 213, 216-220, 229, 238-239
  Intersystem comparison, 213, 216-220, 229, 238-239
  See also Scoring symbols C, CC, Cd, C denom, Cdes, Cdet, CDet, CF, Cn, Cp, Csym, F/C, FC, FCarb, FCarbit, FC denial
Computerization, 147-151
Content scores, 71, 84-86, 97, 136, 187, 194, 226
Cut-off whole responses, 59-60, 127, 161, 208

Detail responses, 58-61, 74, 94-95, 128, 140, 161, 182, 189-190, 208-209
  Intersystem comparison, 206-207, 208-209, 232, 233

Divergence, 15-28
  Beck and Binder, 17
  Beck and Hertz, 18-19
  Beck and Klopfer, 16-19, 53
  Beck and Piotrowski, 17, 20, 25, 45-
      46, 53, 122-124, 144
  Form responses, 16, 19, 21
  Hertz and Klopfer, 19, 44, 53
  Klopfer and Rapaport, 53
  Movement, 17-20
  Piotrowski and Hertz, 20, 25
  Piotrowski and Klopfer, 20, 25, 45-
      46, 53, 122-124, 144
  Shading, 17, 19, 21
  Standardization, 22-25

Ego operations. *See* Form responses;
      Erlebnistypus
Erfassungstypus, 103
Erlebnistypus, 6, 77-78, 107-108, 112,
      115-117, 143, 194-195, 221
Experience, actual, 115-117, 195
Experience balance. *See* Erlebnistypus

First Grade Normal Details, 59-60
Form Level Rating, 36, 61
Form responses, 17-18, 21, 61-62, 67-68,
      78-79, 98, 104, 111, 130, 135,
      136, 142, 186, 191-192, 210-
      212
Free association period, 54, 92, 124, 158,
      178, 201-204

Global interpretation. *See* Interpretation
Great Man Awards, 52, 90

Hertz System, 155-173
  Administration, 158-160
    Analogy period, 159
    Inquiry, 159-167
    Testing the Limits, 159
  Blind analysis, 171
  Early development, 41-45, 155-158
  Interactionist approach, 168-171
  Interpretation, 168-171, 321-374
    Case of Ellen, 321-374
    Sequence analysis, 330-348
  On administration, 23
  On standardization, 23, 34, 42-43

Scoring, 160-168
  Determinants, 160, 162-167
  Location responses, 160-161
  Organizational activity, 167
  Original responses, 167-168
  Popular responses, 167

Idiographic features, 247-248
  See also Interpretation, sign and global
Inquiry
  Analogy period, 58, 159
  Beck System, 93-94
  Hertz System, 159-167
  Intersystem comparison, 203-205
  Klopfer System, 55-58
  Rapport-Schafer System, 179-180
  Rorschach, 54
  Testing the Limits, 55-57
Interpretation
  Beck System, 97, 101-118
  Global interpretation, 72-73, 86-87,
      105, 109, 110, 139, 156-157,
      168-171, 180-181, 188-190, 229
  Hertz System, 168-171
  Intersystem comparison, 228-245
    Blind analysis, 228-231
    Color responses, 238-239
    Content, 243
    Form responses, 234-235
    Location responses, 232-234
    Movement responses, 235-238
    Original responses, 242
    Popular responses, 242
    Shading responses, 239-242
    Verbalizations, 243
  Klopfer System, 71-86
  Piotrowski System, 137-147
  Rapaport-Schafer System, 188-198
  Sign interpretation, 71-72, 86, 105,
      108, 156-157, 188-190

Klopfer System, 52-89
  Administration, 54-58
  Case of A. S., 258-282
  Early development, 29-37, 52-54
  Form responses, 36, 61, 67-68
  Instructions, 35
  Interpretation, 71-86, 258-282
    Blind analysis, 71, 87

Configuration principle, 72
Content analysis, 84-86
Proportional occurrence, 72
Quantitative analysis, 73-83, 271-275
  Color responses, 79-81
  Erlebnistypus, 77-78, 272-273
  Form responses, 78-79
  Location responses, 74-75
  Movement responses, 75-78
  Ratios, 83
  Shading responses, 81-83
Multiple determinants, 36
On standardization, 22-25, 34-36
Phenomenological orientation, 8-9, 20-22
Scoring, 58-71
  Content, 71
  Determinants, 61-71
    Animal movement, 68-69
    Color responses, 64-65, 69-70
    Form responses, 61-62, 67-68
    Movement responses, 62-63, 68
    Shading responses, 65-66, 70-71
  Location responses, 58-61
  Popular responses, 71

Life style. See Interpretation for movement responses; Erlebnistypus
Location responses. See Whole responses; Detail responses; Space responses
Location sheet, 58

Movement responses, 17-20, 62-63, 75-78, 98, 104-105, 111-112, 127, 129-130, 134, 142-145, 192
Intersystem comparison, 212-215
See also Scoring symbols M, FM, m, Ms
Multiple determinants
  Beck System, 96
  Klopfer System, 36
  Piotrowski System, 137
  Rapaport-Schafer System, 187-188
  Rorschach, 96

Nomothetic interpretation, 247-248
See also Interpretation, sign and global

Oppositional tendencies. See Space responses
Organizational activity, 92, 101, 103, 111, 167
Overview, 246-256
  Administrative procedures, 252-253
  Interpretation, 254-255
  Scoring, 253-254
  Teaching Rorschach, 255

Perceptanalysis. See Piotrowski System
Piotrowski System, 121-154
  Administration, 124-126, 201-205
    Free association, 201-205
    Inquiry, 125-126, 203, 205
    Instructions, 202, 204
    Seating, 201-204
  Blind analysis, 26
  Case of Delia, 297-314
  Computerization, 147-151
  Early development, 45-47, 121-124
  Interpretation
    Color denial, 145-146
    Color naming, 145
    Color projection, 145-146
    Color responses, 134, 145-146
    Form responses, 142
    Location responses, 140-142
    Movement responses, 142-145
    Ratios and percentages, 147, 303
    Shading responses, 146-147
  Pre-test procedures, 35
  Scoring
    Content, 136
    Determinants, 127-137
      Color responses, 131, 132, 134
      Form responses, 130, 135-136
      Movement responses, 127-129, 130, 134
      Shading responses, 135
    Location responses, 127-128
    Multiple determinants, 137
    Original responses, 136
    Popular responses, 136
Popular responses, 71, 104, 136, 167, 187, 226
Principle of Interdependence of Components, 139

Procedures, 201-227
  Free association period, 201-205
  Inquiry, 203, 205
  Instructions, 202, 204
  Seating arrangements, 201-204
Projection, 48, 138
Projective hypothesis, 6, 138
Psychodiagnostik, 4, 20, 32, 55, 220

Rapaport-Schafer System, 175-200
  Administration, 178-181
  Early development, 47-49, 175-178
  Interpretation, 188-198, 315-320
    Color responses, 192-194
    Detail responses, 189-190
    Erlebnistypus, 194-195
    Form responses, 191-192
    Movement responses, 192
    Original responses, 195
    Popular responses, 195
    Ratios and percentages, 319
    Shading responses, 194
    Verbalizations, 196-198
    Whole responses, 189
  On standardization, 24, 25, 48-49
  Projective hypothesis, 177
  Response process, 177-178
  Scoring, 181-188
    Content, 187
    Determinants, 183-187
      Color responses, 185-187
      Movement responses, 183-184, 187
      Shading responses, 186-187
    Location responses, 181-183
    Multiple determinants, 187-188
    Original responses, 187
    Popular responses, 187
  Test battery, 27
  Test hierarchy, 47
Ratios and percentages
  Beck System, 107-108
  Erlebnistypus, 6, 77-78, 83
  Hertz System, 348-353
  Intersystem comparison, 221, 226
  Klopfer System, 77, 83, 270-271
  Piotrowski System, 141-142, 147
  Rapaport-Schafer System, 189-190,
    195-196, 198, 319

Reflex hallucinations, 3
Rorschach, H.
  Early history, 1-13
  On administration, 54
  On Color, 80-81
  On Form, 61
  On Multiple Determinants, 96
  On Scoring, 59
  Vulgar responses, 71
Rorschach Institute, 16, 31-33, 90, 137
Rorschach Research Exchange, 16-18,
    21, 29-31, 36-37, 39, 53, 90,
    155
Rorschach Volunteer Unit, 32

Scoring symbols
  C, 64, 69, 70, 79-81, 96, 98, 105, 131,
    134, 163, 185, 216
  (C), 65, 70, 79-81, 99, 132, 135, 165,
    222
  c, 66, 70, 81-82, 133, 135, 165, 224
  C', 66, 70, 82-83, 186, 225
  c', 132, 135, 225
  CC, 64, 98, 131
  Cd, 131, 134, 216
  C denom, 163, 185, 217
  Cdes, 64, 79-81, 163, 185, 217
  C Det, 164, 216
  C det, 185
  CF, 65, 79-81, 96, 99, 105, 132, 134,
    163, 185, 217
  Cg, 133, 225
  (C)F, 164, 186, 222
  Ch', 165, 225
  Ch'', 165, 225
  Cn, 64, 69, 79-81, 163, 185, 217
  Cp, 131, 134, 216
  Csym, 64, 79-81, 163, 185, 217
  Cw, 133, 135, 225
  D, 58-60, 74, 94-95, 161, 182, 209
  d, 59-60, 74, 128, 208
  Dd, 59, 94-95, 161, 182, 209
  dd, 59, 60, 209
  de, 59, 60, 209
  De, 182, 209
  di, 59, 60, 209
  Do, 59, 94, 95, 128, 161, 209
  DW, 59, 61, 95, 103, 128, 161, 182,
    208

F, 61-62, 67-68, 78-79, 98, 104, 130, 135-136, 162, 184

FC, 65, 69, 79-81, 96, 99, 105, 132, 134, 163, 185, 218

F(C), 164, 186, 222

F͞C, 186, 218

F/C, 185, 218

Fc, 133, 135

Fc', 132, 135

FC arb, 186, 218

FC arbit, 164, 218

FC denial, 164, 218

FM, 62, 68, 76-78, 122, 130, 134, 162, 184

g, 167

K, 65, 70, 81-82, 223

k, 66, 70, 81-82, 223

M, 62, 75-77, 96, 98, 104, 129-130, 134, 162, 184, 214

(M), 162

M̲, 162

m̄, 63, 69, 76, 122, 131, 163, 215

Ms, 184, 214

S, 58, 59, 75, 94-95, 128, 161, 182, 209

s, 59, 61, 161, 182, 209

T, 96, 100, 223

V, 96, 99, 105, 223

W, 58-59, 74, 94-95, 128, 161, 182, 208

Cut-off whole, 59-60, 127, 161, 208

Y, 96, 99, 105-106, 222

Z, 92, 103

Seating, 201-204

Second Grade Details, 60

Shading responses, 17, 19, 21, 65-66, 70, 81-83, 99-100, 132-135, 146-147, 186-187, 194, 220-222, 223-225, 239-242

Intersystem comparison, 220-225, 239-242

See also Scoring symbols (C), c, C', c', Ch', Ch", Cg, Cw, K, k, T, V, Y

Sign interpretation. *See* Interpretation

Society for Projective Techniques, 52, 90

Space responses, 58-59, 61, 75, 94-95, 113, 128, 140-141, 161, 182, 206-207, 209, 233

Intersystem comparison, 206-209, 233

Standardization, 22, 23-25, 34

Test "45," 2

Texture responses, 66, 70, 81-82, 96, 100, 133, 135, 165, 220-221, 223-224, 240

See also Scoring symbols c and T

Third Grade Details, 60-61

Typological approach, 5

Validation, 248-250

See also Standardization

Verbalizations, 189, 191, 196-198

Vista responses, 65, 70, 81-83, 96, 99, 105, 220-221, 223, 240-241

See also Scoring symbols K and V

Whole responses, 58-59, 60, 74, 94-95, 103, 127-128, 140, 161, 181, 182, 189, 208, 232, 233

Intersystem comparison, 206-208, 232-233

Z Score, 92, 103

See also Organizational activity